T0254917

BRAIN AND BEHAVIOR COMPUTING

BRAIN AND BEHAVIOR COMPUTING

Edited by

Mridu Sahu and G. R. Sinha

CRC Press
Taylor & Francis Group
Boca Raton London New York

CRC Press is an imprint of the
Taylor & Francis Group, an **informa** business

MATLAB® is a trademark of The MathWorks, Inc. and is used with permission. The MathWorks does not warrant the accuracy of the text or exercises in this book. This book's use or discussion of MATLAB® software or related products does not constitute endorsement or sponsorship by The MathWorks of a particular pedagogical approach or particular use of the MATLAB® software.

First edition published 2021 by
CRC Press
6000 Broken Sound Parkway NW, Suite 300, Boca Raton, FL 33487-2742

and by CRC Press
2 Park Square, Milton Park, Abingdon, Oxon, OX14 4RN

© 2021 Taylor & Francis Group, LLC

The right of GR Sinha and Mridu Sahu to be identified as the authors of the editorial material, and of the authors for their individual chapters, has been asserted in accordance with sections 77 and 78 of the Copyright, Designs and Patents Act 1988.

Reasonable efforts have been made to publish reliable data and information, but the author and publisher cannot assume responsibility for the validity of all materials or the consequences of their use. The authors and publishers have attempted to trace the
copyright holders of all material reproduced in this publication and apologize to
copyright holders if permission to publish in this form has not been obtained. If any copyright material has not been acknowledged please write and let us know so we may rectify in any future reprint.

Except as permitted under U.S. Copyright Law, no part of this book may be reprinted, reproduced, transmitted, or utilized in any form by any electronic, mechanical, or other means, now known or hereafter invented, including photocopying, microfilming, and recording, or in any information storage or retrieval system, without written permission from the publishers.

For permission to photocopy or use material electronically from this work, access www.copyright.com or contact the Copyright Clearance Center, Inc. (CCC), 222 Rosewood Drive, Danvers, MA 01923, 978-750-8400. For works that are not available on CCC please contact mpkbookspermissions@tandf.co.uk

Trademark notice: Product or corporate names may be trademarks or registered trademarks and are used only for identification and explanation without intent to infringe.

Library of Congress Cataloging-in-Publication Data
Names: Sinha, G. R., 1975- author. I Sahu, Mridu, author.
Title: Brain and behavior computing / authored by: GR Sinha and Mridu Sahu.
Description: First edition. I Boca Raton, FL : CRC Press, 2021. I Includes
bibliographical references. I Summary: "Brain and Behavior Computing
provides an insight into the functions of the human brain. This book
provides emphasis on brain and behavior computing with different
modalities available such as signal and image processing, data science,
statistics, distributed computing including fundamentals, model,
algorithms, case studies, and research scope. It further illustrates
brain signals sources and how the brain signal can process, manipulate
and transform in different domains to extract information about the
physiological condition of the brain. Emphasis is on real challenges in
brain signal processing for variety of applications for analysis,
classification, clustering and identification"-- Provided by publisher.
Identifiers: LCCN 2020055208 (print) I LCCN 2020055209 (ebook) I ISBN
9780367552978 (hardback) I ISBN 9781003092889 (ebook)
Subjects: LCSH: Computational neuroscience. I Neurosciences--Data
processing. I Brain--Computer simulation. I Electroencephalography. I
Brain-computer interfaces. I Human behavior--Computer simulation. I
Behavioral assessment--Data processing.
Classification: LCC QP357.5 .S56 2021 (print) I LCC QP357.5 (ebook) I DDC 612.8--dc23
LC record available at https://lccn.loc.gov/2020055208
LC ebook record available at https://lccn.loc.gov/2020055209

ISBN: 978-0-367-55297-8 (hbk)
ISBN: 978-0-367-55299-2 (pbk)
ISBN: 978-1-003-09288-9 (ebk)

Typeset in Times
by MPS Limited, Dehradun

Dedicated to Jesus Christ – Mridu Sahu

Dedicated to my Grandparents, Teachers, and Swami Vivekananda –
G. R. Sinha

Contents

Contents

Preface

Brain and behavior modeling is one of the interesting and challenging domains of today's era. We are living in the era of artificial intelligence (AI) and machine learning (ML) which makes life sophisticated and fast-solution oriented. This book focuses on recent advances in brain and behavior modeling and also attempts to provide application-based learning for an in-depth understanding of the subject. The initial chapters of book provide the details of simulation tools and technology used to analyze the brain along with processing techniques. The discussion includes image modalities and tools for analysis of the brain signal. The brain computer interface (BCI) is also an emerging communication technology in this field along with different applications such as epileptic seizure, motor imagery task, and neuro-rehabilitation application, which are discussed in this book with real-time implementation. Deep learning and optimization techniques are introduced by researchers to improve the brain imaging techniques especially for disease and disorder detection. The single-trial classification approach for Devanagari, a script-based visual P300 speller using knowledge distillation and transfer learning, is also introduced to provide speller-based paradigm understanding. The details of functional brain network and behavior modeling methods are also presented. Chapter-wise brief descriptions are as follows.

Chapter 1 deals with important characteristics of each toolbox and then performs independent analysis using electroencephalogram (EEG) signal datasets. The analysis will tend to reveal the support of these toolboxes for the computational study of various brain-related applications such as BCIs. Chapter 2 identifies the deep learning challenges of longer training time and higher accuracies. To improve the optimality in training time and accuracies, an extreme learning machine (ELM) approach is considered as an optimal generalization algorithm with minimum training error and the smallest norm of the weights. Further, Chapter 3 deals with stress identification, how to select EEG features based on neurobiological grounding, and how to decide on an appropriate ML pipeline. Chapter 4 addresses the numerous BCI technologies that regulate an area as communications and biosensor technology. Expanding efficiency of data distribution, the feasibility of the power of transmitting, and optimizing the energy of knowledge in the environment are discussed in detail. Chapter 5 describes signal modeling using spatial filtering and matching wavelet feature extraction for classification of brain activity pattern. Chapter 6 compares the SP tool and manual feature extraction method for P300 based BCI. Chapter 7 presents an original approach of realizing the adaptive rate signal acquisition and processing chain for the cloud-based BCI to achieve a real-time compression gain in order to attain effective EEG signal processing, transmission, and analysis in the context of realizing a proficient cloud-based BCI framework. Chapter 8 provides an introduction to the BCI concept, followed by the design and development of neural-driven BCI systems using EEG signals. Chapter 9 describes tunable Q wavelet transform (TQWT) entropy-based epileptic seizure detection methodology that shows significant classification results. Chapter 10 provides an efficient compact model for single-trial P300 detection, channel-wise convolution to provide sparse connectivity, first time utilization of knowledge distillation to compensate the loss and reduce the trade-off between accuracy and number of trainable parameters, and transfer learning to handle inter-trial and inter-subject variability. Chapter 11 aims to collate major deep learning algorithms that played a decisive role in functional blocks of brain image analysis, such as in registration, segmentation, and classification. Evolutionary optimization-based automatic skull stripping and brain tumor segmentation approach has been developed in Chapter 12. In Chapter 13, a car racing game has been designed for neurofeedback (NF) training to enhance the focus level (FL) of the participants The game is designed with two difficulty levels, and different game elements have been used to enhance the interest of the participants. In Chapter 14, detection of K-complexes and sleep spindles (DETOKS) and their modifications are proposed to improve the existing sleep stage identification methods. Chapter 15 presents directed functional brain networks for characterization of information flow direction during cognitive function using non-linear granger causality; this chapter may contribute towards designing better information search and retrieval systems. Chapter 16 proposed a research study on the growth of mobile technologies, smart sensing devices, and ubiquitous learning environments that have led to the development of context aware adaptive learning education; this chapter relates the behavior modeling for the given scenario.

Acknowledgments

Dr. Mridu Sahu expresses her sincere thanks to God, her parents, and son Mukund for their wonderful support and encouragement throughout the completion of this important book. The completion of the book would not be possible without Samrudhi, her contribution is sincerely appreciated and gratefully acknowledged. She would also like to thank all the contributors and well-wishers for the book.

Dr Sinha too expresses his gratitude and sincere thanks to his family members, wife Shubhra, daughter Samprati, parents, and teachers.

We would like to thank all our friends, well-wishers, and all those who keep us motivated in doing more and more, better and better. We sincerely thank all contributors for writing relevant theoretical background and real-time applications of brain and behavior computing.

We express our humble thanks to Dr. Gagandeep Singh, Engineering editor and all the editorial staff of CRC Press for great support, necessary help, appreciation, and quick responses. We also wish to thank Lakshay Gaba and all the CRC team for the support and publishing, for giving us this opportunity to contribute on some relevant topic with a reputed publisher. Finally, we want to thank everyone, in one way or another, who helped us in editing this book.

Last, but not least, we would like to thank God for showering us with his blessings and strength to do this type of novel and quality work.

Editors' Biographies

Dr. Mridu Sahu has completed her graduation in Computer Science and Engineering in 2004 from **Maulana Azad National Institute of Technology, Bhopal**. She completed her post-graduation Master of Technology in Computer Science and Engineering from RIT, Raipur, in 2011, and completed the Ph.D. in Computer Science and Engineering in 2018 from the National Institute of Technology Raipur, India. She has more than ten years experience in teaching; presently she is working as Assistant Professor in the Department of Information Technology, **RIT, Raipur**. She has published more than 25 research articles in various journals and conferencess and book chapters in the field of data mining, brain computer interface, sensor devices, and visual mining techniques.

G. R. Sinha is Adjunct Professor at the International Institute of Information Technology Bangalore (IIITB) and currently deputed as Professor at the Myanmar Institute of Information Technology (MIIT) Mandalay, Myanmar. He obtained his B.E. (Electronics Engineering) and M.Tech. (Computer Technology) with a Gold Medal from National Institute of Technology, Raipur, India. He received his Ph.D. in Electronics and Telecommunication Engineering from Chhattisgarh Swami Vivekanand Technical University (CSVTU) Bhilai, India. He has been Visiting Professor (Honorary) in Sri Lanka Technological Campus Colombo for 2019-2020.

He has published 259 research papers, book chapters, books, and nine edited books. He is Associate Editor of three SCI journals: *IET-Electronics Letters*, *IET-Image Processing Journal*, and *IEEE Access-Multidisciplinary Open Access Journal*. He has 22 years of teaching and research experience. He has been Dean of Faculty and an Executive Council Member of CSVTU, and is currently a member of the senate of MIIT. Dr. Sinha has been delivering ACM lectures as ACM Distinguished Speaker in the field of digital signal processing(DSP) since 2017 across the world. His few more important assignments include Expert Member for Vocational Training Program by Tata Institute of Social Sciences (TISS) for two years (2017-2019); Chhattisgarh Representative of IEEE MP Sub-Section Executive Council (2016-2019); Distinguished Speaker in the field of Digital Image Processing by Computer Society of India (2015). He served as Distinguished IEEE Lecturer on the IEEE India council for Bombay. He is the recipient of ten national and international level awards. He is Senior Member of IEEE, Fellow of Institute of Engineers India, and Fellow of IETE India. He has delivered more than 50 keynote/invited talks and chaired many technical sessions in international conferences across the world such as Singapore, Myanmar, Sri Lanka, and India. His special session on "Deep Learning in Biometrics" was included in the IEEE International Conference on Image Processing 2017. Dr. Sinha has supervised eight Ph.D. scholars, 15 M.Tech. scholars and has been supervising one more Ph.D. scholar. His research interest includes biometrics, cognitive science, medical image processing, computer vision, outcome-based education (OBE) and information communication technology (ICT) tools for developing employability skills.

Contributors

Sai Darahas Akkineni
Department of Electrical Engineering
National Institute of Technology
Andhra Pradesh, India

Han Shen Chong
Universiti Tunku Abdul Rahman
Faculty of Engineering and Green
  Technology
Kampar, Malaysia

Rig Das
DTU Health Tech
Technical University of Denmark
Kongens Lyngby, Denmark

Suma Dawn
Jaypee Institute of Information
  Technology (JIIT)
Noida (UP), India

Jia Tina Du
Science, Technology, Engineering and
  Mathematics (STEM)
University of South Australia
Adelaide, Australia

Kusumika Krori Dutta
Department of Electrical and Electronics
  Engineering
M.S. Ramaiah Institute of Technology
  (MSRIT)
Bengalaru, India

Sanjay R. Ganorkar
Savitribai Phule Pune University
Maharashtra, India

Chuang Huei Gau
Universiti Tunku Abdul Rahman
Faculty of Arts and Social Science
Kampar, Malaysia

Zahra Ghanbari
Biomedical Engineering Department
Amirkabir University of
  Technology
Tehran, Iran

Anandi Giridharan
Indian Institute of Science
Bengalaru, India

John Paulin Hansen
DTU Management
Technical University of Denmark
Kongens Lyngby, Denmark

Yeap Kim Ho
Universiti Tunku Abdul Rahman
Faculty of Engineering and Green
  Technology
Kampar, Malaysia

Komal Jindal
Department of Electronics and Communi-
  cation Engineering
Thapar Institute of Engineering and
  Technology
Patiala, Punjab, India

Dr. V. Karan
Ambedkar National Institute of Tech-
  nology (NIT)
Jalandhar, Punjab, India

Dr. S.P.K. Karri
Department of Electrical Engineering
National Institute of Technology
Andhra Pradesh, India

Muhammad Ahmed Khan
DTU Health Tech
Technical University of Denmark
Kongens Lyngby, Denmark

Ghanahshyam B. Kshirsagar
Department of Electrical Engineering
National Institute of Technology
Raipur, Chhattisgarh, India

Narendra D. Londhe
Department of Electrical Engineering
National Institute of Technology
Raipur, Chhattisgarh, India

Samrudhi Mohdiwale
Department of Information Technology
National Institute of Technology
Raipur, Chhattisgarh, India

Mohammad Hassan Moradi
Biomedical Engineering Department
Amirkabir University of Technology
Tehran, Iran

Dr. Deepak Nagaria
British Institute of Engineering Tech-
   nology (BIET)
Jhansi, India

D. (Nanda) Nandagopal
Science, Technology, Engineering and
   Mathematics (STEM)
University of South Australia
Adelaide, Australia

Humaira Nisar
Universiti Tunku Abdul Rahman
Faculty of Engineering and Green
   Technology
Kampar, Malaysia

Prabin Kumar Padhy
Electronics and Communication Engi-
   neering Discipline
Indian Institute of Information Technology
   Design and Manufacturing
Jabalpur, MP, India

Y. Saty Prakash
Dr. B.R. Ambedkar National Institute of
   Technology (NIT) Jalandhar
Punjab, India

Sadasivan Puthusserypady
DTU Health Tech
Technical University of Denmark
Kongens Lyngby, Denmark

Saeed Mian Qaisar
College of Engineering
Effat University
Jeddah, Saudi Arabia

Vyom Raj
Department of Information
   Technology
National Institute of Technology
Raipur, Chhattisgarh, India

Omprakash S. Rajankar
Savitribai Phule Pune University
Maharashtra, India

Supriya O. Rajankar
Savitribai Phule Pune University
Maharashtra, India

Reem Ramadan
College of Engineering
Effat University
Jeddah, Saudi Arabia

Vijayalakshmi Ramasamy
University of Wisconsin-Parkside
Kenosha, WI, USA

Munaza Ramzan
Jaypee Institute of Information
   Technology (JIIT)
Noida (UP), India

Vrushali G. Raut
Savitribai Phule Pune University
Maharashtra, India

Mridu Sahu
Department of Information Technology
National Institute of Technology
Raipur, Chhattisgarh, India

Dr. Arun Sasidharan
Scientist-C (Neuroscience), Center for
Consciousness Studies,
Neurophysiology
National Institute of Mental Health and
Neuro Sciences (NIMHANS)
Research Collaborator for Axxonet Brain
Research Laboratory (ABRL)
Bengaluru, Karnataka, India

Shreya Sharma
Department of Information Technology
National Institute of Technology
Raipur, Chhattisgarh, India

Md. Hedayetul Islam Shovon
Science, Technology, Engineering and
Mathematics (STEM)
University of South Australia
Adelaide, Australia

Hari Shankar Singh
Department of Electronics and Comm-
unication Engineering
Thapar Institute of Engineering and
Technology
Patiala, Punjab, India

Savita Srivastava
British Institute of Engineering Tech-
nology (BIET)
Jhansi, India

Rahul Upadhyay
Department of Electronics and Comm-
unication Engineering
Thapar Institute of Engineering and
Technology
Patiala, Punjab, India

K.A. Venkatesh
Myanmar Institute of Information
Technology
Mandalay, Myanmar

K. Vijay
Dr. B.R. Ambedkar National Institute of
Technology (NIT)
Jalandhar, Punjab, India

1 Simulation Tools for Brain Signal Analysis

Munaza Ramzan and Suma Dawn

1.1 INTRODUCTION

The human brain contains 86 billion neurons with an average of 7,000 connections (synapses) to each other. The coordination and interaction of neurons with specific brain regions incorporate the functioning and working of the central nervous system (CNS) [1]. Therefore, it's not possible to analyze the information transmission and compare experimental results without simulation tools. To analyze such coordination and turn them into transformative gains of various practical and clinical applications, we need ongoing processing tools and data structures. With brain simulation tools, the brain-related mathematical theory, principles, and signals are returned out into new insights and improve computational validation of input data. They can be used for both online and offline data analysis, connectivity analysis, and visualization [2]. Brain-computer interface (BCI) is an integrated system comprised of analyzed brain signals and a computer to predict and monitor a particular state of a person. The brain signals which are produced by the CNS are acquired, analyzed, and translated into desired actions in three different ways [3]. First, the active BCIs are controlled by users consciously, and the output is directly extracted from conscious brain waves. Second, the reactive BCIs are stimulus-dependent in which the user reacts to an external stimulus, and the brain waves are modulated and analyzed indirectly to control an application. Third, the passive BCIs or implicit BCIs arbitrarily derive the output from extracted brain activities without the user control, such as monitoring of user intention and interpretation of different emotional states. To predict or monitor the person's cognitive state using brain signals, researchers and experimenters need to measure and analyze these signals in a well-defined manner. With this monitoring, different types of BCIs can be developed such as active, reactive, or passive BCIs. The basic requirement for each BCI system is the acquisition of brain signals and the commonly studied signals may include: electrical and magnetic signals [4]. The procedure for capturing such signals are EEG and MEG, respectively. To allow the processing and analysis of these signals, a collection of tools such as EEGLAB, BCILab, Fieldtrip, etc., as shown in Table 1.1, has been developed by different neuroscience communities [5]. Most of the tools are freely available for the analysis of multimodal signals with advanced signal processing techniques and methods.

The brain is continuously involved in cognitive activities, and to identify the certain task or hypothesis-related patterns and aspects, good quality signals need to

1

TABLE 1.1
BSTs for EEG/MEG signals

Toolbox	Version	License	Open-source	Framework	Procedures supported	Download link
EEGLAB	14 & 2019	GNU	Yes	MATLAB®	EEG, MEG	https://sccn.ucsd.edu/eeglab/download.php
BCILAB	1.0-beta	GNU	Yes	MATLAB®, EEGLAB-Plugin	EEG, MEG	ftp://sccn.ucsd.edu/pub/bcilab
Fieldtrip	–	GNU	Yes	MATLAB®	EEG, MEG, NIRS, ECoG	http://www.fieldtriptoolbox.org/download/
BrainNet Viewer	1.7	GNU	Yes	MATLAB®	Brain Network Visualization Toolbox.	https://www.nitrc.org/projects/bnv/
SIFT	1.4.1	GNU	Yes	MATLAB®	EEG, MEG, ECoG	https://www.nitrc.org/frs/downloadlink.php/9394
PyEEG	–	GNU	Yes	Python	EEG, MEG	https://github.com/forrestbao/pyeeg

be acquired and analyzed properly. The general protocol for analysis includes brain signal acquisition (EEG, MEG), pre-processing (detection and removal of artifacts, and noise), computation of statistical features, and then apply different learning algorithms and procedures.

1.2 TOOLBOXES FOR ANALYSIS OF BRAIN SIGNAL (EEG/MEG) RECORDINGS

1.2.1 EEGLAB-TOOLBOX

The EEGLAB is an interactive graphical user interface (GUI) MATLAB® toolbox for the analysis of electrophysiological signals such as EEG and MEG. It runs under different operating systems such as Windows, Unix, Linux, and Mac OS X. It is developed at Swartz Center for Computational Neuroscience (SCCN) and freely available at https://sccn.ucsd.edu/eeglab/download.php. It allows importing, exporting, loading, saving, manipulating, artifact rejection, time-frequency analysis, independent component analysis (ICA), and visualization of continuous and event-related EEG/MEG signals [6]. For special analysis and modeling, different EEGLAB plug-ins are available such as EMDLAB for empirical mode decomposition analysis, ERPLAB for event-related potential (ERP), and CSP for the analysis of common spatial patterns. It is accessible via three ways: (a) EEGLAB-GUI, (b) EEGLAB data structure and command history, and (c) EEGLAB scripting [7].

The below steps need to follow for installing EEGLAB-toolbox on your machine:

- After downloading this toolbox, open MATLAB® and add EEGLAB-Toolbox path to its search path as:
  MATLAB® Home -> Set Path -> Add with Subfolders -> Popup dialogue box will appear -> Select EEGLAB-Toolbox folder -> Click Ok -> Save.
- In the command window of MATLAB®, type eeglab; and hit enter as shown in Figure 1.1.

1.2.1.1 EEGLAB-GUI

The EEGLAB GUI enables users to apply various signal processing techniques and methods to EEG/MEG data without writing their own scripts. Menu shortcuts are incorporated in this toolbox, which allows users to import datasets with different formats, choose multiple datasets, extract data epochs, creating various plots and studies, compute statistics, etc. as shown in Figure 1.1.

1.2.1.2 Data Importing

1.2.1.2.1 Load Data as MATLAB® Array

To import MATLAB® array EEG data (.mat), we need to store the data file in a MATLAB® path and then open EEGLAB-GUI, click on the File menu, import data using EEGLAB functions and plug-ins, from the ASCII/float file or MATLAB® array as shown in Figure 1.2.

A dialogue box will prompt where we need to input dataset information such as the number of channels, sampling rate, epoch start time, etc. as shown in Figure 1.3.

To load an already saved or existing dataset, click on the file menu, then click on load existing dataset as shown in Figure 1.4.

FIGURE 1.1 EEGLAB-GUI.

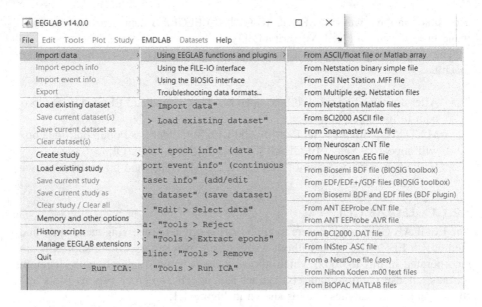

FIGURE 1.2 Import data in any format.

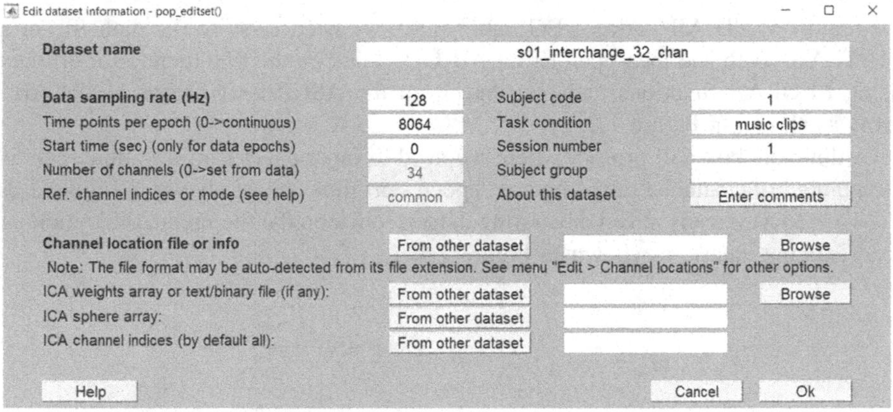

FIGURE 1.3 Input dataset information.

A dialogue box will appear where we can choose a file that we want to load with (.set) format. EEGLAB has default (.set) format.

The plot menu in EEGLAB-GUI enables different plotting and visualization options as shown in Figures 1.5a and b.

We can plot channel or sensor locations either by name or number. Similarly, other options like channel spectra map plot spectral plots of different channels. Channel ERP image, Channel ERPs, ERP map series, and sum/compare ERPs are used for time-domain event-related potential analysis. Component-related activities are used to visualize components that are created via different component analyses

FIGURE 1.4 Import saved dataset.

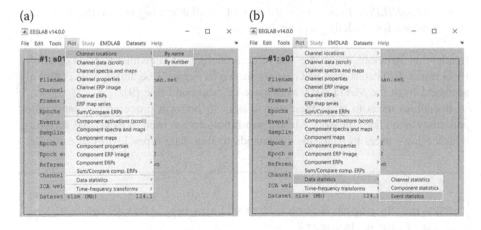

FIGURE 1.5 (a) Data visualization/plotting menu. (b) Data statistics with three sub-options.

such as independent component analysis (ICA). Data statistics option is also available under plot option which is used to plot statistical properties of input dataset such as mean, median, skewness, etc. It has three sub-categories: Channel statistics, component statistics, and event statistics. Time-frequency transforms option is used to characterize the spectral properties of time-series data. It has also three sub-options: channel time-frequency, component time-frequency, and component cross-coherence. Channel time-frequency detects inter-trial coherence (ITC) and event-related spectral distributions. Component time-frequency plots time-frequency decompositions of components. Component cross-coherence plots coherence between pairs of scalp electrodes [8].

1.2.1.3   EEGLAB Data-Structure

After loading the datafile using GUI, a data structure called EEG is created automatically. It stores the parameters of a dataset such as number of channels and locations, sampling-rate, number of events and epochs, etc., as shown in Figure 1.6a.

Once the interactive GUI is called by writing eeglab; in the MATLAB® command-line, different variables are created automatically in MATLAB® workspace as in Figure 1.6b. These reserved variables are defined as [8]:

- *ALLCOM*: It describes the commands which are issued from the EEGLAB-menu.
- *ALLEEG*: It describes all the loaded EEG/MEG datasets.
- *CURRENTSET*: It describes the index of the dataset which is currently used.
- *CURRENTSTUDY*: Study menu is used for parallel processing of multiple datasets. It describes the current study of datasets.
- *EEG*: It describes the data structure of the loaded EEG/MEG dataset with all information about it.
- *eeglabupdater*: It describes the current version, release date, etc. of the EEGLAB toolbox.
- *LASTCOM*: It describes the command which is issued from the EEGLAB lastly.
- *STUDY*: It describes the study.
- *PLUGINLIST*: It describes the list of available plug-ins of the EEGLAB toolbox for modeling and analysis.

Inside this structure, there are sub-structures like EEG.chanlocs, EEG.chaninfo, EEG.reject, EEG.stats, and EEG.etc, as shown in Figure 1.6c and d. This is directly accessed from the MATLAB® workspace or command line [9].

It enables users to write their own scripts to perform processing computations and analysis on their datasets. Mostly pop-functions are used in EEGLAB scripting, which allows users to adapt the commands to new data types [10]. For example:

```
EEG-data= pop_loadset ('Datafilename', 'DatafilePath');
% load input dataset
Preprocess1-data = pop_eegfilt (EEG-data, 4, 0) % input
data is highpass filtered above 4Hz
Preprocess2-data = pop_eegrej (EEG-data, [100 315]) %
reject some portions of data
Chan-locs = pop_chanedit (EEG-data.chanlocs, 'load',
{'/   E:\MATLAB\eeglab14_0_0b\sample_locs\  chanlo-
c_32.locs','filetype'}); % Add channel locations
Plot-data= pop_eegplot (EEG-data, 1, 1, 1) %plot
input data
```

FIGURE 1.6 (a) EEG data structure. (b) EEGLAB variables in MATLAB® workspace. (c) Chanloc data structure under EEG. (d) Chaninfo data structure under EEG.

1.2.2   BRAIN COMPUTER INTERFACE LAB TOOLBOX (BCILAB)

The BCILab is an open-source MATLAB® toolbox for the experimentation, analysis, and evaluation of BCI systems [11]. It is developed at SCCN and freely available at ftp://sccn.ucsd.edu/pub/bcilab. With EEGLAB, it can be used as a plug-in for designing and testing BCI frameworks. The BCILab-GUI appears on the screen with different menu items such as Data Source, Offline Analysis, Online Analysis, etc. The BCI systems predict the cognitive states of a person from brain signals that are measured through various direct and indirect measures such as EEG. Toolboxes like BCILab accelerate and simplify the research analysis in such areas. This toolbox offers GUI, MATLAB®-based scripting, and application programming interfaces (APIs) for real-time analysis. It also efficiently supports machine learning and statistical analysis of biosignal recordings as shown in Table 1.2 with the integration of plug-in frameworks for advanced modeling [12].

1.2.2.1   Installation

The below steps need to follow for installing the BCILab toolbox on your machine:

TABLE 1.2

Signal processing, feature extraction, and machine learning algorithms supported by BCILab

Signal preprocessing algorithms	Feature extraction algorithms	Machine learning algorithms
Remove baseline	Common spatial patterns (CSP)	Support vector machine (SVM)
Independent component analysis (ICA)	Covariance and coherence features	Variational logistic regression
Generalized principal component analysis (GPCA)	Phase synchronization Indexing (PSI)	Regularized linear and logistic regression
Surface Laplacian	Statistical feature extraction	Linear discriminant analysis (LDA)
Moving window averaging	Lagrangian regression	Quadratic discriminant analysis (QDA)
Re-referencing and re-sampling	Multi-band feature extraction	Bayesian classification
Channel selection or removal	Spatio-spectral dynamics	Gaussian mixture models with clusters
Wavelet analysis	–	–
Power spectral density (PSD)	–	–
Artifact rejection (e.g. eye movement peak removal)	–	–

- After downloading this toolbox, open MATLAB® and add the BCILab Toolbox path to its search path as:
  MATLAB® Home -> Set Path -> Add with Subfolders -> Popup dialogue box will appear -> Select BCILab -Toolbox folder -> Click Ok -> Save.
- In the command window of MATLAB®, type bcilab; and hit enter as shown in Figure 1.7.

1.2.2.2 BCILab-GUI

The BCILab-GUI offers most of the features for analysis such as loading and saving of recordings, computation of predictive models using source data, online analysis for prediction of real-time states, and also provides post-hoc analysis via offline analysis of recorded data. The three main components of GUI are Data Source, Offline Analysis, and Online Analysis. The Data Source menu offers to load of recordings for analysis; Offline Analysis allows us to define computational approaches and predictive models from saved data recordings, evaluate its performance and visualization of different aspects of the developed model; Online Analysis allows real-time analysis using predictive models as shown in Figure 1.8a–c.

For beginners and experimenters, BCILab-GUI provides rapid set-up to perform both offline and online analysis to design BCIs for cognitive monitoring.

1.2.2.3 BCILab Scripting

The BCILab scripting boosts computational productivity and allows us to automate the workflow of loading data, define approaches for model building, model learning,

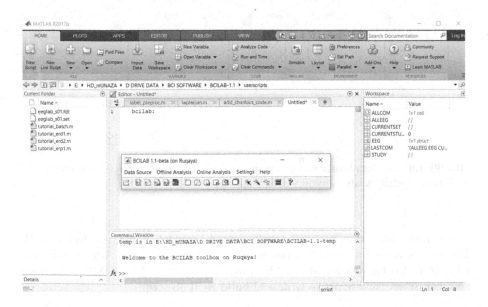

FIGURE 1.7 BCILab-GUI.

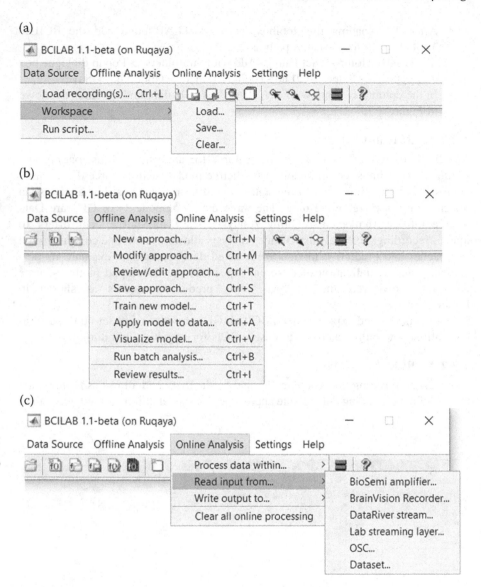

FIGURE 1.8   (a) Data Source menu with sub-options. (b) Offline Analysis menu with sub-options. (c) Online Analysis menu with sub-options.

performance estimation, plot and visualize model, model saving, and testing [13]. The scripts invoke user-defined functions or built-in functions. After adding the BCILab to the appropriate MATLAB® directory, click on MATLAB® File menu and then select New Script to write and build BCILab scripts.

1.2.2.3.1 Example

```
bcilab;
sub1_data= io_loadset('bcilab:/s01/data.set') %load
dataset
new_approach = 'CSP' % specify the approach such as
Common Spatial Patters (CSP)
bci_visualize (model) %visualize model
test_data = io_loadset('bcilab:/s01/test/data.set');
[model_predictions, testloss, teststats, targets] =
bci_predict (model, test_data)
disp(['training-mis-classification-rate:'num2str
(loss*100,3)'%']);
disp(['testing-mis-classification-rate:'num2str
(loss*100,3)'%']);
disp(['classes-predicted:'num2str(model_predictions
{2}* model_predictions {3})')]);
disp(['classes-actual:'num2str(targets)')]);
```

1.2.3   PYEEG

Python is gaining popularity in scientific research, such as in computational neuroscience with simple syntax and high-level libraries [14]. For example, in disease diagnoses, such as epilepsy and other neurodegenerative diseases, these libraries support the development of computational systems in less time with more accuracy. PyEEG has been introduced for feature extraction to save time and cost for computational neuroscientists [15,16]. It is an open-source Python module to extract features from EEG/MEG recorded signals. It has two sets of functions: preprocessing and feature extraction functions as depicted in Table 1.3. The installation steps and guidelines to PyEEG are available at https://github.com/forrestbao/pyeeg and https://pip.pypa.io/en/latest/reference/pip_install/#git.

1.2.3.1   Example

```
import pyeeg
import numpy*
data_id = open('S01.txt', 'r')
temp= data_id.readlines()
data=[float(i) for I in temp]
```

```
print pyeeg.embed_seq(data,2,6)
print pyeeg.dfa(data)
print pyeeg.pfd(data)
print pyeeg.hurst(data)
print pyeeg.svd_entropy(data)
```

1.2.4   FIELDTRIP TOOLBOX

The Fieldtrip toolbox is an open-source MATLAB® toolbox for the analysis of brain signals (EEG, MEG, and NIRS). It doesn't have a GUI like other toolboxes (EEGLAB and BCILab), but MATLAB® scripting is necessary as it contains all the functions of this Toolbox [17]. It is developed at Donders Centre for Cognitive Neuroimaging (DCCN) and freely available at http://www.fieldtriptoolbox.org/download/.

1.2.4.1   Installation

Follow the below steps for installing Fieldtrip-toolbox on your machine:

- After downloading this toolbox, open MATLAB® and add the Fieldtrip-Toolbox path to its search path as:
  MATLAB® Home -> Set Path -> Add with Subfolders -> Popup dialogue box will appear -> Select Fieldtrip-Toolbox folder -> Click Ok -> Save.

It provides broad functionality for analysis of signals such as preprocessing, sensor-level analysis, source reconstruction, and supports invasive BCI analysis such as electrocorticography (ECoG) or intracranial-EEG monitoring, analysis of

TABLE 1.3
Preprocessing and feature extraction functions supported by PyEEG

Pre-processing function	Pre-processing name	Feature function	Feature name
embed_seq()	Embedding sequence	Pdf()	Petrosian fractal dimension (PFD)
first_order_diff()	First order differential sequence	dfa()	Detrended fluctuation analysis (dfa)
–	–	fisher_info()	Fisher information
–	–	bin_power()	Power spectral intensity
–	–	hfd()	Higuchi fractal dimension (HFD)
–	–	spectral_entropy()	Shannon's spectral entropy

transcranial magnetic stimulation-EEG, analysis of functional near-infrared spectroscopy (fNIRS), various statistical analysis procedures, and whole-brain connectivity analysis [18]. The collection of functions for this analysis are categorized into various categories as shown in Table 1.4.

The above functions implement specific algorithms with a configuration structure of the parameters. All functions have their own configuration structures and are executed within it. For example, the configuration structure for an EEG recording for a particular subject (say S01) is defined as:

```
addpath<fieldtrip_path> %add Fieldtrip directory to
MATLAB path
Cfg=[]; %use default options
Cfg.dataset='S01.m';
Cfg. trialdef.eventvalue=1;
Cfg.trialdef.prestim=0;
Cfg.trialdef.poststim=2;
Cfg =ft_preprocessing(Cfg);
```

After correctly setting the path of a Fieldtrip toolbox in MATLAB®, write help <function-name> in the command window to get an understanding of a particular function and its configurable settings.

1.2.4.2   Reading the MEG/EEG Recording Using Fieldtrip

The recording data can contain epochs with linked triggers or continuous epochs without specifying trigger locations [19]. To read MEG/EEG data files in Fieldtrip, we should call the high-level functions such as ft_definetrial, which then call low-level functions such as ft_read_header/data. For example:

```
Cfg.dataset="S01.eeg"; %dataset specifies the combina-
tion of multiple recorded data
header= ft_read_header('S01.eeg') %return header in-
formation with sampling rate, number of channels, number
of samples, number of trials, labels attached tor da-
taset, etc.
data=  ft_read_data('S01.eeg');  %  a  3D  matrix
(Channels*Data-samples*trials)
```

TABLE 1.4

Some functions supported by Fieldtrip for different types of analysis [17]

Type of analysis	Function category example	Description
Pre-processing	ft_ preprocessingft_ definetrialft_ artifact_eogft_ resampledata	ft_ preprocessing reads input (EEG, MEG) recordings and applies various preprocessing methods which are specified by the user. For example, [data_s01] = ft_ preprocessing (cfg; datafile); where "cfg" is the configuration and "datafile" is the file containing input data. ft_ definetrial defines the data segments for analysis, ft_ artifact_eog identifies EOG artifacts from input data, and ft_ resampledata resample or downsample the input data.
Time-domain analysis (e.g. event-related potentials (ERPs))	ft_ timelockanalysisft_ timelockgrandaverageft_ singleplotERft_ topoplotER	ft_ timelockanalysis computes averaged potentials (ERP), ft_ timelockgrandaverage computes averaged potentials and variance over subjects or trials, ft_ singleplotER plots ERP of a single channel, ft_ topoplotER plots 2D–3D topographical distributions of ERPs.
Frequency/time-frequency analysis	ft_ freqanalysisft_ freqbaselineft_ freqgranda-verageft_ freqstatistics	ft_ freqanalysis performs frequency or time-frequency analysis on input data over different trials. ft_ freqbaseline performs baseline normalization (either percent power change/decibel) on time-frequency signals, ft_ freqgrandaverage evaluates the cross subject power-spectrum of time-frequency data, ft_ freqstatistics performs various statistical procedures such as parametric or non-parametric permutation testing.

(Continued)

TABLE 1.4 (Continued)

Type of analysis	Function category example	Description
Statistical analysis	ft_timelockstatisticsft_statfun_meanft_statfun_rocft_statfun_diff	ft_timelockstatistics computes time-lock significant probabilities and critical values by applying statistical tests, ft_statfun_mean computes average over all conditions in input data, ft_statfun_roc computes Area Under Curve (AUC) of the Receiver Operator Characteristics (ROC) to distinguish conditions in input data, ft_statfun_diff computes the mean difference in two conditions.
Source localization analysis	ft_sourceanalysisft_dipolefittingft_dipolesimulationft_sourcestatistics	ft_sourceanalysis performs beamformer dipole analysis of EEG, MEG data, ft_dipolefitting performs a grid search and finds the location of dipole model which defines the topography of extracted signals, ft_dipolesimulation simulates the spatial distribution of dipoles, ft_sourcestatistics computes dipole statistics and perform hypothetical testing.
Plotting and visualization	ft_multiplotERft_clusterplotft_layoutplotft_mvaranalysis	ft_multiplotER plots ERP over, and oscillatory activities over different frequency bands, ft_clusterplothighlight clusters in different 2D–3D topoplots, ft_layoutplot plots 2D channel locations, ft_mvaranalysis performs multivariate autoregressive modeling.
Real-time analysis	ft_realtime_average	ft_realtime_average performs real-time averaging over data. For example, ft_realtime_average(cfg).

1.2.4.3   Reading Event Information

After defining the segments of data that we want to analyze using the ft_definetrial function, the ft_read_event function can be used to read event information [19]. It actually reads the trigger information that is located with epochs. For example:

```
event_info=ft_read_event ('S01.eeg');
event_info(2) % to access the second event information.
```

1.2.4.4   Re-Referencing EEG Recordings

EEG recordings can be re-referenced while MEG recordings are reference-free [20]. In EEG acquisition, referencing refers to the recorded signals at each electrode relative to voltages recorded at other electrodes. The reference electrode needs to be chosen carefully because the activity recorded by the reference electrode is reflected in all other electrodes. The position of a reference electrode should not be close to the electrode where we expect the main effects of the task-related activity. Also, it should not be referenced to one of the hemisphere locations, as it may add laterality bias to our recordings [21]. We can re-reference the recorded data in an "offline" mode, for example in the EEGLAB toolbox simply click on the tools menu in EEGLAB-GUI and click on the re-reference option and in Fieldtrip we can re-reference as:

```
Cfg.implicitref = 'CZ'; % Cfg.implicitref is the option
in ft_preprocessing for implicit reference.
Cfg.reref = 'yes;
Cfg.ref channel = {'CZ' 'LM'}; % CZ and LM are the common
reference channel and Left Mastoid respectively.
Data-s01= ft_preprocessing(cfg);
```

1.2.4.5   Visualize Electrode Locations

There is an international system known as the 10/20 System for describing the location of EEG sensors over the scalp. It defines the locations based on the underlying area of the cerebral cortex [20]. For example, channel location "FP1" identifies the frontal lobe on the left hemisphere because the odd number refers to the left hemisphere and even numbers refer to the right hemisphere. In EEG, these locations are adjusted according to the experimental goal, and to visualize their position we can use Plot-menu in EEGLAB-GUI and then click on channel locations either by name or number and in Fieldtrip these locations can be visualized as:

```
Cfg = [];
cfg.layout='ordered';
cfg.width=3.0;
cfg.height=2.5;
Chan_loc= ft_prepare_layout(Cfg)
```

To use the Fieldtrip toolbox for analysis, an analysis protocol needs to be defined that is basically a MATLAB® script containing application-specific functions. In Figure 1.9, an example of analysis protocol for three different analyses namely ERP Analysis, Time-Frequency Analysis, and Source Analysis is depicted.

1.2.4.6 Example

```
Cfg=[]; %use default options
Cfg.dataset='S01.m';
Cfg =ft_definetrial(Cfg);
Disp(Cfg.trl) % Cfg.trl is the matrix of trial segments
that are selected for analysis using ft_definetrial.
Prep_data= ft_preprocessing(Cfg);
Plot(Prep_data.time{1}, Prep_data.trial{1});
```

1.2.5 BRAINNET VIEWER

It is a graph-theoretical visualization tool for topographical architectures of human brain connectomes. It helps to visualize the functional and structural connectivity patterns from different views [22]. It is freely available at https://www.nitrc.org/projects/bnv/. It has a user-friendly GUI and is developed under MATLAB®. Its functions are as [23]:

- Connectivity patterns are displayed as brain surfaces with a combination of nodes, edges, and volumes.
- According to the connectivity strength, color, and size of nodes and edges are adjustable.
- Interactive options such as zoom-in, zoom-out, and rotation are provided.

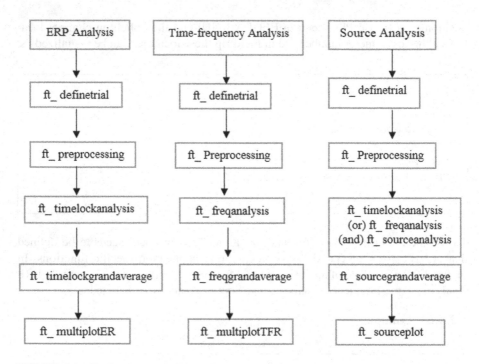

FIGURE 1.9   Basic steps to build analysis protocol in Fieldtrip toolbox.

- Different types of image format exporting and demonstration videos options are available.
- It supports command line calling.
- Node files can be generated from the NIfTI atlas using available codes.

1.2.5.1   Installation

The below steps need to follow for installing the BrainNet Viewer toolbox on your machine:

- After downloading this toolbox, open MATLAB® and add the BrainNet Viewer path to its search path as:
  MATLAB® Home -> Set Path -> Add with Subfolders -> Popup dialogue box will appear -> Select BrainNet Viewer folder -> Click Ok -> Save.
- In the command window of MATLAB®, type BrainNet and hit enter as shown in Figures 1.10 and 1.11.

1.2.5.2   File Menu

To visualize the brain connectomes, we require to load a surface file, node file, edge file, and volume file. Figure 1.12 illustrates the file menu and its sub-options.

All files need not be loaded together, but a combination of these files is also acceptable and they generate different networks [24]. For example, we can load the

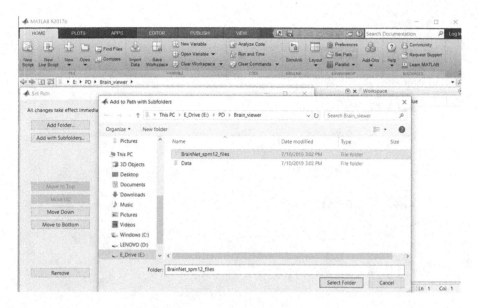

FIGURE 1.10 Add BrainNet Viewer to MATLAB® path.

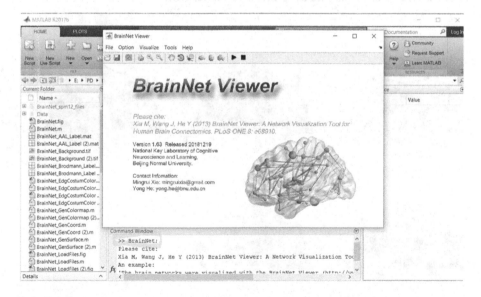

FIGURE 1.11 BrainNet Viewer-GUI main window.

surface and node file only, or surface, node, and edge files to draw and visualize connectivity patterns as shown in Figure 1.13.

The node and edge files can be generated according to the activity tasks. There are several brain surface template files, node and edge files provided in the BrainNet Viewer folder which you can upload directly.

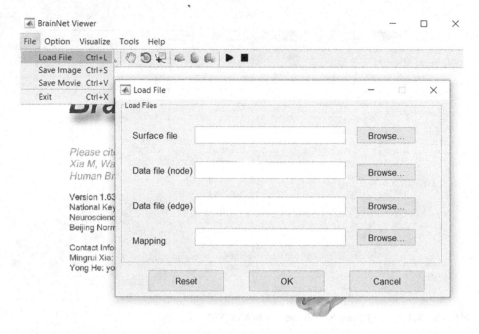

FIGURE 1.12 Load input files using BrainNet Viewer GUI.

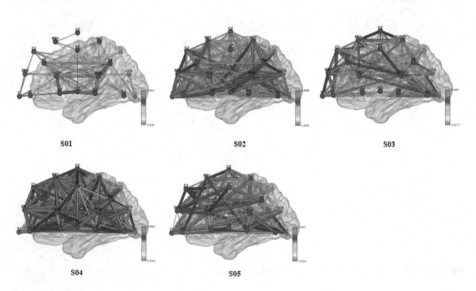

S01   S02   S03

S04   S05

FIGURE 1.13 Connectivity patterns for different subjects (S01, S02, S03, S04, and S05) using surface, node, and edge files.

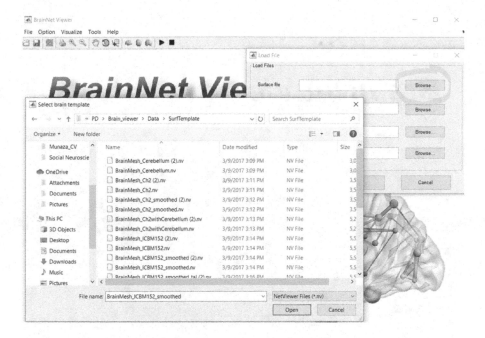

FIGURE 1.14   Load surface templates.

1.2.5.2.1 Load Surface File

To load the surface file, click on the Browse button and select one of the surface templates from the popup dialogue box as shown in Figure 1.14.

These surface files are based on two brain templates (ICBM152 and Colin27) and right or left hemispheres.

1.2.5.2.2 Load Node File

The node file represents the information of nodes or channels. BrainNet Viewer file provides the node files which are obtained from AAL90, Power264, Fair34, etc [24]. To load the node file, click on the Browse button next to the node file and select one of the node templates from the popup dialogue box as shown in Figure 1.15.

Each node file has six columns: the first three columns are the node coordinates, the fourth column represents its color, the fifth represents the size and the sixth represents the node labels.

1.2.5.2.3 Load Edge File

The edge file represents the connectivity matrix among the region of interest (ROI) such as correlation, phase synchronization value (PSV), coherence, etc [24]. The dimension of the matrix corresponds to the number of nodes. To load the edge file, click on the Browse button next to the edge file and select one of the edge templates from the popup dialogue box as shown in Figure 1.16.

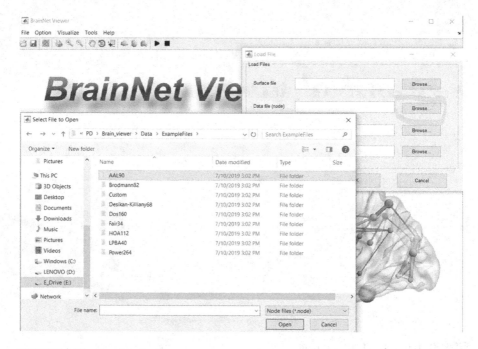

FIGURE 1.15   Load node files.

1.2.5.3   Option Menu

In the options menu, the option panel represents different aspects of image visualization such as "Layout," "Global," "Surface," "Node," "Edge," "Volume," and "Image" as shown in Figure 1.17a–g.

1.2.5.3.1 Layout Option Panel

In the Layout option, a user can set different views such as Single view, Lateral and medial view, Lateral, medial, and dorsal view, Lateral, medial, and ventral view, and Full view. In Single view, there are sub-options for view direction like Sagittal view (Left-side), Axial view (dorsal-side), Coronal view (frontal-side), and Custom view as shown in Figure 1.17a.

In a Single view, there is only one brain model with one view in the figure such as the Sagittal view (left-side), Axial view (dorsal-side), Coronal view (frontal-side), and Custom view [25]. In the Lateral and medial view, the lateral view in the upper row and medial view in the lower row of the left and right hemispheres are shown. Similarly, in the Lateral, medial, and ventral view, the lateral view in the upper row, medial view in the middle row, and ventral view in the lower row of the left and right hemispheres are shown. In the Lateral, medial and dorsal view, the lateral view in the upper row, and medial view in the lower row of the left and right hemisphere are shown with the whole brain view displayed from the dorsal side in the middle. In Full view, either six or eight views of brain connectomes are displayed. In the six view model, the top row from left to right are left side, top side and frontal side, while the bottom row from left

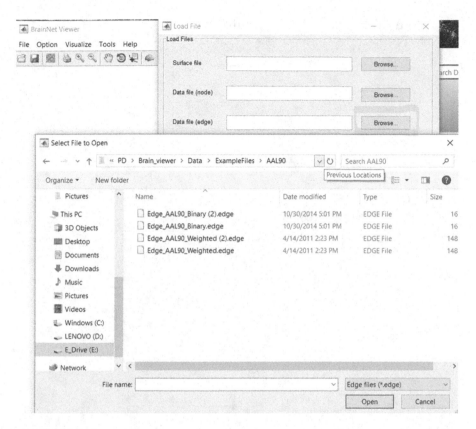

FIGURE 1.16 Load edge files.

to right are right sides, bottom side, and backside. In the eight view model, the first row from left to right is the lateral view of the left hemisphere, topside, lateral view of the right hemisphere, the second row from left to right are the medial view of the left hemisphere, bottom side, the medial view of the right hemisphere, and the third row are frontal side and backside [25].

1.2.5.3.2 Global Option Panel

The Global option Panel provides the display properties of the figure such as background color, object material, shading properties, lighting algorithm, light direction, renderer, graph detail, and the mark left and right as shown in Figure 1.17b.

The Background Color option offers to change the color of the background. Object Material option has four sub-options: Shiny, Dull, Metal, and Custom for brain surfaces. Shading properties include Flat, Faceted, and Interp. Lighting algorithms include Flat, Gouraud, Phong, and None. Light direction sets the direction of light and provides three options: Headlight, Right, and Left. Renderer provides OpenGL and zbuffer options. Graph detail sets the level of objects by adjusting the

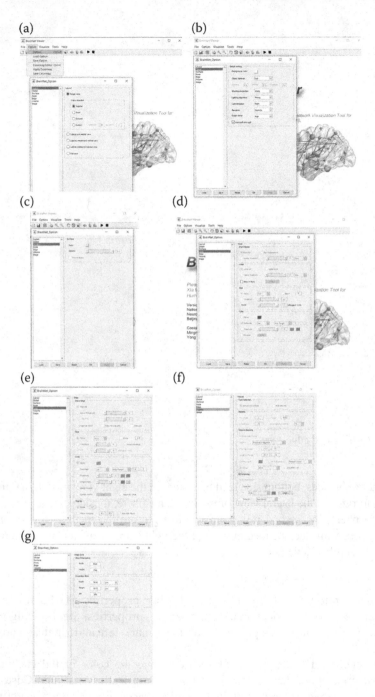

FIGURE 1.17   (a) Layout option Panel under Option Menu. (b) Global option Panel under Option Menu. (c) Surface option Panel under Option Menu. (d) Node option Panel under Option Menu. (e) Edge option Panel under Option Menu. (f) Volume option Panel under Option Menu. (g) Image option Panel under Option Menu.

number of nodes and edges. It has three options: High, Moderate, and Low. Mark left and right displays the "L" and "R" markers in the figure.

1.2.5.3.3 Surface Option Panel

To adjust the properties of the brain surface, the Surface panel provides different options such as Color, Opacity, and Double Brain as shown in Figure 1.17c.

Enabling the Color option changes the color of the brain surface. The opacity option changes the transparency of the brain surface by entering the desired number range in the edit box or dragging the slider bar. The double Brain option is used to show the relationship between nodes by displaying two brain models. The node and edge file need to be arranged for displaying these models. For example, in a node file, the information is duplicated according to input data. On the left side of the brain model, the first half of node information is displayed and on the right side of the brain model, the second half of the node information is displayed. Similarly, the edge file, which contains the intra- and inter-connectivity association matrix, needs to be arranged for both left and right brain models.

1.2.5.3.4 Node Option Panel

The Node option Panel is divided into four zones: Node drawing, Labels, Size, and Color as shown in Figure 1.17d.

These options are enabled according to nodal information in the node file. In Node drawing or draw nodes, there are sub-options such as Draw All, Has Connections, and Above Threshold. Label options contain four sub-options: Label All, Label None, Above Threshold, and Show in Front. Node size option contains Value, Equal, Above Threshold, and Scale. Node Color option contains Same, Colormap, Above Threshold, Modular, and Load Custom Color. The Threshold option enables us to set the threshold value for color and size for drawing the nodes higher than the enabled value.

1.2.5.3.5 Edge Option Panel

The Edge option Panel is similar to the node panel with four zones: Edge drawing, Edge Size, Edge Color, and Opacity as shown in Figure 1.17e.

These options are enabled according to the connectivity matrix information in the edge file. The edge strength is drawn as per the association value of edges between nodes. In edge drawing or draw edges, there are sub-options such as Draw All, absolute value, inter-hemi edges, directed, and Above Threshold. Edge size option contains Value, Equal, Above Threshold, and Scale. The Edge Color option contains the Same, Colormap, Threshold, Length, Nodal Module, and Custom matrix. The Threshold option enables us to set the threshold value for a color, and size for drawing the edges higher than the enabled value. Edge opacity contains the same, mapping and absolute value sub-options.

1.2.5.3.6 Volume Option Panel

This panel enables us to draw brain volume surfaces and ROI clusters. It is also divided into four zones: Type of selection (Volume to Surface or ROI drawing),

Statistic (Threshold, P-value, Cluster size, Connectivity criterion), Volume mapping (Display, Positive and negative range, Map algorithm, and colormap), and ROI Drawing (Draw All, Custom, and smooth) as shown in Figure 1.17f.

In the Statistic zone, the threshold value is used to set a particular range of voxels, P-values are related to statistical volumes, cluster size is used to display the size of the cluster, and connectivity criterion is used to set the voxel connections. In the Volume Mapping zone, the Volume Data range depicts the minimum and maximum values of the input volume file. The display has three drop-down-list options: "Positive and Negative," "only Positive," and "only Negative." These options set the range of the colorbar from minimum negative to maximum positive. Map algorithm is used to find the vertex values in the brain surface. It has eight algorithms: "Nearest Voxel," "Average Vertex," "Average Voxel," "Gaussian," "Interpolated," "Maximum Voxel," "Minimum Voxel," and "Extremum Voxel." In the ROI drawing zone, there are four sub-options: Draw All, Custom, Color, and Smooth. All these options are related to the ROI volume surface.

1.2.5.3.7 Image Option Panel

This panel is used to set the properties of an output image. It has two zones: Pixel dimension and Document size, as shown in Figure 1.17g.

In the pixel dimension, height and width are used to adjust the pixel dimensions. In document size, the resolution of an output image is set in dots per inch (DPI).

1.2.5.4 Visualize Menu

There are three options in the Visualize menu: View Matrix, Clear Figure, and Redraw as shown in Figure 1.18.

View Matrix enables us to view the connectivity or association matrix, Redraw is used to redraw the image with previously loaded files, and Clear Figure is used to remove the network and display the default information [24].

1.2.5.5 Tools Menu

The Merge Mesh option under the Tools menu in BrainNet Viewer-GUI is used to merge the Left-Mesh and Right Mesh hemispheres of the brain surface files [24]. Figure 1.19 depicts the Tools menu with the Merge Mesh sub-menu.

FIGURE 1.18 Visualize or plotting menu.

FIGURE 1.19 Tools menu with merge mesh sub-option.

1.3 CONCLUSION

In this study, some of the open-source toolboxes for analysis of EEG/MEG signals have been introduced. The past few decades have seen neuroscience with the computer-aided diagnosis of cognitive states, restore communication, augmentation in BCI systems using EEG signals as an emerging field of research. In order for continuing the advances in this area, there is a need for powerful and cost-effective platforms for the analysis, evaluation, and deployment of new systems and methods. In this study, such platforms and frameworks for the analysis of EEG/MEG recorded signals have been discussed. These frameworks accelerate the pace of innovations in computer-aided neuroscience research areas. Application-specific analysis such as time-domain ERP analysis, time-frequency analysis, and statistical procedures over EEG/MEG signals can be performed with relative flexibility and versatility of these frameworks. With both GUI and scripting interfaces, both beginners and experienced researchers can innovate their ideas in this area of research. Also, some frameworks allow both online and offline analysis of recordings and shorten the time required to develop a well-founded and reasonably complete theoretical and empirical basis for real-time analysis of brain signals for a wide range of purposes.

REFERENCES

1. Domschke, Angelika, and Frank Josef Boehm. "Application of a conceptual nanomedical platform to facilitate the mapping of the human brain: a survey of cognitive functions and implications." In *The Physics of the Mind and Brain Disorders*, pp. 741–771. Springer, Cham, 2017.
2. Hill, Sean. "Whole-brain simulation." In *The Future of the Brain: Essays by the World's Leading Neuroscientists*, 111. Princeton University Press, 2016.
3. Mousavi, Mahta, and Virginia R. de Sa. "Spatio-temporal analysis of error-related brain activity in active and passive brain-computer interfaces." *Brain-Computer Interfaces* 6, 4 (2019): 118–127.
4. Blundell, Inga, Romain Brette, Thomas A. Cleland, Thomas G. Close, Daniel Coca, Andrew P. Davison, Sandra Diaz-Pier et al. "Code generation in computational neuroscience: a review of tools and techniques." *Frontiers in Neuroinformatics* 12 (2018): 68.
5. Arnaud Delorme, Tim Mullen, Christian Kothe, Zeynep Akalin Acar, Nima Bigdely-Shamlo, Andrey Vankov, Scott Makeig, "EEGLAB, SIFT, NFT, BCILAB, and ERICA: new tools for advanced EEG processing", *Computational Intelligence and Neuroscience*, 2011. doi:10.1155/2011/130714.
6. Delorme Arnaud, and Makeig Scott "EEGLAB: an open-source toolbox for analysis of single-trial EEG dynamics including independent component analysis." *Journal of Neuroscience Methods*, *134*(1), (2004): 9–21.
7. Valipour, Shaligram, and Kulkarni "Detection of an alpha rhythm of EEG signal based on EEGLAB". *International Journal of Engineering Research and Application*, *4*(01), (2014): 154–159.

8. Brunner, Clemens et al. "Eeglab—an open-source Matlab toolbox for electro-physiological research." *Biomedizinische Technik. Biomedical Engineering*, 58 Suppl 1 (2013). doi:10.1515/bmt-2013-4182

9. Mullen Tim, Delorme Arnaud, Kothe Christian, & Makeig Scott "An electrophysiological information flow toolbox for EEGLAB". *Biological Cybernetics*, 83, (2010): 35–45.

10. Sosa, O., Y. Quijano, M. Doniz, and J. E. C. Quero. "Development of an EEG signal processing program based on EEGLAB." *2011 Pan American Health Care Exchanges* (2011): 199–202. doi: 10.1109/PAHCE.2011.5871881. https://ieeexplore.ieee.org/document/5871881.

11. Kothe, C. and Scott Makeig. "BCILAB: a platform for brain-computer interface development." *Journal of Neural Engineering* 10 5 (2013): 056014.

12. Choudhury, Tanupriya, Amrendra Tripathi, Bhawna Arora, and Archit Aggarwal. "Implementation of common spatial pattern algorithm using EEG in BCILAB." In *International Conference on Recent Developments in Science, Engineering and Technology*, pp. 288–300. Springer, Singapore, 2019.

13. Kinney-Lang, E., S. Murji, D. Kelly, B. Paffrath, E. Zewdie, and A. Kirton. "Designing a flexible tool for rapid implementation of brain-computer interfaces (BCI) in game development." In *2020 42nd Annual International Conference of the IEEE Engineering in Medicine & Biology Society (EMBC)*, pp. 6078–6081. IEEE, 2020.

14. Bao, F. S., Xin Liu, and Christina Zhang. "PyEEG: an open-source python module for EEG/MEG feature extraction." *Computational Intelligence and Neuroscience* 2011 (2011).

15. Thara, D. K., B. G. Premasudha, and Fan Xiong. "Auto-detection of epileptic seizure events using a deep neural network with different feature scaling techniques. Pattern Recognition Letters 128 (2019): 544–550.

16. Desai, Rahul, Pratik Porob, Penjo Rebelo, Damodar Reddy Edla, and Annushree Bablani. "EEG data classification for mental state analysis using wavelet packet transform and Gaussian process classifier." *Wireless Personal Communications* 115 (2020): 1–21.

17. Oostenveld, R., P. Fries, E. Maris, and Jan-Mathijs Schoffelen. "FieldTrip: open source software for advanced analysis of MEG, EEG, and invasive electrophysiological data." *Computational Intelligence and Neuroscience* 1 (2011).

18. Litvak, V., J. Mattout, S. Kiebel, C. Phillips, R. Henson, J. Kilner, G. Barnes, R. Oostenveld, J. Daunizeau, G. Flandin, W. Penny, and Karl J. Friston. "EEG and MEG data analysis in SPM8." *Computational Intelligence and Neuroscience* (2011).

19. Lee, Chungki, R. Oostenveld, S. H. Lee, L. Kim, Hokun Sung, and J. Choi. "Dipole source localization of mouse electroencephalogram using the fieldtrip toolbox." *PLoS ONE* 8 (2013).

20. Mahjoory, Keyvan, V. Nikulin, L. Botrel, K. Linkenkaer-Hansen, M. Fato, and S. Haufe. "Consistency of EEG source localization and connectivity estimates." *NeuroImage* 152 (2017): 590–601.

21. Costa, Madalena et al. "Multiscale entropy analysis of biological signals." *Physical Review. E, Statistical, Nonlinear, and Soft Matter Physics*, 71.2 Pt 1 (2005): 021906. doi:10.1103/PhysRevE.71.021906

22. Xia, Mingrui, Jinhui Wang, and Y. He. "BrainNet Viewer: a network visualization tool for human brain connectomics." *PLoS ONE* 8 (2013): e68910. doi: 10.1371/journal.pone.0068910.

23. Xia, Mingrui et al. "BrainNet Viewer: a network visualization tool for human brain connectomics." *PLoS ONE* 8,7 e68910. 2013, doi:10.1371/journal.pone.0068910

24. Xia, M. (2014). BrainNet Viewer Manual.

25. Urquhart, Elizabeth L., Hashini Wanniarachchi, Xinlong Wang, George Alexandrakis, and Hanli Liu. "Functional connectivity changes from transcranial infrared laser stimulation measured by functional near-infrared spectroscopy." In *Microscopy Histopathology and Analytics*, pp. JW3A–33. Optical Society of America, 2020.

2 Processing Techniques and Analysis of Brain Sensor Data Using Electroencephalography

Munaza Ramzan and Suma Dawn

2.1 INTRODUCTION

What makes us humans is the essence of emotions that are characterized as intense mental activities and feelings. The emotions range between arousal and valence such as confrontation of fearful or life-threatening events for example stimulus arised from high sexual appeal increases the levels of arousal or valance [1]. Human behavior is comprised of three main components: emotions, actions, and cognitions. The interaction between them enables us to perceive, respond, and have relations with other people in our surroundings. The emotions heavily affect human behavior, intelligence, and decision making; therefore, they need to be captured either using qualitative or quantitative analysis [2]. The information processing of brain functions with the advancement in artificial intelligence (AI) and signal-processing techniques open up a plethora of opportunities in the field of computational neuroscience for making applications that can make decisions autonomously and accurately.

In recent years, modeling the brain functions from the nonstationary nature of electrochemical signals has been proven to be a hard problem. But computational neuroscience forms a meeting ground for mathematics and the study of cognitive functions that are produced by the population of neurons. To capture the neurocognitive dynamics and processes, various high-resolution techniques are used such as electroencephalography (EEG), functional magnetic resonance imaging (fMRI), magnetoencephalography (MEG) and so on. The specific applications, properties, and characteristics of these techniques will be discussed one by one. Among these techniques, EEG is a noninvasive method that contains the rhythmic activities of the brain which reflects the neural oscillations. These oscillations are the fluctuations in the excitability of neuron populations. The information of frequency, power, and phase is extracted using these oscillations. The human brain is a highly nonstationary processing unit in which 100 billion neurons communicate through electrochemical signals. It uses the same amount of power as a 10-watt light bulb and can store five times as much information as Wikipedia. It is a very complicated and mysterious information processing system; to know how to analyze neuro-cognitive data efficiently and make an inference about where in the brain the activities may come from is the main aim of computational neuroscience. The main application areas are—home automation, operator monitoring, forensics, entertainment, and brain–computer interfaces. The brain data usually capture a large volume of samples, high dimensional features (statistical, temporal and spatial) and multi-modal characteristics of different states of brain functions. To analyze such features, the traditional supervised techniques have a fast training time but lower accuracies, while deep learning methods have longer training time and high accuracies. To improve the efficiency and optimality in training and accuracies, the extreme learning machine (ELM) approach is considered an optimal generalization model with high learning accuracy and speed. The ELM has better generalization performance with minimum training error and the smallest norm of weights. The hidden nodes are randomly generated with any continuous sampling distribution probability, independent of training samples and also not iteratively tuned while learning.

2.2 BUILDING BLOCKS OF THE HUMAN BRAIN

The human brain lies in the category of the central nervous system (CNS). It is divided into different regions such as cerebrum, cerebellum, brainstem, limbic system, etc. as shown in Figure 2.1.

Each brain region is discussed below:

1. Cerebrum/cortex: It is the largest and most forward portion of the brain with a highly convoluted topography of sulci and gyri. It has two hemispheres and is generally associated with higher functioning such as sensory processing. The cerebral cortex is further divided into four lobes: frontal, temporal, occipital and parietal.
   - Frontal lobe: This lobe is associated with conscious thoughts, voluntary limb and eye movements, and decision making. The dopamine sensitive

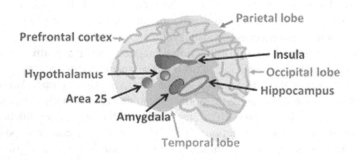

FIGURE 2.1   Different brain regions
Source: https://commons.wikimedia.org/wiki/File:Some_brain_areas.png (https://creativecommons.org/licenses/by-sa/3.0/

neurons are mostly present in this lobe due to which it is responsible for planning, motivation, attention, and short-term memory processes.

- Temporal lobe: It is associated with long-term memory, language (both written and spoken), emotional and visual memories [2].
- Occipital lobe: It is located at the rearmost portion of the brain known as a visual processing unit. It is associated with vision color, and motion perception.
- Parietal lobe: It is responsible for relating our body with environmental sources. For example, without the functioning of this lobe, to grasp an object by our hand would not be possible. It is associated with integrate external sources with internal sensory processes.

2. Cerebellum/little brain: It is associated with posture, fine movements, and balance. It integrates the inputs from spinal cord sensory systems and other brain areas to fine-tune motor activity.
3. Brainstem: The lower part of the brain comprising the medulla, pons, and midbrain controls body processes such as breathing, heartbeat, sense of equilibrium, etc. It controls everything that our body does consciously or unconsciously.
4. Limbic system/emotional brain: It is associated with emotions and excitement such as job interviews, marriage ceremonies, shopping, etc. It includes the thalamus, amygdala, and the hypothalamus.

The 85 billion neurons are responsible for communicating, supporting, and facilitating neural signaling processes. Each neuron consists of a cell body, axons, and synapses as shown in Figure 2.2.

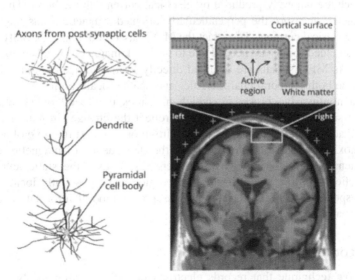

FIGURE 2.2   Electric potential generation with neural activations [3]

Synapses are considered gateways of excitatory (increased neuron signaling chances) or inhibitory (decreased neuron signaling chances) activities [4]. There is a voltage change across a cell membrane due to the release of neurotransmitters by synaptic transmissions. Also, the postsynaptic potentials or electrical fields occur in synchrony by synaptic activities which last for hundreds of milliseconds. The electric field is summing up and rapidly propagated over the scalp and then eventually measured by an EEG-like procedure [4,5]. All the electrical potentials are not strong enough to spread over the scalp and get measured by EEG sensors [4]. The synchronized activity of the pyramidal cells in cortical regions of the brain (frontal, temporal, occipital and parietal) can be measured. The cell body and dendrites make the unique orientation of these cells by heading away from the grey matter and towards the surface, respectively. With such specific orientation, the generated electrical fields are very stable and spread into various directions and can then be measured easily by EEG sensors. It is an ideal imagining technology for the analysis of precise time-course emotional and cognitive processes.

2.3   BRAIN SIGNAL ACQUISITION TECHNIQUES

The advanced technology of brain–computer interfaces (BCIs) enables us to establish a direct communication pathway between the brain and the computer. The BCI covers a huge variety of applications starting from gaming to helping people with disabilities. To recover the mental state and control capabilities of disabled persons through various patterns, BCI translates them into computer commands. The patterns of such mental states can be extracted via different procedures such as EEG, EMG, MRI, and fMRI. These data acquisition methods for extraction of brain data are discussed next.

Magnetoencephalography (MEG) data acquisition techniques record the magnetic fields which are naturally produced by electrical currents in the brain. The sensitive magnetometers measure the perpendicularly oriented magnetic fields that are generated by electrical currents. To extract the MEG-based brain data, specially designed magnetic shielded rooms are needed due to the weak magnetic signals emitted by the brain [6]. As MEG signals are obtained directly from electrical neuronal activities, they provide both temporal characteristics and spatial localization.

It is a noninvasive procedure which measures the blood oxygenation-level-dependent signals (BOLD). These signals reflect the changes in neuronal activity during the activation of neurons by some stimuli or tasks. At the time of activation, carbon dioxide production intensifies and the dependence of magnetic resonance signal intensity with the oxygen level increases. It uses the static and gradient magnetic field to align nuclei in the brain region and to spatially locate different nuclei, respectively [3]. This technique has poor temporal information but more accurate spatial localization.

2.3.1   LOCAL FIELD POTENTIAL (LFP)

An invasive technique that records electrical potentials within the brain cortical tissue using metallic, silicon, or glass micropipettes. It relatively samples a localized population of neurons. Unlike EEG signals, the LFP signals are not contaminated with muscular activities [7]. The LFPs mainly acquire the synchronized synaptic currents which arise on cortical pyramidal neurons. The widespread availability of this technique in research is under-used due to its invasive nature.

2.3.2   Positron Emission Tomography (PET)

A noninvasive brain imagining technique for capturing brain functionality by absorbing radioactive tracers into the bloodstream. These radioactive tracers are attached with the glucose-like component and the active areas of the brain utilizing glucose at a higher rate than inactive regions [8]. The radiotracer creates radionuclide called fluorodeoxyglucose. It traces the biomedical changes in brain functioning.

2.3.3   Electroencephalography (EEG)

The synaptic events occur in the human brain each second and recorded as an electrophysiological signal by an EEG with several electrodes attached on the scalp. These electrodes, set across an area of cortex, measure the spatiotemporal field synchrony or near-synchrony which emerges simultaneously as a dynamic phenomenon for some particular event [9]. These synchronous or near-synchronous field activities are conveyed towards the scalp electrodes by the phenomenon of volume conduction. The recordings are then measured through intervening conductive media including cortical grey and white matter, cerebral-spinal fluid (CSF), skull, and skin. The recorded EEG signals are the sum of source activities on the scalp and a contribution of different artefacts or nonbrain source activities, such as cardiac artefacts, eye movements or blinks, scalp muscle movement, and so on. The portion of local field synchrony activity measured by EEG as electrophysiological signals depends on the number of electrodes or channels used and their distance from brain sources [10].

2.3.4   Functional Near-Infrared Spectroscopy (fNIRS)

This is an optical noninvasive brain signal visualization technique that passes laser beams with light wavelengths close to infrared from about 700–2500 nm through the skull. With this technique, brain functionality is analyzed through hemodynamic responses associated with neuron behavior [11,12]. As fMRI, it measures the oxygen level increase in active regions of the brain. The downside of this technique is that it does not have a good temporal resolution, as EEG and also spatial resolution is not as good as fMRI.

2.4   ELECTROENCEPHALOGRAM (EEG)

The brain allows us to remember past events, process present scenarios, and project thoughts and estimations into the future. It drives and controls our behavior based on our experiences, thoughts, and desires. To analyze the underlying structure and

functions of it, we need to understand its basic building blocks and how they interact with each other. With the advanced imagining technologies and processing
procedures and algorithms, one can dive into its depth of structure and functioning.
One such imagining technology used by both researchers and neurologists is EEG
[13]. It captures the interaction of the brain cells (neurons) in the form of electrical
potentials by using sensors placed on the scalp. The reason behind its academic and
commercial use includes:

- It captures the high temporal resolution cognitive, perceptual, and motor
  imaginary processes with hundreds of milliseconds in the time frame in which
  they occur [5,14]. However, it has a less spatial resolution as compared to
  other brain imagining techniques such as MRI or CT-scan.
- It picks up tiny electrical signals related to cognition or attentional processing
  from the scalp in a noninvasive manner.
- Its flexible data collection procedure, portability, inexpensiveness, and light-
  weight allows it to use not only in healthcare but also in real-world applications such as human-machine or machine-to-machine systems.
- In the absence of behavioral responses, it monitors ongoing cognitive processing by different activation patterns with different frequencies.

2.4.1 EEG Sensor Data Collection

EEG signals are microvolt relative voltage potentials over the scalp from the different electrodes or sensor arrays within a second. The sensor arrays vary from
experiment to experiment and range from 10 to 500 sensors. These sensors are
mounted on the scalp either by using wet or dry electrode arrays. The wet electrodes
are usually made up of silver (Ag), and are attached on the scalp by applying
conductive gel or cream as shown in Figure 2.3a and b. The dry electrodes don't use
the conductive gel as shown in Figure 2.3c, but they are embedded in elastic caps,
headsets, meshes, and rigid grids with long wires attached to an amplifier [15].

The sensor/electrode placement follows a specific 10–20 system standard provided by the American EEG Society [13,16,17]. According to this system, the

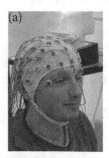
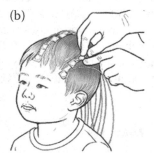

FIGURE 2.3   (a) Elastic EEG head caps. (b) Wired EEG-sensors attached on scalp with
conductive gel or cream. (c) Wireless emotive headset, connected via Bluetooth

electrodes are placed at 10–20 percent points along vertical and horizontal lines of latitude and longitude as shown in Figure 2.4a. The nasion (front) and inion (back) are connected via vertical line, and left and right pre-auricular sides are connecting via the horizontal line [15]. Each electrode is named in alpha-numeric order indicating the brain lobe and hemisphere position (right/left) as in Figure 2.4b. For example, FP1-> frontal-polar left hemisphere, T7-> left temporal region, and so on. At the midline, electrodes are labelled with Z (zero) such as CZ, FZ, PZ, etc.

The electrical activity is not only obtained from the particular single electrode, but it is measured between the site and the ground electrode. As the ground electrode is attached to the ground circuit in the amplifier, it always introduces some noise. As a result, the measured electrical potentials contain both brain activity as well as noise. Therefore, to reduce this noise, EEG uses a reference electrode and records the potential between the site, reference, and ground electrode as well. The pre-auricular sides are usually referred to as reference electrodes [18]. The amplifier gives the output signal by computing the difference between these electrodes. For example, [FP1-Gr]-[Ref-Gr] = FP1-Gr-Ref + Gr = Fp1-Ref (Final EEG signal).

As the brain is constantly generating continuous fluctuations of electrical currents, the EEG procedure takes discrete samples of data with a particular sampling rate [19]. The sampling rate is defined as the number of samples per second with unit Hertz (Hz). For example, if the data are collected at 128 Hz, then 128 samples are collected per second. The sampling rate depends on the objective of an experiment, such as for higher time precision [14], the EEG sampling rate should be >500 Hz, for frequency-based analysis, 128 Hz can be sufficient. The recorded electrical signals are digited before forwarded to an amplifier due to the tiny nature of these signals. Once the signals are amplified, they are displayed as voltage values in a continuous flow-through wired or wirelessly on a computer screen as shown in Figure 2.5.

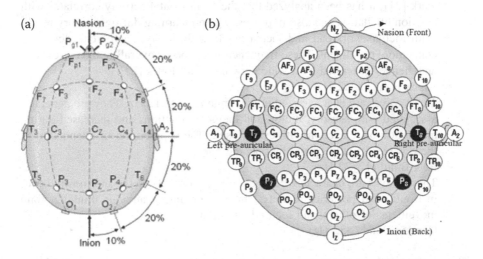

FIGURE 2.4 (a) 10–20 system standard provided by American EEG Society [17]. (b) Array of EEG sensor placement on scalp [17]

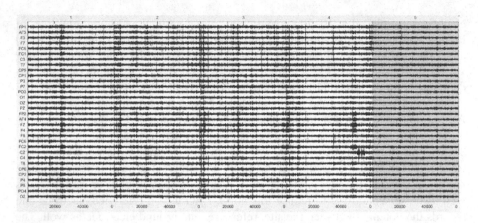

FIGURE 2.5 EEG-sensor recordings from different channels

The extracted signal from each sensor reflects certain cognitive activities with a mixture of underlying frequencies. These frequencies are classified into several bands [9,20]: Delta (1–4 Hz), Theta (4–8 Hz), Alpha (8–12 Hz), Beta (12–32 Hz), and Gamma (>32 Hz) as shown in Figure 2.6.

- Delta Band (1–4 Hz)
  These waves are characterized in the range from 1–4 Hz with the highest amplitude and slowest brain wave. These waves occur during sleep and are stronger in the right brain hemisphere. The source of these waves is typically localized in the thalamus and plays a key role in the formation of biographic memory.
- Theta Band (4–8 Hz)
  These waves are characterized in the range from 4–8 Hz. As in our previous work [21], it has been analyzed that the theta-frontal activity correlates with emotion elicitation and also in processing and learning during memory recall. With mental workload and increasing task difficulty, such frequencies become more prominent. These frequencies also occur overall in the cortex area and, hence, generated by a wide network of all lobes [22].
- Alpha Band (8–12 Hz)
  These waves are characterized in the range from 8–12 Hz. They are generally associated with sensory, motor, and memory functions and increased during meditation or relaxation with eyes closed. The suppression or attenuation of these waves usually occurs by opening eyes.
- Beta Band (12–32 Hz)
  These waves are characterized in the range from 12–32 Hz and mostly occur in frontal and posterior regions. They occur during anxious thinking, limb movements of others, and focused attention.
- Gamma Band (>32 Hz)

These waves are characterized as the fastest rhythms with a range above 32 Hz. They are associated with universal love, spirituality, consciousness, higher virtues,

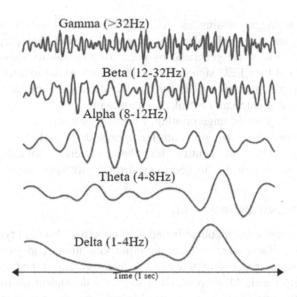

Gamma (>32Hz)

Beta (12-32Hz)

Alpha (8-12Hz)

Theta (4-8Hz)

Delta (1-4Hz)

Time (1 sec)

FIGURE 2.6 Classification of frequency bands [7]

and altruism. Their generation remains a mystery due to higher frequencies, which are above the frequencies of neuronal firing.

2.4.2 APPLICATIONS OF EEG SIGNALS

Electrical signals in the brain are spreading through the head and reach to the scalp, which then can be recorded via different brain acquisition methods (as discussed earlier). Electroencephalogram is one of the techniques which has millisecond temporal resolution and can be obtained noninvasively [5]. There have been vast areas of research applications in which EEG-like signals can be used, such as BCIs. With the advancement in technology, EEG-BCIs can be used for the classification and detection of emotion recognition tasks, motor-imagery tasks, mental workload tasks, seizure detection tasks, event-related potential tasks, and steady-state visually evoked potential tasks [23]. Some of the common applications are:

- In clinical environments, the spontaneous EEG signals can help diagnose tumors, epilepsy, epileptic seizures, genetic dysfunctions, and abnormal brain states.
- Neuromarketing is one of the emerging fields where economists use EEG signals to detect consumer decisions and brain states while exploring physical or virtual stores [24,25].
- To monitor human factors such as social anxiety, intro/extroversion behavior, cognitive and attentional states [23].
- To gain deeper insights about social interactions by "hyper-scanning" multiple people at once by recording their EEG signals.

- To analyze trigger or stimulus-based psychological studies for understanding attention, learning, and underlying memory [26]. For example, event-related potentials (ERPs) are generated by presenting stimuli to a specific group of subjects and then EEG signals like p300 (surprise) are extracted.
- To develop noninvasive BCIs for paralyzed patients, military scenarios, lie detection, and entertainment like game playing.
- Forensics (e.g. brain fingerprinting, trust assessment)
- Entertainment (e.g. thought control, response detection)
- Communication and control for the severely disabled (e.g. severe disabilities—tetraplegia, locked-in syndrome, prosthetic control).

2.4.3   EEG SIGNAL PREPROCESSING

The EEG signals are usually contaminated with noise and different types of artifacts such as muscle artifacts, edge artifacts, amplifier saturations, and line noise [27,28]. Before analysis, preprocessing with many transformations and reorganizations needs to be performed. All preprocessing steps are dependent on the detailed experiment design, type of analyzes we need to perform, and equipment used in the process of collection of EEG signals. The signals are never completely noise or artifact-free, but we can try to minimize them and maximize the ratio of signal to noise. After the data collection, each subject file includes information about the number of channels or sensors used, data-points (time), and trials performed. The following are some of the preprocessing steps which one can apply on the EEG sensor data:

- Epoch extraction from continuous signals. For example, to extract epoch start-time or stimulus onset for each trial, baseline-time, and activity time [19].
- Epochs with artifacts need to be removed. For example, to remove eye blink artifacts, muscle artifacts, and edge artifacts [27,28].
- Extraction of particular frequency bands by applying different temporal and spatial filters. For example, either to apply a low-pass filter with a cut-off frequency of 20 Hz or a high-pass filter for higher frequencies.
- Manual trial rejection by visualizing signals manually through topographical maps.
- Run independent component analysis (ICA) to remove bad electrodes [29].
- Either to include baseline period or subtracting it from the post-stimulus activity.
- To reduce the potential biases, trial count across different conditions should be the same.
- Each EEG sensor records voltage potential relative to other reference sensor electrode [18]. The effect of this electrode is direct on all other scalp sensors, therefore we need to choose such electrode very carefully such as earlobes or mastoids are usually referenced.
- Subjects under experimentation can be properly trained before signal extraction by explaining or visualizing them how their jaw clench, eye blink, muscle movements, smile, sneezing, etc., affect EEG signals.

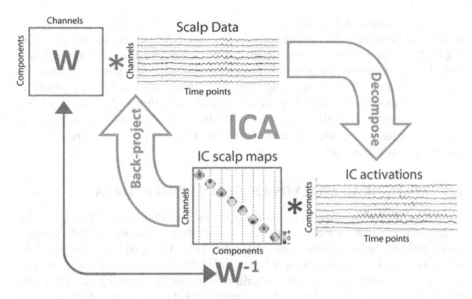

FIGURE 2.7   ICA decomposition methodology for EEG data analysis [29]

2.4.3.1   ICA Algorithm

For all the EEG channels, a set of weights to isolate EEG brain activity sources are assigned such that each independent component is a weighted sum of activity at all electrodes as shown in Figure 2.7.

To each electrode location, the scalp component maps interpret the projection strengths or relative weights of the projection from the component processes. At each time point, the relative polarity and amplitude of the activity of the components are given by the component activation time series [14]. A scalp component map remains constant over time. The number of components is equal to the number of electrodes or channels e.g. for 32 channels there are 32 components. The "N" recorded mixtures at different electrodes are defined as:

$$X = \{x_1(t), x_2(t), ...X_n(t)\} = U_s$$

where $s = \{s_1(t), s_2(t),...s_n(t)\}$, is the independent vector of source signals and linearly mixed with an unknown matrix U, $R = WX$, is the ICA activation components of time courses, and the columns of the inverse matrix W^{-1} give the component projection strengths onto the scalp sensors. The location of sources are on the scalp topographies of the components.

$X' = (W)^{-1}R'$, where X' are the recovered EEG signals and R' is the matrix of activation waveforms, R, with rows set to 0 representing the artefactual components. The correlation of the dynamic characteristics of EEG oscillations and behavior changes can be revealed with the independent component analysis and time-frequency analysis [5]. The EEGLAB software toolbox provides the functionality of automated infomax ICA decomposition function runica() for both single and group level EEG data analysis [30].

Each component is analyzed by its scalp map, time course, and power spectrum activity to determine the cognition relation and type of artifact as shown in Figure 2.8a. The component scalp maps are not constrained to have any relationship. They may or may not give information or relative projections of the source to the scalp channels. The artifacts can also be relatively identified by the visual inspection of time-course data of each component as in Figure 2.8b–d. Trials that contain artifacts such as electromyography (EMG) or muscle movements, cognitive noise, or artifacts that are less correlated with EEG data, etc., can be removed manually or automatically.

2.5 STATISTICAL ANALYSIS OF BRAIN SENSOR DATA

To some extent, the qualitative visual inspection of brain sensor data, like EEG signals, are important for understanding the underlying information and dynamics about different brain activities and conditions [10]. The qualitative statistical inspection of data facilitates the appropriate interpretation and significance of findings. To do the empirical research on brain sensor data for assessing the statistically significant effects, we need to perform appropriate statistical procedures. For significant results, we need to maximize the signal-to-noise (SNR) ratio [5]. For example, if we want to show that there is a significant difference between the power of two particular brain regions for some condition, then we need to infer this difference statistically by assuming a hypothesis among them. The assumption is to start with a null hypothesis, say the difference between the power of sensor-FP1 and sensor-O1 are identical (H0 = FP1 = O1 = 0) and an alternative hypothesis (H1 = FP1 ≠ O1). The null hypothesis is accepted only if and if the probability value (p-value) is greater than the significance level ($\alpha = 0.05$) as shown in Figure 2.9.

There are two ways to generate the null hypothesis distribution for brain sensor data analysis: Parametric and nonparametric statistics. The main difference between these two statistical approaches is regarding the assumptions of the distribution of data and their parameters.

2.5.1 PARAMETRIC TEST

This analytical test based on some parameters, such as mean and variance, needs strong underlying assumptions for generating distributions. The assumptions may include:

- From a given population, data need to be sampled randomly
- Known parameter distributions for the population
- Variance needs to be homogenous across repeated measurements
- Sample variance and error need to be independent

2.5.2 NONPARAMETRIC TEST

This test is more reliable, generic, and without any assumption for the null hypothesis distribution of data. The permutation test distribution approach is followed

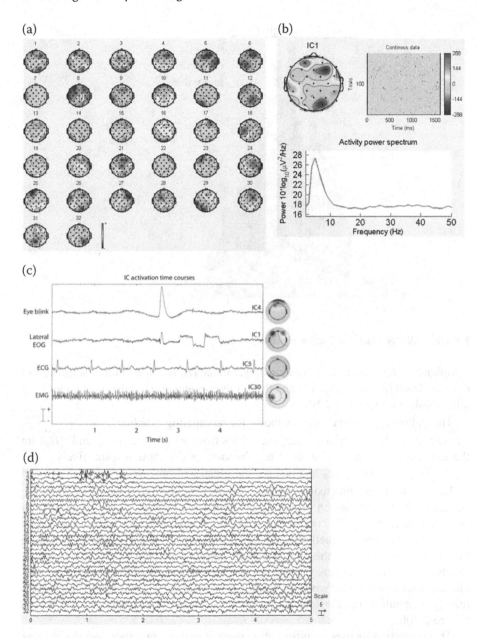

FIGURE 2.8   (a) ICA 2D-component maps for 32 channels. (b) Activity component map and power spectrum of component1 for channel FP1. (c) Independent component with a time-course signal. (d) Visual inspection of time course data of each individual component

by randomizing or shuffling all possible conditions on the observed data recordings. To accept the null hypothesis (H0), the values for the two observed signals (e.g. FP1 and O1) should follow the same distribution and therefore the values are exchangeable between them. To evaluate whether the data distribution is statistically

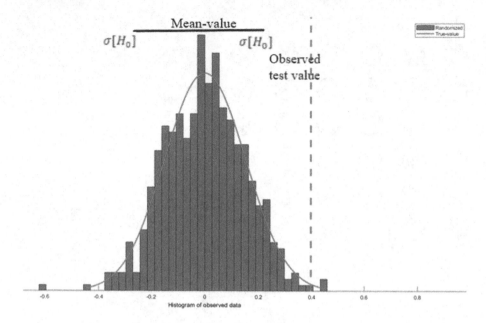

FIGURE 2.9   Normal distribution example

significant or not, we need to compute the Z-value (zobs while random shuffling) in empirical null hypothesis testing and then convert them into p-value using a look-up table as shown in Figure 2.10a.

The following are the two methods for computing z-value: $Z_{val} = \frac{z_{obs} - \mu(H_0)}{\sigma[H_0]}$; where z_{obs} are the observed test statistic values from actual data, $\mu(H_0)$ and $\sigma[H_0]$ are the mean and standard deviation of null-hypothesis distribution respectively. $P = \frac{\Sigma(H_0 > obs)}{N_{H_0}}$, where H_0 and obs are the mean and observed values.

Due to the large dimensions of EEG signals (Chan*data-points*trials), there occurs multiple comparison problems over time-points with the huge number of permutation tests [5]. To correct this problem, a common approach known as a cluster-based correction method is used. The basic assumption under this method lies in the cluster size with some threshold value. If the autocorrelation value of pixels in the time-frequency plane is below the specified threshold then that cluster is set to zero otherwise the finding is significant. Therefore, this method is mainly dependent on clusters rather than a single pixel value as shown in Figure 2.10b.

This correction focuses on information present in the data rather than the number of tests and also provides the corrected threshold p-value which remains sensitive enough to detect effects in multidimensional data.

In the cluster correction method, permutation testing is performed normally. However, at each iteration of the null hypothesis test statistic generation during permutation testing, a threshold is applied to the time-frequency map at an uncorrected level such as $p < 0.05$, known as the precluster threshold. The clusters with a value less than a specified threshold are removed from the

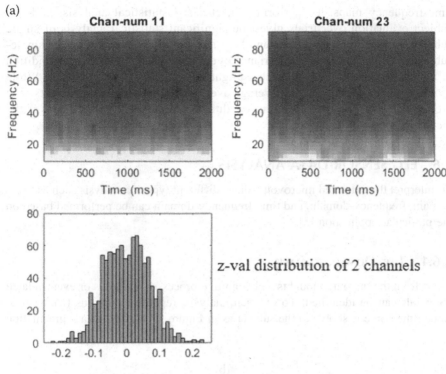

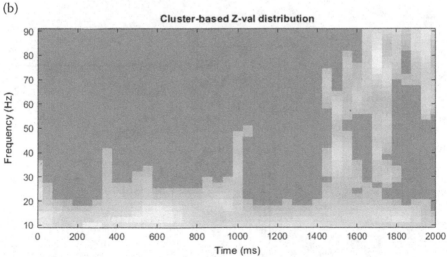

FIGURE 2.10   (a) Nonparametric permutation test. (b) Cluster based statistics for correct multiple comparison problem

time-frequency maps. To perform subject-based statistical analysis, with in-subject evaluation over trials gives the significant statistical analysis of single subjects for different conditions and facilitate group-level analysis. The single-subject analysis deals with the variance of data over trials. If there is a condition in which variance is high, then that might be statistically insignificant. While group-level analysis deals with average over trials across different subjects. The group-level analysis over different conditions is statistically significant if the means are consistent.

2.6 EEG SENSOR DATA ANALYSIS

To interpret the extracted microvolt values, different types of analysis such as time-domain, frequency-domain, and time-frequency-domain can be performed based on the particular application [5].

2.6.1 TIME-DOMAIN ANALYSIS

Apart from the ongoing thoughts and cognitive processes, stimulus or event-related potentials can be identified. To do such analysis, repetitive stimulus (trials) with some time range is shown to the subject as in Figure 2.11a. The data segmentation

(a)   (b)

(c)   (d)

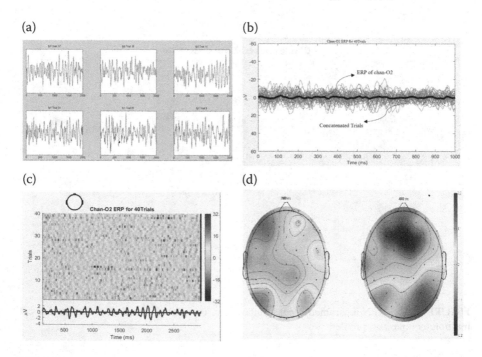

FIGURE 2.11   (a) Individual trial data for Channel FP1. (b) Computed ERP over 40 trial data for channel FP1. (c) Channel FP1 ERP representation over 40 trials. (d) 2D ERP to-pographical representation

or epoching is performed on the collected continuous EEG signals and all trials are averaged sample by sample as shown in Figure 2.11b–d.

With such averaging, only stimulus-related potentials are collected from each electrode and reflect specific stimulus activity [31]. In the noninvasive EEG procedure, the event-related potentials (ERP) identify the continuous processing between an external stimulus and response [5,26,32]. With these potentials, the individual trial voltage fluctuations are averaged and then the ERP is smaller in magnitude as compared to individual trials. Signal averaging has been done to improve the SNR. $ERP(t) = s(t) + \frac{1}{N} \Sigma_{k=1}^{N} (t, k)$; where k represents trial, t is the elapsed time after kth event, $s(t)$ is the signal and $n(t, k)$ is the noise.

Figure 2.11 depicts the ERP of electric potentials and 2D scalp maps recorded from channel O2 with 40 trials and 8064 time-points. It is computed in MATLAB® as:

Trials $_{O2}$ = [tr$_1$, tr$_{2,}$ tr$_3$,…, tr$_{40}$]; T = [T$_1$, T$_{2,}$T$_3$,…, T$_{8064}$];

ERP = mean (μ) [EEG.data ("O2," T, Trials $_{O2}$), 3 -> Trials $_{O2}$];

where Trials$_{O2}$ depicts the number of trials, T is the number of EEG data points, and O2 is the channel name.

The brain is the continuous oscillator of cognitive activities, even during sleeping, and generates them with specific frequencies. The ERP analysis is computationally simple and has a good time precision, but the downside is that it can't interpret the activities in terms of frequency change [5,32]. Also, it is limited to cross-frequency coupling, synchronization, and the average of source distributions may not lead to a realistic or useful underlying distribution model. Therefore, a different analytical approach such as frequency-based analysis is required. The frequency-based analysis is more likely associated with brain functionality and structure such as to analyze the underlying behavior of cognitive mental states, emotions, thoughts, and motivations.

2.6.2 FREQUENCY DOMAIN ANALYSIS

As the raw EEG signals are in time domain with voltage values in microvolts, it needs the transformation into frequency band. Fourier Transform is one of the techniques to transform time-domain signals into frequency domain. The dot product between the kernel (sine wave) of different frequencies and the input signal (EEG signal) is computed [5]. As the sine wave has three main components: frequency, power, and phase, the output signal results in a three-dimensional representation. The output signal is decomposed into a sum of sine waves of different frequencies, amplitudes (power), and phases as shown in Figure 2.12.

It contains all the information in the time series data and perfectly reconstructed via Inverse Fourier Transform. To apply the Fourier Transform to the given EEG time-series signal, we want to compute which sine waves with which phases, amplitudes, and frequencies can be computed. The sine waves and the Fourier Transform is computed as:

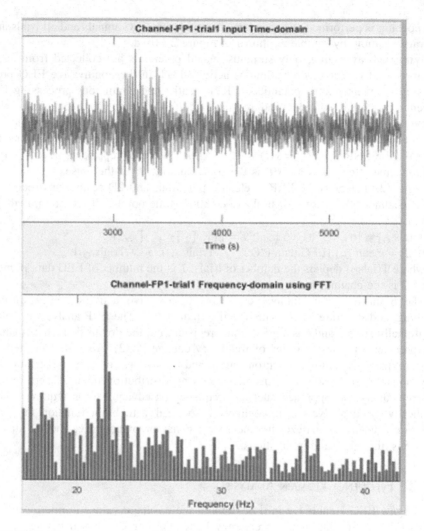

FIGURE 2.12 Frequency domain representation via Fast Fourier Transform for channel 1 data

$$\text{Sine-wave} = A sin (2\pi ft); F_{\text{coeff}} = \sum_{i=1}^{n} \text{tr}_i e^{-i2\pi f (i-1)n^{-1}}$$

where A is the amplitude of sine wave, f is the frequency, t is the time, tr_i is the vector of data-points in trial_i, F_{coeff} is the Fourier coefficient of time points of trial_i at frequency f.

2.6.2.1 Fast Fourier Transform

The algorithm for Frequency domain analysis using DFT and FFT to project the data from time domain $F(t)$ to frequency domain $F(\omega)$ is summarized as:

Step 1. Given: N samples of EEG time series data:
Data = EEG.data;
Step 2. Initialize Fourier time and coefficients:
$F_f = \sum_{k=1}^{n} S_i e^{-i2\pi f\,(k-1)n^{-1}}$ and $F_t = ((1:N) - 1)/N$; where $N = $ length(Data)
Step 3. Create complex sine wave and compute the dot product between
the sine wave and input data:
$\text{Sine}_W = e^{(-1i*2\pi\,(f_i-1))}$. $_*F_t$ and $F_i = $ sum (Sine_W.* Data)
Step 4. To reconstruct original signal, use inverse Fourier Transform:
$S_i = \sum_{k=1}^{n} F_k e^{i2\pi f\,(k-1)n^{-1}} R_s = ifft(F_t)* N$;

The brain data is highly nonstationary due to the happening of events that change over time [33]. This nonstationary nature is not only due to the external events, but also due to the switching of the metastable state of neuronal behavior [22]. This switching behavior is analyzed by observing the abrupt transitive processes in EEG traces. However, the Fourier Transform assumes the stationary nature of data, which is violated with nonstationary data such as EEG data and also to visualize the dynamic changes in the frequency structure over time, is not possible because the kernel (sine wave) used in this method has no temporal localization. Therefore, the time-frequency decomposition is performed via several methods such as wavelet analysis.

2.6.3 Time-Frequency Domain Analysis

To analyze how frequency structure changes over time in EEG data, multiple time-frequency domains analyzing methods can be used such as wavelet transform (e.g. Morlet wavelet), Hilbert transform and Short Time Fourier Transform can be used [5]. The wavelet analysis has a good temporal localization of frequency characters at different time points by moving the non-zero kernel (wavelet) over each data point of the EEG signal which remains constant. This kernel is like a sine wave that is tampered with Gaussian and the processed results are known as Convolution. Convolution produces the frequency band intersection between the EEG time-series signal and the wavelet kernel which are tuned for specific frequencies. In the averaged ERPs, the correlation between characteristic dynamism of specific frequency bands in EEG traces with behavioral changes can't be revealed [26]. These dynamic changes at multiple frequencies can be accompanied by using time-frequency analysis. Relatively large low- and high-frequency activities can be seen in the time-frequency windows with time locking events [9].

Unlike sine waves that are smooth, predictable, and extend towards infinity, wavelets are asymmetric, irregular, and a limited duration waveform that has an average value of zero [20]. Wavelet analysis is a windowing technique with short and long intervals for analyzing the high- and low-frequency information, respectively. The two important properties of wavelets known as multiresolution analysis (MRA), and local analysis. The MRA helps to analyze the information at multiple resolutions simultaneously, and local analysis helps to analyze the localized area of a large signal such as recorded EEG time-series signal [34]. With wavelet analysis, a signal can be de-noised or compressed, revealing discontinuities in a signal, self-similarities, and so on. Wavelet transforms decompose signals into two separate series known as approximations and details. The approximations are high-scale and low-frequency components, while details are low-scale and high-frequency components [20]. Approximations merge from the scaling functions $\varphi(x)$ known as the Father function and details originating from the underlying wavelet function $\Psi(x)$ known as the Mother function. These two functions make the bases of wavelet analysis and act as a hallmark of wavelet transforms, because in other transforms such as Fourier transform, Z transform, etc, the parameters of kernel function or bases function can't be scaled or translated. With these two functions, a specific part of a signal can be analyzed. Scaling is defined as a stretching or shrinking of a wavelet. To capture the slowly varying changes in a signal, a wavelet is stretched and to capture abrupt changes in a signal, a compressed or shrinking wavelet is used. Shifting is defined as delaying or advancing the onset of the wavelet along the length of the signal. Scaling and shifting are defined as: $\Psi(t/a)$; a > 0; "a" is a scaling factor which corresponds how much a signal is scaled in time. $\varphi(t-k)$; shifted and centered at "k".

2.6.3.1 Complex Morlet Wavelet

Morlet wavelet is defined as a sine wave which is windowed with a Gaussian tapered to zero at both of the ends. It helps us to localize the changes in the frequency characteristics over time in the extracted input signal in terms of power and phase information [5]. According to the literature, the time-frequency analysis of neural time series data is convolved with complex Morlet wavelet analysis. These wavelets have both real and imaginary components and are defined as:

$$\Psi(x) = \frac{1}{\sqrt{\pi s}} e^{2i\pi f t} . \ e\frac{-t^2}{2_* s^2}; s = \text{wavelet} - \text{cycles}/2\pi f;$$

where $\frac{1}{\sqrt{\pi s}}$ is a frequency band-specific scaling factor, "s" is the standard deviation parameter of Gaussian which represents number of cycles for a wavelet, $e^{2i\pi f t}$ is the complex sine wave and $e\frac{-t^2}{2_* s^2}$ represents Gaussian window, "t" is the time.

The CMW algorithm is summarized as:

Step 1. N samples of EEG time series data :
Data = EEG.data;
Step 2. Create complex sine wave and Gaussian window:

$$\left\{ \begin{array}{l} \text{SW=exp}(i_* 2_* \text{pi}_* f. \ _* t); \\ \text{GW} exp\{(-t.\ ^2).\ /(2_* s^2)\} \end{array} \right\} \text{(in MATLAB}^{\circledR})$$

Step 3. Create complex Morlet wavelet:

$$\Psi(x) = \frac{1}{\sqrt{\pi s}}e^{2i\pi f t} \cdot e^{\frac{-t^2}{2_* s^2}};$$

CMW =SW.*GW
; (in MATLAB®)

Step 4. Perform Convolution operation:
Con-op= (kernel (length(Data) + length(
CMW)-1), CMW).

Step 5. Take the Fourier transform between data and convolution operation:
FT = fft (Data, Con-op)
Step 6. The convolution result will be the dot product between FT and Con-op:
Con-res = FT. * Con-op;

2.7 EXTREME LEARNING MACHINE (ELM)

The learning speed of Feedforward neural networks is slow with gradient-based learning and iteratively tuning of all network parameters. For example, the sigmoid or additive feed-forward neural networks and radial basis function (RBF) feed-forward neural networks require the tuning of parameters for universal approximation. The learning methods required to adjust the tuning of parameters at hidden nodes include gradient descent or iterative approach (such as backpropagation), least-square for RBF network, Quick-net, and support vector machine (SVM), etc. To overcome this problem, ELM has been proposed for single-hidden layer Feedforward neural networks (SLFNs) [35]. The ELM randomly chooses hidden nodes and analytically determines the output weights of SLFNs. The input weights and hidden layer biases are randomly generated with the infinitely differentiable activation functions at the hidden layer as shown in Figure 2.13.

It has a fast learning speed, smallest training error, the smallest norm of weights and obtains a good generalization performance as compared to traditional feedforward neural networks. The ELM involves network learning without iteratively tuning the hidden neurons [35,36]. With any nonconstant piecewise continuous function $p(x)$, if the continuous target function $T(x)$ can be approximated by single layer feedforward networks (SLFNs) with adjustable hidden nodes "m" then the hidden node parameters of such SLFNs need not be tuned. These parameters are randomly generated without training data and are independent of each other. That is, any randomly generated

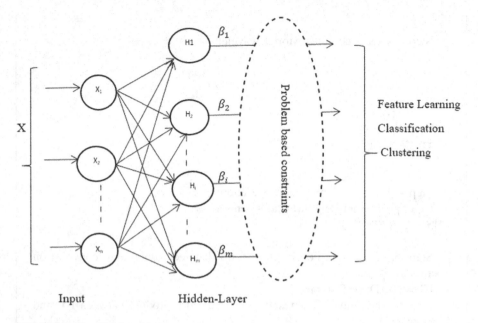

FIGURE 2.13 ELM architecture

sequence $\{(x_i, b_i)_{i=1}^m\}$, $\lim_{m \to \infty} | |p(x) - T_m(x)|| = \lim_{m \to \infty} | |p(x) - \Sigma_{i=1}^m \beta_i G(x_i, b_i, x)|| = 0$; holds with probability "1" if β_i is chosen to minimize $||p(x) - T_m(x)||$, $\forall\ i$ [5].

The standard SLFNs with m hidden nodes and activation function $g(x)$ can approximate the n samples with zero mean error, that is, there exists β_i, w_i, and b_i such that:

$$\sum_{i=1}^{m} \beta_i g(w_i \cdot x_j + b_i) = a_j; \ \sum_{i=1}^{m} (||\text{pred}_{\text{out}} - a_j||) = 0;$$

The H_m random hidden nodes at hidden layer mapping space is defined as $H[(w_1, b_1, x_1), (w_2, b_2, x_2)...,(w_m, b_m, x_i)]$ and the hidden node output function can be sigmoid, RBF, Fourier Series, wavelets, and polynomial functions. The compact form of the above equations are:

$$H\beta = A;$$

where $H = \begin{bmatrix} g(w_1 \cdot x_1 + b_1)...............g(w_m \cdot x_1 + b_m) \\ g(w_1 \cdot x_2 + b_1)...............g(w_2 \cdot x_2 + b_m) \\ ... . \\ ... . \\ g(w_1 \cdot x_i + b_1)...............g(w_m \cdot x_i + b_m) \end{bmatrix} \beta = \begin{bmatrix} \beta_1 \\ \beta_2 \\ . \\ . \\ \beta_m \end{bmatrix}$ and $A = \begin{bmatrix} a_1 \\ a_2 \\ . \\ . \\ a_i \end{bmatrix}$

To summarize, the hidden nodes are randomly generated with any continuous sampling distribution probability, independent of training samples and also not iteratively tuned while learning. In different hidden nodes, the output function may not be unique. The ELM has two main steps to train SLFNs: random feature mapping and linear parameter solving. The hidden layer is initialized randomly for mapping the input into an ELM feature space with some nonlinear piece-wise continuous functions such as sigmoid function, hard limit function, and so on [37]. The hidden node parameters are randomly generated instead of being explicitly trained as compared to traditional learning techniques such as back-propagation neural networks. The Moore-Penrose generalized inverse of hidden matrix "H" is solved for the optimization of output weights [38]. With this, the ELM not only achieves the smallest training error but also the smallest norm of output weights.

2.7.1 ELM ALGORITHM

Input: A given training samples $\{(x_i, a_i)|\ x_i{\in}R^D$ and $a_i{\in}R^M;\ i = 1,2,3,...N\}$, with hidden output node function for "m" hidden nodes is modeled as:

$$T_m(X) = \sum_{i=1}^{m} \beta_i g_i(x_j) = \sum_{i=1}^{m} \beta_i g(w_i \cdot x_j + b_i)(j = 1,2,3, ...)$$

where w_i and β_i are the weight vectors connecting ith input nodes with mth hidden nodes and mth hidden nodes with output node respectively. b_i is the threshold of mth hidden node.

Step 1: Hidden node parameters random assignment: (w_i, b_i), $i = 1,2,3,$ ...m.

Step 2: Output matrix H of the hidden layer is computed.

Step 3: Computation of output weight matrix β=HA.

2.7.2 DATASET DESCRIPTION

The database for emotion analysis using physiological signals (DEAP) captures emotion-related brain signals of 32 participants by watching one-minute extracts of 40 different trials/movie clips with a sampling rate of 128 Hz [1] as shown in Table 2.1.

TABLE 2.1
EEG dataset description

Total no. of participants	32
EEG channels	32 (FP1, AF3, F3...)
Sampling rate	128 Hz
Trials/video clips	40
Labels	40*4 (valence, arousal, dominance, liking)
Baseline	3 s
Trial recording	60 s = 63 s with baseline period

The subjects would rate the video clips on a scale of 1–9 based on their feelings of valence, arousal, dominance, liking, and familiarity. For example, valence being characterized as unhappy/ happy with rating <5 and >=5 respectively. The dataset contains 32 EEG sensors placed on the scalp of 32 different subjects according to the 10–20 international system.

2.7.3 RESULTS

All the 32 channels such as FP1, AF3, FP2, etc. were used for the classification of emotions. With the extracted features, ELM, radial basis kernel-support vector machine (RBF-SVM), and K-nearest neighbor (KNN) were used for the classification of valence and arousal emotions as shown in Figure 2.14.

The different statistical features like mean, standard deviation, kurtosis, skewness, energy, entropy, and power spectral density of input EEG signal were extracted for various labels as depicted in Figure 2.15a and b.

The valence emotion has been divided into two groups of high valence low valence (HVLV) and arousal into high arousal low arousal (HALA) groups. The accuracy and training time were recorded for each classifier. The results show that the ELM has almost the same accuracy with a significantly shorter time.

For both the emotions, the ELM classifier showed promising results using EEG signals in terms of accuracy and training time as in Figure 2.16a and b.

The Figure 2.17a and b showing the classification results of valence and arousal emotions by evaluating different classifiers.

The similar accuracies to the traditional machine learning methods have been achieved with less training time. As the ELM's performance is directly affected by the features extracted, its comparison with deep learning methods is a challenging task.

2.8 CONCLUSION

The goal of the study is to understand the acquisition techniques for capturing brain signals via sensors, their applications, preprocessing and functional analysis methods. The volume, velocity, variety, and veracity of brain data is high due to the electrical activity of neurons, because it captures a large volume of samples, high-dimensional features (statistical, temporal and spatial) and multimodal characteristics of different states of brain functions. To deal with such a massive amount of data and to analyze various features, we need scalable algorithms and processing techniques. We implement a case study using EEG signals (emotion-related signals) and show how a researcher can capture brain data via sensors, feature extraction, and also a comparison among various machine learning algorithms. As emotions reflect the perception of humans, in the area of affective computing, neuroscience, and computer science, the recognition of these emotions play an important role. To recognize emotions using the sensor data such as EEG is a challenging task due to the differences in individual variations in emotions and fuzzy boundaries. For the emotion detection system,

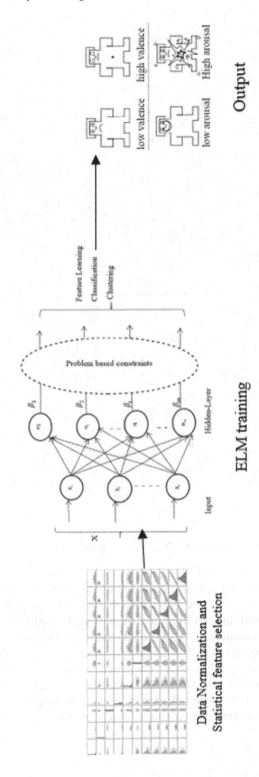

FIGURE 2.14 Classification of valence and arousal emotion using ELM

(a)

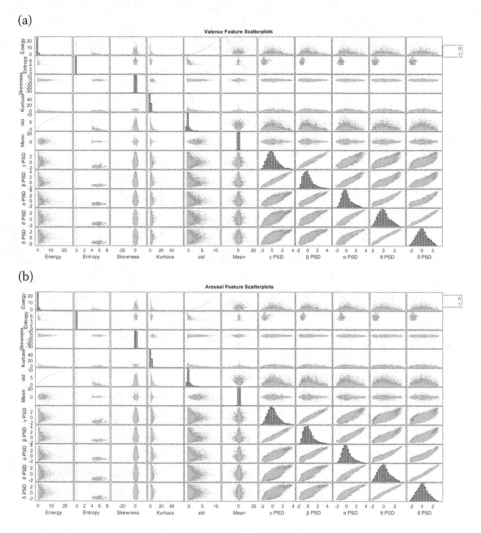

FIGURE 2.15 (a) Valence feature map. (b) Arousal feature map

the subjective nature of the nonphysiological signals like voice tones and facial expression conceals the intrinsic behavior of a person. To make this system more reliable and robust, the physiological signals such as EEG have emerged in the field of affective computing. With the advancement in artificial intelligence, both machine learning and deep learning approaches are applicable for emotion detection using physiological signals. The machine learning methods have fast training but lower accuracies, while deep learning has higher accuracies with lower training times. It has been shown in this study that ELM satisfies both training time and accuracies comparable to machine learning and deep learning methods.

(a)

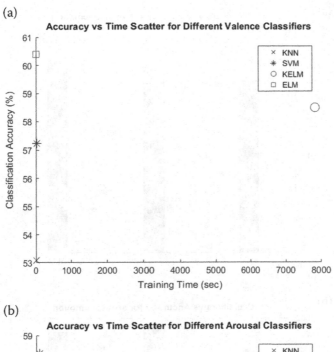

(b)

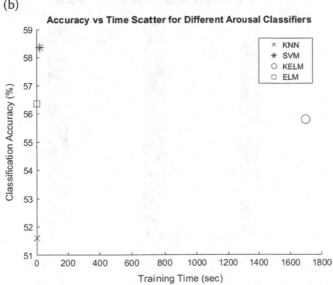

FIGURE 2.16 (a) Comparison between accuracy and training time of valence emotion. (b) Comparison between accuracy and training time of arousal emotion

(a)

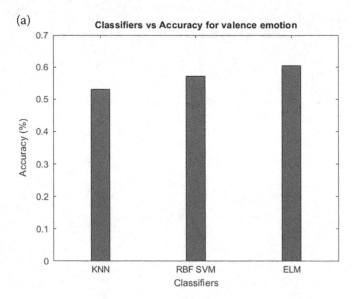

(b)

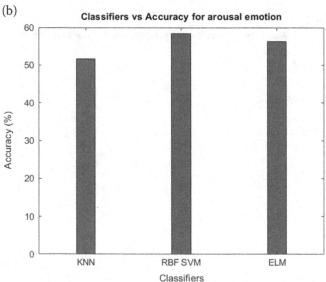

FIGURE 2.17   (a) Comparison between accuracy and classifier type of valence emotion. (b) Comparison between accuracy and classifier type of arousal emotion

REFERENCES

1. Koelstra, Sander, Christian Muhl, Mohammad Soleymani, Jong-Seok Lee, Ashkan Yazdani, Touradj Ebrahimi, Thierry Pun, Anton Nijholt, and Ioannis Patras. "Deap: a database for emotion analysis; using physiological signals." *IEEE Transactions on Affective Computing* 3, 1 (2011): 18–31.

2. Stikic, M., Johnson, R. R., Tan, V., and Berka, C. (2014). EEG-based classification of positive and negative affective states. *Brain-Computer Interfaces*, *1*(2), 99–112.
3. Tang, I-Chun, Yu-Ping Tsai, Ying-Ju Lin, Jyh-Horng Chen, Chao-Hsien Hsieh, Shih-Han Hung, William C. Sullivan, Hsing-Fen Tang, and Chun-Yen Chang. "Using functional magnetic resonance imaging (fMRI) to analyze brain region activity when viewing landscapes." *Landscape and Urban Planning* 162 (2017): 137–144.
4. Buzsáki, György, Costas A. Anastassiou, and Christof Koch. "The origin of extra-cellular fields and currents—EEG, ECoG, LFP and spikes." *Nature Reviews Neuroscience* 13, 6 (2012): 407–420.
5. Cohen, Mike X. *Analyzing Neural Time Series Data: Theory and Practice*. MIT Press, London, 2014.
6. Baillet, Sylvain. "Magnetoencephalography for brain electrophysiology and imaging." *Nature nEUROSCIENCE* 20, 3 (2017): 327–339.
7. https://raphaelvallat.com/bandpower.
8. Tanaka, Takuma, and Kouichi C. Nakamura. "Focal inputs are a potential origin of local field potential (LFP) in the brain regions without laminar structure." *Plos ONE* 14, 12 (2019): e0226028.
9. Ramzan, Munaza, and Suma Dawn. "A survey of brainwaves using electro-encephalography (EEG) to develop robust brain-computer interfaces (BCIs): processing techniques and algorithms." In *2019 9th International Conference on Cloud Computing, Data Science and Engineering (Confluence)*, pp. 642–647. IEEE, 2019.
10. Ramzan, Munaza, and Suma Dawn. "Temporal measures for analysis of emotional states from human electroencephalography signals." In *2019 Twelfth International Conference on Contemporary Computing (IC3)*, pp. 1–6. IEEE, 2019.
11. Treglia, Giorgio, Barbara Muoio, Gianluca Trevisi, Maria Vittoria Mattoli, Domenico Albano, Francesco Bertagna, and Luca Giovanella. "Diagnostic performance and prognostic value of PET/CT with different tracers for brain tumors: a systematic review of published meta-analyses." *International Journal Of Molecular Sciences* 20, 19 (2019): 4669.
12. Pinti, Paola, Ilias Tachtsidis, Antonia Hamilton, Joy Hirsch, Clarisse Aichelburg, Sam Gilbert, and Paul W. Burgess. "The present and future use of functional near-infrared spectroscopy (fNIRS) for cognitive neuroscience." *Annals of the New York Academy of Sciences* 1464, 1 (2020): 5.
13. Niedermeyer, Ernst, and FH Lopes da Silva, eds. *Electroencephalography: Basic Principles, Clinical Applications, and Related Fields*. Lippincott Williams and Wilkins, Philadelphia, 2005.
14. Cohen, Michael X. "It's about time." *Frontiers in Human Neuroscience* 5 (2011): 2.
15. Saab, J., B. Battes, M. Grosse-Wentrup, R. Scherer, M. Billinger, and A. Kreilinger. *Simultaneous EEG Recordings With Dry and Wet Electrodes in Motor-Imagery*. 2011.
16. J. N. Acharya, A. Hani, J. Cheek, P. Thirumala and T. N. Tsuchida, "American clinical neurophysiology soc ety guideline 2: guidelines for standard electrode position nomenclature," *Journal of Clinical Neurophysiology*, 33, 4, pp. 308–311, 2016.
17. Ahmad, Tahir, and Vinod Ramachandran. "Hyperspherical manifold for EEG signals of epileptic seizures." *Journal of Applied Mathematics* 2012 (2012): 1–22. doi: 10.1155/2012/926358.
18. Lepage, Kyle Q et al. "A statistically robust EEG re-referencing procedure to mitigate reference effect." *Journal of neuroscience methods* 235 (2014): 101–116. doi:10.1016/j.jneumeth.2014.05.008
19. Byford, G. "Signal variance and its application to continuous measurements of e.e.g. activity." *Proceedings of the Royal Society of London. Series B. Biological Sciences* 161 (1965): 421–437.

20. Klimesch, W. (1996). Memory processes, brain oscillations and EEG synchronization. *International journal of psychophysiology*, 24(1-2), 61–100.
21. Ramzan, Munaza, and Suma Dawn. "Learning-based classification of valence emotion from electroencephalography." *International Journal of Neuroscience* 129, 11 (2019): 1085–1093.
22. Kahana, Michael J., Robert Sekuler, Jeremy B. Caplan, Matthew Kirschen, and Joseph R. Madsen. "Human theta oscillations exhibit task dependence during virtual maze navigation." *Nature* 399, 6738 (1999): 781–784.
23. Stevens, Ronald H., Trysha Galloway, and Chris Berka. "EEG-related changes in cognitive workload, engagement and distraction as students acquire problem solving skills." In *International Conference on User Modeling*, pp. 187–196. Springer, Berlin, Heidelberg, 2007.
24. Astolfi, Laura, F. De Vico Fallani, Febo Cincotti, Donatella Mattia, Luigi Bianchi, M. G. Marciani, Serenella Salinari et al. "Neural basis for brain responses to TV commercials: a high-resolution EEG study." *IEEE Transactions on Neural Systems and rehabilitation engineering* 16, 6 (2008): 522–531.
25. Ramsøy, Thomas Z. *Introduction to Neuromarketing and Consumer Neuroscience*. Neurons Inc., Denmark, 2015.
26. Acunzo, David J., Graham MacKenzie, and Mark CW van Rossum. "Systematic biases in early ERP and ERF components as a result of high-pass filtering." *Journal of Neuroscience Methods* 209, 1 (2012): 212–218.
27. Singh, Balbir, and Hiroaki Wagatsuma. "A removal of eye movement and blink artifacts from EEG data using morphological component analysis." *Computational and Mathematical Methods in Medicine* 2017 (2017).
28. Zou, Liang, Xun Chen, Ge Dang, Yi Guo, and Z. Jane Wang. "Removing muscle artifacts from EEG data via underdetermined joint blind source separation: A simulation study." *IEEE Transactions on Circuits and Systems II: Express Briefs* 67, 1 (2019): 187–191.
29. Makeig, Scott and Onton, Julie "ERP features and EEG dynamics: an ICA perspective". *The Oxford Handbook of Event-Related Potential Components* (2012): 10.1093/oxfordhb/9780195374148.013.0035.
30. Paszkiel, Szczepan. "Data analysis of human brain activity using MATLAB environment with EEGLAB." In *Analysis and Classification of EEG Signals for Brain–Computer Interfaces*, pp. 33–39. Springer, Cham, 2020.
31. Hjorth, B. "EEG analysis based on time domain properties." *Electroencephalography and Clinical Neurophysiology* 29,3 (1970): 306–310. doi:10.1016/0013-4694(70)90143-4
32. Burgess, Adrian P. "Towards a unified understanding of event-related changes in the EEG: the firefly model of synchronization through cross-frequency phase modulation." *PloS ONE* 7, 9 (2012): e45630.
33. Kaplan, A., A. Fingelkurts, S. Borisov and B. Darkhovsky. "Nonstationary nature of the brain activity as revealed by EEG/MEG: Methodological, practical and conceptual challenges." *Signal Process.* 85 (2005): 2190–2212.
34. Misiti, M., Misiti, Y., Oppenheim, G., and Poggi, J. M. (Eds.) "*Wavelets and their Applications*" (2013): John Wiley and Sons, New York.
35. Huang, Guang-Bin, Qin-Yu Zhu, and Chee-Kheong Siew. "Extreme learning machine: theory and applications." *Neurocomputing* 70, 1-3 (2006): 489–501.
36. Kübra, E. R. A. T., Pınar Onay Durdu, and Orhan Akbulut. "The role of extreme learning machine in multi classification based emotion recognition using EEG signals." In *2019 Innovations in Intelligent Systems and Applications Conference (ASYU)*, pp. 1–6. IEEE.

37. Samara, Anas, Maria Luiza Recena Menezes, and Leo Galway. "Feature extraction for emotion recognition and modelling using neurophysiological data." In *2016 15th international conference on ubiquitous computing and communications and 2016 international symposium on cyberspace and security (IUCC-CSS)*, pp. 138–144. IEEE, 2016.
38. Soleymani, Mohammad, Frank Villaro-Dixon, Thierry Pun, and Guillaume Chanel. "Toolbox for emotional feature extraction from physiological signals (TEAP)." *Frontiers in ICT* 4 (2017): 1.

3 Application of Machine-Learning Techniques in Electroencephalography Signals

Arun Sasidharan and Kusumika Krori Dutta

3.1 INTRODUCTION

Humans are highly intelligent species which is attributed to their complex brains. Trying to understand or predict the brain's activities has been one of the greatest challenges of mankind. Ever since the invention of electroencephalography (EEG) about 100 years ago, there has been significant progress towards this goal. Electroencephalography continues to be an affordable and easy-to-use device for objective assessment of human brain activities, used in clinics and research labs across the globe. However, in clinics, EEG-based brain activity prediction has mostly remained subjective through expert visual inspection, despite several advances in signal processing-based evaluation in research labs. The main reason for this dichotomy is that the manual evaluation by an expert is inherently flexible in adapting their rules based on several contextual information ("learning through experience") [1], which is seldom captured by the prefixed rules programmed into signal processing algorithms ("no learning"), despite their mathematical rigor. Over recent years, machine learning (ML) techniques have tried to address this issue in fields like image processing and have begun to show high promise in EEG interpretation [2]. There is a general consensus that the effective incorporation of ML techniques into EEG-based brain activity classification and prediction will require an interdisciplinary effort bringing together both EEG experts and ML data scientists, which is currently a rarity. The current chapter is a humble effort to emphasize this point, by initially providing a simplified neurobiological grounding on the brain and EEG activity, then introducing the basic principle behind ML techniques and finally showing these are used in two neuroscience applications (seizure prediction and sleep-stage classification).

3.2 BRAIN AND ELECTROENCEPHALOGRAPHY (EEG)

The human brain is a complex machine which processes many inputs at a time. The activities of the brain can be partially understood by analysing EEG signals. In this section, we discuss the human brain and how to measure its activities using EEG.

3.2.1 HUMAN BRAIN

The brain is the main "biological computer" of our body, capable of enormous amounts of information processing, storage, and complex predictions. The human brain brings about a myriad of functions, including the processing of sensory information from external and internal sources, controlling body movements, and bringing about cognitive functions such as ability to think, learn new ideas, memorize facts, remember past events, speak to other people, and make complex decisions. Different parts of the brain specialize in different sub-functions. Some of the evolutionarily conserved brain regions control basic bodily activities like respiration (brainstem), hormone regulation (hypothalamus), information flow (thalamus), etc. Whereas, the cerebral cortex is a brain region that is more evolved and enlarged (forming the bulk of brain), with specialization for auditory processing (in temporal cortex), visual processing (in occipital cortex), touch processing (in parietal cortex), movement (in frontal cortex), thinking (in pre-frontal cortex), so on and so forth.

3.2.2 FUNDAMENTALS OF BRAIN ACTIVITIES AND THEIR ELECTRICAL NATURE

Despite functional divisions, the brain is dominated by electrically active microscopic cells called neurons. The human brain is estimated to contain around 100 billion neurons with trillions of massively parallel interconnections. Throughout such interconnections, a neuron communicates with other neurons through a complex series of electro-chemical signalling. The electrical nature of the neuron is attributed to its two main features [3]. First, it can actively maintain a concentration gradient for biological ions across its membrane at rest—more positive ions outside than inside making the neuron relatively negatively charged (typically −70 mV to −80 mV). Second, it has three functional zones with differential distribution of ion channels—input zone (fine receptive projections called dendrites and part of its cell body), integrative zone (starting segment of output projection called axon hillock), and conductive zone (long output projections called axons). The input zone receives stimulations from other neurons, at small membrane junctions called synapses through chemicals called neurotransmitters. This causes an opening of ion channels (ligand-gated) and a graded passive inflow of positive ions from the neuronal surrounding, making local pockets of neuron slightly positively charged (0.1–10 mV change); this is called post-synaptic potential. Multiples of such post-synaptic potentials occurring in close succession can get summated at the integrative zone, triggering a much stronger "all-or-none" inflow of positive ions through another type of channel (voltage-gated), making larger areas inside neurons more positively charged (70–110 mV change); this is called an action potential. This short-lived depolarized state (1 ms), then propagates along the conductive zone. Further ion channel openings will quickly repolarize the neuron and bring it back to its resting state (in another 2–3 ms), getting it ready for the next firing. Action potential firing can be thought of as the firing of a "gun" creating a resting membrane potential is like loading the gun, getting ready to fire, and pulling the trigger is like firing an action potential. Whereas, this firing requires post-synaptic potentials from multiple neurons (involving thousands of synapses) to summate, either due to repeated firing from few synapses or concordant firing from several synapses. Taken together, post-synaptic potentials allow a flexible and accurate way to determine stimuli features, and action potentials allow a quick and effective way to respond to important stimuli.

3.2.3 Principles of EEG and What They Measure

A common way to measure such electrical activity is to determine the voltage difference around a neuron, called local field potential (LFP). Due to the extremely brief (1–2 ms) and localized (few micrometers) nature of action potentials, they can be effectively derived from LFP only if we place small sensors close to such neurons. On the contrary, post-synaptic potentials are much more spread in time (5 ms to minutes) and space (over several centimeters), whereby a summated signal can be well detected in LFP as well as over longer distance by volume conduction called far-field potentials. Far-field potentials, when captured noninvasively over scalp sensors or electrodes, are usually called electroencephalography (EEG), though in principle even LFPs and similar measurements are also EEG. Neurons are of many sizes and shapes, depending on their location within the brain and their functional role. Pyramidal neurons are the largest and more numerous of the neurons present in the cerebral cortex. They are also aligned more regularly, lying parallel to the cortical surface. This makes their receptive portion (called dendrites) forming a thick sheet-like layer, closer to the cortical surface. This alignment pattern and the fact that the cortex covers most of the area underneath the skull, makes pyramidal neurons the largest contributor to EEG signals (contributions from other neurons, interneurons, glia, etc., are believed to be indirect). Figure 3.1 summarizes the neural basis of EEG genesis. The movement of charged ions differentially across the pyramidal neuron causes a sink-source phenomenon in the immediate surrounding of this neuron, generating instantaneous dipole states. Collective activation of several pyramidal neurons can get summated to be detectable to an EEG electrode placed on the scalp. Volume conduction property of biological tissues allows such signals to spread to more further regions of the scalp with varying intensities or polarity. The EEG thus captures neuronal activities as blurred electrical field changes over the scalp due to movement of charged molecules (ions) around the neural tissue.

Measurement of EEG requires extremely sensitive voltage sensing devices, which compare the tiny differences in scalp voltages (within microvolts) between two regions. Figure 3.2 illustrates this process. These sensing devices typically consist of a differential amplifier connected to the intact scalp through conductive inert metal sensors called electrodes. The contact between skin and the electrode surface usually has a conductive electrolytic medium, where the ion movement is recreated. Each EEG amplifier requires at least three electrode inputs to measure a single EEG signal accurately: an active electrode at the scalp region of interest, a reference electrode at a comparison site (like the ear lobe), and a ground electrode for DC calibration. Most EEG devices have multiple amplifiers within them (termed channels), to capture EEG signals from multiple scalp regions. Such EEG signals

(a)   (b)   (c)

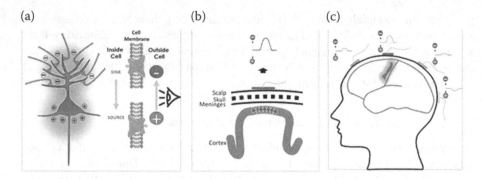

FIGURE 3.1   Neural basis of EEG: (a) Sink-source phenomenon and dipole formulation of pyramidal neuron, (b) dipole summation in a cortical patch and its effect on surface electrode, (c) volume conduction of signals to different scalp electrodes.

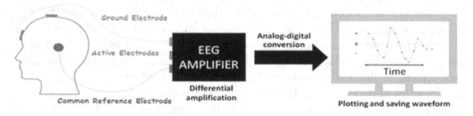

FIGURE 3.2   Measurement of EEG.

are sampled at a high temporal resolution using analog-to-digital converters built into the device (a typical EEG sampling rate of 1000 Hz means a sample is captured at every one millisecond). A routine clinical EEG device captures from around 19 scalp locations, whereas research EEG devices may capture from up to 256 scalp locations simultaneously.

3.2.4   Importance of EEG and Its Signal Processing Features

The EEG can give millisecond resolution information of brain activity, which many other neuroimaging tools (like functional magnetic resonance imaging) fail to capture. As a noninvasive, affordable medical device, EEG has been in clinical use for the last several years. From a clinical context, the main use of EEG is to diagnose brain activity abnormalities, mainly with respect to epileptic seizures and sleep disorders. Other clinical uses of EEG are in the diagnosis of coma, brain death, encephalopathy, etc. From a research context, the analysis of EEG signals has found innumerable applications such as understanding the mechanism behind several mental disorders, emotional processing/regulation, substance abuse, altered consciousness (like coma), mental training (like mediation and music), the effect of cognitive training, lie detection, neuromarketing, so on and so forth. Thus, EEG patterns capture many aspects of mental processes like cognition, behavior, and emotions, across the illness to wellness spectrum.

For signal processing, such EEG patterns are commonly considered as sine waves, and hence described in terms of frequency (number of waves per second), amplitude (magnitude of the wave), and phase (position of the values in the wave). These are called the spectral features of EEG and are represented in Figure 3.3. Commonly, many brain activity patterns have been described by grouping the EEG spectral features into frequency bands like delta (0.5–4 Hz), theta (4–7 Hz), alpha (8–12 Hz), beta (13–30 Hz), and gamma (>30 Hz).

Fast Fourier transform (FFT) [4] is the most widely used algorithms that extract spectral features from EEG segments, by decomposing them into sinusoidal versions. Discrete wavelet transform (DWT) [5] is another common algorithm, where EEG signals are decomposed into scaled and shifted versions of signal templates called wavelets. Unlike FFTs, DWTs can extract the temporal dynamics of oscillatory patterns as well as detect the presence of short transient signals, and hence is preferred for time-frequency analysis. But, compared to FFT, DWT is more computationally intensive for applying across long datasets. Hilbert transform (HT) [6] is another useful algorithm for time-frequency analysis, where the EEG signals are filtered into narrow bands of interest, before extracting their instantaneous oscillatory characteristics. The HT is less computationally intensive compared to DWT, and could provide equivalent results if the filters are appropriately chosen [6]. There are also some derivatives of FFT, which provide added capabilities to FFT. Multi-taper FFT (MFFT) [7] does multiple FFTs on the same EEG segments, orthogonally resampling each time by applying a different windowing function or taper, and then taking the average estimate of these FFTs, which improves the inter-frequency resolution of the data, especially for higher frequencies. The MFFT applied as a sliding window function is useful for time-frequency analysis. Stockwell transform (ST) [8] is another FFT derivative that varies window sizes for each frequency content, adding some of the features of DWT to FFT, and making it useful for time-frequency analysis. Besides examining spectral features within each scalp site separately, their distribution across the scalp (topography) could also give simple yet important information on the source of this pattern and thereby the underlying brain processes. Interactions between scalp sites could be quantified as correlations between spectral features in terms of power (like power coherence and amplitude envelope correlations), as well as that of phase (like imaginary coherence and phase lock value), all interpreted as measures of brain connectivity or synchronization [9]. Interactions between spectral contents, either within the same scalp site or between sites, are an important feature to understand the underlying brain state. This is especially useful when some spectral contents (generally higher frequencies) are too weak to be directly detected, and yet couples with a higher intensity spectral content (usually a lower frequency). For instance, the amplitude of the high-frequency oscillations (HFOs; 80–150 Hz), which is a spectral feature suggestive of seizure disorder, shows modulation with the phase of a low-frequency content like theta (4–7 Hz) [10,11]. Furthermore, there are spatial filters which help to demix the EEG patterns and improve the signal-to-noise ratio, before spectral feature extraction. These include those that demix based on statistical properties like principal

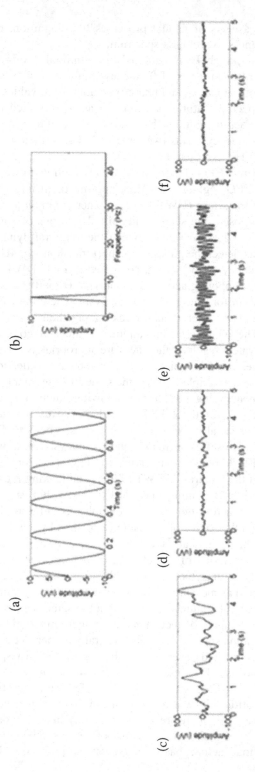

FIGURE 3.3 Spectral features of EEG (a) Voltage change across time, (b) Average magnitude of each frequency component, (c) Delta activity (0.5–4 Hz), (d) Theta activity (4–7 Hz), (e) Alpha activity (8–12 Hz), (f) Beta/Gamma activity (>13 Hz).

component analysis (PCA) and independent component analysis, as well as those that take account of signal spread like Laplacian transform or current source density (CSD). There are more advanced spatial filters that help in estimating the source location of the EEG features, using a combination of forward head conduction models (like the Boundary Element Model [BEM] and Finite Element Model [FEM]) and inverse source models (like low-resolution electromagnetic tomography [LORETA]) [12]. These can increase the interpretability of the EEG feature, but significantly increases the computation time.

3.3 INTRODUCTION TO MACHINE LEARNING TECHNIQUES

Machine learning (ML) is a branch of computer science, where computers are programmed in a way that they can learn from data without explicit instructions [13]. It is most useful when there is a problem that is either too complex for traditional approaches or has no known algorithm, which is quite common when one tries to predict a complex brain activity using an EEG signal. The ML-based approaches can be broadly grouped into: (1) supervised learning, (2) unsupervised learning, and (3) reinforcement learning.

1. *Supervised learning:* In case of supervised learning, labeled input data is presented during the training phase (as shown in Figure 3.4) and based on the labels, the model groups the output (target). This type of learning is further categorized as (1) classification and (2) regression models. The classification model is mainly used if it is required to decide to which type or class a given sample belongs. For example, let us consider a dataset that has several images of four types of brain waves and their names are provided as labels. The brain waves types are delta, theta, alpha, and beta. Now, given a new wave image, if we need to identify to which among those four waves types used for training it belongs, then this is a classification problem. Whereas, if we had provided the names as well as the quantity-wise frequencies of those waves as labels during training and then use the model to calculate the frequency of a new test wave, then this is an example of a regression model. Considering the recent COVID-19 scenario as another example, to determine if a person is COVID positive or not (diagnosis based on symptom and test report) is a classification problem, whereas, to predict over a certain period of time how many people could get affected is a regression problem.

2. *Unsupervised learning:* In the case of unsupervised learning, the input data is unlabeled. Based on the input features, the model generates different clusters (as shown in Figure 3.5). The number of clusters depends on the number of features extracted. Let us consider the same example of four brain waves. If we train a model giving all the four varieties of brain wave images without providing the names of the waves, then the model groups them into several clusters based on features. Taking the example of COVID-19, if the mortality rate and its reasons are provided for unsupervised training, then it can find the people at high risk by clustering based on medical history, staying in the containment zone, travel history, etc. There are five popular clustering algorithms used by

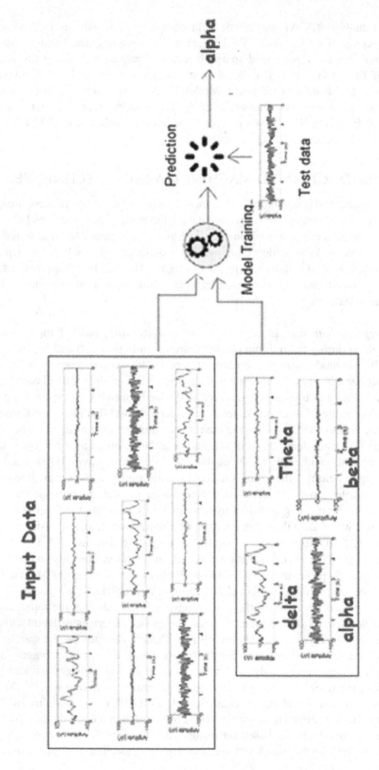

FIGURE 3.4   Supervised training and testing process.

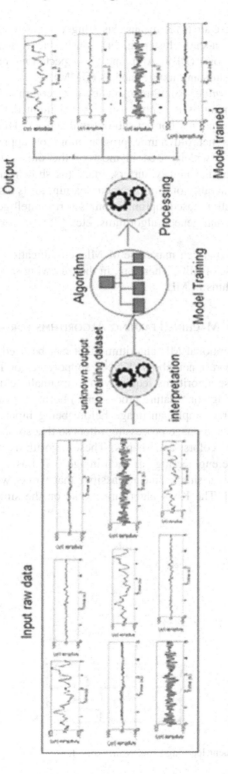

FIGURE 3.5 Unsupervised training process.

data scientists. These are (1) K-means clustering, (2) agglomerative hierarchical clustering, (3) mean-shift clustering, (4) density-based spatial clustering of applications with noise (DBSCAN), and (5) expectation–maximization (EM) clustering using Gaussian mixture models (GMM).

3. *Reinforcement learning:* Reinforcement learning contradicts supervised and unsupervised learning as it neither uses labeled input data for training nor does it require to explicitly correct sub-optimal actions. This type of learning is also known as neuro-dynamic programming or approximate dynamic programming. It is widely used in most of the online games like backgammon, flappy birds, subway surfers, maze (as shown in Figure 3.6), etc. Because of the generality of reinforcement learning, it is also used in various fields like simulation-based optimization, swarm intelligence, multi-agent systems, statistics and genetic algorithms, etc.

Among the many tasks that can make use of ML, classification problems are the most common in the case of EEG. Therefore, in the following section we will focus on classification algorithms in ML.

3.3.1 CONVENTIONAL MACHINE LEARNING ALGORITHMS FOR CLASSIFICATION

There are several conventional ML algorithms that can be used for classification problems, such as k-nearest neighbors (KNN), support vector machines (SVM), decision trees, etc. These algorithms require you to manually extract relevant features ("feature engineering" or "feature processing") before they can start learning to classify the data. For example, an image before being input into the SVM or KNN must go through some image processing filters so that some features might be extracted such as edges, colors, and shapes. These algorithms work linearly and require time for "feature engineering" as each image is fed as a single entity.

The KNN classifier is a simple linear classifier that works well on basic classification problems [14]. The KNN algorithm works on the simple principle that

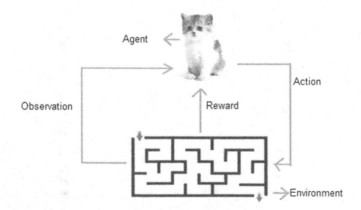

FIGURE 3.6   Reinforcement learning process in game theory.

similar data are closer to each other in data space. So, it tries to predict the label of a new instance by finding the most common label among the k-nearest neighbors from the training data labels [15]. Despite the simplicity of this algorithm, it has several disadvantages. First, at each prediction, this algorithm needs to compute the distance measures and sort all the training data, which can significantly slow down the process, especially when there are numerous training examples. Second, this algorithm groups patterns specific to the training data, but do not learn features that are generalizable ("lazy learner"), and is also not robust to noise in the data. Furthermore, changing the value of K can change the classification output. The SVM is another linear classifier [16], with more complex logic useful in several classification applications. The main disadvantage of this algorithm is that it requires the optimal tuning of several key parameters to achieve a good classification outcome. So, a given parameter setting could give high classification accuracy for problem A, but low performance for problem B. The user, therefore, needs to experiment with several parameter settings before achieving a satisfactory result.

Artificial neural networks (ANNs) are another prominent ML algorithm useful for data classification, which (as their name suggests) were inspired by the efficient functional logic of neurons and early success in creating their basic computational models [17]. They are multi-layered networks of artificial neurons acting as nodes and interconnected through several input and output links that have weights as parameters. During learning, ANNs optimize the weights of their links. Thus, these algorithms are useful in solving nonlinear classification problems, which are common with biological signals. Despite the superior performance, ANNs have some disadvantages like the features identified by them are not interpretable (unlike ML algorithms like decision trees), their development can be extremely difficult due to poor control over the algorithm details, and they require much larger amounts of training data and greater computational power.

3.3.2 DEEP LEARNING ALGORITHMS FOR CLASSIFICATION

But, when dealing with huge datasets, there could be thousands of features that need to be engineered (like image spectrograms), which can slow down most ML classification algorithms and their accuracy plateaus. Deep learning algorithms like convolutional neural networks (CNNs) and recurrent neural networks (RNNs) are improved versions of ANNs, which can automatically learn features directly from raw data, without the requirement of a feature engineering step from the user [18]. They are inherently parallel and achieve higher training speed and efficiency in classification. For example, we could give many pictures of cats and dogs to this algorithm and it can automatically learn several distinct features for each class. Both the models are computationally efficient for large datasets, where RNNs have memory storage options in its architecture and also can overcome vanishing gradient crises [19]; in the case of CNNs, the efficiency due to usage of special convolutions and pooling operations and parameter sharing ability. There are several read-to-use CNN models through cloud services enabling them to be run universally from many types of devices, making them incredibly attractive.

The architecture of any typical CNN consists of a convolution layer, activation function, pooling layers, and output layer.

3.3.2.1   Convolution Layer

Convolution is the distinguishing feature of a CNN. Its main parameter is a set of learnable filters (or kernels), which usually have a small window size, but strides through the full depth of the input data. During the forward pass, the filter is applied on overlapping patches of the input data in both directions (left to right and top to bottom). This application results in element-wise multiplication between the filter with the input array, and their averaging gives out a single result per filter overlap region. This process is called convolution. The filter gets convolved multiple times across the input array, resulting in a smaller two-dimensional array as output. This output array represents some of the features of the input array in a smaller data space called a feature map.

Figure 3.7 represent the input image and the filter/kernel represents a filter of size 3×3, after first convolution the feature map is the sum of overlapping values as in Eq. (3.1).

$$\text{Feature map} = (1 \times 2) + (4 \times 2) + (9 \times 3) + (-4 \times 2) + (7 \times 1) + (4 \times 4)$$
$$+ (2 \times 1) + (-5 \times 1) + (1 \times 2) = 51 \qquad (3.1)$$

Typically, CNNs do not just use a single filter, instead they convolve the input data using multiple filters in parallel, thereby learning multiple features quickly. This makes the feature extraction of such models very rich and effective.

3.3.2.2   Activation Function

The activation function is a node that is put at the end of or between activation in CNNs. The activation functions which are widely used in neural networks are rectified linear units (ReLU), hyperbolic tangent, etc. An activation example using ReLU is shown in Figure 3.8, and is defined by equation 3.2.

$$f(x) = \max(0, x) \qquad (3.2)$$

It replaces the negative values of the activation map with zeros. This improves the decision function of the overall model without affecting the receptive fields of the convolution layer.

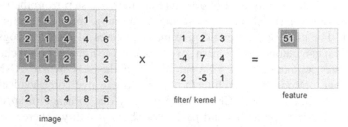

FIGURE 3.7   Feature map and convolution filter/kernel.

0.77	-0.11	0.11	0.33	0.55	-0.11	0.33
-0.11	1.0	-0.11	0.33	-0.11	0.11	-0.11
0.11	-0.11	1.0	-0.33	0.11	-0.11	0.55
0.33	0.33	-0.33	0.55	-0.33	0.33	0.33
0.55	-0.11	0.11	-0.33	1.00	-0.11	0.11
-0.11	0.11	-0.11	0.33	-0.11	1.00	-0.11
0.33	-0.11	0.55	0.33	0.11	-0.11	0.77

0.77	0	0.11	0.33	0.55	0	0.33
0	1.00	0	0.33	0	0.11	0
0.11	0	1.00	0	0.11	0	0.55
0.33	0.33	0	0.55	0	0.33	0.33
0.55	0	0.11	0	1.00	0	0.11
0	0.11	0	0.33	0	1.00	0
0.33	0	0.55	0.33	0.11	0	1.77

FIGURE 3.8 Activation function.

3.3.2.3 Pooling Layer

Though convolution causes the compactness within the feature maps, pooling is responsible for the reduction in the dimensionality across such feature parameters. The principle behind pooling is that the rough relative location of a feature is more important than its exact location. During pooling, each feature map gets down-sampled independently, causing a reduction in their height and width, without affecting their depth. This step substantially reduces the size of the parameter space, thereby reducing the memory footprint of the model and the amount of computation required in the network. Hence, the training time shortens and prevents the model from over-fitting. The most common pooling method is max pooling. Like a convolution filter, it has a window size and stride, which then slides across the data and extracts the max value within in pooling window.

Figure 3.9 shows the result of max pooling using a window size of 2 × 2 and stride of 2. Each color represents a different window. After a round of convolution and pooling (sometimes after multiple such rounds), the output will be pushed into a couple of fully connected neural network layers. But, the output of a convolution and pooling round is a 2D matrix, and a fully connected layer works on a 1D vector. Therefore, the output 2D matrix of the final pooling layer will need to be flattened to a 1D vector, before entering a fully connected layer. Flattening is achieved by simple reshaping of the 2D matrix into a 1D vector as shown in Figure 3.10.

3.3.2.4 Post Processing of Predicted Label

Post-processing the class labels after processing a stream of data through the defined pipeline of preprocessing and classification plays an important role in preventing the false alarming of the proposed system, because no deep neural network can be made to achieve 100% accuracy and especially in the case of medical applications it is very important to handle the false triggering of the system due to

FIGURE 3.9 Max pooling.

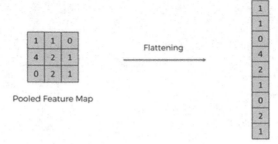

FIGURE 3.10   Pooling and flattening.

some wrong output. To overcome this problem, we propose to use a simple method that we name as "k of n". It states that the alarm will be triggered only when k predictions out of last n output labels were positive.

In Table 3.1 the samples correspond to nine spectrograms formed before feeding to the classification algorithm; the predicted output is the output value from the classification model for each spectrogram—value 1 is coded as preictal state and 0 is coded as an interictal state. In Table 3.1 if $n = 5$ and $k = 3$, meaning that 3 predicted outputs in a window of 5 samples are positive, the alarm for successful prediction of preictal state of epileptic seizure is triggered, while if $k > 3$ for $n = 5$, the alarm will not be triggered. To find the optimum value of k and n, we must analyze the preictal segment results used in training deep neural networks.

3.3.3   DECIDING ON A CLASSIFICATION ALGORITHM

Overall, it is important to note that there is no ML algorithm that can be claimed "perfect" for all classification problems. For each problem, a certain method may be better suited and achieves good results, while another method fails heavily. For instance, in a problem where performance is critical (like predicting a deadly disease) with high data availability and computation resources, a CNN approach would be an ideal choice. On the contrary, some of the simpler ML algorithms (like KNN or decision trees) would be more effective for classification on small and simple datasets working on low-resource devices (not connected to cloud services), with greater interpretability of the classification strategy. This is because, unlike the traditional ML algorithms, deep learning approaches require hundreds of thousands or millions of data points for the best results, and are computationally intensive, often requiring a high-performance graphical processing unit (GPU).

TABLE 3.1
Post-processing technique

Sample	1	2	3	4	5	6	7	8	9
Predicted output	1	1	1	0	0	1	1	0	0

3.4 NEUROSCIENCE APPLICATION OF MACHINE LEARNING USING EEG SIGNALS

This section will guide you through the application of ML, using seizure and sleep stage classifications as examples. In each case, first, we will provide some background knowledge, and then walk through the selection of EEG features and application of a suitable ML pipeline.

3.4.1 SEIZURE DETECTION

Scalp and intracranial EEG, accelerometric and motion sensors, electro-cardiography (ECG), audio/video captures, and electrodermal activity have been utilized towards detection of seizure over the past few decades. But, till today, not a single such technology can be considered as the best confirmatory test for seizure, because of its uncertain nature of the occurrence. In this section, seizure and its detection methodology will be discussed.

3.4.1.1 Background: What Are Seizures?

Epilepsy is the fourth most common neurological disorder characterized by an abrupt and recurrent dysfunction of the brain called a "seizure," which has a worldwide prevalence of around 65 million [20]. Every year, about 48 out of 100,000 people are estimated to develop epilepsy, globally. It can occur in a wide range of age groups (from very young to very old), irrespective of ethnicity or geographical location. In the U.S. alone, about 1 in 100 people is believed to have had at least a single unprovoked seizure or been diagnosed with epilepsy. Figure 3.11 shows worldwide epilepsy cases [21].

Chronologically, young children (mostly in the first year of their life) have the highest incidence of epilepsy. The incidence gradually declines until about the age of 10 years, plateaus for a while, and further increases after the age of 55 years. The increased incidence in elderly is strongly associated with the incidence of other illnesses like strokes, brain tumors, or Alzheimer disease, which can themselves be

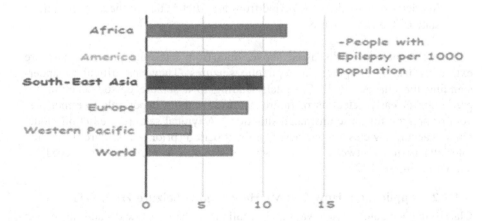

FIGURE 3.11 Statistics of worldwide epilepsy cases.

secondary causes for epilepsy. Based on behaviorally visible motor symptoms, the seizures are classified into two major groups [22]. They are as follows:

1. Seizures with motor symptoms that include muscles becoming tense or rigid (tonic), muscles undergoing sustained rhythmic jerky movements (clonic), muscles becoming weak or flaccid (atonic), muscles having brief twitches (myoclonic), or whole-body muscles undergoing repeated flexion and extension (spasmodic).
2. Seizures with no motor symptoms. They are usually called absence seizures, either typical or atypical, and are characterised by "staring spells." Though absence seizures can also have brief twitches (myoclonus), unlike motor seizures, these affect a specific part of the body or just the eyelids.

Seizure type and epilepsy syndrome can be determined with the help of EEG and thereby helping to choose appropriate anti-seizure drugs (ASD) and allow prognosis prediction. In practice, clinicians generally diagnose based on history provided by the patient or the attendee who witnessed the episode. But it becomes extremely difficult for clinicians when patients suffer from "blackout" (loss of consciousness or brief impairment of awareness) and also absence of any witness around at that time as EEG can only show a person has seizure syndrome or not. In such situations, auto-classification of epilepsy from given EEG signals aids proper clinical diagnosis, leads to appropriate medication, as ASDs have tremendous side effects.

Another side of seizure is the different stages of its occurrence. There are four major phases (or states) of seizures which can be classified as follows:

1. Preictal state this is the time before the seizure. Some sufferers use this as a warning signal to prepare for an impending seizure.
2. Ictal state—this refers to the entire period of the seizure attack.
3. Postictal state—this is the period immediately after a seizure. This phase can last for seconds, minutes, hours and sometimes even days.
4. Interictal state—this is the period from a postictal state to the start of preictal state of the next seizure.

Among the four states discussed above, data from ictal and preictal states are extremely useful for predicting epileptic seizures. They are critical to understanding the changes in EEG signals leading to a seizure episode, helping in prediction or early detection of future seizures, making it possible to either prevent or prepare for these unwanted situations. A typical seizure prediction model aims to accurately classify between a preictal period (prior to a seizure onset) and interictal period (between seizures when nonseizure syndrome is observed) as shown in Figure 3.12.

3.4.1.2 Application: How Can ML Help Predict Seizure From EEG?

Classifying accurately was always a big challenge. The past few decades have seen several advances in the field of ML, allowing extensive data mining and using them

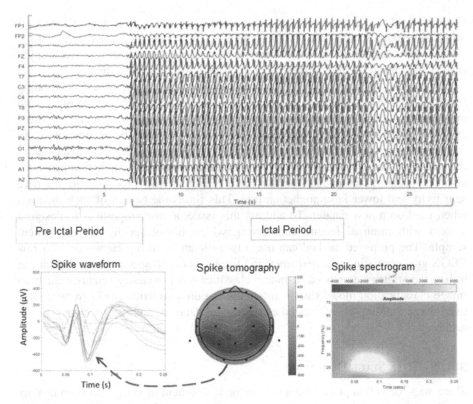

FIGURE 3.12   Epileptic EEG pattern and its features.

for predictive analytics, which is very promising in healthcare practice. Even though the currently available methods do not convincingly pinpoint the source of epileptic seizures, a recent study [23] used spectral features of each channel as features for seizure prediction, and trained them using an SVM classifier to learn the feature differences between preictal and interictal data. Testing with the large Freiburg Hospital dataset [24], they achieved a sensitivity of 98.3% and false positive rate of 0.29/h. Another study [25] additionally added between-frequency spectral power ratios as features to achieve a sensitivity exceeding 98% and false positive rate lower than 0.05/h. As this approach also involved independent tailoring of features for each patient, their impressive results may not be that generalizable. Such patient-specific feature engineering processes often involve manual intervention by domain experts, and therefore, are highly time-consuming and effortful. Overall, the above study ended up using 44 features and a set of 91 cost-sensitive linear SVM classifiers to determine the best performing feature combinations for each patient. Algorithm performance in both these studies depended heavily on the best combination of features and classifiers, which not only cannot be known for every patient, but even when known, will be suboptimal for a future time point due to the inherent dynamics of brain activity. Hence, there is an obvious need for a seizure-detection system that is more generalizable, uses minimal resources, does not involve patient-specific manual feature engineering, suitable for long period usage and usable in a home setting, thereby facilitating early intervention as well as prevention of seizure-related side effects.

To improve the plight of patients with drug-resistant epilepsy and debilitating seizures, there has been growing interest around seizure prediction. Most of such outstanding works have been focusing on developing ways to indirectly (warning systems) or directly (closed-loop neural stimulation) control the occurrence of refractory seizures, with some achieving impressive results. However, as discussed in the case of studies on classification problems, many works on prediction problems also rely heavily on patient-specific feature engineering processes to improve sensitivity and lower false prediction rate. This limits the benefit of such methods when used on a new dataset. To address this issue, a new proposal is to design a system with minimal feature engineering which is not specific to any patient sample. The proposed method can use a two-dimensional representation of a raw EEG signal consisting of a frequency and time axis called spectrograms, which can utilize the strategy employed in image classification to classify seizures. Such an image classification model can do automatic feature extractions and can be trained using large training sets of preictal and interictal datasets, and can promise superior accuracy.

3.4.2 SLEEP STAGE DETECTION

Sleep stage detection plays a vital role in the assessment of sleep quality in healthy people and more importantly to confirm the presence of a sleep disorder. In this section we will provide a brief overview about sleep and its dynamics, leading to the need for using ML in sleep stage detection.

3.4.2.1 Background: What Is Sleep?

Sleep is a natural state that occupies at least a third of one's daily life. It is not a passive, monotonous physiological event [26,27]. Instead, it is a dynamic process wherein the brain cyclically passes through various phases of activity that are termed sleep stages [28]. Modern sleep research that is based on laboratory-based sleep evaluation termed polysomnography (PSG), allowed the characterisation of sleep stages [29]. Polysomnography combines the electrical patterns observed in scalp-recorded EEG along with those observed from the movement of eyeballs and eyelids (called electrooculography or EOG) and muscle activity under the chin (called electromyography or EMG), to determine the sleep stage. Other physiological measurements like cardiac, respiratory, and autonomic recordings, may also be captured to assess sleep-associated processes, but they are not required for sleep staging. From a PSG recording, a sleep expert/technician scores every consecutive 30 s segments/epochs into one of four sleep stages, as per standard scoring guidelines, most widely used being from American Academy of Sleep Medicine (AASM) [30]. The plot of a scoring time-series is called a hypnogram (as shown in Figure 3.13).

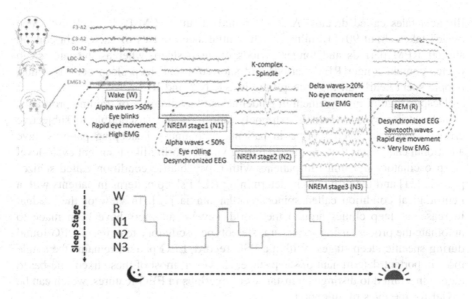

FIGURE 3.13 Sleep stage scoring.

Sleep has been divided into 3–4 nonrapid eye movement (NREM) sleep stages and one REM sleep stage, with the NREM-REM cycle repeating many times throughout the night's sleep. The normal neural state transition from wake to sleep is characterized by behavioral changes as well as some stereotypic EEG changes. Sleep starts with entry into NREM stage 1 (N1), where EEG spectral content shows a reduction in the faster alpha (8–13 Hz) band power and rise in the slower theta (4–8 Hz) band power. Behaviorally, subjects feel drowsy, muscles relax, breath slows down, and eyes start rolling. They can be awakened easily in this state. During this stage, some experience fragmented visual images while drifting in and out of sleep, and feel like falling with sudden muscle jerks (hypnagogic jerks). Following this transitional state, as subjects enter true sleep (NREM stage 2 or N2) eye movement stops and EEG waves become slower, with short and recurrent bursts of fast activities called sleep spindles (11–16 Hz). Further, subjects descend into slow wave sleep (SWS or NREM stage 3 or N3), when scalp EEG is predominated by large-amplitude slow brain waves called delta frequency waves (>100 μV; 0.5–4 Hz). This stage has high awakening threshold, and show no eye movements or muscle activity. When awakened during this stage, people report feel tired and confused for a long time before getting adjusted. During this descent through NREM sleep stages (N1–N3) subjects also show a progressive decrease in respiratory rate, heart rate, blood pressure, and body temperature. Next, subjects switch into REM sleep, where EEG shows "active pattern" resembling that of wake, but eyes show rapid multi-directional jerks (REMs), and body muscles become temporarily limp. During this stage, breathing becomes more rapid, irregular, and shallow, heart rate and blood pressure increases, and males develop penile erections. When people are awakened during REM sleep, they often report bizarre and illogical tales called dreams. A single round of an NREM-REM cycle or "sleep cycle" takes about 90–110 minutes. The initial sleep cycles of each night contain shorter REM periods and longer periods of deep sleep, whereas the later sleep cycles contain longer REM periods and shorter/absent deep sleep periods. Thus, people spent nearly all their sleep time in N1, N2, and REM.

Despite regular improvement in guidelines and availability of training programs, visual scoring by an expert is extremely laborious and susceptible to subjective errors. Moreover, sleep scoring in patients with unusual sleeping patterns have additional challenges that are missed during visual scoring like transient cycle-level sleep oscillatory dynamics in patients with a psychiatric condition called schizophrenia [31] and the difficulty in determining REM sleep patterns in patients with a neurological condition called spinocerebellar ataxia [32]. In view of the gradual increase in sleep clinics around the world, several attempts have been made to automate the process using the several stereotype oscillatory features of EEG found during specific sleep stages. Within a PSG record, EEG pattern remains the single most important determinant of sleep stage. However, most of these fixed rule-based algorithms failed to distinguish instances of overlaps in EEG features, which can be trivial for the eyes of an expert.

3.4.2.2 Application: How Can ML Help Classify Sleep Stages From EEG?

There are several ML algorithms that are suitable for this classification problem. The most common classification strategy is to make use of known PSG features that even a scoring expert relies on for visual scoring. Spectral features (frequency domain) like delta (0.5–4 Hz), sigma, or spindle frequency (11–16 Hz), alpha (8–12 Hz), theta (4–7 Hz) oscillations are most used. Other salient nonspectral features of sleep stages like eye movements (rapid and slow), eye blinks, and muscle activity (tonic and phasic) are also used. Such feature engineering procedures for ML algorithms can have several advantages like reduction in the amount of training data, improving the speed of the model, and making the results more interpretable. Some earlier studies used simple decision trees [33,34] and Bayesian decision trees [35]. Others added nonlinear EEG measures (like correlation dimension, Kolmogorov entropy, Lyapunov exponent) to improve the classification [36]. Availability of large public datasets made some groups (SIESTA group; around 200 controls and 90 sleep disorder patients) [37] improve their detection accuracy using decision trees [38]. The more sophisticated approaches that employ artificial neural networks (ANNs) allowed inclusion of more PSG features and attained accuracies around 90% [39–41]. The common aspect of all these ML approaches was that they require carefully engineered features, which limited their application to research labs, whereas sleep clinics would not have the time and expertise for this process.

With the advent of novel deep learning methods like convolutional neural networks (CNNs), it became possible for algorithms to automatically learn complex patterns from PSG signals without the need for engineering features. This means raw data can be used for training, where several implicit local temporal features, as well as global structure of the PSG data, can be learned by such an algorithm. Therefore, deep neural networks (DNNs) working with raw data have been shown to perform better than feature-based methods [42].

3.5 SUMMARY

Machine learning techniques are emerging as highly promising in the classification of complex EEG signals, but they are currently underutilized, especially in the clinical settings. One major reason for this scenario is the lack of awareness about their usability among the EEG domain experts. Visual inspection has remained the gold standard for diagnosis and classification of clinically relevant brain states as in epileptic seizures and sleep disorders. But given the enormous amount of data collected in this regard, the subjective bias involved, and the valuable time required to do this process manually, it is imperative to make use of ML tools. Proper implementation of ML in such a setting would require a good deal of crosstalk between EEG domain experts and ML data scientists that, in turn, require ML resources that cater to both these groups. More research needs to occur with regard to improving the usability and accuracy of ML techniques, based on the specific requirements and limitations of regional clinical settings (solutions for a tertiary-care hospital in a tyre-III city will not be effective in a rural primary health center). With ML tools becoming available in more and more user-friendly forms, it is not too far from reality that ML will be used routinely, integrated into most clinical EEG applications. Though the main focus of this chapter is ML application on EEG signals, the same concepts will be applicable in several other time-series data (like fMRI BOLD signals, audio signals, etc.).

REFERENCES

1. Younes, Magdy. 2017. "The case for using digital EEG analysis in clinical sleep medicine." *Sleep Science and Practice* 1 (1): 2. doi:10.1186/s41606-016-0005-0.
2. Gemein, Lukas A.W., Robin T. Schirrmeister, Patryk Chrabąszcz, Daniel Wilson, Joschka Boedecker, Andreas Schulze-Bonhage, Frank Hutter, and Tonio Ball. 2020. "Machine-learning-based diagnostics of EEG pathology." *NeuroImage* 220 (October): 117021. doi:10.1016/j.neuroimage.2020.117021.
3. Giuliodori, Mauricio J., and Gustavo Zuccolilli. 2004. "Postsynaptic potential summation and action potential initiation: function following form." *Advances in Physiology Education* 28 (2): 79–80. Doi:10.1152/advan.00051.2003.
4. Cooley, James W., and John W. Tukey. 1965. "An algorithm for the machine calculation of complex Fourier series." *Mathematics of Computation* 19 (90): 297–301.
5. Schiff, Steven J., Akram Aldroubi, Michael Unser, and Susumu Sato. 1994. "Fast wavelet transformation of EEG." *Electroencephalography and Clinical Neurophysiology* 91 (6): 442–455. doi:10.1016/0013-4694(94)90165-1.
6. Bruns, Andreas. 2004. "Fourier-, Hilbert- and wavelet-based signal analysis: are they really different approaches?" *Journal of Neuroscience Methods* 137 (2): 321–332. doi:10.1016/j.jneumeth.2004.03.002.
7. Mitra, P.P., and B. Pesaran. 1999. "Analysis of dynamic brain imaging data." *Biophysical Journal* 76 (2): 691–708. doi:10.1016/S0006-3495(99)77236-X.
8. Stockwell, R.G., L. Mansinha, and R.P. Lowe. 1996. "Localization of the complex spectrum: the S transform." *IEEE Transactions on Signal Processing* 44 (4): 998–1001. doi:10.1109/78.492555.
9. Bastos, André M., and Jan-Mathijs Schoffelen. 2016. "A tutorial review of functional connectivity analysis methods and their interpretational pitfalls." *Frontiers in Systems Neuroscience* 9 (January): 175. doi:10.3389/fnsys.2015.00175

10. Amiri, Mina, Birgit Frauscher, and Jean Gotman. 2016. "Phase-amplitude coupling is elevated in deep sleep and in the onset zone of focal epileptic seizures." *Frontiers in Human Neuroscience* 10 (August): 387. doi: 10.3389/fnhum.2016.00387.

11. Anderer, Peter, Georg Gruber, Silvia Parapatics, Michael Woertz, Tatiana Miazhynskaia, Gerhard Klösch, Bernd Saletu, et al. 2005. "An E-health solution for automatic sleep classification according to rechtschaffen and kales: validation study of the somnolyzer 24 × 7 utilizing the siesta database." *Neuropsychobiology* 51 (3): 115–133. doi:10.1159/000085205.

12. Michel, Christoph M., and Denis Brunet. 2019. "EEG source imaging: a practical review of the analysis steps." *Frontiers in Neurology* 10 (April): 325. doi:10.3389/fneur.2019.00325.

13. Géron, Aurélien. 2019. *Hands-On Machine Learning with Scikit-Learn, Keras, and TensorFlow: Concepts, Tools, and Techniques to Build Intelligent Systems.* O'Reilly Media, Inc., Newton

14. Altman, N.S. 1992. "An introduction to Kernel and nearest-neighbor nonparametric regression." *The American Statistician* 46 (3): 175–185. doi:10.1080/00031305.1992. 10475879.

15. Dutta, Kusumika Krori, Kavya Venugopal, and Sunny Arokia Swamy. 2017. "removal of muscle artifacts from EEG based on ensemble empirical mode decomposition and classification of seizure using machine learning techniques." In *2017 International Conference on Inventive Computing and Informatics (ICICI)*, 861–866. Coimbatore: IEEE. doi:10.1109/ICICI.2017.8365259.

16. Cortes, Corinna, and Vladimir Vapnik. 1995. "Support-vector networks." *Machine Learning* 20 (3): 273–297. doi:10.1007/BF00994018.

17. Ivakhnenko, A.G., and V.G. Lapa. 1973. *Cybernetic Predicting Devices.* Jprs Report. CCM Information Corporation. https://books.google.co.in/books?id=FhwVNQAACAAJ.

18. LeCun, Yann, Yoshua Bengio, and Geoffrey Hinton. 2015. "Deep learning." *Nature* 521 (7553): 436–444. doi:10.1038/nature14539.

19. Dutta, Kusumika Krori. 2019. "Multi-class time series classification of EEG signals with recurrent neural networks." In *2019 9th International Conference on Cloud Computing, Data Science & Engineering (Confluence)*, 337–341. Noida, India: IEEE. doi:10.1109/CONFLUENCE.2019.8776889.

20. WHO, International League against Epilepsy, and International Bureau of Epilepsy, eds. 2005. *Atlas: Epilepsy Care in the World.* Geneva: WHO Press, World Health Organization.

21. Vetrikani, R., and T. Christy Bobby. 2017. "Diagnosis of epilepsy – a systematic review." In *2017 Third International Conference on Biosignals, Images and Instrumentation (ICBSII)*, 1–5. Chennai: IEEE. doi:10.1109/ICBSII.2017.8082300.

22. Halabi, Nashaat el, Roy Abi Zeid Daou, Roger Achkar, Ali Hayek, and Josef Borcsok. 2019. "Monitoring system for prediction and detection of epilepsy seizure." In *2019 Fourth International Conference on Advances in Computational Tools for Engineering Applications (ACTEA)*, 1–7. Beirut, Lebanon: IEEE. doi:10.1109/ACTEA.2019.8851094.

23. Park, Yun, Lan Luo, Keshab K. Parhi, and Theoden Netoff. 2011. "Seizure prediction with spectral power of EEG using cost-sensitive support vector machines." *Epilepsia* 52 (10): 1761–1770. doi:10.1111/j.1528-1167.2011.03138.x.

24. Klatt, Juliane, Hinnerk Feldwisch-Drentrup, Matthias Ihle, Vincent Navarro, Markus Neufang, Cesar Teixeira, Claude Adam, et al. 2012. "The EPILEPSIAE database: an extensive electroencephalography database of epilepsy patients: European EEG database 'EPILEPSIAE.'" *Epilepsia* 53 (9): 1669–1676. doi:10.1111/j.1528-1167.2012. 03564.x.

25. Zhang, Zisheng, and Keshab K. Parhi. 2016. "Low-complexity seizure prediction from IEEG/SEEG using spectral power and ratios of spectral power." *IEEE Transactions on Biomedical Circuits and Systems* 10 (3): 693–706. doi:10.1109/TBCAS.2015.2477264.

26. Gulia, Kamalesh K. 2012. "Dynamism in activity of the neural networks in brain is the basis of sleep-wakefulness oscillations." *Frontiers in Neurology* 3 (March). doi:10. 3389/fneur.2012.00038.

27. Kumar, Velayudhan Mohan. 2012. "Sleep is an auto-regulatory global phenomenon." *Frontiers in Neurology* 3. doi:10.3389/fneur.2012.00094.

28. Sasidharan, Arun, Sathiamma Sulekha, and Bindu Kutty. 2014. "Current understanding on the neurobiology of sleep and wakefulness." *International Journal of Clinical and Experimental Physiology* 1 (1): 3. doi:10.4103/2348-8093.129720.

29. Dement, William, and Nathaniel Kleitman. 1957. "Cyclic variations in EEG during sleep and their relation to eye movements, body motility, and dreaming." *Electroencephalography and Clinical Neurophysiology* 9 (4): 673–690. doi:10.1016/ 0013-4694(57)90088-3.

30. Iber, Conrad, Sonia Ancoli-Israel, Andrew L. Chesson, Stuart F. Quan, and others. 2007. *The AASM Manual for the Scoring of Sleep and Associated Events: Rules, Terminology and Technical Specifications.* Vol. 1. American Academy of Sleep Medicine Westchester, IL.

31. Sasidharan, Arun, Sunil Kumar, Ajay Kumar Nair, Ammu Lukose, Vrinda Marigowda, John P. John, and Bindu M. Kutty. 2017. "Further evidences for sleep instability and impaired spindle-delta dynamics in schizophrenia: a whole-night polysomnography study with neuroloop-gain and sleep-cycle analysis." *Sleep Medicine* 38: 1–13. doi:10. 1016/j.sleep.2017.02.009.

32. Seshagiri, Doniparthi Venkata, Arun Sasidharan, Gulshan Kumar, Pramod Kumar Pal, Sanjeev Jain, Bindu M. Kutty, and Ravi Yadav. 2018. "Challenges in sleep stage R scoring in patients with autosomal dominant spinocerebellar ataxias (SCA1, SCA2 and SCA3) and oculomotor abnormalities: a whole night polysomnographic evaluation." *Sleep Medicine* 42: 97–102. doi:10.1016/j.sleep.2017.09.030.

33. Martin, W.B., L.C. Johnson, S.S. Viglione, P. Naitoh, R.D. Joseph, and J.D. Moses. 1972. "Pattern recognition of EEG-EOG as a technique for all-night sleep stage scoring." *Electroencephalography and Clinical Neurophysiology* 32 (4): 417–427. doi:10.1016/0013-4694(72)90009-0.

34. Louis, Rhain P., James Lee, and Richard Stephenson. 2004. "Design and validation of a computer-based sleep-scoring algorithm." *Journal of Neuroscience Methods* 133 (1–2): 71–80. doi:10.1016/j.jneumeth.2003.09.025.

35. Stanus, E., B. Lacroix, M. Kerkhofs, and J. Mendlewicz. 1987. "Automated sleep scoring: a comparative reliability study of two algorithms." *Electroencephalography and Clinical Neurophysiology* 66 (4): 448–456. doi:10.1016/0013-4694(87)90214-8.

36. Fell, Jürgen, Joachim Röschke, Klaus Mann, and Cornelius Schäffner. 1996. "Discrimination of sleep stages: a comparison between spectral and nonlinear EEG measures." *Electroencephalography and Clinical Neurophysiology* 98 (5): 401–410. doi:10.1016/0013-4694(96)95636-9.

37. Penzel, T., M. Glos, C. Garcia, C. Schoebel, and I. Fietze. 2011. "The SIESTA database and the SIESTA sleep analyzer." In *2011 Annual International Conference of the IEEE Engineering in Medicine and Biology Society*, 8323–8326. Boston, MA: IEEE. doi:10.1109/IEMBS.2011.6092052.

38. Klosh, G., B. Kemp, T. Penzel, A. Schlogl, P. Rappelsberger, E. Trenker, G. Gruber, et al. 2001. "The SIESTA Project polygraphic and clinical database." *IEEE Engineering in Medicine and Biology Magazine* 20 (3): 51–57. doi:10.1109/51.932725.

39. Längkvist, Martin, Lars Karlsson, and Amy Loutfi. 2012. "Sleep stage classification using unsupervised feature learning." *Advances in Artificial Neural Systems* 2012: 1–9. doi:10.1155/2012/107046.
40. Pardey, James, Stephen Roberts, Lionel Tarassenko, and John Stradling. 1996. "A new approach to the analysis of the human sleep/wakefulness continuum." *Journal of Sleep Research* 5 (4): 201–210. doi:10.1111/j.1365-2869.1996.00201.x.
41. Schaltenbrand, Nicolas, Régis Lengelle, and Jean-Paul Macher. 1993. "Neural network model: application to automatic analysis of human sleep." *Computers and Biomedical Research* 26 (2): 157–171. doi:10.1006/cbmr.1993.1010.
42. Malafeev, Alexander, Dmitry Laptev, Stefan Bauer, Ximena Omlin, Aleksandra Wierzbicka, Adam Wichniak, Wojciech Jernajczyk, Robert Riener, Joachim Buhmann, and Peter Achermann. 2018. "Automatic human sleep stage scoring using deep neural networks." *Frontiers in Neuroscience* 12 (November): 781. doi:10.3389/fnins.2018.00781.

4 Revolution of Brain Computer Interface
An Introduction

Y. Saty Prakash, K. Vijay, and V. Karan

4.1 INTRODUCTION

The Brain-computer interface also known as a brain machine interface (BMI), it consists of software and hardware communication system through which the human beings interacting with their neighbouring, without any help of peripheral nerve and muscle, with the help of control signals those are rises from electroencephalographic. A BCI is a device which regulates the human intention from brain activities and creates an alternate communication channel. For interaction with environment, brain computer interface does not allow requirement of the "output pathway of brain's simple peripheral nerve and muscle". Communication provided by BCI is non-muscular channels which creates a direct path from brain to computers. Brain-computer interface contains the sensor and the tool for signal processing which convert brain activities into command signal or message signal [1]. BCI uses in the multimedia communications and human-computer interactions [2]. The general block diagram of BCI is illustrated in the Figure 4.1. Hans Berger was the first The German scientist who shows that the human brain was generating an electrical current in the 1920. With the help of electrodes, we can measure these currents that produced by brain activities. In 1929, the ideas of EEG were developed by the Berger [3]. In 1968, Kamiya has studies the behaviours of the EEG with considering the alpha wave that can be control by the human. In 1973, the term BCI was given by J. J. Vidal. He explained about the brain-computer interface as "utilizing the brain signals in a man-computer dialogue" and "as a mean of control over external processes such as computers or prosthetic devices" [4].

In 1988, another seminal paper was published by The Farwell and Donchin that became very popular and used brain-computer interface paradigm which are known as "P300-speller" [5]. Sensori Motor Rhythms (SMR) that works on the principle of the oscillatory EEG activity was developed by the researchers of USA and Europe. In 1991, the BCI for the one-dimension cursor controls that was based on the conditioning developed by the Jonathan Wolpaw and his colleagues. BCI is a specific machine learning control tools were suggested by different groups for classifying the EEG signal in the robust way. The famous Common Spatial Pattern (CSP) was developed in 2000 as a spatial filtering control algorithm, which is a type of gold standard was developed by back then. In 1999, First international meeting on the brain-computer interface was held in the USA. In 2000, approximate 22 research groups which

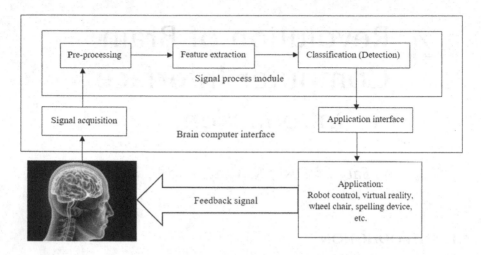

FIGURE 4.1 General block diagram of the BCI.

consist bout 50 participants then the BCI defined as "a communication system in which messages or commands that an individual send to the external world do not pass through the brain's normal output pathways of peripheral nerves and muscles." In 2016, approximate 400 participants, from the 188 researcher groups and different organizations was gathered in the six-international BCI meeting [6]. In 2013, the journal that was based on the "Brain-Computer Interfaces" was generated and published in 2014. In 2015, the international society for the brain-computer interface was established in order to "to foster research and development leading to technologies that enable people to interact with the world through brain signals". The development of the brain-computer interface provides some new results that was including new visual or auditory evoked potentials-based BCI or Hybrid BCI that combined one Brain-computer interface with another interface or another BCI. The application of the brain-computer interface including the stroke rehabilitation, HCI (Human-Computer Interaction), gaming, real-time EEG decoding, intelligent systems etc. [7].

4.2 NEUROIMAGING APPROACHES IN BCIS

Brain-computer interface collect the information with the help of brain signals. The recording of BCI signals in term of electrical signal, first we measure the activities of the brain. The brain activities classified into two categories as the electro-physiological and the hemodynamic.

Electrophysiological activities are produced through electro-chemical transmitters which exchange the information between the neuron. Neuron produced the ionic current that flow between the neuron's assemblies. The different types of signal in term of current that can be developed when the dipole is in the conducting mode. There are two types of current known as the primary current and secondary current. Primary current is also known as the intracellular current and secondary current is also known as the extracellular current [8]. Generally, the measurement of Electrophysiological activity is done by EEG.

Hemodynamic response is a process in which glucose is delivers to active neuron by blood in huge rate than neuron which are inactive. The state of oxyhaemoglobin change into the oxyhaemoglobin when the oxygen and glucose in large amount enter into the blood stream [9]. The neuroimaging is spectroscopy methods whose functional magnetic resonance and infrared uses to balance the state of blood those was unbalance by large amount of glucose and oxygen. These types of methods are known as indirect method. Summary of different neuroimaging method with spatial resolution, temporal resolution, risk, portability and method of measurement are disused as in the Table 4.1.

Non-invasive method is generally used with the partially paralyzed patient for communication and to control neuroprocessing. Invasive methods like intracortical electrocorticography in which the neuron recording was used. The quality of brain signal can be improved and monitored by brain-computer interface. Invasive approaches are used for movement re-establishment for the multiple degrees of freedom. There are two invasive process that is used in BCI are known as electrocorticography and intracortical.

4.3 TYPES OF BCIS

The classifications of brain-computer interface are divided as exogenous, endogenous, dependent, independent, synchronous or cue-paced and asynchronous self-paced. Here, we discussed about the exogenous, endogenous, synchronized and asynchronized as shown in the Tables 4.2 and 4.3. The table containing the approaches, signals, advantages and the disadvantages.

TABLE 4.1

The different features of Neuroimaging method

Neuroimaging Method	Indirect/ Direct Measurement	Spatial Resolution	Activity Measured	Temporal Resolution Range	Portability	Risk
EEG	Direct	10mm	Electrical	0.04s to 0.06s	Portable	Non-invasive
ECOG	Direct	1mm	Electrical	0.002 to 0.04s	Portable	Invasive
FMRI	Indirect	1mm	Metabolic	0s to 1.5s	Non-portable	Non-invasive
MEG	Direct	5mm	Magnetic	0.04s to 0.06s	Non-portable	Non-invasive
NRIS	Indirect	5mm	Metabolic	0s to 1.5s	Portable	Non-invasive
Intracortical neuron recording	Direct	0.04 mm to 0.15mm	Electrical	0.002s to 0.04s	Portable	Invasive

TABLE 4.2
Basic differences between Endogenous and Exogenous BCI

Approach	Advantage	Disadvantage	Signal
Endogenous BCI	1. It is independent of any particular task	1. It has low information transfer rate.	1. SCP
	2. It is useful for patients of sensory deficit.	2. It is required large number of electrodes for EEG signal	2. Frequency band
	3. It is useful for cursor control application.	3. Multichannel EEG recording provide good performance	3. Sensorimotor Rhythms
Exogenous BCI	1. It has minimal training period	1. Incase subject is not attending to the stimuli, System is said to failure	1. ERP
	2. It has high (SNR) signal to noise ratio	2. Fatigue occurs in subjects.	2. P300
	3. It has high rate of transfer and feasible with few EEG channel		3.SSVEP

TABLE 4.3
Basic differences between Asynchronous and Synchronous BCIs

Approach	Advantage	Disadvantage
Synchronous BCI	1. It reduces the overhead bit.	1. For the poor operation receiver can be starting to sample the line at the correct instant.
	2. Designing and the Performance analysis is simple.	2. There is limited number of natural nodes of interaction.
	3. It increased the efficiency and reduce the error.	3. More expensive.
Asynchronous BCI	1. No requirement to wait for external cause.	1. Overhead of start and stop bit.
	2. The Transmitting and receiving period are independent of each other.	2. The designing and the evaluation are more complex.
	3. There is large number of natural modes of interaction	3. Increased the error.

When the neuron activities are obtained by the external stimulus as visual evoked potential then we use the exogenous brain-computer interface [10]. This system is not requiring the extensive training because this control signal can be easily set-up. In The exogenous brain-computer interface the cursor cannot moves at any points in two-dimension space but in the endogenous brain-computer interface we can use the cursor at any points in the two-dimension space. Analysis of brain signals done in synchronous BCIs during pre-defined time window [11]. Mental activity is known in advancement and related to the particular synchronized brain-computer interface that is the benefits of a synchronous brain-computer interface [12]

4.4 NEUROPHYSIOLOGIC SIGNALS

The aim of brain-computer interface is monitoring the cerebral activities. The signal generated from brain has various simultaneous phenomena relating to cognitive task. There are many signals whose source is unknown. Some brain signals can be decoding to enable the brain-computer interface system to infer their objectives.

4.4.1 EVENT-RELATED POTENTIAL (ERP)

The spatiotemporal pattern of the brain activities is the event-related potential that is produced period-lock for an event. The motor-related potential (MRP) and the steady state visual evoked potential (SSVEP) are the examples of the ERP which is used in brain-computer interface. Analysis of the system that can be used this type of signal is given in [13].

4.4.2 NEURONAL ENSEMBLE ACTIVITY (NEA)

Basic unit of information in the brain is action potential. The communication between one neuron to another neuron is done through the action potential. In brain-computer interface, the action potential per time that is known as the firing rate can be used to forecast the behavior of subjects. Rate of firing is responsible for the finding the hand velocity and the hand position. This activity can be implemented as neurophysiological signals in brain-computer interface by microelectrodes array [14]

4.4.3 OSCILLATORY BRAIN ACTIVITY (OBA)

This activity in the electroencephalography is divided into many frequency band or rhythm. The rhythms as the Δ(delta), Θ(theta), $\bar{\alpha}$(alpha), β(beta), and Υ(gamma) having the frequency range as 1–4 Hz, 4–8 Hz, 8–13 Hz, 13–25 Hz, 25 - 40 Hz. The research group of pfurstcheller in Austria has been introduced imagined actions of feet, hand, or tongue in BCI system [15]. In United States, of worked on similar systems and the sensorimotor rhythm which allows brain-computer interface for fast controlling of 2-Dimension cursor are analysed in [16].

4.4.4 VISUAL EVOKED POTENTIAL (VEP)

When the visual stimulus is receiving in the visual cortex then the visual evoke potential is generated [17]. These signals are very simply detected because the magnitude of this potential is increased after the stimulus is reached near the field of central visual. The classification of this potential is done with the different criteria as on the basis of the morphology of the optical stimulation, on the field stimulation and on the visual stimulation frequency [18]. On the basis of the frequency visual

TABLE 4.4
Types of VEP modulations: f-VEP, t-VEP and, c-VEP

Modulation	Highlights
c-VEP	1. Synchronous signal is necessary
	2. Highest data Transfer rate speed (>100 bits/min.).
	3. It required the user training.
t-VEP	1. Synchronous signal is necessaly
	2. Low Data Transfer rate (<30bits/min.).
	3. It does not require user training.
f-VEP	1. It has signal and also, it's harmonic.
	2. Medium data transfer rate (30bits/min<60bits/min).
	3. It does not require user training.

stimulation the visual evoke potential are divided as SSVEP (steady-state visual evoke potential) and the TVEP (transient visual evokes potential). TVEP arises when the visual stimulation frequency is lower than 6Hz and at the higher SSEVP occurs [19]. On the basis of field stimulation, the visual evoke potential are divided as partial field visual evoke potential (PFVEP), half field visual evoke potential (HFVEP) and whole field visual evoke potential (WFVEP). On the basis of specific stimulation sequences SSVEP can be divided as the frequency modulated VEP (f-VEP), time modulated VEP (t-VEP) [20]. The different types of VEP modulations like as t-VEP, f-VEP and, c-VEP are explained in the Table 4.4.

4.4.5 P300 EVOKED POTENTIAL

Positive peak in the EEG are P300 evoked potential which is occurring due to infrequent auditory or visual stimulation. The responses of this potential are obtained approximate in the range 280 to 320 ms [5]. The BCI, which are based on the P300 is not required of training. Due to the use of infrequently stimulation the magnitude is decreasing therefor the performance characteristics of the P300-based BCI is reduced [21]. The application of a BCI based on this potential containing the number, symbol and command. It provides low rate of transmission due to the accuracy of this potential is too small [22].

4.4.6 SLOW CORTICAL POTENTIAL (SCP)

This potential has slow voltage that can move in the electroencephalography, having the frequency band range of 1–2 Hz. It can be controlled through the feedback training subject. This signal is self-regulated through the paralyzed patient or healthy people. Movement of cursor and selection of the target that is presented on the screen is done through the slow cortical potential. In this potential the self-regulation training depends on the different factor as physical state, relationship between the trainer and the patient and motivation. The testing of Amyotrophic Lateral Sclerosis (ALS) Patient is done through the self-regulation of slow cortical potential [23,24].

TABLE 4.5
Summary of control signals

Signals	Choices	Range of data transfer rate (bits/min)	Physiological Phenomenon	Training
SCP	Low	4.14	Slow voltages swing in the brain signal.	Yes
Rhythms of sensorimotor	Low	Feb-37	Sensory motor rhythms matched to motor actions.	Yes
P300	High	18-27	Infrequent stimulus causes Positive peaks.	NO
VEP	High	55-100	Modulation of brain signal in visual cortex.	NO

4.4.7 SENSORIMOTOR RHYTHM

Beta and mu rhythm comes under the sensorimotor rhythms. The mu rhythm is also known as the rolandic rhythm. The frequency range of the beta and mu rhythm are 13–30 Hz and 7–13 Hz respectively. The beta rhythm is harmonic and also independent [25]. The magnitude of the sensorimotor rhythm changes according the cerebral activity. The amplitude modulation of sensorimotor rhythm is done through the ERS (event-related synchronization) and the ERD (event-related desynchronization) that are produced according to stimulation [26]. The summary of different control signals is explained in the Table 4.5.

4.5 SIGNAL PROCESSING AND MACHINE LEARNING

Grouping of signals to specific user according to the training dataset is done through the machine learning algorithm in the brain-computer interface. Signal processing is a part of machine leaning that is also known as the feature extraction and classification.

4.5.1 FREQUENCY DOMAIN FEATURE (FDF)

FDF depends on the oscillatory movement. The period of oscillatory action is not period-lock for the appearance of stimulation. Generally, the FDF depend on the changes in the magnitude of the oscillatory activities. There are many methods are used for finding the band power as Morlet Wavelet Method [27], Welch's Method [28] and the Adaptive Autoregressive Method [29].

4.5.2 TIME DOMAIN FEATURE (TDF)

TDF depends on the change in the magnitude of the neurophysiologic signals. It is period-lock for the presentation of stimulation. The example of TDF as P300 evokes potential and the slow cortical potential. BPF (band pass filter) or LPF (low pass filter) or is used for separating these signals from the noise signal. Instead of filtering we can also uses the wavelet transformation as continuous wavelet transformation and discrete wavelet transformation.

4.5.3   Machine Learning Feature (MLF)

MLF is used for the calculation of figures out signal to determining the order of particular client. Generally, support vector machine is used for the calculations [30]. With the help of Kernel, we can be easily implemented support vector machine for the good accuracy of non-linear function. There are many other machine learning algorithms used in the BCI [31].

4.5.4   Spatial Domain Feature (SDF)

The aim of SDF method is finding the efficient combination of feature from more than one electrode. The one electrode is used for feature extraction of univariate time series and does not used in bivariate time series. The easiest way to perform the extraction with SDF is used only electrode which contains the important information to differentiation of the set of cognitive tasks. This feature is depending on the P300 peak and change in the band power.

4.6   THE CHALLENGES IN THE BRAIN COMPUTER INTERFACE:

There are several challenges in the BCI control for the real-life applications are explained as below:

4.6.1   Information Transfer Rate ("ITR")

The average information handover rates for subject and tuned brain-computer-interface system is low. Generally, 24 b/min which are approximate three characters per minutes [32]. This rate is very slow for natural interactive conversation. Therefore, some researchers are searching the way for optimizing the information transfer rate.

4.6.2   High Error Rate ("HER")

Normally, in the brain computer interface the ITR remains low. Thus, it provides the high error rate. Signal produced by the brain highly variable due to the medication, fatigue and spasms. If the subject has not communication channel or very low communication outside of the brain computer interface system then it generated an error known as the self-reporting error.

4.6.3   Autonomy

Ideally, a correspondence framework for an individual with extreme incapacities ought to be totally constrained by its client. Tragically, BCI frameworks require broad help from guardians who need to apply cathodes or sign accepting gadgets before a client can impart. Besides, most BCI frameworks are framework started, implying that the client can't turn off and on freely. Outcomes are named as the "Midas contact" issue the Brain Computer Interface framework deciphers complete cerebrum movement as information, therefore in what manner can the client convey the goal to control the framework? A BCI client might have the option to play out a choice to kill the BCI framework, yet walking out on again is an issue.

4.6.4 Cognitive Burden

BCI frameworks remain tried in calm lab situations, wherever clients can focus on the job that needs to be done with insignificant interruptions. BCI clients in reality need to manage considerably more intricate circumstances, including the subjective heap of the undertaking being performed, enthusiastic reactions, and conceivably even wellbeing contemplations. We are examining the impacts of psychological burden on the viability of BCI controls so as to decide if BCI's could be utilized for in-home regular day to day environments.

4.6.5 Training Process

Training is a tedious movement in managing the client over the procedure or in the number of records meetings. It happens any stage like classifier alignment or in the primer stage [33]. Client is educated to manage the framework just as to regulate cerebrum criticism flags in fundamental stage, although in alignment stage, prepared subject's sign has been utilized to gain proficiency with the pre-owned classifier. One of the frequently addressed solutions to this delayed problem is to use a single pre-liminary rather than a multi-preliminary test, which is used to upgrade the symbol to clamour apportionment [34], and putting the weight of little preparing size on resulting BCI framework parts to deal with different zero and versatile preparing classifiers have been evaluated as arrangements as referenced [35].

4.7 THE DEVELOPMENT OF BIOSENSING TECHNIQUES FOR BCI APPLICATIONS

4.7.1 Wet Sensor

Conventionally, this type of electrode is frequently used sensor for measurement of the EEG signal. The block diagram of classification of wet electrodes is given in the Figure 4.2.

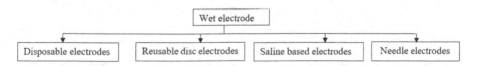

FIGURE 4.2 The block diagram of classification of wet electrodes.

Typically, wet anode is covered with the Ag–AgCl and having the breadth run 1 to 3 mm. This lead is adaptable thusly it tends to be effortlessly connected to the readout circuit gadget. The needle anode is utilized for long chronicle and is obtrusively embedded under the scalp.

The factor that can be considered during the improvement of successful and agreeable EEG sensors talked about as: 1: Sensor connection, long length between application sensor dependability and the client comfort issues. 2: Common sense thought like as straightforwardness of use and the expense. 3: Capacity for securing top notch signal from wide ranges with various sizes, shapes, length and scalp properties. 4: The impacts of long haul utilize on sensor security or toughness and the head or scalp.

NovelWet Approaches: Recently, the upside of cross-connected polyacrylate gel at the skin interface or the terminals is investigated by Alba et al. [36]. The polyacrylate gel might be assimilate an electrolyte arrangement and swell to a degree a long way past commonplace contemporary cathode materials, giving a solid hydrating impact to the skin surface. Cross-connected sodium polyacrylate gel was blended utilizing a technique suggested by Sohn et al. [37]. Advancement of water-based sensor for EEGbased BCI application remained concentrated by Volosyak et al. [38]. This gathering had indicated that water-based sensor could quantify EEG-movement utilizing faucet water to the scalp. This gathering has additionally presumed that ideal plans of the cathode and the terminal materials for keeping up low impedance despite everything require future improvement.

4.7.2 DRY BIOSENSOR

The correct skin planning, the employments of conducting gel, the quality signal from sensor is great. Skin planning process utilizes for decreasing the skin-terminal connection interface resistivity that can be tedious and awkward for the client. The nature of EEG signal corrupts after some time as the skin recovers as well as the conductive gel dries and the issues likewise emerge when estimating an area of intrigue which is secured with hair that can prompt deficient skin-cathode contact zone, particularly for long haul applications. For limit these issue noncontact type and dry-contact-type EEG sensor created to improve EEG estimations. The square chart of order of dry contact sensors is appeared in the Figure 4.3.

The characteristics and dependence of the electrode skin electrode of dry microelectromechanical systems (MEMS). EEG sensors are elaborated in detail [39]. The performance of dry MEMS sensors for measurement of EEG signal when applied to the hairless and forehead sites is good. For measurement of

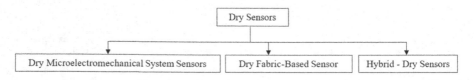

FIGURE 4.3 The block diagram of classification of dry contact sensors.

biopotential signal fabric-based sensor was developed. Foam based sensor enfolded in the conducting fabric material for finding the forehead EEG signal is discussed by Lin et al. [40].

The hybrid dry sensor proposed by matthews et al. for the measurement of the EEG signal [41]. This type of sensor has large-impedance capacitive and resistive physiognomies between the electrodes and scalp. This sensor has the hard substrates that created the uneasiness or even torment on the scalp surface and because of the hard substrate EEG signal mutilated. The minimal effort dry EEG sensor fabricated of adaptable metal covered polymers bristle. Novel dry spring stacked interacts lead EEG sensors proposed by Liao et al. for estimating EEG signals [42,43]. The spring-stacked tests are utilized to connected the sensor firmly to the surface of scalp. These tests were intended to be embedded into a meagre plate for extra conductivity and furthermore it is the slight plate adaptable in this manner when power is applied to sensor that fits to scalp surface. Capacitive sensor or noncontact sensor that has the spaces between the body and the cathode and without skin planning likewise can possibly secure EEG signal.

4.7.3 Nano- and Microtechnology Sensors

In the advancement of novel sensors, straightforward, adaptable and the savvy wraps, wearable elite gadgets, radiation hard hardware, optoelectronics, correspondence, on-chip electronic-optical coupling and handling hardware the nano-hardware assume significant jobs. The analysts in the United Kingdom and the Spain have built up the new strategy for estimation of the electrical movement in the cerebrum that utilizes sensor which are developed from carbon nanotubes (CNTs) and furthermore showed the utilization of carbon nanotube based dry sensor in biopotential signal investigations. These gadgets are likewise concentrating as an innovation for attractive memory applications, and might be additionally utilized as radio recurrence (RF) sources and touchy attractive field identifiers [44]. Nanoelectromechanical and Maturing smaller scale framework (NEMS/MEMS/) advancements likewise hold guarantee for novel activation gadgets and state-estimation gadgets. Later on, carbon-based or other bio-compatible nanoscale detecting advances might be infused into cell, vein, append to the particular neuron, cross the blood-mind boundary, detect the ideal signals and send to an outer collector however the intact skull.

4.7.4 Multimodality Sensors

There are a few sensors which is utilized for the estimation of EEG signal, the synchronous account of the reaction of hemodynamic utilizing neural movement and NIRS utilizing EEG through multimodality sensor. For accepting the incitement is a basic issue in the neuroscience area. NIRS and EEG procedures depend on various imaging standards and in this manner, cross-approval may advance our comprehension of together the connection between hemodynamic reactions and neural action hidden cortical initiation and behind the biophysics the estimation strategies themselves. Takeuchi et al. built up top head for both EEG and EEG entire cerebrum -imaging, neuro hemodynamic deviations have been tended to in detail. Cooper et al. additionally suggested a novel test structure for concurrent NIRS and EEG imaging of cortical enactment in human being cerebrum [45]. The dry or non-contact EEG gadgets had not been proposed for clinic application, numerous business gadgets use EEG estimations for diversion.

4.8 INTEGRATION OF SENSING DEVICES AND BIOSENSORS INTO BCI SYSTEMS

4.8.1 PRESENT DEVELOPMENTS IN BIOSENSING DEVICE TECHNOLOGIES

4.8.1.1 Essential System Design

Traditionally, EEG framework has utilized generally massive, clinically situated gear or wired research Centre for estimating the EEG signal. The simple type of the EEG sign can be legitimately transmitted to a detecting gadget with the assistance of wire. Presently a day a little wearable EEG securing gadget are accessible which is proficient for recording the EEG signal without thwarting the client in the presentation of routine assignments in ordinary operational condition. The wearable EEG framework created utilizing headband, tops, headset, earphone, caps and the cat ears. The state of wearable EEG framework decides the potential situation of the cathodes, that can constrain their usefulness. usefulness and the appearance both are considered during the structure of wearable EEG framework.

4.8.1.2 Simple Front-End

For finding the high sign to calm or proportion an instrumentation intensifier is utilized. The basic mode dismissal proportion is typically utilizing for assessing the intensifier instruments. Generally, the usage of intensifier utilizes a three-operation amp design that require the exact coordinating of the resistor utilized in the criticism organize for getting the high regular mode dismissal proportion. This kind of coordinating is commonly costly laser-cut resistors that devour a lot of chip territory. For limiting this issue utilizes current criticism instrumentation speakers [46].

During the information securing of EEG signal, which contains low frequencies, glint clamor and info alluded dc counterbalances which is unfortunate sign. The glint commotion is contrarily corresponding to the clamor and the information alluded dc counterbalances are because of the terminal polarization. For lessening the clamor and the information alluded dc counterbalance utilizes the chopper enhancer. Autozeroing intensifier work in one of two stages: the inspecting stage or the yield stage. Autozeroing can't be appropriate for low-power applications on the grounds that it requires the balance to be put away on a capacitor. This issue ought to be limited if this enhancer is utilized with the low pass channel [47].

4.8.1.3 Transmission Medium

The gadget which is utilized for EEG procurement, typically intended for minimal effort and low-power utilization. A large portion of the venture is utilized regular remote innovation like as the Bluetooth, RF transmitters, 802.15.4/Zigbees. Bluetooth was produced for substitution of the link yet it has overwhelming convention stack and the powerful utilization. The convention heaps of RF is light and increasingly effective regarding their capacity. The transmission of EEG with the multichannel having the powerful utilization and the high information rate. Lossy pressure plans have high pressure proportions yet present ancient rarity issues. Signal processing requires high power and is handled by host. In this way, procurement gadgets could be actualized with minimal effort microcontrollers. Microcontrollers secure digitized EEG signals from an Analog to digital converter through sequential interfaces. As indicated by the Nyquist-Shannon testing hypothesis, examining ratio ought to more noteworthy than double greatest recurrence of procured EEG signal.

4.8.2 ADVANCES OF FUTURE BIO-SENSING TECHNIQUE IN BCI

4.8.2.1 Scaling Down of Power Sources

The scaling down of intensity source will empower the improvement of inconsequential, li-particle batteries innovation, compact sensor advances. Scientists at the U.S. ARL (Armed force Research Laboratory) has created advancement electrolyte which consider activity of high voltage lithium nickel manganese spinel oxides at 4.7V compared to Li with 99 percent coulombic proficiency and 85 percent limit maintenance after 200 cycles [48]. Force sources utilizing fiery materials dependent on atomic isomers are being researched for future force age. Radioisotopes have natural vitality stockpiling that is in excess of multiple times more noteworthy than that of power modules and battery, and that has the potential capacity to discharge that vitality upon request. Late outcomes have exhibited an actuated vitality discharge with the help of some isomer utilizing neutron [49]. Complementary metal oxide semiconductor (CMOS) plan strategies, for example, explicit gatekeeper ring and drifting well, that empower on-chip treatment of in excess of 20 V in a 130-nm 1.2-V CMOS method has shown [49] and the high voltage required for new actuator. Novel methods utilizing hair like wicking is utilized to attractive and the high dielectric constant which is the nanoparticle into complex with the 3-D microstructure. Nanoelectronics gadgets are likewise being investigated, including supercapacitors for vitality stockpiling [50] and MIM (grapheme-based metal-protector metal) diode structure for gathering vitality or redressing receiving wire structure. Plan of intensity productive regulate hypothesis is alternative way to deal with accomplishing diminished force necessities for sensor cluster data preparing.

4.8.2.2 Real Life Applications of Human Brain Imaging

Neuro-Scientific ways to deal with estimating and tomography, hemodynamic joined to neural movement. It allows just negligible development of the members' hands or feet. This limitation of the members development run is important to stay away from development of the sign producing volume. Moreover, mind imaging technique that directly measures electrical activity originating from the neural population underlying cognitive processing further confines the development of the members' head and eyes. Psychological procedures are firmly coupled to physical movement and utilize our physical structure to arrive at conduct objectives.

The outcome from conventional imaging approaches can just clarify the neural premise of subjective procedures that are limited to explicit chronicle situations and don't really reflect common intellectual preparing. New outcomes from creatures moving, in any case, exhibit an immediate coupling of social states with mind states [51]. The mind elements going with dynamic spatial direction including physical pivot will give novel bits of knowledge into the cerebrum elements related with idiothetic data handling and will consequently assist us with bettering comprehend the cerebrum elements related with spatial direction. To beat the limitations of customary imaging draws near and to research the cerebrum elements going with dynamic conduct in people, our gathering, as of late created and exhibited a portable mind/body imaging (MoBI) approach [51]. Analysis of human brain dynamics for subject who are standing and walking at different speed was demonstrated. Exemplary models incorporate EEG investigations of shooting that have been generally restricted to static focuses instead of responsive, powerful targets; investigations of golf that have been to a great extent constrained to putting rather than investigations and driving of ball which restricted to free-toss shooting rather than some other part of game-play.

Display Technology and Flexible Electronic: The headways in advancements, for example, adaptable gadgets and showcases, which are developing to give insubstantial, tough, and ultralow-power adaptable imaging frameworks for high return producing forms, will empower such improvement. Organic light-emitting diode (OLED) which exhibited on plastic substrate, and sub-atomic OLED frameworks has incorporated to adaptable presentations into drastically upgrade the charge infusion and transport property of natural gadgets. Adaptable intelligent presentations for framework level combination have changed in industry to meet developing data innovation requirements for the versatile fighter. Huge zone conveyances of adaptable discrete -component, electronic circuit, and sensor is being coordinated through adaptable sun powered cells, radio wires, and strong state lighting to improve cutting edge shows. Upgrades in transporter transport, speed and splendor is examine through the utilization of adaptable and stretchable with metal or silicon innovations [52]. This innovation will empower the formation of elite comparable circuit which are required for progressively consistent mix of BCI into garments just like cutting-edge ideas for keen garments and body armor. Stretchable silicon-incorporated circuit which may be applied legitimately to the skin have as of late been exhibited.

4.9   BCI TECHNOLOGY

4.9.1   FUNCTIONAL NEAR INFRARED TECHNOLOGY (FNIR)

This is the non-intrusive optical methods which measure the neural movement of cerebrum. The neural exercises of the mind are identifying with the hemodynamic reactions inside the cortex. This technique utilize light inside the 700nm to 900nm, set at the scalp for empowering the non-obtrusive optical strategy and legitimate estimation of progress in the overall proportions of the oxygenated hemoglobin and deoxygenated hemoglobin in the narrow beds during the mind exercises. The oxygenated hemoglobin and the deoxygenated hemoglobin are identified with the cerebrum exercises because of the oxygen utilization by the neuron. This innovation took into consideration the structure of safe, non-obtrusive, convenient, insignificantly meddling observing framework and furthermore for the reasonable checking framework. All these qualities make this technology suitable for the studies of hemodynamic change due to the emotional brain activities and the cognitive under ecological conditions or natural conditions. This strategy is utilized for checking the human mind prefrontal cortex for evaluation of working memory, intellectual remaining burden and for the cerebrum PC interface look into [53].

4.9.2 FUNCTIONAL NEAR INFRARED (fNIR) DEVICE

The improvement of this gadget is done in the Optical Brain Imaging Lab of Drexel University is a ceaseless wave framework. Control box equipment is associated with the ten-photograph finder, four light emanating diodes and the adaptable sensor cushion. The sensor cushion is put over the temple of the clients and structuring for test cortical zone basic the brow up to 2Hz.

4.9.3 SHUT CIRCLED, INPUT MANAGED, fNIR BASED BRAIN COMPUTER INTERFACE

In these examinations, the fNIR based mind PC interface framework joins the employments of control box, fNIR sensor, protocol-computer, and information securing PC. The upgrades conveyance programming is utilizing on the convention PC looks as the Maze Suite in the ordinary trial arrangement. The BCI try, the fNIR brain computer interface customer programming on the protocol-computer that utilized for accepting fNIR flags over TCP/IP, and the information determined because of progress the oxygenation is finished with altered Beer Lambert Law. The number between the 0 to 100 known as the mind PC interface list which is determined with the oxygenation information and transmitting to the protocol-computer, that can refresh the visual criticism for making the shut circle [53]. The course of action of trial arrangement of fNIR is discussed in [53].

4.10 APPLICATIONS

Generally, the application of the brain-computer interface is divided into three parts. In the first part that containing the complete locked-in state patient. In this state the patient is lost all motor control and suffering from extreme cerebral palsy or amyotrophic lateral sclerosis. The patient that is completely paralyzed, but having the very small movement likes lip movement, eye movement are categorized into the second part. In the third part, the patient having the ability to control the neuromuscular system and a particular speech.

4.10.1 COMMUNICATIONS

The communication activities are very essential for the human. The applications of brain-computer interface for the communication is related with neurological

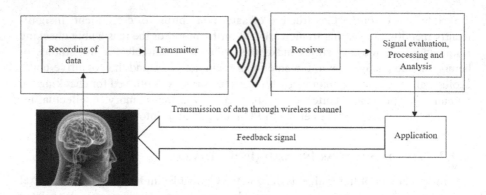

FIGURE 4.4 Block diagram of wireless communication BCI system.

disease. In letter spelling application for communication is related to the P300 evoke potentials. P300 evoke potential is useful for the patients are suffering from amyotrophic lateral sclerosis. The P300 speller is depend on the record of VEP. The paralyzed patients which having the minimum eye control over the movement, auditory stimulation is used in such type of cases [54]. The arrangement of wireless communication BCI system is shown as in the Figure 4.4.

4.10.2 ENTERTAINMENTS

Entertainment based BCI is lower priority in these field. In previous, research of BCI mainly focused on wheel chair control, spelling control rather than application of entertainment purpose. Due to the advancement of the technology researched increased in entertainment application. The best example of entertainment-based application of the brain-computer interface is video games. Internal evoke potential have been also used for games applications. The company Neurosky makes the mind-wave neuroheadset which based on the software application and respond with the brainwave or the mental state of patient. The many software company likes Microsoft take the interest in the development brain-computer interface application.

4.10.3 EDUCATIONAL AND SELF-REGULATION

Neuro-feedback is a procedure for upgrading mind execution by means of converging on human mind movement tweak. It attacks instructive frameworks, which contains cerebrum electrical signs to decide the level of clearness of examined data is decided through the electrical sign of cerebrum. Modified cooperation to every student is built up by resultant reaction practised. Learning to self-regulate through non-invasive BCI has moreover contemplated. It gives an intend to improving subjective helpful methodologies. Exploration in has examined the practicality fMRI for passionate guideline, although have proposed utilization of mixture rtf MRI, EEG Brain computer interface to battle the downturn feelings just as additional neuropsychiatric issue. Moreover, EEG based enthusiastic knowledge have applies in sport rivalries to regulate the going with worry as per inspected in [55].

4.10.4 MEDICAL APPLICATIONS

Medical field has the wide application which may takes the advantages of the brain signal in the different phases as (1) Detection and Diagnosis (2) Prevention (3) Restoration and Rehabilitation.

4.10.4.1 Detection and Diagnosis

BCI framework helps in observing the mental state and helps in detection of various medical problem for example: -anomalous structure of cerebrum, seizure issue, sleep issue and cerebrum growing. Tumour is produced from self-pertaining of cell which is uncontrolled and could be a modest option for MRI. EEG based brain tumour discovery frameworks has the principle objective of the looks into in [56] while have been worried about distinguishing bosom malignancy utilizing EEG signals. Dyslexia, one of the mind issues, can be analysed by estimating mind conduct as depicted in [57]. It impacts the perusing and learning capacity making its revelation at a beginning period spares the youngsters from self-assurance issues and allows to pick up their fundamental aptitudes also, information.

4.10.4.2 Prevention

Various systems for determining the level of consciousness together with his brain studies were developed. Caution have the outcomes of alcohol and smoking on brain waves have been enlighten in [58]. Need of such studies for medical inhibition lies in loss of function and reduced vigilance due to smoking and not alcohol consumption, whereas the authors of [59] has studied the parts of the brain that respond most to consumption of alcohol. Main cause of serious injuries and death are road accident which is started in [60]. Therefore, the level of concentration for those who suffers Motion-Sickness has been studied. Movement disease, which is generated by body due to sending sensory conflicts information such as inner ear and brain, generally occurs in moving transport media.

4.10.4.3 Restoration and Rehabilitation

Mobility rehabilitation is used with patients who have problem with their mobility to regain them lost function and restoration of earlier mobility levels. People suffering with serious injuries and strokes have to fully recover. Lack of oxygen in brain leads to damage the brain cells gives a condition known as strokes. Due to blockage in the bloodstream patient loose capacity to speak.it can leads to memory or paralysis. It was found that structure of brain with strokes injuries can rearrange and may be restored via neuroplasticity. Mobile robots can be used to recover the patient as discussed in [61]. Different approaches to the reality of BCI based rehabilitation training as they have virtual, real and augmented approach. The approach to true rehabilitation has been made use of the signals of brain produced by healthy people. Another approach to the rehabilitation includes VR (virtual reality) through monitor and control action of the avatar generated by output of brain waves.

4.10.5 OTHER BCI APPLICATIONS

There are the wide varieties of the brain-computer interface applications beyond entertainment, environment control, communication. The Neurofeedback is used in the BCI for improving affection, pain management, cognitive performances and the speech skills. The neurofeedback can also be used in the handling of cerebral conditions like alcohol dependent, attention-deficit, epilepsy, attention deficit, depression and schizophrenia. The recording of brain signal is used to determine the status of health and disease of the brain function. There are many companies like as Emsense, Nero-Consult, Nero-Insight, Neuro-Focus are working in the neuro-marketing facilities. It's also drawing attentions amongst scientists.

4.11 FUTURE SCOPE

4.11.1 THE FUTURE OF BCI TECHNOLOGIES

Future errand situated BCIs, in view of advances in sensor innovations, examination calculations, man-made reasoning, multisport perceiving of the mind and condition over unavoidable developments, and registering calculation, can be equipped for crowd and separating cerebrum info for broadened timeframes and are required to get predominant in abundant part of normal life. When client is regularly tiring the mind sensor for explicit purpose, sharp BCI, that is the BCI advancements which give the clients a benefit, so far donât legitimately encourage the assignment the performance of user, may applied short of additional above your head.

4.11.1.1 Direct Control (DC)

The absolute furthermost prompt idea for cerebrum PC border the application focused on knowing the DC. Models initiate from the medical application like as wheelchairs, gadgets, correspondence application and basic mind control games. Sooner rather than later, buyer request is probably going to retain forcefully on BCI, particularly in beguilement and individual fulfilment application, to look for after DC. Since a clinical position, there are masses of patient who may unbelievably benefited by capability to intentionally govern their personal turns of events and contraptions in their general environmental factors. From a preoccupation position, individuals seem to have an enthusiasm with the ability to control dissents by authentically using their mind, appeared by the point that these thoughts, for instance, extraordinary force, are embedded in our standard society. To a restricted degree, this intrigue seems to originate from the possibility that prompt access to the brain will give us unimaginably improved capacities. As self-sufficient route and automated coordination capacities advance in BCI for control of only or numerous planned mechanical gadgets.

4.11.1.2   Circuitous Control or Indirect Control (CC or IC)

Urgent thoughts which genuinely affect upcoming BCI is the usage of recording brain which give info that isn't quickly or enthusiastically accessible to various channel. Cerebrum shapes are potential hotspot for this information which is connected through the human-being perspective on barros, or may be blends of sign related with bungles, for instance, disappointment/shock, thought/responsibility. Human may see directly off the bat into the processes and position of robot hand is utilized fitting for fitting the exact portal, although the figuring that regulate the computerized limb browsing various elective handle control, picking another control style subject to the botch signals got from the human customer. Indirect control application access the neural correlates associated with the users error to influence the robotic controllers choice of manipulation strategy. It does not engage the operation directly in control task. The achievement of this sort of utilization will, as it were, depend on the energy and common sense of perceiving signals that exhibit customer objective or advancing toward bungles.

4.11.1.3   Communications

An extensive the trade's space offers perhaps the greatest potential district of influence in BCI. Initial correspondence BCI was planned for allows a scientific mass with for all intents and purposes no exchanges capacity. From various perspectives these applications resemble the early quick control application for clinical masses. We imagine future BCI such as a component of arrangement which use correspondences express developments, similarly as various advances, for instance, unavoidable identifying and preparing. BCIs may support a far-reaching approach to manage correspondence applications through three thoughts:

1. Expanding the data transfer capacity between the human and computer and the viability of that transmission capacity: As human–computer interfaces extend past mouse and console and into naturalistic UIs, the data transfer capacity between the human and computer will increment. One of the forward leaps of characteristic UI ideas is the possibility that in up close and personal human correspondence, significantly more data is transmitted than simply the words being verbally expressed. Signs describing these parts of human correspondence could be joined with neural signs giving extra knowledge into the neural condition of the administrator and in this manner extra logical data to human–computer correspondence.
2. Improving or predicting the energy about information in setting: For customer's comprehension of the information, a phase forward BCI take future thoughts. Example, neural imprints is a method which states that whether a term in sentences is seen by the customer as right. Envision a contraption which could follow the frequencies of the semantics misjudging in the discussion, be it dispersed and replacement for instructor. With this sort of information, the systems are being anticipated from this information which gives pointers of thankfulness, correspondence adequacy in party. Additional,

structures can flag customer to go over, rephrase discussions, or uniform prescribe choices rather than wording that was dubious, beguiling, or erroneous.

3. Supporting the plan of considerations: Technology is moreover emerging which can enable PC to explore and also envision. The range from PC web searcher propels that usage of aggregate filters for searching terms, to PC idea computations which use graphs speculation to finding protests. Model of BCI at present use for expand idea of PC computations to support directors with finding entities inside a circumstance. Extension of BCI includes the different types of signal. This signal helps in the formation of human computer semantic. Human computer semantic would be tailorable to individual users.

4.11.1.4 Brain-Process Modification (BPM)

BCI technologies provides user to adapt the own states or process of brains. The neurofeedback method can previously permit the individual for the adjusting their own function of brain to accomplish the extra desirable state. The sensors technology and the analytical approached are used for improving the potential, which is the advantage of the neurofeedback. It is probable for distinguish among the brain process of novice and the various tasks which are moreover actually challenging. There is some mental ailment, which is predominantly affecting the disorder like as sadness, can be repairable through a discrete modulating their states of the mental that can help in the advancement of the neurofeedback-based BCI. In neural degradation there is delay in the age or ailment through entering specific brain states. In neuro-feedback based methods, imminent change of the brain-process in BCI technology. The current neural stimulus explore is based on invasive probe, The technique which is based on magnetic field is non-invasive neural stimulation and ultrasound, or the infrared light.

4.11.1.5 Mental State Detection (MSD)

Current melodies in BCI are detection and uses of mental states rather than the neural processing like as ERP for modifying the system [204]. The accurately and the reliability notice the arousal, fatigue, and the affecting levels can allow for adapting states of the patients [205] or help the users achievement as emotional or a desired mental. These intellectual education technologies could significantly the advantage from state detection system (SDS) which can recognize the state of brain like as the low arousal, fatigue, strong negative affect, frustration, and the state of the brain which is related with the learning. SDS is also the advantageous for the medical applications.

4.11.1.6 Opportunistic State-Based Detection (OSBD)

The wide range of state-based application may be established when the technologies reach that point where the very useful opportunistic BCI may be comprehended. The monitoring of the neural-state may be uses in the mixture with the inescapable intelligence for the opportunistically changes the location. The alarm clock comprehensively go-off whatever the user sleep stage, the regardless of fact on awakening energy level of a person is strongly linked with the sleep period unbiased before waking. In the same way, sleep-related BCI monitors rapid sleep movement of eye, that can work a dangerous task which is relating with the memory association for the enhance of the memory performance. The monitoring of the medical areas could also the advantage from utilizing the OSBD technology. This type of technology also probable for increasing the frequency of brain monitoring for recuperation patient or for supporting the home care, hypothetically for making the higher quality medical-care and self-governing living easier.

4.11.2 FUTURE BCI APPLICATIONS BASED ON ADVANCED BIOSENSING TECHNOLOGY

The future application of the BCI in the upcoming decade like as homecare, and recuperation engineering application. The major advancement of the BCI is doing in the gaming and prevailing prototype establish the possibility of game controlling is done by BCI. BCI device which is based on the EEG with the original EEG sensor which can accomplished of understanding the intellectual significance of the neuron connections in the brain will be presented and reliable in the near future. Remote monitoring is another future scope of the BCI that may be used in the homecare and recuperation engineering application. The ill and the elderly which is prefer for living in their own house for existence in a hospital, but it is dangerous for the living alone due to the random accident like as the epileptic seizure and the falling.

4.12 CONCLUSIONS

Here author studied the different steps of brain-computer interface as Neuroimaging Approaches, Classification, Neurophysiologic Signals, Signal Processing and Machine Learning, Challenges, Biosensors. We also discuss about advantages, disadvantages, latest advancement and application of BCIs and we provide technology used in the scientific literature to design the BCI. A limited examination has introduced in this paper in regards for development of BCI applications area i.e. medical field like as Detection and diagnosis, prevention, restoration and rehabilitation. Communication, Entertainments, and Security fields are discussed. We have overviewed the huge assemblage of writing that talks about investigations in which biosensing advances and gadgets have been effectively utilized and also significant study on BCI and their uses. Improvement of BCIs is a quickly extending arena which is ceaselessly advancing to grasp modern advances or genuine uses. We described the P300 evoke potential that tested with the help of data from the disable patients in the brain-computer system and discussed about the future scope in term of communication, brain process modification, mental state detection and also the biosensing technology. The important feature of this system is that it consists of the advancement in the Bayesian machine learning tool that provides the training of classifier become more reliable, fast and the simple. The P300 based system is one of the examples for obtaining the performance. There are some problems in the brain-computer interface that also discussed.

REFERENCES

1. Wolpaw, Jonathan R., Niels Birbaumer, William J. Heetderks, Dennis J. McFarland, P. Hunter Peckham, Gerwin Schalk, Emanuel Donchin, Louis A. Quatrano, Charles J. Robinson, and Theresa M. Vaughan. 2000. "Brain-Computer Interface Technology: A Review of the First International Meeting." *IEEE Transactions on Rehabilitation Engineering* 8 (2): 164–173. doi:10.1109/TRE.2000.847807.
2. Ebrahimi, Touradj, Jean Marc Vesin, and Gary Garcia. 2003. "Brain-Computer Interface in Multimedia Communication." *IEEE Signal Processing Magazine* 20 (1): 14–24. doi:10.1109/MSP.2003.1166626.
3. Berger, Hans. 1934. "Über Das Elektrenkephalogramm Des Menschen." *Deutsche Medizinische Wochenschrift* 60 (51): 1947–1949. doi:10.1055/s-0028-1130334.
4. Vidal, J. J. 1973. "Toward Direct Brain-Computer Communication." *Annual Review of Biophysics and Bioengineering* 2: 157–180. doi:10.1146/annurev.bb.02.060173. 001105.
5. Farwell, L.A.; Donchin, E. 1988. "Talking off the top of your head: Toward a mental prosthesis utilizing event-related brain potentials". *Electroencephalogr. Clin. Neurophysiol. 70*, 510–523.
6. Huggins, Jane E., Christoph Guger, Mounia Ziat, Thorsten O. Zander, Denise Taylor, Michael Tangermann, Aureli Soria-Frisch, et al. 2017. "Workshops of the Sixth International Brain–Computer Interface Meeting: Brain–Computer Interfaces Past, Present, and Future." *Brain-Computer Interfaces* 4 (1–2): 3–36. doi:10.1080/2326263 X.2016.1275488.
7. Girouard, Audrey, Erin Treacy Solovey, Leanne M. Hirshfield, Evan M. Peck, Krysta Chauncey, Angelo Sassaroli, Sergio Fantini, and Robert J. K. Jacob. 2010. "From Brain Signals to Adaptive Interfaces: Using FNIRS in HCI," *Brain-Computer Interfaces*, pp. 221–237. doi:10.1007/978-1-84996-272-8_13.
8. Baillet, Sylvain, John C Mosher, and Richard M Leahy. 2001. "Electromagnetic brain mapping." *IEEE Signal Processing Magazine*, 18 (6): pp. 14–30.
9. Hirsch, Joy. 2005. "Functional Neuroimaging during Altered States of Consciousness: How and What Do We Measure?" *Progress in Brain Research* 150 (212): 25–43. doi:10.1016/S0079-6123(05)50003-7.
10. Fabio, Babiloni. 1900. "Brain Computer Interfaces for Communication and Control." *Frontiers in Neuroscience* 4: 767–791. doi:10.3389/conf.fnins.2010.05.00007.
11. Pfurtscheller, G., C. Neuper, G. R. Muüller, B. Obermaier, G. Krausz, A. Schloögl, R. Scherer, et al. 2003. "Graz-BCI: State of the Art and Clinical Applications." *IEEE Transactions on Neural Systems and Rehabilitation Engineering* 11 (2): 177–180. doi:10.1109/TNSRE.2003.814454.
12. Tsui, Chun Sing Louis, and John Q. Gan. 2007. "Asynchronous BCI Control of a Robot Simulator with Supervised Online Training." *Lecture Notes in Computer Science (Including Subseries Lecture Notes in Artificial Intelligence and Lecture Notes in Bioinformatics)* 4881 LNCS: 125–134. doi:10.1007/978-3-540-77226-2_14.
13. Lalor, E. C., S. P. Kelly, C. Finucane, R. Burke, R. Smith, R. B. Reilly, and G. McDarby. 2005. "Steady-State VEP-Based Brain-Computer Interface Control in an Immersive 3D Gaming Environment." *Eurasip Journal on Applied Signal Processing* 2005 (19): 3156–3164. doi:10.1155/ASP.2005.3156.
14. Hochberg, Leigh R., Mijail D. Serruya, Gerhard M. Friehs, Jon A. Mukand, Maryam Saleh, Abraham H. Caplan, Almut Branner, David Chen, Richard D. Penn, and John P. Donoghue. 2006. "Neuronal Ensemble Control of Prosthetic Devices by a Human with Tetraplegia." *Nature* 442 (7099): 164–171. doi:10.1038/nature04970.
15. Pfurtscheller, G., and C. Neuper. 2001. "Motor Imagery and Direct Brain-Computer Communication." *Proceedings of the IEEE* 89 (7): 1123–1134. doi:10.1109/5.939829.

16. Wolpaw, Jonathan R., and Dennis J. McFarland. 2004. "Control of a Two-Dimensional Movement Signal by a Noninvasive Brain-Computer Interface in Humans." *Proceedings of the National Academy of Sciences of the United States of America* 101 (51): 17849–17854. doi:10.1073/pnas.0403504101.
17. Dekker, Marcel. 1989. "Cell Surface Antigen Thy-1: Immunology, Neurology and Therapeutic Applications Electrophysiology: Evoked Potentials and Evoked Magnetic Fields in Science and Medicine HTLV-1 and the Nervous System."
18. Yin, Jinghai, Derong Jiang, and Jianfeng Hu. 2009. "Design and Application of Brain-Computer Interface Web Browser Based on VEP." FBIE 2009 - 2009 International Conference on Future BioMedical Information Engineering, 77–80. doi:10.1109/FBIE. 2009.5405788.
19. Gao, Xiaorong, Dingfeng Xu, Ming Cheng, and Shangkai Gao. 2003. "A BCI-Based Environmental Controller for the Motion-Disabled." *IEEE Transactions on Neural Systems and Rehabilitation Engineering* 11 (2): 137–140. doi:10.1109/TNSRE.2003.814449.
20. Bin, Guangyu, Xiaorong Gao, Yijun Wang, Bo Hong, and Shangkai Gao. 2009. "VEP-Based Brain-Computer Interfaces: Time, Frequency, and Code Modulations." *IEEE Computational Intelligence Magazine* 4 (4): 22–26. doi:10.1109/MCI.2009.934562.
21. Birbaumer, N., N. Ghanayim, T. Hinterberger, I. Iversen, B. Kotchoubey, A. Kübler, J. Perelmouter, E. Taub, and H. Flor. 1999. "A Spelling Device for the Paralysed." *Nature* 398 (6725): 297–298. doi:10.1038/18581.
22. Rivet, Bertrand, Antoine Souloumiac, Virginie Attina, and Guillaume Gibert. 2009. "XDAWN Algorithm to Enhance Evoked Potentials: Application to Brain-Computer Interface." *IEEE Transactions on Biomedical Engineering* 56 (8): 2035–2043. doi:10. 1109/TBME.2009.2012869.
23. Hinterberger, Thilo, Stefan Schmidt, Nicola Neumann, Jürgen Mellinger, Benjamin Blankertz, Gabriel Curio, and Niels Birbaumer. 2004. "Brain-Computer Communication and Slow Cortical Potentials." *IEEE Transactions on Biomedical Engineering* 51 (6): 1011–1018. doi:10.1109/TBME.2004.827067.
24. A Kübler, Kotchoubey B, Hinterberger T, Ghanayim N, Perelmouter J, Schauer M, Fritsch C, Taub E, and Birbaumer N. 1999. "'The Thought Translation Device: A Neurophysiological Approach to Communication in Total Motor Paralysis.'" *Experimental Brain Research* 124 (2): 223–232. http://www.citeulike.org/user/sebwills/article/244747.
25. Pfurtscheller, G.; Lopes da Silva, F.H. 1999. "Event-related EEG/MEG synchronization and desynchronization: Basic principles". *Clin. Neurophysiol. 110*, 1842–1857.
26. Pfurtscheller, Gert, and Christa Neuper. 2001. "Motor Imagery Direct Communication." *Proceedings of the IEEE* 89 (7): 1123–1134. doi:10.1109/5.939829.
27. Lemm, Steven, Christin Schäfer, and Gabriel Curio. 2004. "BCI Competition 2003 - Data Set III: Modeling of Sensorimotor μ Rhythms for Classification of Imaginary Hand Movements." *IEEE Transactions on Biomedical Engineering* 51 (6): 1077–1080. doi:10.1109/TBME.2004.827076.
28. Lalor, E. C., S. P. Kelly, C. Finucane, R. Burke, R. Smith, R. B. Reilly, and G. McDarby. 2005. "Steady-State VEP-Based Brain-Computer Interface Control in an Immersive 3D Gaming Environment." *Eurasip Journal on Applied Signal Processing* 2005 (FRIED19): 3156–3164. doi:10.1155/ASP.2005.3156.
29. Schlögl, Alois, Felix Lee, Horst Bischof, and Gert Pfurtscheller. 2005. "Characterization of Four-Class Motor Imagery EEG Data for the BCI-Competition 2005." *Journal of Neural Engineering* 2 (4). doi:10.1088/1741-2560/2/4/L02.
30. T. Hastie, R. Tibshirani, and J. Friedman. 2009. "The Elements of Statistical Learning - Data Mining, Inference, and Prediction".
31. Bashashati, Ali, Mehrdad Fatourechi, Rabab K. Ward, and Gary E. Birch. 2007. "A Survey of Signal Processing Algorithms in Brain-Computer Interfaces Based on Electrical Brain Signals." *Journal of Neural Engineering* 4 (2). doi:10.1088/1741-2560/4/2/R03.

32. McFarland, Dennis J., and Jonathan R. Wolpaw. 2011. "Brain-Computer Interfaces for Communication and Control." *Communications of the ACM* 54 (5): 60–66. doi:10.1145/1941487.1941506.
33. Panoulas, Konstantinos J., Leontios J. Hadjileontiadis, and Stavros M. Panas. 2010. "Brain-Computer Interface (BCI): Types, Processing Perspectives and Applications." *Smart Innovation, Systems and Technologies* 3: 299–321. doi:10.1007/978-3-642-13396-1_14.
34. Pfurtscheller G, Lopes da Silva F.H. 1999. "Event-related eeg/meg synchronization and desynchronization: basic principles". Clin Neurophysiol 110(11):1842–1857.
35. Gao, Shangkai, Yijun Wang, and Xiaorong Gao. 2014. "Visual and Auditory Brain – Computer Interfaces" *IEEE Transactions on Biomedical Engineering*, 61 (5): pp. 1436–1447.
36. Alba, Nicolas Alexander, Robert J. Sclabassi, Mingui Sun, and Xinyan Tracy Cui. 2010. "Novel Hydrogel-Based Preparation-Free EEG Electrode". *IEEE Transactions on Neural Systems and Rehabilitation Engineering*, 18 (4): pp. 415–423. doi: 10.1109/TNSRE.2010.2048579.
37. Sohn, Ohgun, and Dukjoon Kim. 2003. "Theoretical and Experimental Investigation of the Swelling Behavior of Sodium Polyacrylate Superabsorbent Particles." *Journal of Applied Polymer Science* 87 (2): 252–257. doi:10.1002/app.11360.
38. Volosyak, Ivan, Diana Valbuena, Tatsiana Malechka, Jan Peuscher, and Axel Gräser. 2010. "Brain-Computer Interface Using Water-Based Electrodes." *Journal of Neural Engineering* 7 (6). doi:10.1088/1741-2560/7/6/066007.
39. Griss, Patrick, Heli K. Tolvanen-Laakso, Pekka Meriläinen, and Göran Stemme. 2002. "Characterization of Micromachined Spiked Biopotential Electrodes." *IEEE Transactions on Biomedical Engineering* 49 (6): 597–604. doi:10.1109/TBME.2002.1001974.
40. Lin, Chin Teng, Lun De Liao, Yu Hang Liu, I. Jan Wang, Bor Shyh Lin, and Jyh Yeong Chang. 2011. "Novel Dry Polymer Foam Electrodes for Long-Term EEG Measurement." *IEEE Transactions on Biomedical Engineering* 58 (5): 1200–1207. doi:10.1109/TBME.2010.2102353.
41. Sellers, Eric W., Peter Turner, William A. Sarnacki, Tobin McManus, Theresa M. Vaughan, and Robert Matthews. 2009. "A Novel Dry Electrode for Brain-Computer Interface." *Lecture Notes in Computer Science (Including Subseries Lecture Notes in Artificial Intelligence and Lecture Notes in Bioinformatics)* 5611 LNCS (PART 2): 623–631. doi:10.1007/978-3-642-02577-8_68.
42. Liao, Lun De, I. Jan Wang, Sheng Fu Chen, Jyh Yeong Chang, and Chin Teng Lin. 2011. "Design, Fabrication and Experimental Validation of a Novel Dry-Contact Sensor for Measuring Electroencephalography Signals without Skin Preparation." *Sensors* 11 (6): 5819–5834. doi:10.3390/s110605819.
43. Ruffini, G., S. Dunne, L. Fuentemilla, C. Grau, E. Farrés, J. Marco-Pallarés, P. C.P. Watts, and S. R.P. Silva. 2008. "First Human Trials of a Dry Electrophysiology Sensor Using a Carbon Nanotube Array Interface." *Sensors and Actuators, A: Physical* 144 (2): 275–279. doi:10.1016/j.sna.2008.03.007.
44. Katine, J. A., and Eric E. Fullerton. 2008. "Device Implications of Spin-Transfer Torques." *Journal of Magnetism and Magnetic Materials* 320 (7): 1217–1226. doi:10.1016/j.jmmm.2007.12.013.
45. Cooper, R. J., N. L. Everdell, L. C. Enfield, A. P. Gibson, Alan Worley, and Jeremy C. Hebden. 2009. "Design and Evaluation of a Probe for Simultaneous EEG and Near-Infrared Imaging of Cortical Activation." *Physics in Medicine and Biology* 54 (7): 2093–2102. doi:10.1088/0031-9155/54/7/016.
46. Martins, Rui, Siegfried Selberherr, and Francisco A. Vaz. 1998. "A CMOS IC for Portable EEG Acquisition Systems." *IEEE Transactions on Instrumentation and Measurement* 47 (5): 1191–1196. doi:10.1109/19.746581.

47. Costa, Guillermo, Alfredo Arnaud, and Matías Miguez. 2010. "A Precision Autozero Amplifier for EEG Signals." *SBCCI'10 – Proceedings of the 23rd Symposium on Integrated Circuits and Systems Design*, 28–32. doi:10.1145/1854153.1854162.
48. Von Cresce, Arthur, and Kang Xu. 2011. "Electrolyte Additive in Support of 5 V Li Ion Chemistry." *Journal of The Electrochemical Society* 158 (3): A337. doi:10.1149/1. 3532047.
49. Karamian, S. A., and J. J. Carroll. 2011. "Cross Section for Inelastic Neutron 'Acceleration' by 178Hfm2." *Physical Review C - Nuclear Physics* 83 (2): 1–8. doi:10. 1103/PhysRevC.83.024604.
50. Le, Linh T., Matthew H. Ervin, Hongwei Qiu, Brian E. Fuchs, and Woo Y. Lee. 2011. "Graphene Supercapacitor Electrodes Fabricated by Inkjet Printing and Thermal Reduction of Graphene Oxide." *Electrochemistry Communications* 13 (4). Elsevier B.V.: 355–358. doi:10.1016/j.elecom.2011.01.023.
51. Niell, Cristopher M., and Michael P. Stryker. 2010. "Modulation of Visual Responses by Behavioral State in Mouse Visual Cortex." *Neuron* 65 (4). Elsevier Ltd: 472–479. doi:10.1016/j.neuron.2010.01.033.
52. Kim, Dae Hyeong, Nanshu Lu, Roozbeh Ghaffari, and John A. Rogers. 2012. "Inorganic Semiconductor Nanomaterials for Flexible and Stretchable Bio-Integrated Electronics." *NPG Asia Materials* 4 (4). Nature Publishing Group: e15–e19. doi:10. 1038/am.2012.27.
53. Ayaz, Hasan, Patricia A. Shewokis, Scott Bunce, Maria Schultheis, and Banu Onaral. 2009. "Assessment of Cognitive Neural Correlates for a Functional near Infrared-Based Brain Computer Interface System." *Lecture Notes in Computer Science (Including Subseries Lecture Notes in Artificial Intelligence and Lecture Notes in Bioinformatics)* 5638 LNAI: 699–708. doi:10.1007/978-3-642-02812-0_79.
54. Furdea, A., S. Halder, D. J. Krusienski, D. Bross, F. Nijboer, N. Birbaumer, and A. Kübler. 2009. "An Auditory Oddball (P300) Spelling System for Brain-Computer Interfaces." *Psychophysiology* 46 (3): 617–625. doi:10.1111/j.1469-8986.2008. 00783.x.
55. Márquez, Bogart Yail, Arnulfo Alanis, Miguel Ángel Lopez, and José Sergio Magdaleno-palencia. 2012. "Sport Education Based Technology: Stress Measurement in Competence," 247–252.
56. Selvam, V Salai, and S Shenbagadevi. 2011. "Brain Tumor Detection Using Scalp EEG with Modified Wavelet-ICA and Multi Layer Feed Forward Neural Network," 6104–6109.
57. Fadzal, C. W. N. F. C. W., W Mansor, L Y Khuan, Universiti Teknologi Mara, and Shah Alam. 2011. "Review of Brain Computer Interface Application in Diagnosing Dyslexia," 124–128.
58. Taib, Mohd Nasir, Noor Hayatee, and Abdul Hamid. 2010. "EEG Pattern of Smokers for Theta, Alpha and Beta Band Frequencies," no. SCOReD: 13–14.
59. Shooshtari, M Alavash. 2010. "Selection of Optimal EEG Channels for Classification of Signals Correlated with Alcohol Abusers," 1745–1748.
60. Fan, Xin, Luzheng Bi, and Zhi Wang. 2012. "Detecting Emergency Situations by Monitoring Drivers' States from EEG," 245–248.
61. Barbosa, Alexandre O G, David R Achanccaray, and Marco A Meggiolaro. 2010. "Activation of a Mobile Robot through a Brain Computer Interface," 4815–4821.

5 Signal Modeling Using Spatial Filtering and Matching Wavelet Feature Extraction for Classification of Brain Activity Patterns

Vrushali G. Raut, Sanjay R. Ganorkar,
Supriya O. Rajankar, and Omprakash S. Rajankar

5.1 INTRODUCTION

Brain computer interface (BCI) emerging from the past four decades as a specialized medium that offers the effective control of the environment, which may include devices such as assistive appliances, prostheses, and computers directly controlled by brain signals bypassing muscular pathway [1]. Though it started with the aim of assisting disabled people with severe motor impairments and leading to reduced social costs and improved quality of life, it was found to be applicable in gaming and military applications and many more applications for environment control [2]. Under advanced applications of BCI, it is used to regulate neural and behavioral functions such as attention, pain, and emotion by providing neurofeedback to users [3]. Research on BCI is being done in multidisciplinary fields involving physiology, psychology, engineering, and mathematics [2].

Brain signals capturing the modulations corresponding to the different intentions, acts as the potential input to the BCI. The signal-capturing methodologies are divided into invasive and noninvasive techniques. Under noninvasive methods, the electroencephalogram (EEG) measures the potential using the electrodes placed on the scalp of the subject; the magneto-encephalogram (MEG) measures the change in the magnetic field caused by electrical signals due to neural events [4-7]; functional magnetic resonance imaging (fMRI) monitors the magnetic properties of the blood in response to the functions or stimulus; and near-infrared spectroscopic (NIRS) uses the light near-infrared region to study oxygenation and deoxygenation of the hemoglobin due to brain function [7-10]. Electrocorticograms (ECoG) are the invasive technique placing the electrodes invasively on the small part of the cortex extracting the signals related to a specific function [11]. Noninvasiveness, low-cost set-up, and excellent temporal resolution made EEG the popular method to capture brain signals for research on BCI [12,13].

Brain signals used to drive BCI can be categorized as evoked potential and spontaneous signals. The evoked potential needs the stimulus and thus forms the dependent BCI. Steady-state visually evoked potentials (SSVEP) are one of the efficient signals that can be evoked by providing the visual stimulus. On the other hand, sensorimotor rhythms (SMR) or motor imagery (MI) are the spontaneous signals that can be generated by the intention of the subject and lead to independent BCI [14,15].

5.1.1 Sensorimotor Rhythms (SMR): An Efficient Input to BCI

Sensorimotor rhythms (SMRs) can be detected at the somatosensory cortex and motor cortex of the brain with contralateral variations in the μ band (8–13 Hz) and ipsilateral enhancement in the β band (18–26 Hz). The MI and execution of the movement decrease the amplitude in the μ band, and this is called event-related desynchronization (ERD); synchronization with the movement in the β band is called event-related synchronization (ERS) [7,16]. The SMRs are the beneficial control signal for persons with muscular disorders, as it helps in driving the systems performing motor activities [17]. The applications developed using SMR include prosthesis movement, driving a wheelchair, cursor control, and robot control [18]. Electrodes placed on the parietal and central region of the brain covering the motor cortex captures the variations due to MI [19,20]. The SMR can be placed in the category of independent BCI as no external (e.g., visual) stimuli is necessary [21], resulting in effective communication for different MI [22,23]. The different motor movements used are left and right-hand movement, variations in foot movement, movement of the tongue, or word generation, thus having a good prospect for adding the new distinguishable movements. More motor movements will provide more control in BCI; hence the MI-based BCI suggests a promising alternative for the rehabilitation of the stroke patient [24].

5.2   SIGNAL PROCESSING STRATEGIES FOR BCI

After acquiring the input EEG signals, the most critical part of BCI, which follows is signal processing, it is responsible for representing the intentions of the signal as well as distinguishing them. Other electrophysiological signals like electro-cardiogram (ECG) and electromyogram (EMG) and neighboring neural signals interfere with the EEG signal of interest and mislead the task classification. The relevant features corresponding to motor movement have to be extracted from the signal for representing the uniqueness of the task. The detailed survey of EEG based BCI decides on the requirement of signal processing strategies such as signal modeling, feature extraction, feature selection, and classification.

5.2.1   Signal Modelling Methods

Brain signal collected from the scalp has to pass through three nonconducting layers of the head, thus called volume conducted. This volume conduction leads to interference from neighboring neural signals as well as signals like ECG and EMG that also interfere with the EEG signal collected from the scalp of the subject. Also the EEG signal was contaminated by the reference electrode, as the EEG is a potential difference measured at one brain point with respect to other brain points called as the reference.

Signal modeling or pre-processing works for removing the interfering signals and rebuilding the source-specific signal. Hence, signal modeling plays a significant role in BCI using the EEG signals for diagnostic purposes. The selection of a signal modeling strategy must consider the above-mentioned interferences, as well it must collect the spread of the signal on neighboring electrodes. Temporal filtering using bandpass and notch filter and spatial filtering by common average referencing (CAR) claims the boosting of signal to noise ratio [17]. Spatial filtering using surface Laplacian (SL) emphasized in this work counteracts the volume conduction in EEG representing the source-specific signals.

5.2.1.1 Surface Laplacian (SL) Counteracting the Volume Conduction

The local relation between the potential available on the scalp electrode and the actual electric current produced by the specific brain activity is proportionate and forms the base for SL [25]. Application of the SL will improve the spatial resolution, reproducing electrical activity of a restricted brain source of interest compared to the signals obtained by conventional topography. This is the motivation behind the use of the SL technique.

Physical interpretation of SL: EEG signal taken at the scalp is the potential difference between the electrode and the reference electrode. The electric field E, measuring the force per unit of the charge, is more important in comparison with the potential. The potential V_{AB} can be given in terms of electric field E as in equation (5.1) between two points' r_A and r_B.

$$V_{AB} = \int_{r_A}^{r_B} E(r) \cdot dr \qquad (5.1)$$

But, this potential difference can also be given as equation (5.2), where the function $V(r)$ is the electric potential of the field E.

$$V_{AB} = V(r_A) - V(r_B) \qquad (5.2)$$

When distance $r_B \to \infty$, $V(r_B) \to 0$, potential captured by the electrode with respect to the reference electrode can be considered as the signal potential on the electrode. This will help in writing one important relation between the electric field E and the potential V specified by the gradient operator in the Cartesian coordinate as in equation (5.3), where $\hat{a}_x$, $\hat{a}_y$, $\hat{a}_z$ are the unit vectors along x, y, and z directions, respectively. The spatial derivative $Grad(V(r))$ with respect to space is V at r and given by equation (5.4).

$$E(r) = -Grad(V(r)) \qquad (5.3)$$

$$Grad(V(r)) = \frac{\partial V(r)}{\partial x} \hat{a}_x + \frac{\partial V(r)}{\partial y} \hat{a}_y + \frac{\partial V(r)}{\partial z} \hat{a}_z \qquad (5.4)$$

The maximum rate of change of the potential V is pointed by a vector $Grad(V(r))$; whereas, its rate of change gives the magnitude. Thus, it can be stated that the equipotential field lines are perpendicular to $Grad(V(r))$. It helps in establishing the relation between the function $V(r)$ and electric field $E(r)$. The explanation for the $E(r)$ and $V(r)$ in the form of the charge q and distance r of the equipotential line can be given by equations (5.5) and (5.6) respectively.

$$E(r) = \frac{q}{4\pi\varepsilon_0} \frac{r - r_0}{(r - r_0)^3} \qquad (5.5)$$

$$V(r) = -\frac{q}{4\pi\varepsilon_0} \frac{1}{|r - r_0|} \qquad (5.6)$$

The divergence of electric field E is an estimate of electric charges which are the source of that field, and Gauss's law represents it in equation (5.7), or double differentiation of the potential as in equation (5.8).

$$Div(E) = -Div(Grad(V)) \qquad (5.7)$$

$$Div(E) = \frac{\partial^2 V}{\partial x^2} + \frac{\partial^2 V}{\partial y^2} + \frac{\partial^2 V}{\partial z^2} \qquad (5.8)$$

The divergence of E can also be estimated as the difference in the number of flux lines entering (sink) and leaving (source) the infinitesimally small volume; thus, the positive value of divergence indicates more source lines then sink lines and vice-versa [25]. Concluding on the above-given interpretation, it can be stated that SL implementation of spatial filter will provide us with the source-specific signal.

Advantages offered by SL: The first advantage offered by SL is the reference-free estimates; thus, for variation of reference in EEG recording will not vary the es-timated SL. Second, it effectively reduces the signal distortion due to volume conduction, which commonly distorts the EEG recorded from the scalp. In this way, SL boosts the specificity of the signal by extracting the neural source-specific signal. Third, SL estimate does not require any assumptions about brain func-tioning, brain volume, and tissue conductivity, etc. Though the obtained estimate of the source does not inform the corresponding brain source or neuronal activity, it offers the advantage of representing that source [26].

Methods for implementation of SL: Various methods suggested for im-plementation of SL are elaborated further in this chapter. Hjorth's method works on finite-difference; whereas, Perrin's method uses the concept of the spherical spline.

A. Hjorth's method of finite difference

The finite difference method is a classic scheme for SL estimation. It computes the finite difference between the signal on the electrode and average of the signals on the electrodes physically surrounding it as given in equation (5.9), where *sj* is the number of surrounding electrodes. Though simple mathematics is involved, the assumption of the piecewise planar scalp is unrealistic. Representing unequal electrode separation and estimating for electrodes on borderline was difficult [27].

$$V_j^{lap} = V_j - \frac{1}{n}\sum_{k=sj} V_k \tag{5.9}$$

B. Perrin's SL implementation using spherical spline

Due to the spherical pseudo-spline approach developed by Wahaba et al., this method is generally mentioned as the spherical Laplacian. This spherical Laplacian can work for the random distance between the electrodes and predicts the spread of the Laplacian on the scalp. Fitting the observed data at each site of recording and then estimating the missing data at the inter-mediate surface location is done by spherical Laplacian [28]. Spline flexibility is a fundamental characteristic of these functions [29,30]. The divergence of the gradient is defined as the Laplacian of potential or second spatial derivative of potential V given by equation (5.10).

$$LapV = -Div\,(Grad\,(V)) \tag{5.10}$$

It estimates the voltage at the point by calculating the mean of the voltages around the point of computation. Laplacian of V estimates the divergence of electric field E. Thus, it can be stated that electric field sources can be represented by Laplacian of voltage/potential as shown in equation (5.11).

$$LapV = -4\pi\rho Q \tag{5.11}$$

Surface Laplacian identifies the electrode location on the scalp and computes the *channel X channel* transformation matrix, which will be constant for the specified montage and has to be computed once for that montage. This computation is done using the Legendre polynomial popularly used for solving SL. The obtain matrix, when applied on the signal matrix, gives us the spatially filtered and reference-free signal representing the underlying neural source.

5.2.2 FEATURE EXTRACTION STRATEGIES

The spread of variations due to the motor imagery (MI) signal is in time as well as in the frequency domain. The literature further suggested that planning and execution of the motor movement create the transient and circumscribed attenuation in the μ band (8–12 Hz) identified as event-related desynchronization (ERD) and the central β band (13–28 Hz) identified as event-related synchronization (ERS) [21,31]. The tool representing these rhythms or variations in features will be the perfect choice for feature extraction. The work presented in this chapter suggests wavelet transform (WT) as a tool for extracting the features due to properties like localization in time as well as frequency and ease of implementation. The multiresolution and energy compaction properties of the wavelet transform to make it a capable and flexible tool for the applications ranging from feature detection, feature extraction, and pattern recognition to compression of the signals [32,33].

The processing time of the discrete wavelet transform (DWT) makes it preferable in comparison with the continuous wavelet transform (CWT). The signal decomposition using DWT gives approximate and detail coefficient bands containing wavelet coefficients. It is a tool used effectively for signal compression, and the reason is an appropriate representation of the signal by removing randomness and redundancy from it [32]. The same concept of efficient representation can be used for capturing the uniqueness of the signal which will help in building robust features from the underlying activity. The beauty of this tool is in a variety of available wavelet functions for representing the signals effectively. Literature suggested the use of an empirical selection of Daubechies wavelet for the decomposition of EEG signals to give wavelet coefficients used for the preparation of features [34,35]. Thus, while using the WT, significant effort are spent on the selection of the wavelet function. This work provides the capable technique of wavelet function selection for the signal under test.

5.2.2.1 Wavelet Transform

Wavelets transform a linear transformation shift and dilate the mother wavelet to represent the signal using a set of coefficients. The decomposition of the signal leads to a set of coefficients called wavelet coefficients. A computerized method for implementing the wavelet transform is a discrete wavelet transform (DWT). It decomposes the signal into a sub-band consisting of approximate and detail coefficients [36].

Orthonormal wavelet basis functions $\psi_{jk}(t)$ and scaling function $\phi_{jk}(t)$, given in equations (5.12) and (5.13), are dilations and translations of the mother wavelet, respectively, and help to decompose and discretely expand the signal $x(t)$ [37,38].

$$\psi_{jk}(t) = 2^{-\frac{j}{2}}\psi(2^{-j}t - k) \; j, k \in z \tag{5.12}$$

$$\phi_{jk}(t) = 2^{-\frac{j}{2}}\phi(2^{-j}t - k) \; j, k \in z \tag{5.13}$$

Multiresolution analysis of the signal $x(t)$ represented in equation (5.14), where A_j represents the approximate coefficient and D_j represents detail coefficients at decomposition level j.

$$x(t) = \sum_{k=-\infty}^{\infty} A_j(k)\phi_{j,k}(t) + \sum_{j=J}^{I} \sum_{k=-\infty}^{\infty} D_j(k)\psi_{j,k}(t) \tag{5.14}$$

Equation (5.15) gives the decomposition of the signal in the approximation and the detail coefficients for five-levels of decomposition.

$$x(t) = A_5(t) + \{D_5(t) + D_4(t) + D_3(t) + D_2(t) + D_1(t)\} \tag{5.15}$$

5.2.2.2   Methods for Wavelet Function Selection

Selecting the wavelet function plays a very crucial role in signal classification; it entirely relies on the similarity between the signal under test and the scaled version of the base wavelet. Wavelet band filters characterized by properties like regularity, vanishing moments, and shift variance degree, are used for wavelet basis selection [39]. Another basis for selection criteria is the ratio of maximum energy to Shannon entropy used for mechanical signals [40]. Quantitative approaches also suggested for wavelet basis function selection works on the minimum description length (MDL) principle [41].

"David Salomon," suggested that the energy of correlated data is concentrated in the first few transform coefficients [32], those coefficients gathered in the approximate coefficient band are sufficient for representing the signal and are retained while compressing the signal. This research work uses the concept of "David Salomon," for wavelet function selection. The work searches for the wavelet a function that gathers maximum wavelet band energy when applied on the signal of interest due to correlation with the signal. The wavelet accumulating maximum energy in the approximate coefficient band is considered to be the matching wavelet function.

Wavelet entropy: Wavelet entropy is a measure of uncertainty related to the signal; the different entropy measures are used to select the optimal wavelet basis function for the underlying ECG signal [42]. When the WT is used for signal compression, the requirement is matching wavelet basis function for signal decomposition. The library of such an orthonormal basis was created by collecting the wavelet basis functions for which the signal under test has the lowest wavelet entropy or, in other words, the lowest information cost [43]. Entropy is also used to compare the signal by measuring their complexity, and it was concluded that dissimilarity could be measured using wavelet entropy [44]. The relative measure of wavelet entropy offers information about the associated energy and hence, the importance of frequency bands in the EEG.

The wavelet entropy can be used for gathering evidence about the amount of order/disorder, the grade of similarity between various segments of the signal, and information about the dynamics in the signals [45]. Considering these references this work uses wavelet entropy to measure the randomness of the wavelet decomposed signals and use it to decide on the level of wavelet decomposition as well as for crosschecking the selected matching wavelet function.

Formulating wavelet energy and wavelet entropy using wavelet coefficients: Approximate and detailed coefficients are obtained by decomposing the signal using wavelet transform given by equation (5.14). These wavelet coefficients represent the time and frequency distribution of the signals and are used for calculating wavelet energy and wavelet entropy. Equation (5.16) represents the energy compaction in the approximate coefficient band, using approximate coefficients A and the level of resolution j. Checking for the value of energy compaction for different wavelet functions helps in the selection of matching wavelet function.

$$E_j = \sum_k |A_{j,k}|^2 \qquad (5.16)$$

The wavelet entropy S_w must be an additive cost function such that $S(0) = 0$. Shannon's calculation of wave entropy involves wavelet coefficients belonging to the particular band (approximate or detail coefficient band denoted by $C_{j,k}$). The step-wise calculation of wavelet entropy starts with computing the energy at each time sample k as given in equation (5.17) [46]

$$E(k) = \sum_j |C_{j,k}|^2 \tag{5.17}$$

The second step calculates total energy accumulated in all the bands as in equation (5.18)

$$E_{tot} = \sum_j \sum_k |C_{j,k}|^2 \tag{5.18}$$

the normalized values, given by equation (5.19)

$$P_j = \frac{E_j}{E_{tot}} \tag{5.19}$$

Thus the wavelet entropy can be calculated as given in equation (5.20)

$$S_w = -\sum_j P_j \times \ln(P_j) \tag{5.20}$$

5.2.3 FEATURE FORMATION

Wavelet coefficients and wavelet band energy can be used as the features for the MI task classification, but it will increase the number of features passed to the classifier. The statistical representation of the wavelet coefficients can act as efficient and strong features as well as reduces the number of features.

Statistical and higher-order statistical (HoS) features: The second-order statistical features like mean, variance, and standard deviation are used for representing the wavelet coefficients. Mean measures the central tendency by providing information on the data values at the center of the discrete set of numbers as given by equation (5.21). Variance and standard deviation give the measure of the dispersion of the signal. The variance of the data can be defined as the average squared distance between the mean $\bar{x}$ and each data value x_i given in equation (5.22).

$$\bar{x} = \frac{\sum_{i=1}^n x_i}{n} \tag{5.21}$$

$$\sigma^2 = \frac{\sum_{i=1}^n (x_i - \bar{x})^2}{n} \tag{5.22}$$

Standard deviation is given by the square root of variance in equation (5.23). The spread of the values in the dataset around the mean can be effectively measured by standard deviation, it precisely measures the average distance between the values of the data in the set and the mean.

$$\sigma = \sqrt{\frac{\sum_{i=1}^{n}(x_i - \bar{x})^2}{n}} \qquad (5.23)$$

Though the second-order statistics given earlier are significant for representing the features, they are not effective especially for indicating nonlinearities of the signals. For that, higher-order statistics (HoS) containing higher-order moments (m3, m4,...) and nonlinear combinations of these moments, known as cumulants, can be termed as a valuable descriptor. Skewness, a third-order cumulant, is a measure of symmetry or the lack of symmetry of the distribution given by equation (5.24). Kurtosis, a fourth-order cumulant, is a measure of the distribution in terms of heavy-tailed or light-tailed relative to a normal distribution and given by equation (5.25) [47,48]. These HoS features are suggested for representing the dynamics of the signal in this work.

$$b = \frac{1}{n} \sum_{j=1}^{N} \left(\frac{x_j - \bar{x}}{\sigma} \right)^3 \qquad (5.24)$$

$$b = \frac{1}{n} \sum_{j=1}^{N} \left(\frac{x_j - \bar{x}}{\sigma} \right)^4 \qquad (5.25)$$

Robust features are formed by statistical and higher-order statistical (HoS) representation of the wavelet coefficients, obtained by decomposing the signal using matching wavelet function.

5.2.4 FEATURE SELECTION STRATEGIES

Identifying the task-related variation from the EEG signal is very crucial, and, thus, extracting the relevant features from the captured signal representing the underlying task is very important. Feature selection strategy will help in identifying the important features reducing the computational burden on the classifier. A large number of features lead to poor task classification due to the generalization of noisy EEG signal. Genetic algorithm and mutual information are the preferred strategies for feature selection [49]. As the matching wavelet function can efficiently represent the EEG signal, the wavelet transform is also used for the feature selection [50]. Neighborhood entropy can be used to define the interdependency of the features, as well as redundancy of the features that can be figured out by using it. These established relations are used for feature selection [51]. In this work, the feature extraction from the source-specific electrode/channel, and frequency band of interest are considered which covers the variations related to motor movements. In this way, the spread of the signal in the spatial and frequency domain is collected.

5.2.5 CLASSIFIER

Linear, as well as nonlinear supervised and unsupervised, techniques apply to noninvasive BCI. Selection and proper tuning of the classifier help in boosting the task classification accuracy (CA). A few of the preferred classification tools for BCI are the support vector machine (SVM) classifier with kernel tuning, discriminant analysis, and k-NN. The supervised learning approach for the classifier is widely used for the EEG-based BCI as it got trained from the available subject-wise sample data and subsequently classifies the testing data. A nearest-neighbor technique using supervised learning for classification is used successfully in several areas, such as pattern recognition, big data classification, and categorization of text [52,53].

5.2.5.1 Support Vector Machine for Classification

Basic rules of SVM were developed by Vapnik in 1995; its acceptance increased due to promising empirical performance [54]. Support vector machine, due to the capability of generalization, was found advantageous over the traditional neural network. Instead of separating the data into two classes, SVM works on maximizing the margin i.e., maximizing the distance between the margin and the nearest data point of each class resulting in optimal separating hyperplane, which generalizes well as shown in Figure 5.1 [55].

The SVM maps the input feature vector to the space of a higher dimension if the data is linearly nonseparable. The kernel function acts as an optimal separating hyperplane and is constructed by selecting a nonlinear mapping [56]. The curse of dimensionality can be handled if inner products are not evaluated in the feature space; this is fulfilled by the idea of the kernel function.

Kernel Functions: Various kernel functions mentioned here are considered for this work under the concept of kernel tricking [54].

1. Linear kernel the modest kernel function given in terms of two samples x_1 and x_2 and a constant c in equation (5.26).

$$K(x_1, x_2) = x_1^T x_2 + c \qquad (5.26)$$

2. Polynomial kernel is a nonlinear kernel suited for normalized training data. Its equation has adjustable parameters like slope α, constant c, and degree of polynomial d given by equation (5.27).

$$K(x_1, x_2) = (\alpha x_1^T x_2 + c)^d \qquad (5.27)$$

3. Gaussian kernel, also called a radial basis function (RBF), is given by equation (5.28). Parameter σ plays an essential role in estimating the

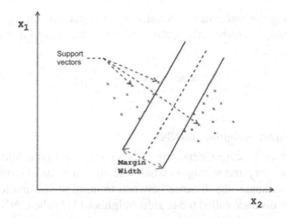

FIGURE 5.1   Support vector machine with separating hyperplanes.

nonlinearity of the kernel function; hence, proper tuning of it is very important to avoid underestimation or overestimation of the decision boundary.

$$K(x_1, x_2) = exp\left(-\frac{\|x_1 - x_2\|^2}{2\sigma^2}\right) \tag{5.28}$$

The highly non-linear classifier can be designed by changing only the kernel functions without making any changes in the algorithm. The local minima of efficient SVM algorithms can be adequately maintained while training the algorithms by nonlinear kernels; this strategy is used for maintaining the robustness of the classifier while taking advantage of kernel variations.

5.2.5.2   Discriminant Analysis for Classification

Multiple regression analysis is at the base of discriminant analysis methodology, where the discriminant analysis deals with a discrete dependent variable. For selecting the beneficial independent variable, they are plotted against the group of the variables. Linear discriminant analysis (LDA) was developed for a 2-class problem and modified for multiclass problems. The LDA implementation involves the following three steps.

1. Computation of class variance as in equation (5.29) between the mean and the sample from each class.

$$S_b = \sum_{i=1}^{g} N_i(\bar{x}_i - \bar{x})(\bar{x}_i - \bar{x})^T \tag{5.29}$$

2. Computation of within-class variance is the distance between the mean and the sample from every class as in equation (5.30).

$$S_w = \sum_{i=1}^{g} \sum_{j=1}^{N_i} (\bar{x}_{ij} - \bar{x})(\bar{x}_{ij} - \bar{x})^T \tag{5.30}$$

3. Constructing the lower dimensional space for maximizing the between-class variance and minimizing the within-class variance given in equation (5.31).

$$P_{lda} = \arg \max_{P} = \left| \frac{P^T S_b P}{P^T S_w P} \right| \tag{5.31}$$

5.2.5.3   K-Nearest Neighbor (k-NN)

The requirement of k-nearest neighbor (k-NN) splits the data into a training set specifying the category and testing set where the classifier has to judge the category. Once trained, it evaluates the distance between training points and testing points to search the lowest distance called the nearest neighbor [57]. The k-NN algorithm had an adjustment for the selection of the number of neighbors, which categorize it as fine k-NN for one neighbor, and coarse k-NN for 100 neighbors whereas medium k-NN uses ten neighbors. Cosine k-NN uses the cosine distance metric, where the cosine distance between two vectors A and B is given by equation (5.32)

$$1 - \frac{A \cdot B}{|A \cdot B'|} \tag{5.32}$$

In cubic k-NN the cubic distance metric is used; it is the distance between two, vectors A and B, given by equation (5.33)

$$\sqrt[3]{\sum_{i=1}^{N} |A_i - B_i|^3} \tag{5.33}$$

5.3   DATASET USED

Dataset IVa provided by BCI competition III is created by Fraunhofer FIRST, Intelligent Data Analysis Group, Department of Neurology, University of Medicine, Berlin. It includes recording on five subjects with small training data thus posing the challenge for signal processing algorithms. Two classes of motor imagery (MI) provided are for the left-hand movement (LHM) and right-foot movement (RFM).

Data is recorded using 118 channel EEG machines placed on the scalp of the subjects seated in a comfortable position. Information about performing left hand and right foot movement is provided by visual cues indicated for 3.5 s. The time-lapse between target cues are of random length for 1.75 to 2.25 s. The 118 EEG electrodes are placed according to standard 10–20 montage for capturing the signal. Continuous signals for 280 cues and markers indicating the time points are provided for each of the subjects [58]. The 118 EEG channels take continuous data recording, intermediately indicated by markers for 280 cues. This process is repeated respectively for all five subjects named *aa, al, av, aw,* and *ay.*

5.4   IMPLEMENTATION METHODOLOGY

The signal processing strategies elaborated in Section 5.2 of this chapter are implemented on the dataset selected for the work. Spherical spline implementation of surface Laplacian is done for signal modeling. The next step of feature extraction proposes wavelet decomposition of the signal up to the level separating the band of interest. In feature extraction, the approach for matching wavelet function selection using wavelet entropy and wavelet energy is proposed. The selected wavelet functions are used for the decomposition of the signal to give features. When applied on the signal, the wavelet accumulating more energy in the approximate band and giving minimum wavelet entropy is considered to be matching wavelet function. Wavelet coefficients extracted using matching wavelets are used for generating statistical and HoS features from a band of interest. The extracted features are passed to the classifier and classification accuracy is evaluated using different kernel functions.

5.4.1   IMPLEMENTATION OF SURFACE LAPLACIAN

The method of surface Laplacian (SL) estimates the scalp current density (SCD) or current source density (CSD) by using a vector form of Ohm's law. It computes the second spatial derivative of the field potential at every electrode and relates it with the brain source as the current generators within an isotropic electrical conductor [29]. Spherical spline estimate is used for the implementation [59-61].

The dataset used for this work consist of signals for left-hand movement (LHM) and right-foot movement (RHM) recorded on five subjects. Out of the available 118 electrodes, the data matrix "Sample X Electrode" with selected 21 electrodes shown in Figure 5.2 is used for spatial filtering by SL. The patch of 21 electrodes is selected based on enhanced system performance after testing for different electrode combinations. Signals on electrodes covering the central region, a region between the frontal and central part, and the region between the parietal and central part of the skull (seven electrodes from each row of C, FC, CP) are transformed using SL.

Implementation flow for SL using spline interpolation is as follows:

1. Coordinates mapping
2. Specifying and extracting an EEG Montage
3. Generating the Matrices G and H for Transformation
4. Preparing input data for SL Transform

1. Coordinates mapping: SL estimate needs to map the direction, position, and intensity of the brain source also called a current generator with the EEG topography. It will help in computing the second order spatial derivation of that generator. Thus the first step for SL identifies the scalp locations using the provided EEG montage. Head is assumed to be a sphere of unit ("1") radius with all EEG scalp sites set on the surface of the sphere. Vector originating at the center of the sphere is used for indicating the location on the surface.
2. Specifying and extracting an EEG Montage: If the dataset uses the standard EEG montage system available for electrode placements such as 10/20, 10/10,

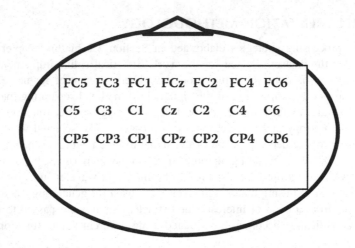

FIGURE 5.2 Selected 21 electrodes for SL transformation.

or 10/5 it can be directly mapped to give Cartesian and spherical coordinates for the placed electrodes. Positions of reference electrodes are also montage specific and thus can be extracted. We have selected 21 from an available 118 electrodes placed according to the 10/20 electrode placement montage of the dataset used in this work.

3. Generating the Matrices G and H for Transformation: The obtained positions of the electrodes are utilized for generation of the "channel X channel" matrices G and H called transformation matrices according to Perrin et al. (1989) algorithm. These matrices are used for the spherical spline interpolation of surface and are derived using the number and relative position of electrode placement included in the EEG montage (i.e., their cosine distances). The equations for G and H are equations (5.34) and (5.35) given here [27].

$$G_{ij} = \frac{1}{4\pi} \sum_{n=1}^{order} \frac{2n + 1}{(n(n + 1))^m} P_n \cos dis_{ij} \qquad (5.34)$$

$$H_{ij} = \frac{1}{4\pi} \sum_{n=1}^{order} - \frac{2n + 1}{(n(n + 1))^{m-1}} P_n \cos dis_{ij} \qquad (5.35)$$

$$Cosdis_{ij} = 1 - \frac{(X_i - X_j)^2 + (Y_i - Y_j)^2 + (Z_i - Z_j)^2}{2} \qquad (5.36)$$

- Pn used in the equations of G and H is Legendre polynomial used for the solution of Laplace's equation.
- n is the order of the polynomial, it decreases the amplitude of polynomial monotonically, letting it work as a Butterworth filter that weighs down high-frequency spatial components.

- m helps filter out more low spatial frequencies.
- *Cosdis* gives cosine distance between all pairs of electrodes [25].

4. Preparing input data for (SL) Transform: After obtaining the G and H matrix, it is required to groom the input data for transformation. Armed with G and H surface Laplacian transform can be computed using equation (5.37). Equations (5.38), (5.39), and (5.40) elaborate the data grooming.

$$lap_i = \sum_{i=1}^{nelec} C_i H_{ij} \tag{5.37}$$

where lap_i is Laplacian for electrode i and one-time point, j is each other electrode, and H_{ij} is H matrix corresponding to electrodes i and j.

$$C_i = d_i - \frac{\sum_{j=1}^{nele} d_j}{\sum_{j=1}^{nele} Gs_j^{-1}} Gs^{-1} \tag{5.38}$$

$$d_i = data_i^{-1} Gs \tag{5.39}$$

$$Gs = G + \lambda \tag{5.40}$$

where λ is the smoothing parameter added to the diagonal element of matrix G. This procedure gives the modeling or processed data matrix representing the source-specific and reference-free signal that can be used for further process. The original and SL transformed signal is represented in Figure 5.3.

5.4.2 WAVELET FUNCTION SELECTION METHODOLOGY

The level of decomposition and matching wavelet function selections are the two strategies to be followed after signal modeling using SL. Wavelet entropy, which measures the randomness of the signal, is applied for selecting the level of decomposition, and wavelet entropy along with wavelet band energy is used for selecting matching wavelet functions as explained in Figure 5.4.

The wavelet coefficients of the signal extracted by applying the matching wavelet are translated into the statistical features; the work flow is explained in Figure 5.5. These features are further passed to the classifier for categorizing the motor movements.

5.4.2.1 Level of Wavelet Decomposition

The entropy is the cost function which selects the level of decomposition. The idea is to decompose the signal into two bands and to check for the value of the wavelet entropy of the approximate band as in Figure 5.4; the approximate band is further

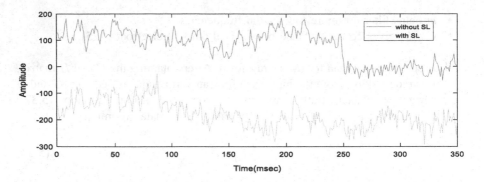

FIGURE 5.3 Time representation of the signal with and without SL transform.

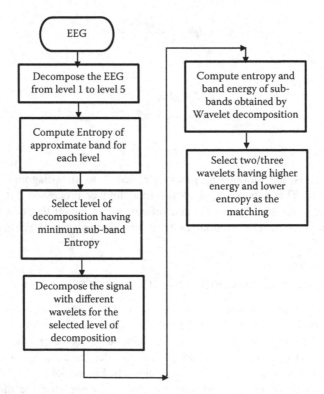

FIGURE 5.4 Flow of proposed scheme for selection of matching wavelet functions and level of wavelet decomposition.

decomposed and again wavelet entropy for the approximate band at the second level is computed. The procedure is repeated until the level of decomposition provides minimum entropy in the approximate coefficient band resulting in minimum randomness as explained by the following pseudocodes.

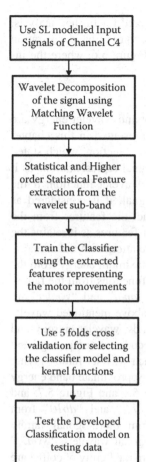

FIGURE 5.5 Optimized feature extraction and motor imagery task classification.

```
#Compute DWT of the signal till it gives minimum wavelet entropy
Input: Data, Wavelet function
Set Entropy to 0
[CA0,CD0] = dwt(Data, 'wavelet function')
For i=0 to n
[CAi+1,CDi+1] = dwt(CAi,'wavelet function')
Eni = wentropy(CAi+1,'shannon')
Update Eni in Entropy
End for
Find_min(Entropy)
```

When this process is repeated with all orthonormal bases from the "biorothogonal," "daubechies," "coiflet," "revere bior," and "symlet" it has been found that the entropy value reduces till the fourth level of decomposition; whereas, it increases for the 5th level, thus concluding on the 4th level as the suitable level with minimum entropy. Exceptional bases, *"bior1.1," db1, "rbior2," symlet2*, gives minimum entropy at the 3rd level of decomposition, thus not considered for further analysis. At the selected 4th level of wavelet decomposition, the structure of band separation considering the 100 Hz sampling frequency is shown in Figure 5.6, where the indicated frequency is in Hz.

5.4.2.2   Wavelet Function Selection

Once the level of decomposition is fixed, wavelet entropy and wavelet energy are used for the selection of a matching wavelet. The work presented in this chapter uses the concept of "David Salomon," for wavelet function selection, which stated that the approximate band coefficients are sufficient for signal representations as it carries a maximum of the signal energy. Hence, for the wavelet function, if the approximate band accumulates more energy from the signal, it is considered as the matching function for further decomposition to extract the features from the signal. This matching wavelet will help in extracting better features as it retains the required variations in the signal due to its maximum correlation with the signal.

The work searches for the wavelet functions gathering maximum energy from the signal in the approximate coefficient band. All the wavelet functions from the family of *"biorthogonal," "daubechies" "coiflet" "revere biorthogonal"* and *"symlet"* are used for experimenting. Every wavelet function from the above-mentioned wavelet families is applied to the signals to get the wavelet subbands; wavelet entropy and wavelet energy are computed for the subbands. The pseudocode for computing band energy is given next. Two/three wavelet functions from each wavelet family giving the comparably higher value of wavelet energy is selected. Approximate band energy of RFM for selected wavelet functions is shown in Table 5.1 and Figure 5.7, and LHM are in Table 5.2 and Figure 5.8. The wavelets *"db9"* and *"db10"* from Daubechies family, *"bior3.1," "bior3.7," "bior3.9"* from biorthogonal family *"rbior3.9," "rbior 5.5," "rbior 6.8"* from reverse biorthogonal wavelets, *"sym7," "sym8"* from the family of symlet, and *"coif4," "coif5"* from the family of coiflet are the selected wavelets with a higher value of approximate band energy. Though *"bior3.1"* is the wavelet function giving maximum band energy as well minimum wavelet entropy at the fourth level of the wavelet decomposition, all the selected wavelets are retained for feature extraction and task classification purposes so as to analyze the performance of the system for the selected wavelets.

```
# Pseudo code to compute Band Energy
Input: wavelet functions (n), Data1
For i=1 to n
If i=1
```

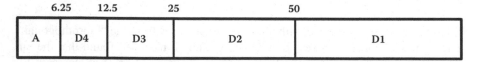

FIGURE 5.6   The frequency band separation at the 4th level of wavelet decomposition for the signal with 100 Hz sampling frequency.

TABLE 5.1

Comparative tabulation of band energy compaction against wavelet functions for right-foot movement

Wavelet function	Band energy (%)				
	App. coefficient band	Detail coefficient band			
		D4	D3	D2	D1
db9	53.0548	11.62148	18.24627	11.33534	5.742097
db10	53.06475	12.59509	17.89705	10.96879	5.474322
bior3.1	**64.41005**	15.26732	13.96486	5.159947	1.197826
bior3.7	47.08865	22.00887	21.31145	7.954695	1.636338
bior3.9	45.18436	23.04662	22.73659	7.537623	1.494814
rbior3.9	49.54941	7.366217	14.35259	15.11669	13.61509
rbior5.5	55.82805	11.02736	18.62502	10.54334	3.976223
rbior6.8	54.74029	10.3209	16.37447	12.1758	6.388541
sym7	56.06403	9.505114	16.98693	11.5309	5.913029
sym8	56.02836	9.100085	17.61403	11.41993	5.837593
coif4	55.20215	11.65975	17.39333	10.51007	5.234705
coif5	55.65427	12.77078	16.94348	9.886897	4.744568

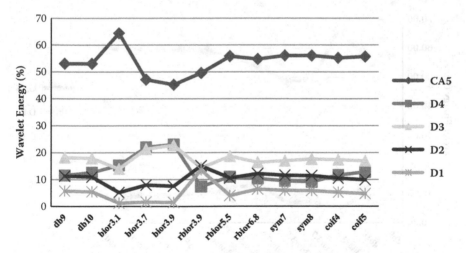

FIGURE 5.7 Plot of wavelet energy compaction against wavelet functions for right-foot movement.

```
wavelet='wavelet function 1';
[CA,CD] = DWT(Data1, wavelet, level of Decomposition=4)
BEi =Band Energy (CA, CD)
A=Accumulate(BEi)
End for
Compare A
```

TABLE 5.2

Comparative tabulation of band energy compaction and wavelet functions for left-hand movement

Wavelet functions	Band energy (%)				
	App. coefficient band	Detail coefficient band			
		D4	D3	D2	D1
db9	57.08	12.19	15.88	9.41	5.45
db10	57.79	12.64	15.06	9.39	5.12
bior3.1	**66.20**	15.91	12.08	4.69	1.12
bior3.7	49.25	22.77	19.22	7.20	1.57
bior3.9	48.54	23.11	19.94	6.96	1.46
rbior3.9	53.34	7.88	13.66	12.85	12.27
rbior5.5	56.88	9.72	13.85	12.43	7.13
rbior6.8	58.93	10.08	14.90	10.13	5.95
sym7	59.65	9.65	15.26	9.81	5.63
sym8	59.76	8.89	15.95	9.85	5.55
coif4	59.71	11.71	14.91	8.88	4.79
coif5	60.13	12.92	14.37	8.26	4.32

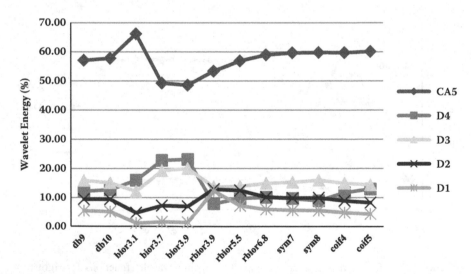

FIGURE 5.8 Plot of wavelet energy compaction against wavelet functions for left-hand movement.

5.4.2.3 Optimized Feature Extraction and Classification

After decomposing the signal using the selected wavelet function, the next important step is to construct the efficient features representing the motor-related variation of the signal. Motor imagery (MI) is prominently observable on electrode C3 and C4 situated on the motor cortex of the brain. Electrodes on the contralateral side are responsible for capturing ERD whereas that on ipsilateral for ERS. Thus, C3 and C4 electrodes can collect ERD from μ band and ERS in the β band of the signal and hence the motor-related variability. Based on performance, signals only from channel C4 are considered for further processing. Applying wavelet transform (WT) to the signals from the selected electrode with a specific wavelet and extracting statistical (mean, variance, and standard deviation), as well as higher-order statistical (HoS) features (skewness and kurtosis) from the band of interest, is covered under feature extraction. Wave energy is one more feature extracted from wavelet bands of interest. This procedure of limiting the electrodes as well as limiting the features is considered a feature optimization as it reduces the complexity of the classifiers, enhancing the classification accuracy.

5.5 RESULTS

The extracted and optimized features are used for training and testing of the following supervised classifiers with different kernel functions. Classification accuracy (CA) is used as the performance indicator.

The support vector machine (SVM) classifier with linear and nonlinear kernel functions are used for mapping the data of much higher dimensionality. The kernels used are linear, Gaussian (RBF), quadratic, and cubic kernel. The wavelet coefficients extracted by applying selected wavelet functions are used for feature formations. The statistical and HoS features along with wavelet band energy used for training the classifier. The classifier is trained using five fold cross-validation; thus, along with training, effective testing of the classifier model takes place, helping in estimating the performance of the classifier model. A medium Gaussian kernel of SVM when applied to the features extracted by wavelet "*bior3.1*" gives the maximum task classification accuracy of 81.4% compared to other kernel functions as shown in Figure 5.9. The scatter plot in Figure 5.9 gives the idea of separable and overlapping features. From the positive predictive rate and false discovery rate (FDR) given in Figure 5.10, it can be concluded that the second motor movement or right-foot movement (RFM) is having a

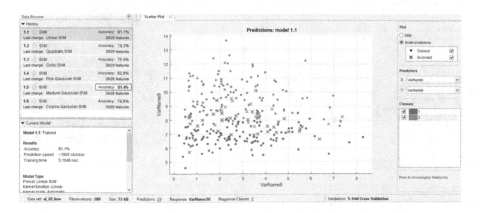

FIGURE 5.9   Scatter plot indicating the separable and overlap wavelet features.

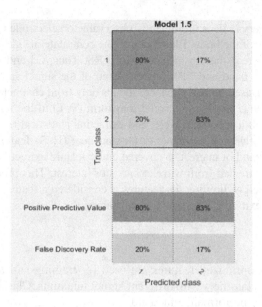

FIGURE 5.10 True positive value and false discovery rate for medium Gaussian SVM.

false discovery rate (FDR) of 16% which is less than the FDR for left-hand movement (LHM) which is 21%.

The next classifier evaluated in this work is k-NN, The k-NN, with variation in the number of neighbors and variations in distance measures like cosine, cubic, medium-fine, is used for training the model. Obtained maximum classification accuracy during training with five-fold cross-validation is 78.2%, FDR is 14% for RFM, and 27% for LHM as shown in Figure 5.11.

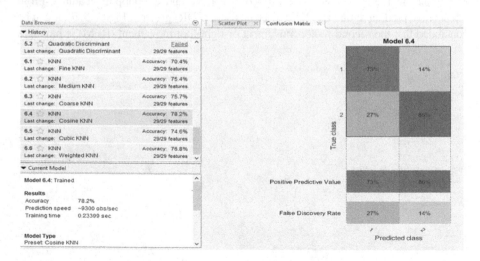

FIGURE 5.11 True positive value and false discovery rate for cosine KNN.

While evaluating the discriminant analysis, the linear discriminant analysis gives the training accuracy of 81.8%, whereas the quadratic discriminant analysis failed for this set of features as in Figure 5.12. The FDR of 17% for RFM and 19% for LHM for five-fold cross-validation is obtained as in Figure 5.13.

Testing classification accuracy is computed for five subjects available in the dataset. Table 5.3 gives a comparative analysis of CA obtained for the variation of wavelet functions and kernel functions. The evaluation of the accuracy involves variations in wavelet functions used for feature extraction and the three classifiers, mentioned earlier, with different kernel functions. Subject "*al*" leads to the maximum classification accuracy of 98.32% for wavelet *bior3.1* and SVM with Gaussian kernel function. Subject

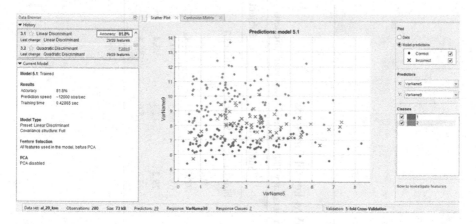

FIGURE 5.12 Scatter plot and training accuracy for discriminant analysis.

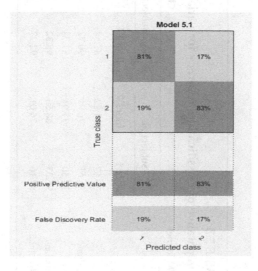

FIGURE 5.13 True positive value and false discovery rate for linear discriminant analysis.

TABLE 5.3

Comparative of classification accuracy for variation in SVM kernel functions

SVM kernel	Classification accuracy (%) for various wavelet functions									
	Subject aa		Subject al		Subject av		Subject aw		Subject ay	
	bior3.1	bior3.7	bior3.1	bior3.7	bior3.1	bior3.7	bior3.1	bior3.7	bior3.1	bior3.7
Linear	78.67	81.82	87.54	93.10	70.4	66.7	90.5	85.3	90.3	92.9
Quadratic	80.61	76.01	90.72	86.12	72.6	71.4	92.1	86.5	93.3	92.1
MLP	79.50	77.91	87.78	87.81	68.4	69.5	90.9	88.5	90.5	88.2
Gaussian	**90.33**	**88.50**	**98.32**	**97.24**	**79.2**	72.4	**93.4**	88	**94.2**	92.3
Polynomial	81.16	76.01	92.27	86.22	73.4	75.6	86.4	87.3	92.5	89.2

av leads to a minimum accuracy of 79% for SVM Gaussian kernel. Whereas, the subject *"aa"* gives task classification accuracy of 90.33% when operated by *bior3.1* for extracting the features and the Gaussian kernel function of SVM is used for classification. Whereas, the subject *"ay"* gives 94.2% classification accuracy on using *bior3.1* for decomposition and SVM for classification.

5.6 CONCLUDING REMARKS

Concluding on the results obtained in terms of classification accuracy (CA) it can be stated that the obtained task of classification accuracy depends on the effectiveness of the signal processing methods used. Signal modeling or the pre-processing method is playing a very important role, as the requirement is a source-specific signal representation, thus the domains of signal spread have to consider it. Surface laplacian have exhaustive computations; it has to be done once for calculating matrix G and H, which can be applied later on the captured signals to get a transformed signal. The task-specific features have to be extracted from the EEG signal with the time spread. This work proposes the method for matching wavelet function selection and uses the matching wavelet function for wavelet decomposition of the signal. The wavelet coefficients obtained by wavelet decomposing the signals are used to form the statistical (HoS) features: skewness, and kurtosis, along with second-order statistical features for representing the dynamics of the signal. This work tries to verify the direct relation of matching wavelet selection with the classification accuracy (CA) obtained and hence emphasize the selection of appropriate wavelet for representing the signal. Feature selection strategies work on selecting the band-specific features and the features from the channel of interest, thus, reducing the burden on the classifier. The classifier selection and tuning play a major role, supervised learning works better for non-invasive BCI as it got tuned to the task-specific variability of the particular subject. When checked for different classifiers and different kernel functions it is concluded that the SVM classifier with linear kernel and linear discriminant analysis works well for the classification.

Subject-wise variation in task classification accuracy leads to the conclusion that, similar brain activity results in similar modulations of the signal, but the depth of the modulation is varying with subjects. Training of the subject can improve the task-related modulations resulting in increased classification accuracy.

REFERENCES

1. M. Anousouya Devi, R. Sharmila, and V. Saranya, 'Hybrid brain computer interface in wheelchair using voice recognition sensors', in *2014 International Conference on Computer Communication and Informatics*, 2014, pp. 1–5, doi: 10.1109/ICCCI.2014. 6921754.
2. S. G. Mason and G. E. Birch, 'A general framework for brain – computer interface design', *IEEE Transactions on Neural Systems and Rehabilitation Engineering*, 11, 1 (2003), pp. 70–85, doi: 10.1109/TNSRE.2003.810426.
3. R. A. Miranda *et al.*, 'DARPA-funded efforts in the development of novel brain-computer interface technologies', *Journal of Neuroscience Methods*, 244 (2015), pp. 52–67, doi: 10.1016/j.jneumeth.2014.07.019.

4. B. W. A. F. J. Holsheimer, 'Volume conduction and EEG measurements within the brain: a quantitative approach to the influence of electrical spread on the linear relationship of activities measured at different locations', *Electroencephalography and Clinical Neurophysiology*, Elsevier, (1977) pp. 52–58.

5. J. R. Millán, F. Renkens, J. Mouriño, S. Member, and W. Gerstner, 'Noninvasive brain-actuated control of a mobile robot by human EEG', *IEEE Transactions on Biomedical Engineering*, 51, 6 (2004), pp. 1026–1033.

6. J. Le Roux and J. Z. Simon, 'MEG signal denoising based on time-shift PCA', in *ICASSP, IEEE Explorer*, 165, 1 (2007), pp. 317–320.

7. G. Pfurtscheller and F. H. Lopes, 'Event-related EEG/MEG synchronization and desynchronization: basic principles', *Clinical Neurophysiology*, 110 (1999), pp. 1842–1857, doi: 10.1016/S1388-2457(99)00141-8.

8. L. Grosenick, B. Klingenberg, K. Katovich, B. Knutson, and J. E. Taylor, 'Interpretable whole-brain prediction analysis with GraphNet', *Neuroimage*, 72, 2 (2013), pp. 304–321, doi: 10.1016/j.neuroimage.2012.12.062.

9. U. Chaudhary, N. Birbaumer, and A. Ramos-Murguialday, 'Brain-computer interfaces for communication and rehabilitation', *Nature Reviews Neurology*, 12, 9 (2016), pp. 513–525, doi: 10.1038/nrneurol.2016.113.

10. A. Bablani, D. R. Edla, D. Tripathi, and R. Cheruku, 'Survey on brain-computer interface', *Association for Computing Machinery*, 52, 1 (2019), pp. 1–32, doi: 10.1145/3297713.

11. P. Brunner, A. L. Ritaccio, J. F. Emrich, H. Bischof, and G. Schalk, 'Rapid communication with a "P300" matrix speller using electrocorticographic signals (ECoG)', *Frontiers in Neuroscience*, 5, 2011, p. 5, doi: 10.3389/fnins.2011.00005.

12. R. J. Huster, Z. N. Mokom, S. Enriquez-Geppert, and C. S. Herrmann, 'Brain-computer interfaces for EEG neurofeedback: peculiarities and solutions', *International Journal of Psychophysiology.*, 91, 1 (2014), pp. 36–45, doi: 10.1016/j.ijpsycho.2013.08.011.

13. N. Yamawaki, C. Wilke, Z. Liu, and B. He, 'An enhanced time-frequency-spatial approach for motor imagery classification', *IEEE Transactions on Neural Systems and Rehabilitation Engineering*, 14, 2 (2006), pp. 250–255.

14. B. Fabio, 'Brain computer interfaces for communication and control', *Frontiers in Neuroscience*, 4 (2010), pp. 767–791, 1900, doi: 10.3389/conf.fnins.2010.05.00007.

15. M. Nakanishi, Y. Wang, Y. Te Wang, and T. P. Jung, 'A comparison study of canonical correlation analysis based methods for detecting steady-state visual evoked potentials', *PLoS One*, 10, 10 (2015), pp. 1–18, doi: 10.1371/journal.pone.0140703.

16. H. Lu, H. L. Eng, C. Guan, K. N. Plataniotis, and A. N. Venetsanopoulos, 'Regularized common spatial pattern with aggregation for EEG Classification in small-sample setting', *IEEE Transactions on Biomedical Engineering*, 57, 12 (2010), pp. 2936–2946, doi: 10.1109/TBME.2010.2082540.

17. Ran Xiao and Lei Ding, 'Evaluation of EEG features in decoding individual finger movements from one hand', *Computational and Mathematical Methods in Medicine*, 2013 (2013), doi: 10.1155/2013/243257.

18. J. R. Wolpaw and D. J. Mcfarland, 'Control of a two-dimensional movement signal by a noninvasive brain–computer interface in humans', *PNAS*, 101, 51 (2004), pp. 17849–17854.

19. E. a. Carlo, A. Porro, Maria Pia Francescato, 'Primary motor and sensory cortex activation during motor performance and motor imagery: a functional magnetic resonance imaging study', *Journal of Neuroscience*, 16, 23 (1996), pp. 7688–7698.

20. E. Gerardin *et. al.*, Lehéricy, 'Partially overlapping neural networks for real and imagined hand movements', *Cerebral Cortex*, 10, 11 (2000), pp. 1093–1104.

21. Christa Neuper and Gert Pfurtscheller, 'Event-related dynamics of cortical rhythms: frequency-specific features and functional correlates', *International Journal of Psychophysiology*, 43, 1 (2001), pp. 41–58.

22. John Karat and Jean Vanderdonckt, *Human-Computer Interaction Series*, vol. 10, 978-1. Springer International Publishing, Cham, 2009.

23. I. Lazarou, S. Nikolopoulos, and P. C. Petrantonakis, 'EEG-based brain – computer interfaces for communication and rehabilitation of people with motor impairment: a novel approach of the 21st century', *Frontiers in Human Neuroscience*, 12, (2018), pp. 1–18, doi: 10.3389/fnhum.2018.00014.

24. K. K. Ang *et al.*, 'Facilitating effects of transcranial direct current stimulation on motor imagery brain-computer interface with robotic feedback for stroke rehabilitation', *Archieves of Physical Medicine and Rehabilitation*, 96, 3 (2015), pp. S79–S87. doi: 10. 1016/j.apmr.2014.08.008.

25. Claudio Carvalhaes and J. Acacio de Barros, 'The surface Laplacian technique in EEG: theory and methods', *International Journal of Psychophysiology*, 97, 3, (2015), pp. 174–188.

26. J. Kayser and Craig E. Tenke, 'On the benefits of using surface Laplacian (current source density) methodology in electrophysiology', *International Journal of Psychophysiology*, 97, 3, (2015), 171, doi: 10.1016/j.ijpsycho.2015.06.001.

27. C. G. Carvalhaes, R. De Janeiro, and P. Suppes, 'A spline framework for estimating the EEG surface laplacian using the euclidean metric', *Neural Computing 23*, (2011), pp. 2974–3000.

28. Grace Wahaba, 'spherical_spline_wahaba.pdf', *SIAM Journal on Scientific and Statistical Computing*, 2, 1 (1981), pp. 5–16.

29. J. Kayser and C. E. Tenke, 'Issues and considerations for using the scalp surface Laplacian in EEG/ERP research: A tutorial review', *International Journal of Psychophysiology*, 97, 3 (2015), pp. 189–209, 2015, doi: 10.1016/j.ijpsycho.2015. 04.012.

30. F. Perrin *et al.*, 'Spherical splines for scalp potential and current density mapping', *Electroencephalography and Clinical Neurophysiology*, (1989), pp. 184–187.

31. T. Wang, J. Deng, and B. He, 'Classifying EEG-based motor imagery tasks by means of time – frequency synthesized spatial patterns', *Clinical Neurophysiology*, 115 (2004), pp. 2744–2753. doi: 10.1016/j.clinph.2004.06.022.

32. U. Salomon David, Department of Computer Science, California State University, Northridge, *Data Compression-The Complete Reference,* third ed. Springer, (1998).

33. S. Mallat, *A Wavelet Tour of Signal Processing-The Sparse Way*, Elsevier. 2009.

34. A. Subasi, 'EEG signal classification using wavelet feature extraction and a mixture of expert model', *Expert Systems with Applications at ScienceDirect*, 32 (2007), pp. 1084–1093, doi: 10.1016/j.eswa.2006.02.005.

35. H. Ullah, A. Aamir, S. Malik, and R. Fayyaz, 'Feature extraction and classification for EEG signals using wavelet transform and machine learning techniques', *Australasian Physical & Engineering Sciences in Medicine*, Springer, (2015), doi: 10.1007/s13246-015-0333-x.

36. M. S. Manikandan and S. Dandapat, 'Wavelet energy based diagnostic distortion measure for ECG', *Bi Comed Signal Processing*, 2, (2007), pp. 80–96, 2007, doi: 10. 1016/j.bspc.2007.05.001.

37. M. S. Sur and S. Dandapat, 'Wavelet-based electrocardiogram signal compression methods and their performances: A prospective review', *Biomedical Signal Processing and Control*, 14, (2014), pp. 73–107, doi: 10.1016/j.bspc.2014.07.002.

38. S. Rajankar and R. Bhanushali, 'A wavelet-based progressive ECG compression using modified SPIHT', *International Journal of Biomedical Engineering and Technology*, 22, 3 (2016), pp. 216–232.

39. D. M. Aleksandra, Mojsilovic, Rackov, 'On the selection of an optimal wavelet basis for texture characterization', *IEEE Transactions on Image Processing*, 9, 12 (2000), pp. 2043–2050.

40. M. Akbari, H. Homaei, and M. Heidari, 'An intelligent fault diagnosis approach for gears and bearings based on wavelet transform as a preprocessor and artificial', *International Journal of Computer Mathematics*, 04, 04 (2014), pp. 309–329.
41. M. S. L. W. K. Ngui, 'Wavelet analysis: mother wavelet selection methods', *Applied Mechanics and Materials*, 393, (2013), pp. 953–958. doi: 10.4028/www.scientific.net/AMM.393.953.
42. H. He, Y. Tan, and Y. Wang, 'Optimal base wavelet selection for ECG noise reduction using a comprehensive entropy criterion', *Entropy*, 17, 9 (2015), pp. 6093–6109. doi: 10.3390/e17096093.
43. R. R. Coifman and M. V. Wickerhauser, 'Entropy-based algorithms for best basis selection', *IEEE Transactions on Information Theory*, 38, 2 (1992), pp. 713–718.
44. P. Xu, X. Hu, and D. Yao, 'Improved wavelet entropy calculation with window functions and its preliminary application to study intracranial pressure', *Computers in Biology and Medicine*, 43, 5 (2013), pp. 425–433. doi: 10.1016/j.compbiomed.2013.01.022.
45. O. A. Rosso *et al.*, 'Wavelet entropy: a new tool for analysis of short duration brain electrical signals', *Journal of Neuroscience Methods*, 105 (2001), pp. 65–75.
46. Osvaldo A. Rosso a, Susana Blanco *et al.*, 'Wavelet entropy: A new tool for analysis of short duration brain electrical signals', *Journal of Neuroscience Methods*, 105, 1 (2001), pp. 65–75. doi: 10.1016/S0165-0270(00)00356-3.
47. Y. Kutlu and D. Kuntalp, 'Feature extraction for ECG heartbeats using higher order statistics of WPD coefficients', *Computer Methods and Programs in Biomedicine*, 105, 3 (2011), pp. 257–267, doi: 10.1016/j.cmpb.2011.10.002.
48. Jerry M. Mendel, Tutorial on higher-order statistics (spectra) in signal processing and system theory: Theoretical results and some applications, *Proceedings of the IEEE*, 79, 3 (1991), pp. 278–305.
49. K. Aswinseshadri and V. T. Bai, 'Feature selection in brain computer interface using genetics method', in *IEEE International Conference on Computer and Information Technology*, (2015), pp. 270–275, doi: 10.1109/CIT/IUCC/DASC/PICOM.2015.39.
50. Y. Yong and N. Hurley, 'Single-trial EEG classification for brain-computer interface using wavelet decomposition', *IEEE Signal Process. Conf. 2013*, Antalya, Turkey, 2005, http://signal.ee.bilkent.edu.tr/defevent/papers/cr1164.pdf.
51. K. Zeng, K. She, and X. Niu, 'Feature selection with neighborhood entropy-based cooperative game theory', *Computational Intelligence and Neuroscience*, 2014 (2014). doi: 10.1155/2014/479289.
52. J. Vitola, F. Pozo, D. A. Tibaduiza, and M. Anaya, 'A sensor data fusion system based on k-nearest neighbor pattern classification for structural health monitoring applications', *Sensors (Switzerland)*, 17, 2 (2017), 412. doi: 10.3390/s17020417.
53. S. Dhanabal and S. Chandramathi, 'A review of various k-nearest neighbor query processing techniques', *International Journal of Computer Applications in Technology*, 31, 7 (2011), pp. 14–22.
54. S. R. Gunn, 'Support vector machines for classification and regression', (1998).
55. G. F. Amal Feltane, 'Automatic seizure detection in rats using laplacian eeg and verification with human seizure signals', *Annals of Biomedical Engineering*, 41, 3 (2014), pp. 645–654, doi: 10.1007/s10439-012-0675-4.Automatic.
56. K. Liao, R. Xiao, J. Gonzalez, and L. Ding, 'Decoding individual finger movements from one hand using human EEG signals', *PLoS One*, 9, 1 (2014), pp. 1–12, doi: 10.1371/journal.pone.0085192.
57. P. E. H. T. M. Cover, 'Nearest neighbor pattern classification', *IEEE Transactions on Information Theory*, 13, 1 (1967), pp. 22–27, doi: 10.1109/TIT.1967.1053945.
58. B. Blankertz *et al.*, 'The BCI competition III: validating alternative approaches to actual BCI Problems', *IEEE Transactions on Neural Systems and Rehabilitation Engineering*, 14, 2 (2006), pp. 153–159.

59. J. Kayser, *Current Source Density (CSD) Interpolation Using Spherical Splines – CSD Toolbox* (Version 1.1). http://psychophysiology.cpmc.columbia.edu/Software/CSDtoolbox. New York State Psychiatric Institute: Division of Cognitive Neuroscience, 2009.
60. C. E. Tenke, 'Principal components analysis of Laplacian waveforms as a generic method for identifying ERP generator patterns: I. Evaluation with auditory oddball tasks', *Clinical Neurophysiology*, 117, (2006), pp. 348–368, doi: 10.1016/j.clinph.2005.08.034.
61. J. Kayser and C. E. Tenke, 'Principal components analysis of Laplacian waveforms as a generic method for identifying ERP generator patterns: II. Adequacy of low-density estimates', *Clinical Neurophysiology*, 117, 2 (2006), pp. 369–380, doi: 10.1016/j.clinph.2005.08.033.

6 Study and Analysis of the Visual P300 Speller on Neurotypical Subjects

Mridu Sahu, Vyom Raj, Shreya Sharma, and Samrudhi Mohdiwale

6.1 INTRODUCTION

Brain computer interfaces (BCI) are modern day devices that bring the power of computation to a wide range of physical world activities, finding scope and implementation in both mundane tasks and medical equipments. The basic idea behind BCIs is the application of machine learning to manipulate and/or affect a person's activities. Some BCI devices may even be limited to just analyzing human activities rather than manipulating them to achieve a predetermined outcome [1,2]. P300 spellers are essential parts of a plethora of BCIs in the medical arena. They provide an efficient way to communicate by spelling words using the letters displayed on a digital alphabet matrix. The idea behind the P300 speller can be explained in layman's terms as follows: rows and columns of the alphabet matrix are flashed sequentially and/or randomly and the user is trained to focus on the row and column being flashed while it contains the desired letter. Event-related potential (ERP) is evoked when the user successfully focuses on the row/column containing the desired letter. In the electroencephalography (EEG) recording of a user participating in P300 spelling, the ERP values can be clearly distinguished. P300 spellers are generally embedded in the BCIs of patients that have some difficulty in normal communication, which may have arose due to a variety of reasons, for example, amyotrophic lateral sclerosis disease. But the effective use of P300 spellers with normal or neurotypical (a brain with no mental anomalies) people also needs to be evaluated [3]. It can come in handy with new silent devices that can extract commands through embedded P300 spellers working with the person's eye movement. Hence, in this work we have taken the task of analyzing the EEG dataset of a visual P300 speller along these lines.

The dataset has been taken from BNCI horizon. It was obtained by evaluating a P300 speller by eight neurotypical subjects, each attempting to spell a word after five minutes of training [3]. The theme of our work revolves around analyzing the dataset obtained from the aforementioned experiment and applying the techniques of data mining and machine learning for identifying useful patterns, characteristics, etc. The broad sequence of steps featured are extraction followed by selection and, ultimately, classification. The approaches are twofold, covering both the manual and semi-automated aspects of the above-mentioned facets. The analysis of this kind is specifically useful in outlining recurrent patterns in various subjects while attempting to do the same task. It is also fruitful in getting a blueprint pattern of EEG signals for a particular kind of activity being performed. Most importantly, our analysis attempts to capitalize on the classification accuracy by intelligent feature extractions and selections. Classification accuracy plays the zenith role in developing any BCI, as the higher the accuracy the greater the efficiency of the given BCI will be. This work explores the ways of maximizing classification accuracy by machine learning.

6.1.1 Goals and Objectives

The underlying objective of this work is to use the EEG dataset obtained from the visual P300 speller for useful classification and description. This aims for the development and deployment of such machine learning and data mining techniques that can deliver results with high integrity and reliability, so that they can be useful for future BCI devices that are finding a place in day-to-day activities of normal people where the need for verbal communication can be eliminated.

Sequential milestone goals were set for the work comprising of two main parts – 1) Manual methods of feature extraction, feature selection, and classification in MATLAB®. 2) Semi-automated methods of feature extraction, feature selection and classification in Rstudio. While both these phases could be executed separately as they are independent of each other, the end results of these phases were needed side by side for matters of comparison. The primary goal was to increase the classification accuracy obtained by both the methods through the alteration of features selected, principle components, etc.

The underlying sections deal with each facet of our work in detail. First and foremost, the literature review that acted as a cue for the course of our work is discussed. Then we move on to discuss the dataset in consideration in Section 3. The basics as well as the details of EEG, BCIs and data mining, and machine learning have been explained in subsequent Sections 4, 5, and 6. The theoretical concepts and the foundations of feature extraction and selection are discussed in Sections 7 and 8. Model fitting with special reference to the support vector machine (SVM) are discussed in Section 9. We have paid special attention to SVM, as it was the basis of the second phase of our work involving semi-automated processes of feature extraction, feature selection, and classification. In Section 10, our focus is shifted to the manual part of the process wherein SPTool in MATLAB® plays a major role. Section 11 discusses and acknowledges the EEG analysis package of Rstudio that played a vital role in the semi-automated part of our work, providing the essential functions of SVM for step wise classification. Finally in Section 12, the overall methodology and the chronological order of the execution and completion of various phases of the work are discussed. This section has been further divided into two important subsections – manual approach and semi-automated approach – both elucidating in detail the two phases of execution. Section 14 deals with the outcome of the proposed methodology, or simply put, the result and analysis part.

This section has again been divided conveniently into three subsections: the first part discusses the results of manual classification; the second discusses the results of semi-automated classification, and, ultimately, the last part compares both these results and inclines a favor towards the better performer. Future scope of our work follows as the aftermath.

6.2   LITERATURE REVIEW

The literature review that we carried prior to the actual advent of our paper helped shape the contours of our paper significantly. A flow of all the relevant literature of our paper is an essential part of its documentation. In Paper [4], the potential of using EEG signals for controlling humanoid robots is discussed. It delves into the potential that EEG manipulation through classification can have on controlling BCI devices. Paper [5] takes the concept of EEG-based BCI devices further, working to improve the adaptation of BCI to different subjects without inducing a separate training for each user that generally accounts for a long period of time during calibration training. In [6], authors demonstrate the power of EEG dataset manipulation. The EEG dataset has been tested through 42 different machine learning algorithms to find the most suitable one for the future prediction of eye state, classification of the testing dataset, based on the classification model that has been formed on the training dataset. Paper [7] deals with the feature extraction from an EEG-based BCI device through the application of continuous wavelet transform on event related potential. This method has the advantage of fully automated detection and quantification of event-related potentials. Paper [8] provides a detailed summary of the BCI developed in Aalborg University. This device is of great interest, as it elucidates the way in which a synchronized BCI system can be developed using steady state potentials. Paper [9] discusses yet another successful implementation of an EEG-based BCI for prosthetic arm control. The real-time analyzes of oscillatory EEG components during right- and left-hand movement imagination allows the control of an electronic device. Paper [10] deals with another way of controlling BCI devices, through motor imagery data. But it is proved that EEG classification offers a more efficient route. Paper [11] discusses a BCI coupled with a P300 speller for helping the spelling system of locked in patients. P300 is an addition to the manipulation advantages of EEG wherein the Event Related Potentials are used to control a P300 speller matrix and act as a substitute for verbal communication. Paper [12] deals with the improvements that can be made in P300 spellers. The authors support the single character paradigm of P300 speller as there are more infrequent instances in this paradigm that cause higher evoked potentials. Paper [13] takes the concept of the P300 speller matrix one step further and demonstrates the control of a 2-D cursor with the help of P300 evoked potential.

 Paper [14] evaluates the effects of some seemingly miscellaneous factors on the event related potential of a P300-based BCI. The effects of matrix size and inter-stimulus intervals on performance has been discussed in detail. The authors in [15] underscore the advantage of having a mobile EEG system instead of a traditional amplifier. The authors compared their mobile 14-channel EEG system with a state-of-the-art wired laboratory EEG system in a popular BCI application. N = 13 individuals repeatedly performed a 6x6 matrix P300 spelling task. Results revealed that the wireless EEG machine was as good as the traditional one and established the importance of the added advantage of a portable EEG recording device. In [16] the authors propose an improvement on the traditional P300 speller by limiting the number of choices to make it more suitable for people with disabilities. A four choice system of commands using yes, no, pass, and end has been implemented. The manual feature extraction and classification techniques in our paper found their ground in the literature we reviewed with respect to various classifiers and some extraction tools in MATLAB®. In their work [17], the authors explore one of the simplest classifiers, the Bayesian network classifiers in Weka. Weka is a machine learning that comes with the ability to perform various kinds of classification ranging from Naive Bayes to decision trees, K star, and more. The authors provide a detailed overview of the use of Bayesian classifiers in Weka and various techniques of getting the most out of these classifiers. In [18], wavelet transformations have been taken into account during manual classification. A combination of wavelet feature extraction has been applied along with expert model for EEG signal classification. Further in paper [19], various feature selection methods have been compared for EEG signal classification. The paper produces very interesting results that show there is very little increase in accuracy when one makes a shift from linear discriminant classifiers to nonlinear classifiers like support vector machines and neural networks. This gives a clear cue that nonlinear classifiers are not a good trade off when manual feature extraction and selection takes place. Paper [20] is yet another paper that reviews various classification algorithms with special reference to the ones suitable for brain computer interfaces. The paper has compared linear classifiers, neural networks, nonlinear Bayesian classifiers, nearest neighbor classifiers, and combinations of classifiers, and reached the overt conclusion that in case of synchronous BCI, an SVM classifier provides the best accuracy. In paper [21], we again revisit the concept of wavelet transformation while classifying EEG signals. The paper uses a novel technique of combining artificial neural network with wavelet transformation to increase classification accuracy. Wavelet transformation has been applied as kind of a preprocessing step. The EEG signals, before being fed into the triple-layered feedforward neural network, undergo wavelet transformation and the results show that this drastically increases classification accuracy. Paper [1] deals with a relatively new domain of affect recognition and explores the classification algorithms best suited for the same. The authors use three classification algorithms to distinguish between ten emotions in the subjects and positive and promising results have been obtained. In [22], a conglomeration of R language and Weka has been discussed as these are the two significant machine learning environments available today. They suggest an aggregate environment RWeka that interfaces Weka's functionality to R.

In paper [23], attempts have been made to study the similarities with which people with disabilities and people without disabilities control a BCI device. They have established that both categories of people control the mu and beta rhythms in the exact same manner and hence research part on how do normal people control some BCI task, say moving a mouse cursor on screen, can be applied to the disabled patients as well. Paper [2] discusses multichannel EEG and the ways of optimizing channel selection to enhance classification accuracy in such channels. They propose a sparse common spatial pattern algorithm for achieving the same. In [24], the ERP components which influence the oddball paradigm the most have been mined. They comprise of N1, P2, N2, P300 and late positive complex. Then wavelet transformation has been applied to decompose these signals into a time-frequency plane. In Paper [25], our focus is shifted to a different classification tool, the SPTool in MATLAB®. In this work, the authors have discussed electromyography (EMG) signals, generated by muscles in a 5 neuromuscular disease and SPTool has been applied for the successful classification of these signals. In paper [26], a new classification technique has been proposed for the classification of EEG signals. A clustering technique based least square support vector machine has been used. The process has two stages, in the first stage the clustering techniques are used for feature extraction and selection and in the second phase least square support vector machine is used to classify the extracted features into two class labels. In paper [27], SVM has been coupled with the Gaussian kernel to see the combined effects. It has been demonstrated that the SVM shows asymptotic behavior in the presence of very large or very small hyper parameters. In paper [28], feature selection algorithms – recursive feature elimination and zero-norm optimization – have been used that are based on SVM. In [29], the problem of classifying EEG related to some responses on visual stimuli has been discussed. To cope with such variability, an ensemble of classifiers approach has been proposed. Paper [30] deals with emotion recognition in BCI devices through EEG signals. Hierarchical binary classifiers have been found to give the best results for the same. Paper [31] deals with the classification of EEG signal with principal component analysis (PCA), independent component analysis (ICA), linear discriminant analysis (LDA), and SVM. The methods PCA, ICA, and LDA were used to reduce dimensionality of data and finally SVM was applied.

The authors in [32] explore the fuzzy support vector machine for EEG classification. It has been found that the fuzzy machine is specifically useful in noisy EEG or the one which has many missing values. In paper [33], SVM has been used in combination with the Fourier and time-frequency correlational domains. The overall approach has been used to classify motor imagery data and gives promising results. In paper [34], SVM has been compared with the other conventional classification schemes and established that SVM yields better results in faster time, requiring only 10 electrodes data and very small amount of pre-processing. In [35], multiclass SVM has been proposed with error correcting output codes. Feature extraction was done using wavelet components and Lyapunov exponents. It was established that wavelet coefficients and Lyapunov exponents expressed the extracted features very well, and combined with multiclass SVM they gave high accuracy for classification. Various machine learning and optimization techniques are also used by researchers to improve the performance of EEG signal classification and prediction for various approaches [36,37,38,39,40,41,42].

6.3   DATASET DESCRIPTION

The EEG dataset of eight subjects using a visual P300 speller has been taken from the BNCI Horizon online. The dataset contains the EEG recordings of all the subjects performing a visual task of spelling. The visual P300 speller used two paradigms: the row-column (RC) and the single character (SC). In the row column paradigm, one row or one column is flashed at one time. In the single character paradigm, every cell in the P300 speller or one character is flashed at one time. Channels 1 to 9 are the EEG channels, channel 10 contains the flash ID, that is the number of row or columns actually flashing, and channel number 11 contains the target information. It is set to 1 if a target row or column flashes and 0 if a nontarget is flashing. P300-based BCI systems are optimal for spelling characters with high speed and accuracy, as compared to other BCI paradigms such as motor imagery. The details of the experiment are provided in [3].

6.4   ELECTROENCEPHALOGRAPHY

Electroencephalography (EEG) refers to the brain signals and their significance. The EEG signals represent the electrical cortical activity of the brain. It directly measures the voltage fluctuations that arise due to ionic current flows in the neurons of the brain. The signal intensity of EEG activity is quite small, often of the order of a few microvolts, which often makes it difficult to correctly measure the exact values and draw relevant conclusions. A routine clinical EEG recording typically lasts 20–30 minutes (plus preparation time) and usually involves recording from scalp electrodes [43]. Routine EEG is typically used in the following clinical circumstances:

- Helps in distinguishing between epileptic seizures from other types of effects such as nonepileptic seizures or fainting.
- To monitor the brain as well as measure the cognitive activities of a person in coma.
- Serves as an additional test of brain death.
- Helps in monitoring sub-cortical movement disorders as well as different types of migraine.

Brainwaves are classified according to their frequencies and have been labelled under five different categories according to the division of bandwidth [44,45]. These are described herewith:

- Infra low waves (frequency range less than 0.5 Hz). They are the basic rhythms that underlie all our brain functions. They have not been studied deeply because of their low frequency which makes them difficult to detect.
- Delta waves (frequency range 0.5–3 Hz). They are low frequency and highly penetrating waves that are observed during deep meditation and dreamless sleeps. Healing and regeneration are stimulated in this state.
- Theta waves (frequency range 3–8 Hz). They are the semi-awake state waves and the times of drifting to sleep or getting awake.
- Alpha waves (frequency range 8–12 Hz). They regulate over-all mental co-ordination, calmness, and alertness. They basically determine the relaxed attentive states.

- Beta waves (frequency range 12–38 Hz). They dominate our nor-mal waking state of consciousness. They direct attentiveness towards cognitive works and the outer world.

6.4.1 EVENT RELATED POTENTIAL

Event-related potential (ERP) is the measured activity of a brain response which is a direct response to a motor event, sensory event, or a sort of cognitive event. More formally, ERP is any common electrophysiological response induced by the brain in response to a stimulus. The ERP study provides a noninvasive or nonsurgical means of monitoring the brain activities of a person suffering from some cognitive disease. They are measured using electroencephalography. Event-related potential uses a simple average technique which is more robust in measuring motor, cognitive or sensory events and therefore is more sophisti-cated. Event-related potentials can be reliably measured using EEG, a procedure that measures electrical activity of the brain over time using electrodes placed on the scalp. The EEG reflects thousands of simultaneous brain processes, and, therefore, the brain's response to a single quantified event is not visible in an EEG recording of a single trial [7,24]. To monitor the brain's response to a particular stimulus we must conduct a number of trials that have to be averaged in order to remove the random waveforms and the remaining waveform can be termed as ERP. The ERP constitutes noises which are bio-signals such as electro oculography (EOG), EMG, and electrocardiography (EKG) that are completely irrelevant to ERP, and, therefore, we can also define the signal to noise ratio (SNR) of an ERP. The reason for the choice of averaging is to increase SNR [46].

6.5 P300 SPELLER

It has been seen that the P300 ERP, generated by the EEG of external stimuli, can be useful to distinguish the target stimuli. In the past, P300 was widely used for lie detection and has been legalized for its wide applications. The signal P300 is measured by the use of electrodes that are placed in the parietal lobe of the brain. Since the beginning of researching P300, it was discovered that P300 has two subcomponents: P3a and the classic P3b.The P3a has a peak latency of 250–280 ms and is associated with attention as well as involuntary shifts to changes in the environment. While the P3b has a peak latency between 250–500 ms and is related to cognitive processes, such as psychology research and how demanding a task is for cognitive workload [11]. The effect of the P300 speller on neurotypical or normal subjects opens a plethora of opportunities for improvements in modern day BCI devices. In the dataset we used, high accuracy has been obtained when the patients used the P300 speller to spell a word after just five minutes of training. This paves the way for more rigorous training and using the P300 speller in a wide range devices, where the need of verbal communication can be eliminated [16].

6.6 MANUAL FEATURE EXTRACTION

SPTool is a digital signal processing tool in MATLAB®. The command, sptool, opens SPTool that includes a suite of four tools: Signal Browser, Filter Design and Analysis Tool, FVTool, and Spectrum Viewer. This tool can be used in the following work:

- Analysis of signals
- Filtering of signals
- Create and analyze signal spectra with the spectrum viewer
- Print the results of signal processing

The signal browser forms the main part of SPTool and is referred to as the scope. It is basically concerned with the time domain analysis of the signals. SPTool provides a wide range of measurement panels; details can be found in the MATLAB® description.

6.7 CLASSIFICATION TECHNIQUES

There are different types of classifiers present that can be used for classification as per the dataset. There are probability based classifiers such as Bayes and Naïve Bayes, lazy classifiers, meta classifiers, and rule-based classifiers. Weka tools provide many inbuilt classifiers for the analysis of data. This tool has been used in the current work to analyze the features used for classification. In the current work, features are classified using the attribute selected classifier, Bayes, Naïve Bayes, Bayesian logistics, classification regression, decorate, discriminative multinominal Naive Bayes (DMNB), hyper pipes, IB1, JRip, Lazy.kstar, Lazy.LWL, LazyKstar, Logistic Function, Logit Boost, Meta.AdaBoostM1, Meta Bagging, Multi Boost, Multi Scheme, Naïve Bayes, and sequential minimal optimization(SMO). These are used in the manual approach of classification. Further in the study, an SVM was used for classification in an automated approach [22,47].

6.8 MODEL FITTING (SUPPORT VECTOR MACHINE)

The SVMs are one of the popular classifiers that take care of a binary characterization issue via looking through a decision boundary that has the maximum margin. The SVMs handle complex choice limits by utilizing complex decision boundaries in a high dimensional space. In this work, linear SVM is considered, because they are known to be well suited to the datasets that we consider, and they offer a clear biological interpretation of the results [48].

6.9 PROPOSED METHODOLOGY

The basic idea behind our work lies in the arena of classification. For finding the best suited classification techniques we have chosen both a manual approach and a semi-automated approach. The reasons for adopting both measures lies in the probability that both of the given measures can prove to be useful for our given dataset. For this reason, we explore both these techniques in detail further. Feature extraction, feature selection, and classification form the three main key points of both the procedures. In our chosen dataset, it is very important to extract and choose features efficiently, because raw EEG dataset is very humungous and random to handle. For this reason, feature extraction becomes absolutely vital in the process. As the dataset is large, naturally the amount of features that can be extracted are very large. For this reason, feature selection, in such a way that only the nontrivial features impacting our dataset greatly are chosen, is essential. Finally classification comes as the backbone of most data mining tasks, because it gives a measure of how well we have extracted and chosen features for our dataset and how far our usage model is able to imbibe the given dataset.

6.9.1 MANUAL APPROACH

The manual approach of our work is executed in three parts as discussed earlier: feature extraction, feature selection, and classification. All three parts in the manual approach have been executed separately and manually to a certain extent the figure is represented as Figure 6.1. In this subsection, we discuss our manual approach intricately in a step by step manner:

6.9.1.1 Feature Extraction

It is carried out extensively in the SPTool arena of MATLAB® software. The dataset is segmented before the feature extraction. This is done because the SPTool cannot process more than 10,000 instances (approximately) at a time and in our dataset, each subject has at least 45,000 data points. Therefore, segmentation of data is carried out and followed by feature extraction.

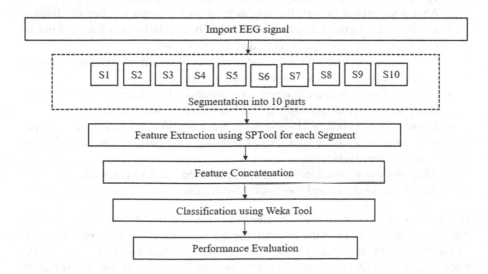

FIGURE 6.1 Manual approach.

6.9.1.2   Feature Selection

After the features have been extracted from our dataset, a large feature set is made that has many features. All these features are not necessarily useful for our purpose of classification as many of them might not have much measureable impact on the visual P300 ERP potentials and many others might be redundant among themselves. Hence, in this step of feature selection we manually select nine features that we deem exhaustive and appropriate for our dataset.

6.9.1.3   Classification

This is the last phase of the manual approach. The data obtained after the feature selection is fed into the Weka machine learning tool and various classification algorithms are applied on it to gauge the highest possible classification accuracy. After the completion of these three steps, the segmented results obtained from the classification part (due to initial partition) are grouped together subject-wise to give a coherent picture of each subject's data classification results. This marks the end of the manual approach, and the results obtained from it are kept aside for further scrutiny and comparison with the semi-automated approach.

6.9.2   SEMI-AUTOMATED APPROACH

The semi-automated approach of our work is again composed of three parts as discussed earlier: feature extraction, feature selection, and classification, as shown in Figure 6.2. All three parts in the semi-automated approach are sort of executed together. This is because the support vector machine of Rstudio used in this part offers all three steps wrapped up in one module of SVM. The work in the semi-automated approach is explained here:

1. The SVM first imports datasets from a local file location.
2. After a successful import, the user is prompted through a series of choices, almost in the form of a questionnaire that is a walkthrough for the kind of feature extraction, selection, etc., that the user wants.
3. In our approach, first we choose the measures of conditional statistics (mean, median, variance, and product) to boost our accuracy.
4. Next we also amalgamate wavelet transformations like Gaussian 1, Gaussian 2, Haar, and Morlet to increase the chances of higher accuracy even further.
5. In the final step before classification, we bring in the concept of principle component analysis and take a last milestone for pushing the classification accuracy even higher.
6. After all these instructions have been embedded, the SVM classifier classifies the data accordingly and the results are obtained.

The reasons for choosing various elements like conditional statistics, wavelet transformations, etc., lies in the concept that we have been offered semi-automated measures of SVM, so it becomes necessary from our work's point of view to explore other facets, like the ones just mentioned, in lieu of increasing classification accuracy even further. As far as principle components are concerned, it is obviously

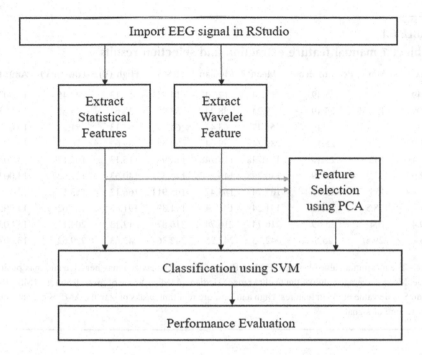

FIGURE 6.2 Semi-automated approach.

intuitive that the higher the number of principle components, the greater will be the classification accuracy; so in a way, the usage of principal components in the end was mandatory, too.

6.10 RESULT AND ANALYSIS

This section deals with the results generated in the due course of our work. The work, as discussed, use two approaches for the classification of datasets – the manual and the semi-automated. The approaches have been applied with the intent of gaining perspective on both the manual efforts for classification and the benefits of packages like that of EEG analysis that provide functions like SVM to do most of the work. In the underlying subsections, we deal with the results and analysis of both approaches one by one, and finally compare the two approaches and discuss both their advantages and disadvantages.

6.10.1 RESULTS THROUGH MANUAL APPROACH

The manual approach, as discussed in proposed methodology, has three main steps: feature extraction and feature selection through SPTool in MATLAB®, and classification of the extracted features through classifiers in the Weka machine learning tool. Table 6.1 shows the feature extraction and selection results obtained after the application of SPTool on Subject 1's dataset. In the table, we have nine selected features: max, min, peak to peak, mean, median, RMS, high (V), low

TABLE 6.1

Subject 1 manual feature extraction and selection results

Max	Min	Peak to peak	Mean	Median	RMS	High (V)	Low (mV)	Amp (V)
25.49	0	25.49	12.74	12.74	14.721	13.13	23.45	13.003
50.99	25.5	25.49	38.24	38.24	38.95	38.63	25.62	13.003
76.49	51	25.49	63.47	63.47	64.17	64.13	51.12	13.003
101.996	76.5	25.49	89.24	89.24	89.55	89.63	76.66	13.003
127.496	102	25.49	114.748	114.748	114.98	115.13	102.127	13.003
152.99	127.5	25.49	140.298	140.298	140.441	140.63	127.627	13.003
178.49	153	25.49	165.74	165.47	165.911	166.13	153.12	13.003
203.99	178.5	25.49	191.24	191.24	191.39	191.63	178.62	13.003
229.49	204	25.49	216.74	216.74	216.87	217.13	204.12	13.003
255	229.5	25.5	242.25	242.25	242.364	242.63	229.62	13.007

Max - The maximum value observed, Peak to Peak - Difference between max negative and max positive value, Mean - Average value of the feature range. Median - Median Value of given features, RMS - Root Mean Sqaure value of given features, High and Low are real time peaks of signals, AMP is the amplitude as a feature of signal

(mV), and amplitude (V). There were more features extracted by SPTool, but these are the top nine features that have been selected based on the fact that for each segment, in each subject's dataset, these features had appreciable values that could be plotted on a graph. It is an evident observation that the value of each feature increases as the segment of the dataset increases. Peak to peak and amplitude values remain constant through all runs in each segment. Table 6.2

TABLE 6.2

Subject 2 manual feature extraction and selection results

Max	Min	Peak to peak	Mean	Median	RMS	High (V)	Low (mV)	Amp (V)
25.58	0	25.58	12.791	12.791	14.77	13.17	24.87	13.04
51.1	25.5	25.58	38.37	38.37	39.08	38.76	25.71	13.04
76.75	51.17	25.58	63.96	63.96	64.38	64.34	51.3	13.01
102.34	76.75	25.58	89.54	89.54	89.58	89.99	76.88	13.047
127.92	102.34	25.58	115.13	115.13	115.371	115.518	102.4	13.04
153.51	127.93	25.58	140.721	140.721	140.91	141.1	128.05	13.04
179.09	153.51	25.58	166.3	166.3	166.471	166.69	153.64	13.04
204.64	179.1	25.58	191.8931	191.893	192.035	192.27	179.22	13.04
230.27	204.68	25.58	217.47	217.47	217.6	217.86	204.815	13.04
255.83	230.23	25.59	243.061	243.06	243.18	242.94	230.4	12.53

discusses the result of classification accuracy obtained through Weka classifiers. Here, a very interesting trend is observed, the classification accuracy obtained through LazyKstar is significantly higher than the accuracy obtained through any other classifier. Hence, it can be concluded that the LazyKstar classifier has promising model formation and usage in the case of our dataset. Overall, we observed that in the manual approach, we can get a classification accuracy of 87% with the Kstar classifier.

6.10.2 RESULTS THROUGH THE SEMI-AUTOMATED APPROACH

In this part, we analyze the results obtained through the SVM classifier. In the semi-automated approach through the SVM classifier there are three main parts: the choice of conditional statistics, the choice of wavelet transformations, and the number of principle components. In the first run of the of the SVM classifier we choose the measure of conditional statistic to be applied. Table 6.3 shows the classification results in SVM for the subject one, S1, after the application of conditional statistics. It is seen that the highest classification accuracy is obtained with nine channels and uses the variance measure of conditional statistic. There is clearly more scope for improvement so we take into account the wavelet transformations, too. It is observed that Haar, Gaussian 1, and Gaussian 2 show no significant improvement on classification accuracy. But the Morlet transformation increases the accuracy obtained from 59.65% in the previous run to 67.81% in this run. This can be seen in Table 6.5. Although some improvement has been noted, there still lies tremendous scope for increase; and, hence, we introduce the concept of the principle component analysis. Table 6.6 shows the results of Subject 1 obtained through the principle component analysis. In this final run with nine principle components, the classification accuracy has been increased to 81.92%. This is the maximum accuracy obtained through the SVM classifier in the semi-automated approach.

TABLE 6.3

Subject 3 manual feature extraction and selection results

Max	Min	Peak to peak	Mean	Median	RMS	High (V)	Low (mV)	Amp (V)
25.76	0	25.71	12.34	12.34	13.22	13.78	23.56	13.01
51.89	25.16	25.76	39.12	39.12	39.34	39.65	25.68	13.01
77.12	51.89	25.76	64.54	64.54	64.88	65.34	52.87	13.01
102.654	77.23	25.76	90.32	90.32	90.44	90.34	77.43	13.01
128.21	102.876	25.71	115.467	115.467	115.786	115.81	103.76	13.01
153.995	127.85	25.76	140.39	140.39	140.654	140.654	128.4	13.01
179.22	153.45	25.76	166.48	166.4	166.56	166.678	154.23	13.01
204.321	179.32	25.76	193.23	193.23	193.887	192.89	179.31	13.01
230.65	204.87	25.76	220.78	220.78	220.988	221	205.78	13.01
254.1	230.12	25.76	243.87	243.87	243.99	244.453	230.63	13.02

6.10.3 COMPARISON OF THE TWO TECHNIQUES

We have already discussed the results obtained from both the techniques, and it has been clearly established that the classification accuracy obtained from the manual approach is substantially higher than the one obtained from SVM. This could be the case for a variety of reasons. First, in the manual approach, we had the opportunity to hand pick features for the feature selection and this certainly led to better quality of selected features. While in SVM, we had no intervention or say, in feature selection at all. Second, in manual approach, we had the opportunity to choose from a wide range of classifiers available in Weka, while in the automated approach, the entire run was just dependent on one classifier: SVM. For these reasons, the manual approach has a better result in the end than the semi-automated approach.

The manual approach, as discussed in proposed methodology, has three main steps: feature extraction and selection through SPTool in MATLAB®, and classification of the extracted features through classifiers in the Weka machine learning tool.

Overall, we observed that in case of the manual approach, we can get a classification accuracy of 87% with the Kstar classifier using the manual feature selection. While 87% is promising accuracy, there still remains scope for improvement, and this is the reason we explore the SVM classifier in the next section. Tables 6.1 through 6.4 show the results of feature extraction and selection through the SPTool. In every table we have nine selected features: max, min, peak to peak, mean, median, rms, High (V), low (mV), and amplitude (V). There were more features extracted by SPTool, but these are the top nine features that have been selected. The selection is based on the fact that for each segment, in each subject's dataset, these features had appreciable values that could be plotted on a graph.

It is an evident observation that the value of each feature increases as the segment of the dataset increases. Peak to peak and amplitude values remain constant through all runs in each segment. Table 6.5 discusses the result of classification

TABLE 6.4
Subject 4 manual feature extraction and selection results

Max	Min	Peak to peak	Mean	Median	RMS	High (V)	Low (mV)	Amp (V)
25.34	0	25.34	12.353	12.353	12.756	13.78	25.323	13.03
52.12	25.1	25.34	39.11	39.11	39.98	39.89	25.98	13.03
78.34	51.96	25.34	64.24	64.24	64.98	65.66	52.46	13.03
102.45	78.15	25.34	90.23	90.23	90.44	91.12	78.23	13.03
129.78	103.242	25.34	115.35	115.35	115.786	116.56	104	13.03
154.74	128.43	25.34	140.24	140.24	140.654	140.887	129.67	13.03
180.48	154.31	25.39	166.31	166.35	166.56	167.77	155.35	13.03
205.35	180.12	25.34	193.976	193.976	194.09	193.887	180.345	13.03
229.42	205.428	25.34	220.435	220.435	220.76	221.89	206.34	13.03
255.98	230.11	25.34	244.435	244.435	244.88	244.25	230.44	13.03

TABLE 6.5
Manual classification results

Classifier	TP rate	FP rate	Precision	F-measure	ROC	Accuracy
Attributeselectedclassifier	0.5	0.5	0.25	0.33	0.5	50
bayesNaiveBayes	0.438	0.56	0.437	0.435	0.46	43.75
BayesianLogistics	0.56	0.438	0.76	0.45	0.56	56.25
ClassicationRegression	0.5	0.5	0.25	0.33	0.5	50
Decorate	0.56	0.438	0.76	0.45	0.78	56.25
DMNB	0.5	0.5	0.25	0.33	0.68	50
HyperPipes	0.625	0.375	0.66	0.6	0.73	62.5
IB1	0.438	0.56	0.437	0.435	0.438	43.75
JRip	0.5	0.5	0.25	0.33	0.5	50
Lazy.kstar	0.875	0.125	0.9	0.873	1	87.5
Lazy.LWL	0.625	0.375	0.63	0.61	0.625	62.5
LazyKstar	0.438	0.56	0.437	0.435	0.39	43.75
LogisticFunction	0.56	0.438	0.57	0.54	0.53	56.25
LogitBoost	0.875	0.125	0.9	0.873	0.98	87.5
Meta.AdaBoostM1	0.625	0.375	0.63	0.61	0.79	62.5
MetaBagging	0.375	0.625	0.33	0.33	0.52	37.5
MultiBoost	0.56	0.438	0.56	0.56	0.56	56.25
MultiScheme	0.5	0.5	0.25	0.33	0.5	50
NaiveBayes	0.5	0.5	0.5	0.46	0.5	50
SMO	0.438	0.56	0.42	0.41	0.438	43.75

accuracy obtained through Weka classifiers. Here a very interesting trend is observed, the classification accuracy obtained through LazyKstar is significantly higher than the accuracy obtained through any other classifier. Hence, it can be concluded that the LazyKstar classifier has promising model formation and usage in the case of our dataset.

In this part, we analyze the results obtained through the SVM classifier. In the semi-automated approach through the SVM classifier, there are three main parts: the choice of conditional statistics, the choice of wavelet transformations, and the number of principle components. In the first run of the of the SVM classifier, we choose the measure of conditional statistics to be applied. Although some improvement has been noted, there still lies tremendous scope for increase; and hence, we introduce the concept of principle component analysis.

Tables 6.6, 6.7, and 6.8 show the classification results in SVM for the Subject 1, S1; Subject 2, S2; and Subject 3, S3, respectively. It is seen that the highest classification accuracy is obtained with nine channels using the variance measure of conditional statistics. There is clearly more scope for improvement, so we take into account the wavelet transformations, too. Tables 6.9, 6.10, and 6.11 show the classification accuracy obtained in the second run of SVM (for subjects S1, S2, and S3) when wavelet transformations were applied in combination with the conditional statistics. It is

TABLE 6.6

Statistical features and classification accuracy of subject S1

No of Channels	Mean	Median	Variance	Product	Geometric	Harmonic
1	11.25	19.25	21.73	17.32	17.67	16.47
2	14.21	23.75	24.51	19.35	21.54	17.13
3	18.48	24.43	26.73	14.33	23.75	12.65
4	21.75	27.57	29.85	29.33	29.67	19.62
5	28.71	28.95	36.31	27.67	33.31	16.75
6	29.54	31.25	39.54	33.67	37.54	24.57
7	34.64	33.63	47.62	39.61	38.61	21.52
8	37.26	36.78	51.67	47.67	39.43	23.67
9	39.54	41.51	59.65	50.55	40.54	27.67

TABLE 6.7

Statistical features and classification accuracy of subject S2

No of Channels	Mean	Median	Variance	Product	Geometric	Harmonic
1	17.95	11.67	11.37	15.23	18.95	26.95
2	18.32	13.33	14.15	21	20.45	37.33
3	21.75	14.33	22.38	32.97	28.65	32.67
4	24.33	17.8	28.56	39.33	31.25	39.26
5	31.33	18.53	33.33	37.76	34.75	46.57
6	39.67	21.89	37.67	38.95	36.33	54.85
7	43.64	27.75	43.55	49.63	48.26	57.33
8	38.61	33.85	61.67	59.83	59.37	59.67
9	41.65	49.87	69.65	63.33	60.65	65.33

TABLE 6.8

Statistical features and classification accuracy of subject S3

No of channels	Mean	Median	Variance	Product	Geometric	Harmonic
1	17.64	11.78	13.44	14.33	19.12	32.11
2	22.78	14.56	16.78	22.13	21.34	39.32
3	24.56	17.89	19.43	33.11	26.14	41.34
4	28.98	18.54	25.77	41.24	32.33	43.56
5	31.34	25.57	39.83	42.54	37.82	46.78
6	33.54	28.12	43.12	45.12	45.64	52.12
7	36.99	33.45	48.97	55.13	47.12	55.65
8	39.81	45.77	65.22	66.12	58.12	60.23
9	40.32	49.23	68.12	70.13	59.32	64.98

TABLE 6.9
Wavelet transformations and classification accuracy of subject S1

No of Channel	Haar	Gaussian1	Gaussian2	Morlet
1	21.31	22.55	17.7	41.45
2	24.76	23.75	19.12	43.36
3	21.47	27.31	23.32	47.89
4	28.51	28.67	45.12	51.23
5	29.53	32.54	47.78	53.33
6	27.62	39.25	50.14	57.67
7	28.95	43.75	51.74	61.23
8	41.75	47.75	53.87	63.56
9	37.63	49.63	57.85	67.81

TABLE 6.10
Wavelet transformations and classification accuracy of subject S2

No of Channels	Haar	Gaussian1	Gaussian2	Morlet
1	22.13	15.63	18.51	44.67
2	27.83	27.67	25.26	45.61
3	21.75	33.52	31.67	57.33
4	29.15	38.75	37.54	58.55
5	30.55	43.33	42.67	67.23
6	32.67	49.52	45.54	71.76
7	37.59	53.57	51.75	75.67
8	39.57	56.52	58.45	81.33
9	44.33	58.57	61.23	80.67

TABLE 6.11
Wavelet transformations and classification accuracy of subject S3

No of channels	Haar	Gaussian1	Gaussian2	Morlet
1	23.32	25.36	22.15	49.70
2	20.13	29.76	28.16	54.78
3	29.56	30.25	33.85	59.48
4	32.68	33.55	39.43	62.65
5	27.15	37.87	47.27	69.35
6	37.75	43.90	43.45	69.67
7	39.95	44.75	50.25	65.31
8	45.76	56.25	68.54	87.67
9	49.77	59.75	71.35	90.33

TABLE 6.12
PCA component analysis and classification accuracy of subject S1

Components	PCA1	PCA2	PCA3	PCA4	PCA5	PCA6	PCA7	PCA8	PCA9
Accuracy	41.28	51.85	53.67	63.21	65.23	71.54	74.59	78.53	81.92

TABLE 6.13
PCA component analysis and classification accuracy of S2

Components	PCA1	PCA2	PCA3	PCA4	PCA5	PCA6	PCA7	PCA8	PCA9
Accuracy	55.82	49.67	33.32	53.71	59.33	63.75	68.66	76.33	85.67

TABLE 6.14
PCA component analysis and classification accuracy of S3

Components	PCA1	PCA2	PCA3	PCA4	PCA5	PCA6	PCA7	PCA8	PCA9
Accuracy	49.14	50.77	52.34	55.25	60.13	64.78	65.43	77.89	82.15

observed that Haar, Gaussian 1, and Gaussian 2 show no significant improvement on classification accuracy. But Morlet transformation increased the accuracy obtained from 59.65% in the previous run to 67.81% in this run.

Tables 6.12, 6.13, and 6.14 show the results of S1, S2, and S3 obtained through principle component analysis. In this final run, with nine principle components the classification accuracy has been increased to 81.92% (S1), 85.67% (S2) and 82.15% (S3). This is the maximum accuracy obtained through SVM classification through the semi-automated approach.

6.11 CONCLUSION

In the current work we have tried to provide a comparative study on manual or semi-automated methods of BCI control using P300 signals. Through our work we brought the accuracy to approximately 87% in case of a manual approach. The semi-automated approach may still be able to catch up with the manual one if explored even deeper. This will create the benefit of using the semi-automated approach rather than the manual one, as it requires less effort. In fact, hybrid models using both the manual and semi-automated approaches discussed in our paper, can be created and deployed not only in BCI but Android and IOS environments. When the semi-automated and the manual models are performing so well independently, it may be interesting to note their progress collectively. Combined together, they may cancel out each other's drawbacks, if any, and give rise to an even better model of classification that could be used in a lot of application areas like biomedical devices, economic trend analysis, etc. Apart from the hybrid approach, each algorithm can be explored in its own domain, too. The manual approach that has been discussed in our paper, can be enhanced further and holds an exponential scope for improvements in the feature selection parts. This is because the manual approach gives full freedom to the user in the realm of feature selection. And the more we enhance the feature selection, the end classification accuracy will be higher. In fact, a linear increase in the betterment of the feature selection may have an exponential effect in the increasing classification accuracy. The semi-automated approach can be explored further, too. We have used just one classifier, the support vector machine. The approach could be tested with other classifiers that offer such a consolidated approach. In the near future, if new and better classifiers are developed, the semi-automated approach could use one of them and this would greatly enhance the classification accuracy again.

ACKNOWLEDGMENTS

This research is supported by the National Institute of Technology, Raipur, and thanks to the Weka machine learning group, as well as online BNCI Horizon, for providing EEG corpus.

REFERENCES

1. Omar AlZoubi, Rafael A Calvo, and Ronald H Stevens. "Classification of EEG for affect recognition: an adaptive approach." In *Australasian Joint Conference on Artificial Intelligence*, pages 52–61. Springer, 2009.
2. Mahnaz Arvaneh, Cuntai Guan, Kai Keng Ang, and Chai Quek. "Optimizing the channel selection and classification accuracy in EEG-based BCI." *IEEE Transactions on Biomedical Engineering*, 58(6):1865–1873, 2011.
3. Christoph Guger, Shahab Daban, Eric Sellers, Clemens Holzner, Gunther Krausz, "Roberta Carabalona, FurioGramatica, and Guenter Edlinger. How many people are able to control a p300-based brain–computer interface (bci)?" *Neuroscience Letters*, 462(1):94–98, 2009.
4. YongwookChae, JaeseungJeong, and Sungho Jo. "Toward brain-actuated humanoid robots: asynchronous direct control using an eeg-based bci." *IEEE Transactions on Robotics*, 28(5):1131–1144, 2012.
5. Siamac Fazli, Cristian Grozea, Márton Danóczy, Benjamin Blankertz, Florin Popescu, and Klaus-Robert Müller. "Subject independent EEG-based BCI decoding." In *Advances in Neural Information Processing Systems*, 22, pp. 513–521, 2009.
6. Oliver Rösler and David Suendermann. "A first step towards eye state prediction using EEG." Proc. of the AIHLS, 2013.
7. Vladimir Bostanov. "Bci competition 2003-data sets IB and IIB: feature extraction from event-related brain potentials with the continuous wavelet transform and the t-value scalogram." *IEEE Transactions on Biomedical Engineering*, 51(6):1057–1061, 2004.
8. Kim Dremstrup Nielsen, Alvaro Fuentes Cabrera, and Omar Feix do Nascimento. "Eeg based bci-towards a better control. brain-computer interface research at Aalborg university." *IEEE Transactions on Neural Systems and Rehabilitation Engineering*, 14(2):202–204, 2006.

9. Christoph Guger, Werner Harkam, Carin Hertnaes, and Gert Pfurtscheller. "Prosthetic control by an eeg-based brain-computer interface (BCI)." In Proc. *AAATE 5th European Conference for the Advancement of Assistive Technology*, pp 3–6, 1999.

10. Irina-Emilia Nicolae, "MihaelaUngureanu, and RodicaStrungaru. Motor imagery mental tasks in brain-computer interface applications." In *AMI Proceedings*, 2014.

11. Andrea Kübler, Adrian Furdea, Sebastian Halder, Eva Maria Hammer, Femke Nijboer, and Boris Kotchoubey. "A brain–computer interface controlled auditory event-related potential (p300) spelling system for locked-in patients." *Annals of the New York Academy of Sciences*, 1157(1):90–100, 2009.

12. Cuntai Guan, Manoj Thulasidas, and Jiankang Wu. "High performance p300 speller for brain-computer interface." In *Biomedical Circuits and Systems, 2004 IEEE International Workshop* on, pp. S3–S5. IEEE, 2004. 45

13. Yuanqing Li, Jinyi Long, Tianyou Yu, Zhuliang Yu, Chuanchu Wang, Haihong Zhang, and Cuntai Guan. "An eeg-based bci system for 2-d cursor control by combining mu/beta rhythm and p300 potential." *IEEE Transactions on Biomedical Engineering*, 57(10):2495–2505, 2010. 46

14. Eric W Sellers, Dean J Krusienski, Dennis J McFarland, Theresa M Vaughan, and Jonathan R Wolpaw. "A p300 event-related potential brain–computer interface (BCI): the effects of matrix size and inter stimulus interval on performance." *Biological Psychology*, 73(3):242–252, 2006.

15. Maarten De Vos, Markus Kroesen, Reiner Emkes, and Stefan Debener. "P300 Speller BCI With a Mobile EEG System: Comparison to a Traditional Amplifier." *Journal of Neural Engineering*, 11(3):036008, 2014.

16. Eric W Sellers, Andrea Kubler, and Emanuel Donchin. "Brain-computer interface research at the university of south Florida cognitive psychophysiology laboratory: the p300 speller." *IEEE Transactions on Neural Systems and Rehabilitation Engineering*, 14(2):221–224, 2006.

17. Remco R Bouckaert. *Bayesian Network Classifiers in WEKA. Department of Computer Science*, University of Waikato Hamilton, 2004.

18. Abdulhamit Subasi. "EEG signal classification using wavelet feature extraction and a mixture of expert model." *Expert Systems with Applications*, 32(4):1084–1093, 2007.

19. Deon Garrett, David A Peterson, Charles W Anderson, and Michael H Thaut. "Comparison of linear, nonlinear, and feature selection methods for EEG signal classification." *IEEE Transactions on Neural Systems and Rehabilitation Engineering*, 11(2):141–144, 2003.

20. Fabien Lotte, Marco Congedo, Anatole Lécuyer, Fabrice Lamarche, and Bruno Arnaldi. "A review of classification algorithms for EEG-based brain–computer interfaces." *Journal of Neural Engineering*, 4(2):R1, 2007.

21. Neep Hazarika, Jean Zhu Chen, Ah Chung Tsoi, and Alex Sergejew. "Classification of EEG signals using the wavelet transform." *Signal Processing*, 59(1):61–72, 1997.

22. Kurt Hornik, Christian Buchta, and Achim Zeileis. "Open-source machine learning: R meets weka." *Computational Statistics*, 24(2):225–232, 2009.

23. Jonathan R Wolpaw, Dennis J McFarland, and Theresa M Vaughan. "Brain-computer interface research at the wadsworthcenter." *IEEE Transactions on Rehabilitation Engineering*, 8(2):222–226, 2000. 47

24. Tamer Demiralp, Juliana Yordanova, Vasil Kolev, Ahmet Ademoglu, Müge Devrim, and Vincent J Samar. "Time–frequency analysis of single-sweep event-related potentials by means of fast wavelet transform." *Brain and Language*, 66(1):129–145, 1999.

25. Ufuk Ozkaya, Ozlem Coskun, and Selcuk Comlekci. "Frequency analysis of EMG signals with matlabsptool." In Proceedings of the *9th WSEAS International Conference on Signal Processing*, pp 83–89, 2010.

26. Yan Li, Peng Paul Wen, et al. "Clustering technique-based least square support vector machine for eeg signal classification." *Computer Methods and Programs in Biomedicine*, 104(3):358–372, 2011.

27. S SathiyaKeerthi and Chih-Jen Lin. "Asymptotic behaviors of support vector machines with gaussian kernel." *Neural Computation*, 15(7):1667–1689, 2003.

28. Thomas Navin Lal, Michael Schroder, Thilo Hinterberger, Jason Weston, Martin Bogdan, Niels Birbaumer, and Bernhard Scholkopf. "Support vector channel selection in bci." *IEEE Transactions on Biomedical Engineering*, 51(6):1003–1010, 2004.

29. Alain Rakotomamonjy and Vincent Guigue. "BCI competition III: dataset II-ensemble of SVMs for BCI p300 speller." *IEEE Transactions on Biomedical Engineering*, 55(3):1147–1154, 2008.

30. Yuan-Pin Lin, Chi-Hong Wang, Tien-Lin Wu, Shyh-Kang Jeng, and Jyh-Horng Chen. "EEG-based emotion recognition in music listening: A comparison of schemes for multiclass support vector machine." *IEEE International Conference onAcoustics, Speech and Signal Processing* 2009. ICASSP 2009, pp 489–492. IEEE, 2009.

31. Abdulhamit Subasi and M Ismail Gursoy. "Eeg signal classification using PCA, ICA, LDA and support vector machines." *Expert Systems with Applications*, 37(12): 8659–8666, 2010.

32. Qi Xu, Hui Zhou, Yongji Wang, and Jian Huang. "Fuzzy support vector machine for classification of eeg signals using wavelet-based features." *Medical Engineering & Physics*, 31(7):858–865, 2009.

33. Gary N Garcia, Touradj Ebrahimi, and J-M Vesin. "Support vector EEG classification in the fourier and time-frequency correlation domains." In *Neural Engineering, 2003. Conference Proceedings. First International IEEE EMBS Conference on*, pp. 591–594. IEEE, 2003.

34. Matthias Kaper, Peter Meinicke, Ulf Grossekathoefer, Thomas Lingner, and Helge Ritter. "BCI competition 2003-data set IIB: support vector machines for the p300 speller paradigm." *IEEE Transactions on Biomedical Engineering*, 51(6): 1073–1076, 2004.

35. Inan Guler and Elif Derya Ubeyli. "Multiclass support vector machines for EEG-signals classification." *IEEE Transactions on Information Technology in Biomedicine*, 11(2):117–126, 2007.

36. Kumar, Rahul, Mridu Sahu, and Samrudhi Mohdiwale. "Two class motor imagery classification based on ANFIS." In *ICDSMLA 2019*, pp. 703–711. Springer, Singapore, 2020.

37. Mohdiwale, Samrudhi, Mridu Sahu, G. R. Sinha, and Varun Bajaj. "Automated cognitive workload assessment using logical teaching learning-based optimization and PROMETHEE multi-criteria decision making approach." *IEEE Sensors Journal* 20, 22, pp. 13629–13637, 2020.

38. Sahu, Mridu, Samrudhi Mohdiwale, Namrata Khoriya, Yogita Upadhyay, Anjali Verma, and Shikha Singh. "EEG artifact removal techniques: a comparative study." In *International Conference on Innovative Computing and Communications*, pp. 395–403. Springer, Singapore, 2020.

39. Mohdiwale, S., M. Sahu, and G. R. Sinha. "LJaya optimisation-based channel selection approach for performance improvement of cognitive workload assessment technique." *Electronics Letters*, 56, 15, pp. 793–795, 2020. DOI: 10.1049/el.2020.1011.

40. Sinha, Ganesh R. *Cognitive Informatics, Computer Modelling, and Cognitive Science: Volume 2: Application to Neural Engineering, Robotics, and STEM*. Academic Press, London, 2020.

41. Sinha, Ganesh R., and Jasjit S. Suri, eds. *Cognitive Informatics, Computer Modelling, and Cognitive Science: Volume 1: Theory, Case Studies, and Applications*. Academic Press, London, 2020.

42. Sinha, G. R. "Study of assessment of cognitive ability of human brain using deep learning." *International Journal of Information Technology* 9, no. 3 (2017): 321–326.
43. Sanei, Saeid, and Jonathon A. Chambers. *EEG Signal Processing*. John Wiley & Sons, New York, 2013.
44. Subha, D. Puthankattil, Paul K. Joseph, Rajendra Acharya, and Choo Min Lim. "EEG signal analysis: a survey." *Journal of Medical Systems* 34, no. 2 (2010): 195–212.
45. Mohdiwale, Samrudhi, and Mridu Sahu. "Brain–computer interface and neuro-computing." In *Cognitive Informatics, Computer Modelling, and Cognitive Science*, pp. 27–53. Academic Press, 2020.
46. Jung, Tzyy-Ping, Scott Makeig, Marissa Westerfield, Jeanne Townsend, Eric Courchesne, and Terrence J. Sejnowski. "Analyzing and visualizing single-trial event-related potentials." In *Human Brain Mapping*, 14, 3, pp. 166–185, 2001.
47. Holmes, Geoffrey, Andrew Donkin, and Ian H. Witten. "Weka: A machine learning workbench." In Proceedings of *ANZIIS'94-Australian New Zealand Intelligent Information Systems Conference*, pp. 357–361. IEEE, 1994.
48. Tan, Pang-Ning, Michael Steinbach, and Vipin Kumar. *Introduction to Data Mining*. Pearson Education India, 2016.

7 Effective Brain Computer Interface Based on the Adaptive-Rate Processing and Classification of Motor Imagery Tasks

Saeed Mian Qaisar, Reem Ramadan, and Humaira Nisar

7.1 INTRODUCTION AND BACKGROUND

The BCI systems are defined according to the ability of the system to detect, extract and translate pulses produced by the central nervous system, as well as it is a system that acts on the translated commands [1]. The primary objective of BCI is to assist disabled people in their rehabilitation. It helps them to perform the necessary tasks in daily life without any help, including grabbing things, turning on lights, changing TV channels, etc. The balance of social and technical participation between healthy and disabled individuals is not present. People with disabilities face challenges with day-to-day operations, healthcare, jobs, schooling, and even disability related facilities [2]. Globally, the percentage of disabled persons is increasing. It is due to the rise in road accidents, natural catastrophes, and chronic diseases. Almost 15% of the global population has certain types of disabilities [3]. Even though fixing the underlying cause would solve the issue, it would not decrease the trend. Moreover, according to Zickler et al. (2009) [4], activities of daily living was the second aspect of life in which disabled people wanted to improve.

The majority of disabled people face difficulties in being independent to perform activities like healthy people. Their brains are simply disconnected from most of their body muscles. Medical approaches to improving such an issue can be extremely costly and risky. As an alternative solution, creating a BCI system with a wearable headset would help such people to perform daily life activities by using only their brains.

To implement a real-time noninvasive EEG-based BCI system, it has to detect, analyze, and classify different types of motor imagery tasks [1]. Depending on the

163

location of movement, EEG-based BCI can be categorized as limb motor imagery classification [5], detection of arm movement direction [6], decoding of individual finger movement [7], forward-backward hand movement prediction [8], character recognition based on P300 evoked potential [9], and motor imagery classification [10].

Based on the approaches of data collection, the BCI systems can be categorized as invasive and noninvasive. The noninvasive procedure involves placing sensors on the scalp of the subject, and the brain pulses are collected through them. This is called an electroencephalograph (EEG). This technique follows specific protocols, where these sensors are placed intelligently in particular areas of the brain according to the data the researchers need to acquire. This technique is also relatively inexpensive and safe; however, because the pulses are passing through the skull, they can be attenuated, and several factors add noise to them, which means that some data might be compromised [2,3,11].

On the other hand, the invasive method is done by placing electrodes directly in brain tissue to read the brain pulses. This technique might result in cleaner pulses (less noise) but is more dangerous and ethically ambiguous. In addition, since surgery is needed to accomplish this technique of data acquisition, costs are higher. In [2] and [3], the pros and cons of each strategy are described.

The difficulty in EEG analysis not only arises due to its nonstationary nature, but other factors such as changes in physical state, mood, posture, external noise, etc. In spite of all these factors, the BCI is still realizable by analyzing the EEG signals [12]. In order to achieve this objective, a large variety of wearable EEG devices have been proposed [13,14]. However, EEG-based BCI realization is not very straightforward [15]. The data involved in EEG signal recordings are collected from multiple scalp electrodes. Hence, the amount of data may be very high as no electrodes may vary from very few, i.e., 5 to 1,000 [16,17]. Another challenge with EEG signals is that the interferences and physiological artifacts often corrupt EEG signals, hence, decreasing the effectiveness of feature extraction and classification in later stages [15]. A variety of techniques have been proposed for pre-processing and improving the efficiency of the EEG signal [18], such as a Kalman filter [19], orthogonal wavelet filters [20], adaptive filtering [21], and principal component analysis [22].

The commonly used methods for the EEG signal feature mining are the autoregressive (AR) Burg, discrete wavelet transform (DWT), and wavelet packet decomposition (WPD) [15,22,23]. The identifiable characteristics, obtained with the extraction of features, are utilized for automated evaluation of the motor imagery tasks. Various classification tactics have been reported in this framework [24,25].

7.2 MOTIVATION AND CONTRIBUTION

The real-time BCI can be realized with continuous detection of motor imagery tasks. The cloud-based systems can proficiently expand the effective BCI realization [26]. In this framework, the intended patients require constant monitoring. In this context, a wearable EEG sensor is the most suitable device [27,28]. Smartphones could acquire the EEG sensor data and can send findings to a control center [27]. In case of emergencies, the smartphone device may be utilized to instantly contact the concerned authorities with the intended person's GPS location.

Continuous processing and analysis of EEG signals is required for an effective cloud-based BCI realization. Sensors are usually favored in these situations because they allow continuous recording of EEG signals without creating restrictions to the concerned personnel. The significant power effectiveness can be incorporated in a wireless EEG system by reducing the data transmission [27,28]. To accomplish this, numerous methods are suggested such as compression [29,30] nonuniform sampling [31] and event-driven processing [32–35].

Improving the computational efficiency of modern BCI systems will facilitate and aid in the advancement of research in the BCI area of study. The hope is to reach a stage where these systems can be mobile, such that patients can live their life and wear a headset without having to be connected to computers and wires. Researchers are working towards this goal in different ways. The first is through the power aspect, where researchers are working to make longer-lasting batteries and electronics that consume less power. The other is through increasing the efficiency of the system, i.e., the algorithms, classification techniques, and processing methods. This project lies in the following area of study.

The Nyquist theory is the base of conventional BCI. Worst case parametrization should be employed because of the system time-invariant nature [32,36–40]. These systems are time-invariant, and due to this, the processing activity and the processing load remains fixed for these systems regardless of the incoming EEG signal time variations. Consequently, they record and treat redundant information from the incoming signal, and it causes an extra computational load on these systems [37,38]. One way to overcome this issue is the incorporation of event-driven analog to digital converters (EDADCs) [32–35]. Their data acquisition rate could be adjusted as a function of the incoming signal variations. It can produce notable processing effectiveness in contrast to the traditional methods. Inspiration from these features leads towards the realization of original EEG acquisition strategies [32,33]. In this background, the event-driven retrieval and analysis strategies are suggested for BCI realization for cloud-based healthcare. It uses the event-driven signal digitization and conditioning along with hybrid feature extraction and classification.

This work contributes to the realization of computationally efficient BCIs in the cloud environment. The incoming signal time variations control the signal acquisition and transmission processes. It is attained by incorporating the event-driven feature in the designed solution [40]. It notably enhances the performance of postconditioning, features extraction, and classification by only acquiring the appropriate information.

7.3 ELECTROENCEPHALOGRAPHY IN HEALTHCARE AND BCI

The need for brain scanning was a demand in the field of medicine. From the viewpoint of epilepsy (an abnormality in the electrical brain activity [41]), it motivated medical doctors to understand the way brains behave. The first approach considered was in 1895, by physicist Wilhelm Roentgen, using the technology of the clinical x-ray [42]. The clinical x-ray (also known as radiography) uses ionizing radiation to generate images of the body. However, an x-ray can raise health risks; also, the brain tissues remain invisible in an x-ray. In this framework, a variety of methods have been suggested as a replacement of the x-ray such as electro-encephalography and magnetoencephalography.

The EEG is a test used to detect the electrical waves of the brain by sending the electrical impulses absorbed via the transducing electrodes. These electrodes are commonly placed on the scalp of the head via a headset; however, there are other methods which can be partially or fully invasive through surgery implants of such electrodes inside the human skull. The reason why other tests are not as popular as the EEG is due to their high sensitivity to the surrounding environment, lack of portability, bulkiness in size, as well as their high cost. Additionally, the EEG allows one to explore the electrical activity of the brain directly. It rapidly diagnoses any abnormalities in the functionality of the cerebral system. This feature is not available in the blood flow estimation based techniques. Positron emission tomography measures metabolic activities. These are implicit pieces of information about the electrical activity of the brain and can result in a relatively slower identification of changes in the neural activity of the brain in contrast to the EEG-based approach.

According to [43], the valuable spectral content of the EEG signal exists between 0.5 Hz and 60 Hz. As a function of the spectral band, the signal is classified as Delta [0.5, 4] Hz, Theta [1,8] Hz, Alpha [8,14] Hz, Beta [14,31] Hz, and Gamma [31]. Figure 7.1 is a visual representation of the categorized waves.

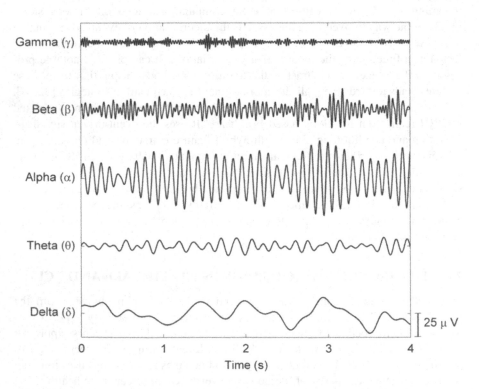

FIGURE 7.1   Example of EEG signals acquired during a rest state with closed eyes

The BCI systems are defined according to the ability of the system to detect, extract, and translate pulses produced by the central nervous system, as well as acting on the translated commands [2].

An important thing to note about how BCI systems work is that, the subject using the system must go through a training period, where the system "trains" to detect and analyze the signals in order to operate correctly and more efficiently [2].

There are two main types of collecting data for BCI systems: invasive and noninvasive. The noninvasive approach involves placing sensors on the scalp of the subject and the brain pulses are collected through them. This is called an electro-encephalograph (EEG). This technique follows specific protocols, where these sensors are placed intelligently in particular areas of the brain according to the data the researchers need to acquire. This technique is also reasonably inexpensive and safe; however, because the pulses are passing through the skull they can be atte-nuated, and a number of factors add noise to them, which means that some data might be compromised [2,3,11].

There is a tradeoff between the use of invasive and non invasive methods. Non invasive methods are cheaper but noisy however, the invasive methods provide cleaner pulses but costlier [2,3]. Researchers have to weigh the advantages and disadvantages of each method against each other to deal with these trade-offs.

The motivation behind this investigation is to enable BCI systems to function in real-time. It will allow providing adequate assistance to disabled persons by transforming their intentions in actions.

7.4 THE PROPOSED APPROACH

The proposed EEG acquisition and processing framework is shown in Figure 7.2.

7.4.1 DATASET

The dataset has EEG collected using the 10–20 system, which is a formal standard. It contains data for the motor imagery of the right hand and the right foot. These pulses were acquired from five healthy subjects under controlled conditions. There

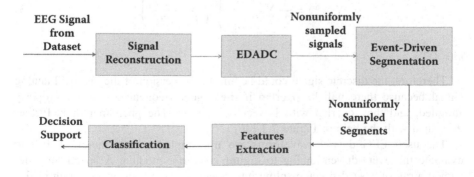

FIGURE 7.2 The proposed system block diagram

are two classes that are used for this project, type 1 is for the motor imagery of moving the right hand, and type 2 is for the motor imagery of driving the right foot. There are 118 channels available in the 10–20 system. Based on the frequency, dataset IVa was obtained from five healthy subjects. These are notated as aa, al, av, aw, and ay [44]. The recording of EEG waveforms is carried out at the rate of 1kHz. The digitization is carried out with a 16-bit resolution analog to digital converter (ADC). The proposed system performance is studied for the case of two subjects, namely aa and ay.

7.4.2 RECONSTRUCTION

In many applications, analog signals are converted into discrete signals (analog to digital) by using sampling and quantization operations (ADC) [45]. Onward, the discrete signals are processed using digital signal processors. Afterward, the processed signals are reconstructed back from digital to analog via utilizing digital to analog converters (DACs).

Using Fourier analysis, the sampling process can be described from a frequency domain perspective, analyze its causes, and discuss the reconstruction phenomenon [45]. Let $x_a(t)$ be an analog signal. Its spectral representation is achievable by using equation (7.1):

$$x_a(j\Omega) \triangleq \int_{-\infty}^{\infty} x_a(t)e^{-j\Omega t}dt. \tag{7.1}$$

Ω is the frequency. Inverse of equation (7.1) inverse is given by equation (7.2).

$$x_a(t) = \frac{1}{2\pi} \int_{-\infty}^{\infty} x_a(j\Omega)e^{j\Omega t}d\Omega \tag{7.2}$$

To find (n) we have to sample $xa(t)$ at sampling interval Ts. The process can be described as: $x(n) \triangleq x_a(nT_s)$. Let $X(e^{jw_n})$ be the frequency domain transformed version of $x(n)$. According to [45] the aliasing formula is:

$$X(e^{j\omega}) = \frac{1}{T_s} \sum_{t=-\infty}^{\infty} x_a\left[j\left(\frac{\omega}{T_s} - \frac{2\pi}{T_s}l\right)\right] \tag{7.3}$$

$\omega = \Omega T$

Therefore, the discrete signal could be an aliased version of the identical analog signal because there will be overlap if the higher frequencies are not properly sampled, and they overlap with lower frequencies. The phenomenon is further described with the help of Figure 7.3 [46].

The used EEG dataset waveforms are up-sampled with a factor of 100 to evaluate the event-driven analog to digital converter module. A specifically designed array of cascaded cubic-spline interpolators is used for up-sampling [25].

7.4.3 THE EVENT-DRIVEN A/D CONVERTER (EDADC)

The reconstructed signal $x(t)$ is conveyed to EDADC. The existing BCI systems are founded on the basis of conventional ADCs. On the other hand, the designed BCI system is founded on the basis of EDADCs. Time-invariant sampling is done by a traditional ADC, which takes samples from a given signal at constant time intervals. However, the acquisition process is time-varying and adjustable in accordance with the changes in the incoming signal [40,47]. This process is depicted in Figures 7.4, 7.5, and 7.6.

The concept behind the event-driven sampling is only to obtain the sample if the reconstructed input signal $x(t)$ intersects with one of the thresholds. The distributed levels among the analog signals are designed to span all of amplitude signal range $\Delta x(t)$. The space between the levels are equally distributed and separated by a quantum q [40]. For clarification of the difference between the acquisition principles of ADCs and EDADCs, the following example is considered.

In the case of ADC, samples are taken at constant intervals. Let us consider the EEG signal, $x(t)$, shown in Figure 7.5. The acquisition process is performed at a

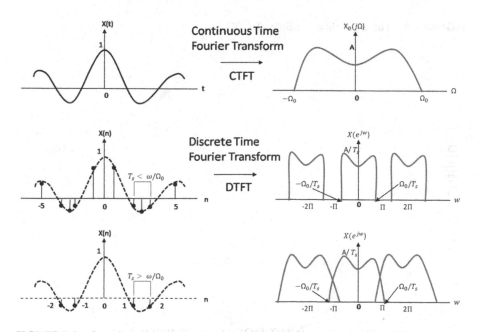

FIGURE 7.3 Sampling and its impact in the time and frequency domains [46]

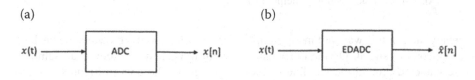

FIGURE 7.4 ADC (a) and EDADC (b)

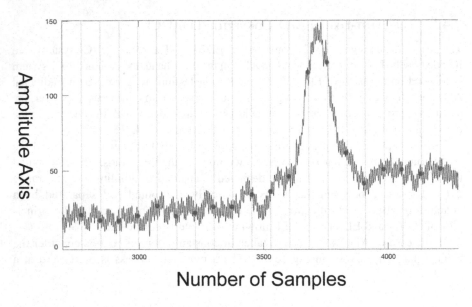

FIGURE 7.5   The acquisition principle of ADC

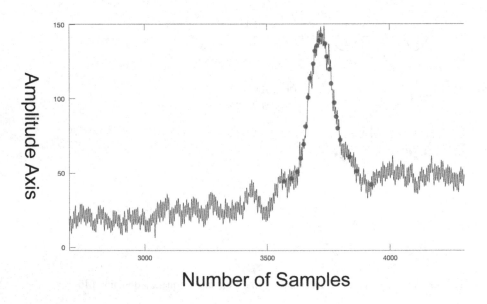

FIGURE 7.6   The acquisition principle of EDADC

steady rate. In this way, not many samples are recorded around the valuable peak of the incoming signal. On the other hand, several unwanted and redundant samples are gathered around the baseline of incoming signal. The dots in Figures 7.6 and 7.7 represent the samples taken at regular time intervals.

In the case of EDADC, samples are not taken at constant intervals. Let us consider the EEG signal, $x(t)$, shown in Figure 7.6. An EDADC is used, and the samples are taken only where there is an activity in the signal. This allows for more efficient sampling such that the samples represent the valuable information. This technique is better than time-invariant ADC because it requires a lower number of samples and does a better job of getting samples that contain data. The dots in Figures 7.5 and 7.6, represent the samples taken at the peak of activity in the signal.

The variation in the count of samples, collected from the incoming signal by utilizing the conventional ADC and the EDADC, is evident from Figures 7.5 and 7.6. For the classical ADC to be able to extract as much of the vital information acquired by the EDADC, the sampling frequency must be multiple times higher than the one shown in Figure 7.5.

7.4.4 THE EVENT-DRIVEN SEGMENTATION

The data obtained from EDADC does not have an equal distance between them in time. So, classical techniques cannot be used to process or analyze the data [37,38]. The windowing is an essential operation, and it is required for the limited time data acquisition to fulfill the practical system implementation specifications [45]. To obtain the windowed version of a sampled signal xn, the picked N sample segment must be centered on τ, as given by the following equation.

$$xw_n = \sum_{n=\tau+\frac{L}{2}}^{\tau+\frac{L}{2}} x_n \cdot w_{n-\tau} \tag{7.4}$$

xw_n is the windowed version of x_n
   L is the length in seconds.
   τ is the central time of wn.
   Fs is the sampling frequency.
   N can be calculated by:

$$N = L.Fs \tag{7.5}$$

Performing digital signal processing and analysis require a finite set of data. Windowing functions are applied to capture a limited frame of data [37]. Figure7.7)

The segmentation of the EDADC output is realized by using the activity selection algorithm (ASA) [37,38]. This is built on the sampling nonuniformity and permits the realization of adaptive rate hybrid features extraction.

7.4.5 EXTRACTION OF FEATURES

The employed features extraction method is shown in Figure 7.8. Each instance's features are extracted in a hybrid fashion using methods called time-domain extraction of features and frequency-domain extraction of features.

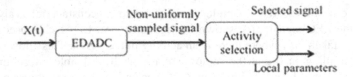

FIGURE 7.7 The sequence of an activity selection based windowing

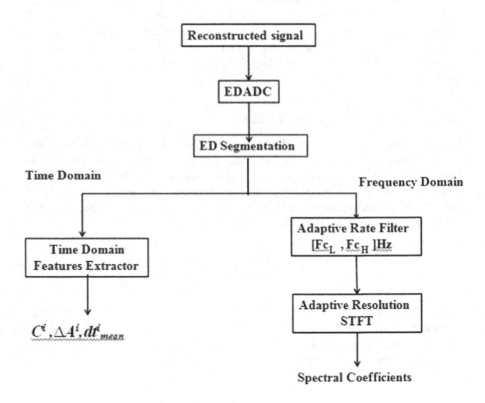

FIGURE 7.8 Features extraction principle

7.4.5.1 Extraction of Time Domain Features

Each selected segment is mined in order to determine its classifiable features. The time-domain level-crossing based sampled signal contains useful information about the frequency content of the signal [38]. It allows the designed system to mine the valuable features in the time domain. Therefore, the system remains computationally effective in contrast to the counterparts, which necessitate the arithmetically expensive operation of frequency-domain transformation and analysis [38,48]. Four parameters are derived for each selected segment W^i namely C^i, ΔA^i, A_{max}^i and dt_{mean}^i. C^i, ΔA^i, A_{max}^i and dt_{mean}^i are the count of threshold crossings, the peak-to-peak amplitude, the maximum positive peak, and the average sampling step for W^i.

7.4.5.2 Extraction of Frequency Domain Features

To enhance the system's classification performance, the frequency domain features are also mined. This method denoises the segmented signal with an adaptive rate digital band-pass filter. It uses the original event-driven adaptive rate filtering and adaptive resolution short-time Fourier transformation (STFT) techniques [45,49]. These are described in the following.

Techniques for adaptive rate filtration are being developed. They are based upon event-driven sensing (EDS) [38]. The sampling frequency of the EDADC follows $x(t)$ temporal disparities. Equation (7.6) represents the mathematical equation of the EDADC maximum sampling frequency [38]. f_{max} is the highest component of $x(t)$ frequency, A_{in} represents the amplitude of the incoming signal, and Fs_{max} is the EDADC maximum sampling frequency.

$$Fs_{max} = 2f_{max}(2^M - 1)\frac{A_{in}}{\Delta V} \tag{7.6}$$

Let the ith selected window acquired with the ASA be W^i and Fs^i represents the sampling frequency of this selected window, then:

$$Fs^i = N^i/L^i \tag{7.7}$$

In equation (7.7), the count of samples and the length in seconds of W^i are respectively presented by N^i and L^i. Locally exploited parameters for each segment are used to adjust the resampling frequency of W^i. Contrasting with the traditional ones, the arithmetic complexity reduction of the suggested technique is thus increased substantially. The selection of the resampling frequency of (W^i), Frs^i, depends on the reference sampling frequency, F_r, and the sampling frequency of the selected window, Fs^i.

Nr^i is known to be the number of samples existing in W^i after the resampling. The resampling is carried out by using the simplified linear interpolation (SLI) technique. In SLI, $\frac{q}{2}$ limits the maximum error per interpolation [47].

For the proposed method, a filters bank is designed offline. It is composed of finite impulse response (FIR) filters. The realization of the architecture for the range of appropriate parameters is obtained when changing the reference sampling frequencies F_{ref}.

The F_{ref} is mathematically given by equation (7.8), where Q is the length of the F_{ref}. The value of Q is always selected to be a weighted binary. Equation (7.9) is then used to calculate the unique offset Δ.

$$F_{ref} = \{Fs_{min}, Fs_{min} + \Delta, ..., Fs_{min} + (Q - 1)\Delta = F_r\} \tag{7.8}$$

$$\Delta = \frac{F_r - Fs_{min}}{Q - 1} \tag{7.9}$$

For each W^i, a proper filter is selected online from the reference set. h_{c_k} represents the selected filter for W^i and F_{ref_c} is its sampling frequency. This choice is made depending on the F_{ref} and Fs^i. F_{ref_c} should be equal to Frs^i to guarantee a proper filtering process [38].

The adaptive resolution STFT (ARSTFT) performs adaptive resolution time-frequency resolution evaluation, which cannot be achieved with the conventional STFT [49].

The STFT weakness is fixed time-frequency resolution. The time resolution (Δt) and frequency resolutions (Δf) are a function of the effective window length (L) [49]. For the conventional STFT the fixed sampling rate (Fs) and L deliver a fixed N and consequently fixed Δt and Δf. N is the count of data points in a segment. Δt and Δf can be respectively given by equations (7.10) and (7.11).

$$\Delta t = L \tag{7.10}$$

$$\Delta f = \frac{F_s}{N} \tag{7.11}$$

Equation (7.11) shows that by increasing N, Δf can be increased for a fixed Fs. Yet increasing N requires an increase in L, which will lead to a reduction in Δt. (cf. equation (7.10)). A larger L, therefore, provides better Δf, but bad Δt, and vice versa. This conflict between Δf and Δt is the reason why multi-resolution analytical techniques were developed, which can be useful for both high- and low-frequency events; it is the most suitable approach for most real-life signals.

The proposed ARSTFT is a smart alternative to the techniques of multiresolution analysis. It provides time-frequency analysis with adaptive resolution, which cannot be achieved with the traditional STFT. In this case, Fs^i, Frs^i, L^i, N^i, and Nr^i varies as a function of x(t). Nr^i is the count of data points, obtained after resampling. In accordance with Nr^i and L^i, the time resolution (Δt^i) and the frequency resolution (Δf^i) of the ARSTFT can be specific for the chosen ith segment and can be given respectively by equations (7.12) and (7.13).

$$\Delta t^i = L^i \tag{7.12}$$

$$\Delta f^i = \frac{Frs^i}{Nr^i} \tag{7.13}$$

Frs^i and L^i adaptation contributes to the ARSTFT's computational advantage compared to the classical counterpart. That is done first by eliminating the collection and processing unwanted samples, and second by eliminating the use of cosine window functions [49]. The coefficients extracted with ARSTFT are also used for the incoming denoised segment classification.

7.4.6 MACHINE LEARNING ALGORITHMS

The features of the incoming selected segment are extracted by using the proposed hybrid features extraction method. Onward, these features, instead of the original waveform, are used for classification.

Many classification techniques used may require tuning the parameters to get maximum results. So we use the basic and common form of validation to configure the classifier's settings during the training process. For the test set, the value that results in the optimal output is used. In the following, we briefly describe the different machine learning classifiers used in our experiments.

7.4.6.1   Support Vector Machine (SVM)

In SVM, the first task is to find those samples that represent the boundary conditions. These are known as support vectors. Onward, these are utilized to search for the optimal hyperplane that separates these vectors from the contrary classes [4,25]. We enhance the distance between the adjacent points, i.e., the points closest to the boundary, to do this. This is done by optimally separating the hyperplane that divides the data of the two classes described in equation (7.14) where x represents the data vector ($x = [x_1, x_2...x_p]$) having attributes. The weight vector is given by $w = [w_1, w_2...w_p]$, and the scalar bias is b.

$$h(x) = sign(w \cdot x^T + b). \tag{7.14}$$

For the case of SVM, the weights w are adjusted in a manner that a test sample x renders either a positive outcome of the classifier h for class one or a negative result of the classifier h for class two. Other parameters are also involved, such as the c parameter (called regularization parameter), which determines the penalty for misclassification during training, and the slack variables.

When the two classes are not linearly separable, a Kernel function [44] is used that transforms samples into a higher dimension where they may be detachable. Moreover, for classifying data with more than two classes, multiple approaches can be used. For instance, we can keep it as a two-class problem by keeping the label of one class (positive class) and relabeling all other classes with the same label (negative class). This may be repeated for each class during classification to identify samples of that particular class. It is known as the One-vs-All approach. Another widely used technique is to consider samples of only two categories at a time and to classify the data using a round-robin fashion. That is known as the One-vs-One approach[4,25].

Figure 7.9 explains how the SVM algorithms work in a straightforward way. In this example, the dataset is composed of stars and circles. The end goal is to divide them into two classes: the star class and the circle class. The two diagonal lines both accomplish the task of separating the dataset into the two categories. However, one is better than the other. According to SVM, the line that has the most considerable distance from the closest point in each set is better. Figure 7.9 illustrates that the gap between the gray line to the nearest data point is Z2. However, the distance between the black line to the closest data point is Z1 because Z2 is superior to Z1. Therefore, as per SVM, the gray line is the smarter splitter and so it will be used to classify the data.

Data is not usually this easy to classify. The SVM, as mentioned before, uses kernel functions to determine the hyperplane that will classify the data in the most

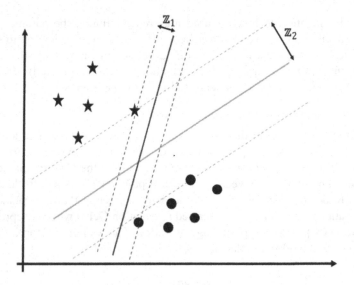

FIGURE 7.9 SVM algorithm concept

optimal way. The following diagrams demonstrate how the kernel function can transform the data from the input space to the feature space. This is done because the data can be classified in a much easier and clearer way.

k-Nearest Neighbors (k-NN)

The k-NN algorithm [25] is a popular classifier that finds the distance of the test data to the k nearest neighbors in the training data to decide its category label. Let v_j represents a sample and $<v_j, l_j>$ represents the pair of the data vector along with its label, $l_j \in [1, C]$ where C denotes the maximum classes in the dataset. Then, the k-NN process to classify a new vector z, is given by Equation (7.15).

$$\underset{j}{\text{argmin}}\ dist\,(v_j, z)\ \forall\ j = 1..\ N \tag{7.15}$$

where $dist(,)$ is a distance measure. The value of k is usually set to a small odd number to ensure a majority consensus. Similarly, any distance metric can be used including classical metrics such as Manhattan, Euclidean, Chebyshev, Hamming, Minkowski, etc. or advanced metrics such as the χ-Sim, Cosine similarity, etc. [25].

Figure 7.10 explains the k-NN algorithm in a basic form. In this example, the dataset is the same set of data as in the SVM, also composed of stars and circles. The circle represents the test sample to be classified. The k-NN algorithm takes the test sample as a center of the circle and the diameter of the circle depends on the variable "k." "k" represents the number of neighbors inside the circle. When "k" is 3 the circle is classified as belonging to the circle class. However, when "k" is increased to 8 then the classification becomes less accurate.

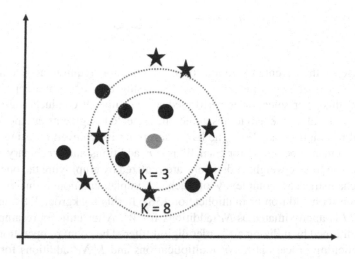

FIGURE 7.10 k-NN algorithm concept

7.5 THE PERFORMANCE EVALUATION MEASURES

The following evaluation measures are used.

7.5.1 Compression Ratio

The count of samples, N, which is recorded for the period L_T, in a traditional case, can be calculated using equation (7.16).

$$N = F_{ref} \times L_T \tag{7.16}$$

The sampling rate for the proposed method [40] is not fixed. The number of samples can vary for a considered time period LT and depend on the signal characteristics [32–35]. Let N_{ED} be the count of collected samples. Then, equation (7.17) can provide the gain in compression, G_{COMP}.

$$G_{COMP} = \frac{N}{N_{ED}} \tag{7.17}$$

7.5.2 Computational Complexity

The front-end processing module's computational complexity is analyzed in detail until the denoising level. The processing effectiveness of feature extraction and classification is assessed by taking into account the compression performance of the designed method. The adaptive rate FIR (ARFIR) method is used to denoise the resampled signal [38]. The processing cost of a traditional K order FIR filter is obvious. The overall processing complexity C_{FIR} is mathematically given by equation (7.18).

$$C_{FIR} = \underbrace{(K-1)}_{\text{Additions}} + \underbrace{K.N}_{\text{Multiplica tions}} \tag{7.18}$$

In the case of the invented solution, online adaptation requires additional operations. First, a filter hc_k is picked up for W^i. Using the successive approximation algorithm, this filter selection is performed in real-time. It conducts $\log_2(Q)$ comparisons. It is also needed to resample the selected segments at the real-time computed resampling rate Frs^i. The live resampling is achieved by using SLI. For SLI, the count of operations for each W^i is Nr^i additions and Nr^i binary weighted divisions. The binary-weighted divisions are realized by employing the one-bit right shift mechanism. The complexity of such an implementation is insignificant in comparison with addition or multiplication [38]. In this background, the arithmetic cost of SLI is approximated as Nr^i additions for W^i. After uniform resampling, the W^i is conditioned by utilizing a K^i order digital filter. The count of operations during the conditioning process is $K^i.Nr^i$ multiplications and $K^i.Nr^i$ additions for W^i. The complexity of a comparison operation is supposed to be equal to that of an addition operation. This assumption allows to evaluate the processing cost of the devised ARFIR with respect to that of the classical one. In this context, equation (7.19) represents the arithmetic cost of the ARFIR.

$$C_{ARFIR} = \underbrace{(K^i - 1).\,Nr^i + Nr^i + \log_2(Q) +}_{\text{Additions}} \underbrace{K^i.\,Nr^i}_{\text{Multiplica tions}} \tag{7.19}$$

7.5.3 CLASSIFICATION ACCURACY

The approach used in this work has many benefits in terms of the performance of the hardware, compression, processing, and transmission. The downside to this, however, is a small decrease in accuracy. We evaluate the work in terms of accuracy to focus on its comparison with actual practice. To ensure the results do not get biased, we use cross-validation. This helps in reducing any abnormal effect that may occur to the dataset used, the particular training-testing split on the dataset, parameter, or classifier bias [25]. We used 10-fold cross-validation and evaluated all the algorithms on the same dataset. In particular, for each training-test in each fold, we save the indices of the training and test set and ensure the same indices are used for all the algorithms. Moreover, to avoid metric bias, we choose to evaluate the results on multiple evaluation metrics, as given below.

7.5.3.1 Accuracy (Acc)

Comparing the findings of the algorithm with the ground reality is achieved with accuracy. It is known as the percentage of properly predicted test-dataset labels. These are utilized to compute the accuracy of classification. The process is given by equation (7.20), where, TP, TN, FP, and FN stand for the true positives, true negatives, false positives, and false negatives.

$$Accuracy = \frac{TP + TN}{TP + TN + FP + FN} \qquad (7.20)$$

7.5.3.2 Specificity (Sp)

It is a measure that computes the number of TN that were correctly classified as a ration of all negatives (i.e., negatives that were classified as negations and negatives that were wrong classified as positives). That is in comparison to the above precision, meaning that measures a basic score except for good. For this cause, Specificity is also often referred to as the "real negative" limit, and provided by equation (7.21).

$$Sp = \frac{TN}{TN + FP} \qquad (7.21)$$

7.6   EXPERIMENTAL RESULTS

The effectiveness of the designed technique is studied for two subjects, namely aa and ay. It is performed for two-class motor imagery (MI) dataset [44]. MATLAB® is utilized to implement and validate the proposed system stages [50]. An example of the EEG instance from class 1 is shown in Figure 7.11a. Zooms of different EEG pulses are shown in Figure 7.11b.

Signal acquisition is an essential operation required in modern BCIs. Commonly, signal identification and processing are fixed-rate. So such mechanisms are not effective in the case of time-varying EEG signals.

This system incorporates the event-driven ADCs (EDADCS). These are focused on event-driven sensing (EDS) and, depending on received signal inequalities, will change their sampling frequency. Acquisition activity is only performed when the signal $x(t)$ passes through any of the pre-fixed thresholds. Therefore, samples are spread over time in a nonuniform fashion [40].

The EDADC output is segmented by the ASA. It separates only the relevant details from an incoming sequence of pooled event-driven samples that are not distributed equally. The $L_{ref} = 5.8$Sec is selected. The chosen segment lengths are adjusted according to the temporal changes of x(t). Figure 7.12a displays examples of the chosen segments. The EDADC and ASA allow the extraction of features to be performed in the time-domain [37,38].

The proposed hybrid features are mined from each segment. The denoising of each segment is carried out by using the ARFIR. Onward, the frequency domain transformation is performed by using the ARSTFT. Examples of the denoised selected segments are displayed in Figure 7.12b.

In this study, the eft EEG MI database [44] is used. There are 100 instances extracted for each subject, namely aa and ay. In the classical case, for a considered segment length of 5.8-sec and a sampling rate of 1kHz, each instance is composed of 5,800 samples. The recording is carried out with a 16-bit resolution ADC. On the

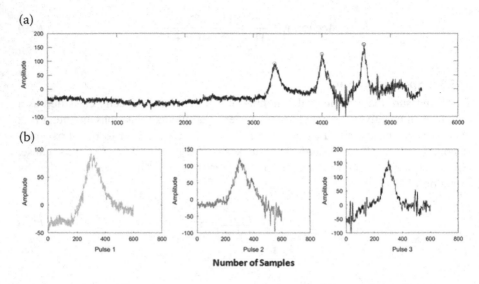

FIGURE 7.11   An example of EEG instance (a). Zoom of EEG pulses (b)

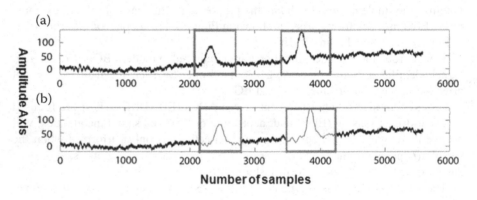

FIGURE 7.12   Examples of selected segments (a) and denoised segments (b)

other hand, the recording is performed with a 5-bit resolution EDADC for the suggested solution. The ASA is used to carry out the adaptive segmentation. $L_{ref} =$ 5.8-second is chosen [37,38]. As a function of the incoming signal variations, the ASA adapts Frs^i ubiquitously. It enables the filter order K^i to be balanced for each W^i and leads to the improved computational efficiency of the suggested tactic. However, for traditional alternatives, the length of the window and the number of observations per instance remain the same. They are not adjusted as per the signal disparities, 5.8-second, and 5,800 samples, respectively. Compared to the proposed solution, it causes a surplus increase in processing and power consumption.

For all 100 instances of each subject, the compression gains are calculated using equation (7.17). These are 11.65, and 15.68 folds for subjects aa and ay, respectively.

Consequently, the average compression gain for both subjects is 13.67-fold. The ASA output is resampled uniformly through the use of the SLI. An ARFIR filtering technique [38] to de-noise the resampled signal is used. Frequencies over 30Hz are often low-energy static, which should be removed for the successful identification of MI tasks. In this context, a bank of band-pass filters is designed offline. The cut-off frequencies of $[F_{Cmin} = 0.5; F_{Cmax} = 30]$ Hz are used for each designed filter. This enables the appropriate EEG band to be focused, thus attenuating the unnecessary noise [33]. Let $Fref$ be the set of frequencies of sampling for which the bank of filters is implemented. Then $Fref$ ranges among $Fs_{min} = 65.5$ Hz > 2. F_{Cmax} to $F_r = 174$Hz. $\Delta = 15.5$ Hz is selected. It permits to realize a bank of $Q = 8$ band-pass FIR filters. Table 7.1 outlines the parameters of these filters. This shows how the change in the sampling frequency influences orders of filters [33]. The adaptation of the online filter is clear from Table 7.1. It enables the signal to be enhanced with a decreased numerical expense relative to the standard approaches, which are of invariant nature [38].

The processing effectiveness of the proposed ARFIR is estimated over the conventional ones by utilizing equations (7.18) and (7.19). The results are reported in Table 7.2. It illustrates that over the traditional counterpart, the proposed ARFIR technique achieves notable numerical complexity reduction. This is accomplished by cleverly adjusting the parameter values such as Frs^i, Nr^i and K^i for each W^i. The incoming signal pilots those alterations.

The average gain for both intended subjects is also computed. For ARFIR, the reduction in the count of additions and multiplications is 30.57 and 32.12 times, respectively.

The proposed hybrid feature extraction is used to mine the discriminative and informative features of the conditioned selected segments. Those attributes are then

---

TABLE 7.1

Summary of the reference filters bank parameters

hc_k	$h1_k$	$h2_k$	$h3_k$	$h4_k$	$h5_k$	$h6_k$	$h7_k$	$h8_k$
$Fref_c$ (Hz)	65.5	81	96.5	112	127.5	143	158.5	174
K^i	20	25	31	36	41	46	51	56

TABLE 7.2

The summary of computational gain of ARFIR over classical filtering

Subject	Gain in additions(ARFIR)	Gain in multiplications(ARFIR)
aa	26.81	28.20
ay	34.32	36.03
Average	30.57	32.12

used for classification. Tables 7.3 and 7.4 illustrate the classification findings obtained by applying the proposed event-driven acquisition and processing-based approach.

Table 7.3 shows the results for subject aa in terms of the classification precision and the specificity values. The highest overall accuracy in the classification of 92.06% is achieved by the k-NN classifier. The average accuracy achieved by the SVM classifier is 86.93%. The highest average specificity value of 0.945 is achieved by the k-NN classifier. The average specificity achieved by the SVM classifier is 0.89. Table 7.4 shows the results for the subject ay in terms of the classification precision and the specificity values for the proposed case. The highest overall accuracy in classification of 91.06% is achieved by the SVM classifier. The average accuracy achieved by the k-NN classifier is 88.91%. The highest average specificity value of 0.943 is achieved by the SVM classifier. The average specificity achieved by the k-NN classifier is 0.91.

7.7 DISCUSSION

Cloud-based biomedical signals processing for BCI is a new trend. Obviously, it will play an essential part in mobile healthcare solutions for the future. From the results section, the benefits of the devised tactic are apparent. It employs a smart assembly of the event-driven acquisition and the methods for adaptive rate processing. The system parameters can be tuned according to variations of the

TABLE 7.3
Classifier performances for subject aa

Evaluation measure	Accuracy (%)			Specificity		
Class	1	2	Average	1	2	Average
SVM	87.65	86.21	86.93	0.90	0.88	0.890
k-NN	92.51	91.61	92.06	0.95	0.94	0.945

Accuracy refers to the correctly identified samples to the total samples. Specificity measures the proportion of negatives that are correctly identified

TABLE 7.4
Classifier performances for subject ay

Evaluation measure	Accuracy (%)			Specificity		
Class	1	2	Average	1	2	Average
SVM	91.43	90.71	91.07	0.94	0.92	0.93
k-NN	89.36	88.46	88.91	0.92	0.90	0.91

incoming signal. This ensures the dynamic parameters of the proposed solution are adapted according to the incoming signal disparities. It is shown how the adaptation of L^i and N^i automates the real-time tuning of Frs^i. This real-time adjustment of Frs^i enhances the processing effectiveness and the power efficiency of the designed approach in contrast to the traditional equal. It is obtained by eviting the needless operations while performing the real-time and online interpolation of the active signal portions. It also avoids the collection and conditioning of irrelevant information and leads towards an effective de-noising mechanism. Additionally, the real-time adoption of filter orders also adds to the effectiveness of the suggested conditioning mechanism [37,38].

The grace of the adaptive rate acquisition, a notable compression gain of 13.67-fold, is attained by the proposed solution. The computational complexity is also reduced at every stage of the system by using adaptive rate processing techniques instead of time-invariant techniques. The average gain for both intended subjects is calculated. The benefit in terms of additions and multiplications for the ARFIR is 30.57 and 32.12 folds, respectively. Reduction of circuit complexity is accomplished by using a 5-bit resolution EDADC as opposed to a 16-bit resolution done in previous studies. As a result of both, power efficiency of the system is inherently improved.

The invented method will derive and manipulate the most appropriate criteria for defining different brain functions. Studies have shown that a clever combination of the algorithms EDADC, ASA, ARFIR, ARSTFT, and k-NN contributes to the highest classification outcomes for the studied dataset. Because of its nonparametric nature, the k-NN achieves the highest precision of classification. Therefore, when identifying an instance, it compares it with each training set element. A designation is rendered in the context of counting the votes of its neighbor. It is necessary for the BCI systems to classify brain instructions correctly. The established model offers the best classification results for an intelligent combination of EDADC, ASA, ARFIR, ARSTFT, and k-NN. Across all subjects tested, it reaches the highest precision of 92.06%.

7.8   CONCLUSION

In cloud-based mobile brain computer interface, one crucial function is consistent and effective monitoring of the electroencephalogram. In this chapter, we developed an event-driven and adaptive rate brain computer interface. It utilizes the electro-cardiogram (ECG) signals for motor imagery task categorization. The suggested approach was checked as being practical, accurate, and successful in the measurement and evaluation of motor imagery tasks. Advances of the smart app and sensor technology provide creative means of enhancing the level of care for disabled individuals. The proposed approach is new and has the ability to improve brain computer interface and medical systems for the next age.

Using results, it is clear that, in contrast to standard equivalents, the mean decreases in the number of operations, both in terms of additions and multiplications, for the ARFIR are respectively 30.57-fold and 32.12-fold. Besides, the proposed approach also attains a notable diminishing in the acquired count of samples. For the studied case, it is 13.67-fold. Notable processing effectiveness of the designed system is evident from these results. Moreover, a significant diminishing in bandwidth usage is also assured by these findings. Furthermore, a simpler 5-bit resolution EDADC is employed in the proposed approach for the recording of EEG signals. In contrast, a relatively complex 16-bit resolution ADC is utilized for the EEG signals recoding in the case of traditional equals. It assures a simpler circuit-level realization of the suggested tactic in contrast to the conventional equals.

On the side of features extraction, the transformation of the 13.67-fold diminished count of samples is realized with a reduced complexity hybrid features extraction approach. It assures a notable lowering in the real-time count of operations of the features extraction process in contrast to the traditional tactics. A similar amount of gain in terms of the processing effectiveness is also expected by the classification stage.

The highest accuracy obtained by the designed frameworks is 92.06%. This suggests that the new solution achieves the same performance of classification compared with the standard equals while making noticeable improvements in compression, processing, and implementation of the hardware.

According to prior studies, the main advantage of this strategy is to achieve reasonably high precision that is comparable with other conventional approaches, while retaining a remarkable numerical advantage over them. It indicates the importance of the method proposed for developing and producing low-power cloud-based BCIs.

The performance of the proposed tactic is dependent on the utilized methods of resampling, conditioning, features mining, and classification. Research on the system effectiveness in terms of processing cost and precision while utilizing the higher-order interpolators is an upcoming task. Another opportunity is to exploit alternative tactics of features mining, such as the round cosine transform and the discrete wavelet transform (DWT). Other research opportunities are to explore the miniaturization, optimization, and integrated development of the proposed solution.

ACKNOWLEDGMENTS

The Effat University funds this work under grant number UC#9/29 April.2020/7.1–22(2) 1. The authors are thankful to Prof. A. Subasi for fruitful discussions. They are also grateful to Engineer M. G. Bahri for assistance during simulations and drawings.

REFERENCES

1. L.F. Nicolas-Alonso, and J. Gomez-Gil. Brain computer interfaces, a review, *Sensors* 12, 2 (2012) 1211–1279.
2. J. J. Shih, D. J. Krusienski, and J. R. Wolpaw. "Brain-computer interfaces in medicine," *Mayo Clinic Proceedings*. 87, 3 (2012): 268–279.
3. I. A. Mirza et al. "Mind-controlled wheelchair using an EEG headset and Arduino microcontroller," in *2015 International Conference on Technologies for Sustainable Development (ICTSD)*, Mumbai, India, pp. 1–5, 2015.
4. Zickler, C., Di Donna, V., Kaiser, V., Al-Khodairy, A., Kleih, S., Kübler, A., …Neuper, C. BCI applications for people with disabilities: defining user needs and user requirements. *Assistive Technology from Adapted Equipment to Inclusive Environments, AAATE*, 25, (2009): 185–189.

5. W. Yi, S. Qiu, H. Qi, L. Zhang, B. Wan, and D. Ming. Eeg feature comparison and classification of simple and compound limb motor imagery, *Journal of Neuro Engineering and Rehabilitation.* 10 (2013).

6. J.-S. Woo, K.-R. Muller, and S.-W. Lee. Classifying directions in continuous arm movement from EEG signals, in: *3rd International Winter Conference on Brain–Computer Interface (BCI), IEEE,* pp. 1–2, 2015.

7. K. Liao, R. Xiao, J. Gonzalez, and L. Ding. Decoding individual finger movements from one hand using human EEG signals. PloS one, 9, 1 (2014): e85192.

8. S.K. Bashar, and M.I.H. Bhuiyan. Identification of arm movements using statistical features from EEG signals in wavelet packet domain, in: *2015 International Conference on Electrical Engineering and Information Communication Technology (ICEEICT), IEEE,* pp. 1–5, 2015.

9. Z. Amini, V. Abootalebi, and M.T. Sadeghi. Comparison of performance of different feature extraction methods in detection of p300, Biocybern. *Biomedical Engineering* 33, 1 (2013): 3–20.

10. S.K. Bashar, A.R. Hassan, and M.I.H. Bhuiyan. Identification of motor imagery movements from EEG signals using dual tree complex wavelet transform, in: *2015 International Conference on Advances in Computing, Communications and Informatics (ICACCI), IEEE,* pp. 290–296, 2015.

11. M. Thulasidas, C. Guan, and J. Wu. "Robust classification of EEG signal for brain–computer interface," *IEEE Transactions on Neural Systems and Rehabilitation Engineering* 14, 1 (Mar. 2006): 24–29.

12. Atkinson, J., and Campos, D. Improving BCI-based emotion recognition by combining EEG feature selection and kernel classifiers. *Expert Systems With Applications* 47, (2016): 35–41.

13. Minguillon, J., Lopez-Gordo, M. A., and Pelayo, F. Trends in EEG-BCI for daily-life: Requirements for artifact removal. *Biomedical Signal Processing and Control* 31, (2017): 407–418.

14. Ahn, J. W., Ku, Y., Kim, D. Y., Sohn, J., Kim, J. H., and Kim, H. C. Wearable in-the-ear EEG system for SSVEP-based brain–computer interface. *Electronics Letters,* 54, 7 (2018): 413–414.

15. Kevric, J., and Subasi, A. Comparison of signal decomposition methods in classification of EEG signals for motor-imagery BCI system. *Biomedical Signal Processing and Control* 31, (2017): 398–406.

16. Samdin, S. B., Ting, C. M., Ombao, H., and Salleh, S. H. A unified estimation framework for state-related changes in effective brain connectivity. *IEEE Transactions on Biomedical Engineering* 64, 4 (2016): 844–858.

17. Long, J., Li, Y., Wang, H., Yu, T., Pan, J., and Li, F. A hybrid brain computer interface to control the direction and speed of a simulated or real wheelchair. *IEEE Transactions on Neural Systems and Rehabilitation Engineering* 20, 5 (2012): 720–729.

18. Hsu, W. Y. Assembling a multi-feature EEG classifier for left–right motor imagery data using wavelet-based fuzzy approximate entropy for improved accuracy. *International Journal of Neural Systems* 25, 08 (2015): 1550037.

19. Bhattacharyya, S., Konar, A., and Tibarewala, D. N. Motor imagery, P300 and error-related EEG-based robot arm movement control for rehabilitation purpose. *Medical & Biological Engineering & Computing* 52, 12 (2014): 1007–1017.

20. Robinson, N., Guan, C., Vinod, A. P., Ang, K. K., and Tee, K. P. Multi-class EEG classification of voluntary hand movement directions. *Journal of Neural Engineering* 10, 5 (2013): 056018.

21. Sannelli, C., Vidaurre, C., Müller, K. R., and Blankertz, B. Ensembles of adaptive spatial filters increase BCI performance: an online evaluation. *Journal of Neural Engineering* 13, 4 (2016): 046003.

22. Bashar, S. K., and Bhuiyan, M. I. H. Classification of motor imagery movements using multivariate empirical mode decomposition and short time Fourier transform based hybrid method. *Engineering Science and Technology, an International Journal* 19, 3 (2016): 1457–1464.

23. Zhang, Y., Liu, B., Ji, X., and Huang, D. Classification of EEG signals based on autoregressive model and wavelet packet decomposition. *Neural Processing Letters* 45, 2) (2017): 365–378.

24]. Datta, A., and Chatterjee, R. Comparative study of different ensemble compositions in EEG signal classification problem. In *Emerging Technologies in Data Mining and Information Security*, pp. 145–154. Springer, Singapore, 2019.

25. Subasi, A. *Practical Guide for Biomedical Signals Analysis Using Machine Learning Techniques: A MATLAB Based Approach.* Academic Press, Cambridge, 2019.

26. Wang, G., Wang, M., Qin, X., and Zhang, L. A brain computer interface control system based on cloud platform for Minitype UAVs. In *Global Intelligence Industry Conference (GIIC 2018)* 10835, p. 108350U. International Society for Optics and Photonics 2018).

27. Blondet, M. V. R., Badarinath, A., Khanna, C., and Jin, Z. A wearable real-time BCI system based on mobile cloud computing. In *2013 6th International IEEE/EMBS Conference on Neural Engineering (NER)*, pp. 739–742. IEEE, 2013.

28. Looney, D., Kidmose, P., and Mandic, D. P. Ear-EEG: user-centered and wearable BCI. *In Brain-Computer Interface Research*, pp. 41–50. Springer, Berlin, 2014.

29. Hejrati, B., Fathi, A., and Abdali-Mohammadi, F. Efficient lossless multi-channel EEG compression based on channel clustering. *Biomedical Signal Processing and Control* 31, (2017): 295–300.

30. Bazán-Prieto, C., Blanco-Velasco, M., Cárdenas-Barrera, J., and Cruz-Roldán, F. (2012). Analysis of tractable distortion metrics for EEG compression applications. *Physiological Measurement* 33, 7 (2012): 1237.

31. Mesin, L. A neural algorithm for the non-uniform and adaptive sampling of biomedical data. *Computers in Biology and Medicine* 71, (2016): 223–230.

32. Mina Qaisar, S., Sidiya, D., Akbar, M., and Subasi, A. An event-driven multiple objects surveillance system. *International Journal of Electrical and Computer Engineering Systems*, 9, 1 (2018): 35–44.

33. Mian Qaisar, S., and Subasi, A. Effective epileptic seizure detection based on the event-driven processing and machine learning for mobile healthcare. *Journal of Ambient Intelligence and Humanized Computing*, (2020): 1–13.

34. Antony, A., Paulson, S. R., and Moni, D. J. Asynchronous level crossing ADC design for wearable devices: a review. *International Journal of Applied Engineering Research*, 13, 4 (2018): 1858–1865.

35. Mian Qaisar, S., and Fawad Hussain, S. Arrhythmia diagnosis by using level-crossing ECG sampling and sub-bands features extraction for mobile healthcare. *Sensors* 20, 8 (2020): 2252.

36. Budiman, Erwin Satrya. "Multi-rate analyte sensor data collection with sample rate configurable signal processing." 2017. U.S. Patent Application No. 15/292,107. Google Patents.

37. S. M. Qaisar, L. Fesquet, and M. Renaudin. "Adaptive rate filtering a computationally efficient signal processing approach," *Signal Process.* 94, (2014): 620–630.

38. Qaisar, S. M. (2019). Efficient mobile systems based on adaptive rate signal processing. *Computers & Electrical Engineering*, 79, 106462.

39. Tan, L., & Jiang, J. *Digital Signal Processing: Fundamentals and Applications.* Academic Press, New York, 2018.

40. Mian Qaisar, S. A proficient Li-Ion battery state of charge estimation based on event-driven processing. *Journal of Electrical Engineering & Technology.* 15, (2020): 1871–1877. doi:10.1007/s42835-020-00458-x.

41. Herzog, Andrew G. "Catamenial Epilepsy: definition, prevalence pathophysiology and treatment." *Seizure* 17, 2 (2008): 151–159.
42. Shorvon, Simon D. "A history of neuroimaging in epilepsy 1909-2009". *Epilepsia* 50, 3 (2009): 39–49.
43. Zeidman, L. A., Stone, J., and Kondziella, D. New revelations about Hans Berger, father of the electroencephalogram (EEG), and his ties to the Third Reich. *Journal of Child Neurology* 29, 7 (2014): 1002–1010.
44. Dornhege, Benjamin Blankertz, Gabriel Curio, and Klaus-Robert Müller. Boosting bit rates in non-invasive EEG single-trial classifications by feature combination and multi-class paradigms. *IEEE Transactions on Biomedical Engineering* 51, 6 (June 2004): 993–1002.
45. Mian Qaisar, S. *Échantillonnage et traitement conditionnés par le signal: une approche prometteuse pour des traitements efficaces à pas adaptatifs* (Doctoral dissertation, Grenoble INPG), 2009.
46. H. Weller. Fourier analysis. 2015. http://www.met.reading.ac.uk/~sws02hs/teaching/Fourier/Fourier_2_student.pdf.
47. S. M. Qaisar, M. Akbar, T. Beyrouthy, W. Al-Habib, and M. Asmatulah, "An error measurement for resampled level crossing signal," presented at the *2016 Second International Conference on Event-based Control, Communication, and Signal Processing (EBCCSP)*, 2016, pp. 1–4.
48. Qaisar, S. M., and Aljefri, R. Event-driven time-domain elucidation of the power quality disturbances. *Procedia Computer Science* 168, (2020): 217–223.
49. Mian Qaisar, S. and Alsharif, F. Signal piloted processing of the smart meter data for effective appliances recognition. *Journal of Electrical Engineering & Technology.* 15 (2020): 2279–2285. doi: 10.1007/s42835-020-00465-y.
50. Knight, A. *Basics of MATLAB and Beyond.* CRC Press, Boca Raton, 2019.

8 EEG-Based BCI Systems for Neurorehabilitation Applications

Muhammad Ahmed Khan, Rig Das,
John Paulin Hansen, and Sadasivan Puthusserypady

8.1 INTRODUCTION

The idea of controlling the environment with the mind was considered to be science fiction. However, technological advancements have paved a platform namely, brain computer interface (BCI), which allows the communication between human brain and environment/machines. A BCI system provides a direct interaction pathway/channel between the brain and a peripheral device by translating the electrical activities (e.g., the electroencephalogram [EEG]) of the brain into control/command signals. Though Dr. Grey Walter introduced BCI in 1964, its research has grown rapidly only in the past few years. The public interest within this field is growing tremendously, several commercial BCI systems are being launched each year, and leading investors have become actively engaged in the BCI industry. Moreover, the impact of BCI systems in medical applications is ever increasing, as it has the potential to be used in rehabilitating the patients suffering from devastating neural injuries and neuromuscular diseases, such as amyotrophic lateral sclerosis (ALS), motor disabilities, spinal cord injuries (SCI), or stroke, etc.

The term "BCI" is very much diversified in nature and hence, can be defined in several possible ways:

BCI systems provide a means to transfer information from the brain to computer by decoding patterns that emerge during mental activities. This allows for interacting with external applications or the environment without the use of the ordinary peripheral neuronal pathways, such as hands, arms or the voice.

In the widely adopted definition, any BCI system must meet four criteria: (1) The system must involve the direct measurement of brain signals; (2) It must deliver feedback to the user; (3) It must operate in online mode; and (4) Rely on the 'user's thought control,' i.e., the system must get control by the input commands produced by the user's imagination to perform the specific task [1].

A more recent definition describes BCI as a system that measures central nervous system (CNS) activity and converts it into an artificial output that replaces, restores, enhances, supplements, or improves natural CNS output and thereby changes the ongoing interactions between the CNS and its external or internal environment [2].

8.1.1 CLASSIFICATION OF BCI SYSTEMS

The BCI systems are classified into five different categories, based on the invasiveness, external stimulus, synchronization, dependability, and mode of application (Figure 8.1).

8.1.1.1 Invasive, Semi-Invasive and Non-Invasive BCI Systems

Depending on how the brain activities are measured, there are currently three possible types of BCI systems. The first type involves invasive recording, where microelectrodes are inserted into the brain cortex and can record even the firing of a single neuron. However, this type gives the highest possible spatial resolution; it could potentially be a health hazard to already fragile patients and its long-term stability is unknown. The second type, which carries possibly less risk compared to the first type, is the semi-invasive type, which uses electrodes placed mostly below the dura layer of the brain that record the signals from the cortical surface using electrocorticogram (ECoG). Lastly, the noninvasive type, which records signals from the scalp using mostly the electroencephalography (EEG). This method is user-friendly, safe, inexpensive, and has a remarkably high temporal resolution. However, it has a much lower spatial resolution (at cm level), is more sensitive to environmental noise, and has a limited frequency range (less than ~70 Hz).

8.1.1.2 Exogenous and Endogenous BCI Systems

Exogenous BCI systems rely on external stimulus (visual/auditory/tactile) to generate desired brain responses. A good example would be the Steady-State Visual Evoked Potential (SSVEP)-based BCI systems, in which the visual system is used to carry out the signals from the eyes to the occipital region (visual cortex) and triggers the brain activities. The endogenous BCI systems, on the other hand, are not relying on external stimuli to evoke different brain signals and are using the brain's rhythms and other potentials to command an external application. This means that the users must learn the skills of producing specific patterns to control

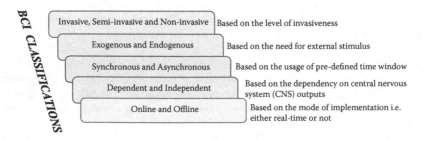

FIGURE 8.1 Classification of BCI systems

the BCI systems with their minds. Motor imagery (MI) is the most common paradigm for endogenous systems in which each mental task is used to evoke unique brain patterns that can be used to perform specific actions.

8.1.1.3 Synchronous and Asynchronous BCI Systems

Synchronous BCI systems use brain signals only during predefined time windows. In this way, users can send control commands only during specific time intervals. The main feature of such a system is that both the beginning and end of the mental activity that are performed is known in advance and can be associated to a start and end point in the data record. The downside, however is that it limits the user from performing mental tasks outside the predefined time intervals. Asynchronous BCI systems, on the other hand, are always active, recording and processing the signals in real-time, irrespective of when the task is performed. They provide a more realistic approach as compared to synchronous systems and can detect EEG signals arising from both the idling state and the active state of a user. This trait comes with a price as asynchronous BCI systems are usually more complex and computationally demanding than the synchronous BCI systems.

8.1.1.4 Dependent and Independent BCI Systems

The BCI systems are classified as dependent/independent, based on the dependency on the natural output of the central nervous system (CNS). The dependent BCI needs natural CNS output to function: for example, a BCI system that uses visual evoked potentials (VEPs) to generate particular brain signals is dependent on the direction of one's gaze and the muscles around the eyes. On the other hand, an independent BCI is not dependent on CNS output for generating the brain signals. This is the case for a MI-BCI system, that requires only the subject's imagination to perform any required task.

The BCI systems are either online or offline, depending on the mode of application. Offline systems act as simulation platform for mimicking an actual BCI system to examine the different BCI parameters like EEG features extraction, classification, the electrode positions, algorithm accuracy, etc. Online systems, however, execute real-time EEG signal processing, and they are the only BCI systems that can facilitate direct control over an external application.

8.2 EEG BASED BCI SYSTEM ARCHITECTURE FOR NEUROREHABILITATION

For neurorehabilitation application, the overall process from designing to implementation of BCI systems is mainly divided into three different phases: (1) pre-rehabilitation phase, (2) rehabilitation phase, and (3) post-rehabilitation phase. To provide an in-depth description regarding specific neural application, a detailed methodology for the BCI-based stroke rehabilitation has been illustrated in Figure 8.2 and is comprehensively described next.

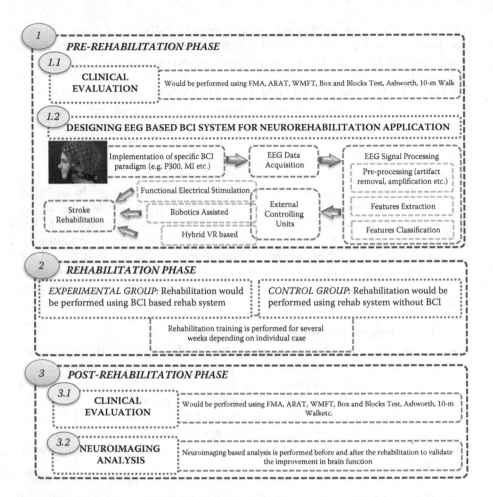

FIGURE 8.2   Schematic for stroke rehabilitation BCI system

8.2.1   Pre-Rehabilitation Phase

This phase mainly consists of "clinical evaluation" and "pilot study to develop BCI systems for stroke rehabilitation." In clinical evaluation, different tests like Fugl-Meyer Assessment (FMA), Action Research Arm Test (ARAT), Box and Blocks Test (BBT), Wolf Motor Function Test (WMFT), Ashworth, 10-m Walk, etc., are performed on stroke patients to determine their present condition [3]. These test scores act as a reference to be compared with post-rehab scores for determining the level of improvement after the rehabilitation therapy. To design a BCI system, EEG data of stroke patients during rehabilitation exercises is acquired and is used to develop an algorithm for controlling the external rehabilitation devices (a pilot study). For developing such a system, three components are of utmost importance, which includes: (1) BCI paradigms, (2) algorithm development for EEG signal processing, and (3) external controlling units.

8.2.2 REHABILITATION PHASE

Once the system is developed, it is tested by carrying out rehabilitation therapy sessions on stroke patients. For this, randomized control trials are performed, whereby the patients are randomly assigned to any of the two groups (experimental group and control group). The experimental group undergoes rehabilitation with the BCI rehab system and the control group undergoes therapy by any other conventional rehabilitation method (without using BCI) [4].

8.2.3 POST-REHABILITATION PHASE

After stroke rehabilitation, the clinical assessment is performed once again by determining the test scores to evaluate the efficiency of the rehab protocol (on both control and experimental groups). The pre- and post-rehabilitation test scores are then compared to identify the recovery level and motor improvements [5,6]. Apart from motor recovery, neuro-functional imaging modalities, such as functional magnetic resonance imaging (fMRI), positron emission tomography (PET), near-infrared spectroscopy (NIRS), magnetoencephalography (MEG), and transcranial magnetic stimulation (TMS), are used to examine the improvements of brain functionalities [7]. This also explains how the BCI trainings affect the stroke rehabilitation by exploring the association between the rehabilitation outcomes and internal brain activities.

8.3 TYPES OF BCI PARADIGMS

8.3.1 STEADY-STATE VISUAL EVOKED POTENTIAL (SSVEP)

8.3.1.1 Introduction

SSVEP is produced in response to external visual stimulus and is widely used in BCI systems. The visual stimulation can be induced by cathode ray tube (CRT), flashing lights, alternating graphical patterns, flickering images or light-emitting diodes (LED) and their frequencies lie in the range of low (1–3.5 Hz) to high (75–100 Hz) frequency bands. SSVEPs are produced in the primary visual cortex, and these signal are acquired by employing the EEG electrodes at the parieto-occipital regions (electrode positions Oz, O1, O2, Pz, P3 and P4) of the brain.

SSVEP based BCI comprises several flickering stimuli and each of them oscillates with a unique frequency. The system allows the person to control the output device or perform a certain task using an eye gaze towards the flickering stimulus. When a user gazes or focuses on the specific flickering stimulus, the EEG signal will show the power increase at that corresponding flickering frequency. Then, feature extraction and classification algorithms will determine which stimulus the subject was observing and executes the predefined task corresponding to the particular frequency. An overview of the advantages, limitations, and applications of the SSVEP-BCI systems is presented in Table 8.1.

TABLE 8.1

SSVEP based BCI systems overview

Advantages	Limitations	Applications
• Higher accuracy.	• Causes fatigue as user	• BCI Speller [8].
• Calibration is done in	must be focused on single	• Mind controlled drone
few minutes.	point.	(act as brain exercise for
• No or minimal training	• Requires high level of eye	neural disorder
is required.	control.	patients) [9].
• Operates on multiple	• Feasible only for short	• BCI-based occupational
frequencies, hence, can	duration experiments.	therapy assist suit
perform wide variety of	• Not appropriate for	(BOTAS) [10].
tasks (one task for each	people with vision related	• Controls a humanoid
frequency).	disorders.	robot [11], prosthesis
		[12], orthosis [13], and
		exoskeleton [14].

8.3.1.2   Case Study for SSVEP-BCI Implementation in Neurorehabilitation: BCI Based 3D Virtual Playground for the Attention Deficit Hyperactivity Disorder (ADHD) Patients

In the presented case study, a novel neurofeedback SSVEP-BCI system was designed and developed to train attention in ADHD subjects [15]. It is a 3D virtual playground created as a 3D virtual classroom having 2D games on the background blackboard. The control in the 2D games utilizes SSVEP, while 3D distractions are being active in the classroom. The results revealed that the subjects were affected by the distractions in the 3D classroom and change of environment, rather than the game elements in the 2D game. Findings revealed that the flickering frequency of 9Hz had longer selection time compared to 7 Hz. The time also increased when attending the same frequency as before. The average selection time was about 3.07 s with the shortest time of 1.33 s and the longest time of 4.98 s. The average accuracy for the experiment was 92.26 percent with the lowest accuracy being 77.41 percent and the highest being 99.26%. The average information transfer rate (ITR) for the system was about 11.85 bits/min.

8.3.1.2.1 Methodology and Experimental Setup

• Frequencies selection for SSVEP paradigm

For the frequencies selection, the method suggested by Mehdi et al. has been adopted [16]. Figure 8.3 illustrates the visual paradigm from the experiment where a small square (fixation point) is located in the middle with flickering squares on either side. The right and left squares flicker at specified frequencies (i.e., 6 Hz,

FIGURE 8.3 Visual paradigm of experiment

7 Hz, 8 Hz or 9 Hz). A number appears at the fixation point at random time intervals showing which number to attend. The experiment consists of 14 sessions where each session runs one of 3 phases in a pseudorandom order. Among all the frequencies, 7 Hz and 9 Hz are selected for the BCI system because their 2nd or 3rd harmonics do not overlap with each other and are easily distinguishable. Another reason for picking 7 Hz and 9 Hz is that they are not as close as the pair 7 Hz and 8 Hz or the pair 8 Hz and 9 Hz. This could give incorrect results in case of a lag affecting the flickering frequencies.

- *Designing 2D game and 3D virtual classroom environment*

The 3D classroom has been designed for introducing realistic disruptions with the possibility of showing different games on the blackboard. Here, only one game was implemented on the blackboard. It is important to understand that the 2D game and the 3D classroom are separate entities, which were combined and provided the training playground for attention training for ADHD subjects.

The 2D game consists of different levels. The first level has only the game appearing where the user uses the flickering squares to move to the left and right to collect fruits and at the same time avoid the danger elements. The screen view is big enough for the user to focus on the game only. The second level has the game placed on the blackboard but there are no distractions except the scoreboard to the right top corner of the blackboard. The user has to get accustomed to the flickering squares in the classroom instead. The user also has to focus on the blackboard game while ignoring the classroom elements. The third level is similar to the previous level with added distractions: teacher, classmates, books, paper planes, etc. These three levels of the game are presented in Figure 8.4. From the top, the first figure shows the 2D game only, the middle picture represents the 3D classroom (empty) with a 2D game on the blackboard and at the bottom, the 3D classroom (containing distractions) is shown with a 2D game on the blackboard.

- *Designing of BCI setup and algorithm development*

The experiments for testing the SSVEP-BCI system used the setup as shown in Figure 8.5. The algorithm, which was developed to play the game via SSVEP stimulus mainly consists of three parts: (a) Artifact removal, (b) Feature extraction via FFT (Fast Fourier Transformation), and (c) Feature classification. The algorithm used a classifier based on the amplitude spectrum and a threshold logic. There were two sets of data ((i) SData – Most recent one second of EEG, and (ii) CData – A concatenation of up to three most recent sets of SData), that were examined in each

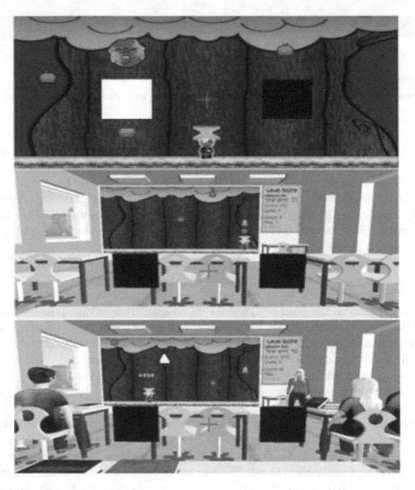

FIGURE 8.4   2D game and 3D class room environment

iteration. Each iteration took originally 2 s, but this has been brought down to 1s in a modified version. This led to lower record time to optimize signal processing and has shown to work better without compromising the results.

8.3.1.2.2 Experimental Results

Experiments were conducted in a dim lit room. The distance between the subject and the stimulus screen was maintained at 60 cm. 12 healthy subjects were selected to perform the experiments and one of them dropped out because of scalp skin disease. The remaining 11 healthy participants were of both genders (8 males and 3 females) within age group of 23–32 years old. The subject participated in 9 tests that are listed in Table 8.2:

Experimental results are shown in Figure 8.6. Figure 8.6a illustrates the average accuracy of all environmental based tests. It is evident that the average accuracy decreases as the environment changed. From all experiments, the highest accuracy

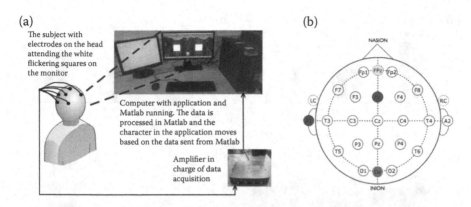

FIGURE 8.5   (a) The visual setting of the BCI system. It shows the subject looking at the SSVEP stimuli. The amplifier acquires the EEG data and sends it to the computer. MATLAB® processes the data and sends a command to the application on the same computer, which then moves the character on the screen, (b) Electrodes placement for EEG acquisition: the top of the head where Oz circle shows the placement for the channel 1 electrode, F_{PZ} circle shows the placement for ground electrode, and A1 & Fz circles show the possible placements for the reference electrode. Only one of the reference circles were chosen.

TABLE 8.2

Tests in the experiment

Tests based on environment	Tests based on game elements
Test 1, 4, 7: Only 2D game	Test 1, 2, 3: No element
Test 2, 5, 8: Empty class with 2D game	Test 4, 5, 6: Contains fruits
Test 3, 6, 9: Full class with 2D game	Test 7, 8, 9: Contains fruits and danger

was found when the tests were running in the 2D environment. The accuracy dropped while changing the environments from 2D to the 3D classroom and decreased further when the distractions increased. This was verified in the average accuracy based on the game elements (Figure 8.6b), where all three groupings show the same pattern. In each group, the first test showed high accuracy, followed by the second test and the last test. The only exception is the test in the no element group, where the full class accuracy is less than the empty-class accuracy. Overall, the pattern shows the same result as before, where the environment affects the accuracy and not the game elements. It is surprising to note that the game elements do not affect the accuracy much, while the change in environment seems to be a drastic change for the subject. However, the results do make sense because the 3D environments are filled with objects and can cause more distraction, which in turn can decrease the task execution accuracy. Moreover, the average accuracy of tasks 1–9 can be found in Figure 8.6c, which indicates that every test has an accuracy of approximately 90 percent or more. Besides, the BCI system's performance was also estimated by analyzing its ITR. Figure 8.6d presents the ITR for each of the subjects

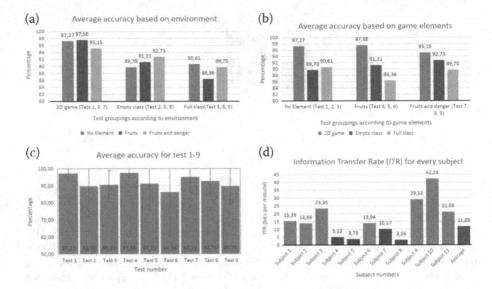

FIGURE 8.6 (a) The accuracy for tests 1–9 sorted into groups based on the application environment. Note that the figure's y-axis begins at 80 percent to clearly show the accuracy difference between the tests, (b) The accuracy for tests 1–9 sorted into groups based on the game elements in the ninja game. Note that the figure's y-axis begins at 80 percent to clearly show the accuracy difference between the tests, (c) The accuracy for tests 1–9. Here, the figure's y-axis begins from 50 percent to clearly show the difference between the tests, and (d) The ITR for every subject executing the tests 1–9. ITR is measured in bits transferred per minute. The last column at the end of the figure is the average ITR calculated on all subjects' ITR. The subjects with an ITR lower than average have dark colored column while the subjects with an ITR higher than average have a light colored column.

where the last bar displays the average ITR. Depending on the subjects, the ITR ranges between the values of 3.26 to 42.24 bits/min, with an average ITR of 11.85 bits/min.

8.3.1.2.3 Case Study Conclusion

An SSVEP-BCI system was developed for attention training for ADHD patients. The system consisted of a 3D training playground with 2D games (different levels) running on the blackboard in a 3D virtual classroom. The idea was to train the subjects to focus and complete the game to attain high scores as well as to advance to the next level in the presence of distractions; thus enabling the subjects to enhance their attention abilities.

Results from this study showed that the subjects were affected by the change of the environment and distractions in the 3D classroom rather than the game elements in the 2D game. The changes in environment and distractions caused their accuracy to fall, increased the number of selections, and also increased the time to finish the test. The 2D game elements play a major role on the subjects' selection time. Together with the environment change and distractions, they make the subjects hesitate before their selection. This resulted in longer selection times because of the subjects' attention to the environment, distractions, and game elements instead of the actual selective target.

8.3.2 P300

8.3.2.1 Introduction

The P300 is an event related potential (ERP) that appears as a positive peak (ranging from 5 to 10 microvolts) around 300 ms after occurrence of a rare or surprising stimulus, which can be visual, tactile or auditory in nature. These activities are strong in the midline areas of the brain and therefore, EEG electrodes are placed over the Fz, Cz and Pz locations to record these signals. The P300 peak is elicited during the "oddball paradigm," where the series of stimuli is classified into two classes: (i) frequently occurring event and (ii) rare/surprising event. Thus, when the brain encounters a surprising event, it will generate P300 ERP after around 300 ms. It has been found that the P300 is stronger if a person performs some tasks during an experiment. Therefore, it is advised to count the number of rare stimuli during trials to achieve a higher and prominent peak of P300 signals.

For P300-BCI systems, the row/column (RC) paradigm is the most commonly used and was first introduced in 1988 by Farwell and Donchin [17]. They have developed the P300 speller, which is now marked as a benchmark paradigm for P300 based BCI systems. IntendiX SPELLER (g.tec, Austria) is the world's first commercially available "Spelling System" based on P300. It is designed to be installed at home settings for patients with neural disorders, such as ALS. It enables the user to select a character or symbol from the screen by means of a RC paradigm. The selected item can be written or spoken by the computer, based on the patient's desire. The system shows remarkable performance, as most of the users were able to spell 5 to 10 characters per minute in their first trial after just 10 minutes of training. Moreover, g.tec has also introduced a special extension tool, named "extendiX," which receives input commands from IntendiX and controls external devices such as music, TVs, games, assistive robots and so on, thus incorporating the BCI technology to improve the patients' everyday lives. The advantages, limitations, and neural applications of P300 based BCI systems are shown in Table 8.3.

8.3.2.2 Case Study for P300-BCI Implementation in Neurorehabilitation: Adaptive Filtering for Detection of User-Independent Event Related Potentials in BCIs

In P300 based BCI systems, several methods have been proposed for spatial filtering and classification of the P300 components. In the presented case study, principal component analysis (PCA), independent component analysis (ICA) and xDAWN algorithm were used along with two classifiers; the Fisher's Linear Discriminant Analysis (FLDA) and Support Vector Machine (SVM) [18]. In addition, an adaptive version of the xDAWN algorithm (axDAWN) that allows previously estimated spatial filters to be adapted to new subjects is implemented and evaluated. The adaptive spatial filtering can reduce the training time considerably without compromising the classification performance. The methods were evaluated using two different datasets: (i) BCI Competition III dataset (P300 speller

TABLE 8.3

P300 based BCI systems overview

Advantages	Limitations	Applications
• Calibration is done in few minutes. • No or minimal training is required.	• Low real-time P300 detection accuracy. • Large number of trials are needed for single task execution. • Possesses low ITR. • Causes fatigue as user has to be focused on single point. • Requires high level of eye control. • Feasible only for short duration experiments. • Not appropriate for people with vision related problems.	• BCI Spellers [18]. • Wheelchair navigation [19]. • Controls a humanoid robot [20]. • Brain-actuated internet browsing [21].

paradigm) [22], which contained EEG recordings from 2 healthy subjects, and (ii) Our own dataset, which was recorded in our BCI laboratory, obtained in the context of this work and contained EEG recordings from 11 healthy subjects. Results indicate that the combination of xDAWN and SVM algorithms achieves the highest performance. Regarding the axDAWN, it is shown that it can achieve comparable performance with xDAWN under the same conditions by incrementally computing the new filters without storing data from old subjects.

8.3.2.2.1 Methodology and Experimental Setup

- BCI competition III dataset
  BCI Competition III dataset consists of EEG signals (P300 based) from 2 healthy subjects. The data was acquired using 64 EEG channels (10/20 electrode placement system) by BCI2000 software at a sampling rate of 240 Hz. The dataset contained signals from 185 characters and was acquired within 5 sessions, with 9 runs each session and single word was spelled in each run [22].
- Our own dataset
  It contains data measured from 11 subjects (students), six females and five males. The EEG electrodes were located at the central, parietal, and occipital areas of the brain. The reference electrode was placed at the earlobe and the ground electrode was positioned at the F_{PZ} position. Figure 8.7 shows the experimental setup and the sixteen electrodes placement (10–20 system).
    The data was acquired in 3 sessions where the subjects were asked to spell a whole sentence. The three sentences used contained 21, 18 and 20 characters,

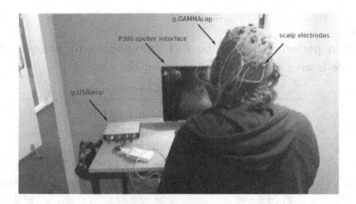

FIGURE 8.7 P300-BCI experimental setup

respectively. For each character, 15 trials were performed producing 15 row/column flashes. Each row/column flashed for 100 ms and after each flash, the P300 speller matrix remained blank for 60 ms. Between stimuli presentation of successive characters, the matrix kept blank for 2.5 ms. The spelling duration of each character was 28.8 s. Each session lasted approximately 10 to 12 minutes while the whole experiment, including the subject preparation, lasted about 45 minutes.

- Data analysis
  The presented study showed the development of spatial filtering and classification schemes for the enhancement of ERP responses in the context of both user-dependent and user-independent analysis. Initially, three widely used spatial filtering techniques (xDAWN, PCA and ICA) were developed (for feature extraction) and the classification performance of classifiers SVM and FLDA is evaluated. To examine the performance of the spatial filtering and classification methods, the Monte-Carlo Cross Validation (MCCV) technique was used. MCCV randomly selects a certain proportion of the available observations to form the training set, while the remaining observations form the test set. The performance was assessed in terms of sensitivity, accuracy, and specificity.

8.3.2.2.2 Experimental Results

Two different scenarios, a user-dependent and user-independent scenario respectively, were investigated in this study. In the user-dependent scenario, the spatial filtering and classification were performed based on observations obtained from the same subject. In the user-independent scenario, spatial filters from an old subject were adapted to enhance the P300 responses for new subjects. The classifiers were trained from scratch using enhanced P300 responses corresponding to both the old and the new subjects. P300 responses were obtained after the spatial filtering of observations from both new and old subjects using the adapted filters.

- Classification performance for user-dependent scenario
  For the user-dependent case, the results were obtained using 30 characters during the training phase and considering 15 trials for each character. Table 8.4 shows the classification accuracy of FLDA and SVM for the

TABLE 8.4

Classification performance for the BCI competition III dataset [22]. The performance figures are the mean values for the subjects

Methods	BCI Competition III		
	Accuracy ± std (%)	Sensitivity ± std (%)	Specificity ± std (%)
xDawn-SVM	93.54 ± 4.13	92.24 ± 4.13	96.20 ± 1.26
ICA-SVM	90.04 ± 5.26	89.68 ± 5.46	90.11 ± 5.22
PCA-SVM	82.35 ± 2.48	79.25 ± 5.39	82.97 ± 1.90
xDawn-FLDA	93.69 ± 5.10	86.71 ± 0.05	95.09 ± 1.62
ICA-FLDA	87.20 ± 4.91	88.02 ± 0.03	87.04 ± 5.13
PCA-FLDA	83.86 ± 0.16	81.00 ± 0.33	84.43 ± 0.12

TABLE 8.5

Classification performance corresponding to our dataset. The performance figures are the mean values for the subjects

Methods	Our Dataset		
	Accuracy ± std (%)	Sensitivity ± std (%)	Specificity ± std (%)
xDawn-SVM	90.16 ± 4.95	84.09 ± 6.60	91.38 ± 4.78
ICA-SVM	87.19 ± 6.09	82.63 ± 6.35	88.00 ± 6.20
PCA-SVM	76.84 ± 7.21	71.12 ± 5.44	77.99 ± 7.75
xDawn-FLDA	86.97 ± 5.16	82.34 ± 0.07	87.90 ± 4.86
ICA-FLDA	84.10 ± 6.07	81.25 ± 0.06	84.67 ± 6.08
PCA-FLDA	80.90 ± 4.87	77.18 ± 0.05	81.65 ± 4.97

different spatial filtering approaches using the BCI Competition III dataset, while Table 8.5 shows the performance obtained by the same methods using our dataset. Results indicate that SVM outperforms the FLDA algorithm. Moreover, the xDAWN method exhibits a better behavior in terms of classification performance as both FLDA and SVM perform better using features that are extracted by the xDAWN algorithm. Meanwhile, the combination of PCA and FLDA performs the worst.

- Classification performance for user-independent scenario

  In the user-independent scenario, xDAWN has been used for feature extraction whereas SVM and FLDA were used as classifiers (only on our dataset). Initially, the spatial filters corresponding to 5 different subjects (termed as old subjects) using 25 randomly selected characters were estimated. Then, the spatial filters of each old subject were adapted to the 6 new subjects using 5 and 10 new randomly selected characters to form the training set. Hence, to assess the classification accuracy of the adapted spatial filters, three different

TABLE 8.6
Classification performance obtained using SVM and FLDA when no adaptation of the initial spatial filters is performed

Subjects	Accuracy ± std (%)		Sensitivity ± std (%)		Specificity ± std (%)	
	SVM	FLDA	SVM	FLDA	SVM	FLDA
1	76.50 ± 8.85	71.10 ± 6.95	34.07 ± 5.27	39.37 ± 7.47	84.99 ± 11.13	77.44 ± 7.31
9	78.72 ± 5.51	72.82 ± 4.68	42.16 ± 0.48	43.96 ± 0.65	89.28 ± 7.38	81.63 ± 6.04
5	80.76 ± 6.21	72.79 ± 9.32	49.85 ± 5.03	49.48 ± 3.84	86.94 ± 8.04	77.46 ± 10.56
8	69.92 ± 11.70	67.23 ± 10.12	40.41 ± 26.68	47.34 ±20.04	75.82 ± 8.98	71.21 ± 8.14
2	79.63 ± 6.43	71.74 ± 4.85	51.03 ± 4.45	56.08 ± 7.37	85.34 ± 7.17	74.88 ± 5.25

TABLE 8.7
Classification performance obtained using SVM and FLDA when 5 new characters are used for adapting the initial spatial filters

Subjects	Accuracy ± std (%)		Sensitivity ± std (%)		Specificity ± std (%)	
	SVM	FLDA	SVM	FLDA	SVM	FLDA
1	84.95 ± 1.84	78.62 ± 2.43	60.05 ± 16.51	63.83 ±11.02	89.93 ± 2.54	81.58 ± 2.73
9	81.55 ± 2.55	75.77 ± 1.80	47.80 ± 0.51	52.62 ± 2.74	88.80 ± 3.50	80.48 ± 2.77
5	88.19 ± 2.55	84.17 ± 2.97	55.98 ± 14.53	58.33 ±10.01	94.63 ± 2.97	89.34 ± 2.64
8	78.71 ± 6.39	74.80 ± 6.06	58.41 ± 17.82	58.91 ±12.47	82.77 ± 4.90	77.97 ± 4.78
2	86.75 ± 4.75	82.85 ± 5.91	64.24 ± 9.56	66.56 ± 9.83	91.25 ± 4.13	86.10 ± 5.39

cases were examined. In the first case, the spatial filters estimated from the old subject were used to filter signals obtained from new subjects without considering any adaptation. In the second case, 5 characters from the new subject were used to adapt the filters. Finally, in the third case, 10 characters were used to adapt the filters.

Tables 8.6–8.8 show the classification performance obtained by SVM and FLDA, when no adaptation, 5-character and 10-character adaptation were performed, respectively. Subjects 1, 9, 5, 8, and 2 correspond to the old subjects. The classification performance is the mean value of the performances achieved from 6 new subjects. Results show that the performance of classifiers improves as the number of characters used for adaptation increases in each case.

8.3.2.2.3 Case Study Conclusion

The main objective of this study was the implementation and validation of spatial filtering and classification techniques for the enhancement as well as classification of P300 components in a P300-BCI spelling system. The discrimination of P300 components was useful as it reveals information regarding the subject's current mental state. However, it was hard to discriminate P300 components because of low signal to noise ratio (SNR). Therefore, series of trials are required to be recorded and averaged for improving the SNR. The drawback of P300 based speller is its "reduced spelling rate." Hence, advanced signal processing techniques are required, which can increase the communication speed (spelling rate) while maintaining high spelling accuracy.

8.3.3   MOTOR IMAGERY (MI)

8.3.3.1   Introduction

According to Mao et al., *"Motor imagery may be seen as a mental rehearsal of a motor act without any overt motor output"* [23]. In MI-BCI, the user imagines a set of pre-defined mental tasks and as a result, different brain signals are generated against every assigned task. The corresponding EEG signals vary with respect to each other and these features are used to design a BCI system. The MI activities are highly noticeable in the primary motor cortex area; hence, the electrodes used for recording MI events are often placed at the C3, Cz and C4 locations. The imagined movement causes event-related synchronization (ERS) and event-related desynchronization (ERD), which can be observed as the changes in the spectral power in the μ (8–12 Hz) and β (18–30 Hz) rhythms. Thinking of actions causes the same activation of brain regions seen when performing the actual movement; therefore, MI plays a vital role in neurorehabilitation BCIs. A detailed overview of MI-based BCIs is described in Table 8.9.

RecoveriX is one of the most used commercial MI-based BCI system for neurorehabilitation. It provides visual feedback, records EEG data for MI events, and delivers functional electric stimulation (FES) to specific areas depending on the received imagination inputs. In many research works, the RecoveriX system has been used to treat post-stroke patients. Rehabilitation based experiments were performed using RecoveriX by Sabathiel et al. [24] and Cho et al. [25] to recover

---

TABLE 8.8

Classification performance obtained using SVM and FLDA when 10 new characters are used for adapting the initial spatial filters

Subjects	Accuracy ± std (%)		Sensitivity ± std (%)		Specificity ± std (%)	
	SVM	FLDA	SVM	FLDA	SVM	FLDA
1	86.19 ± 3.69	81.95 ± 5.76	74.35 ± 13.04	73.46 ±12.03	88.56 ± 2.59	83.65 ± 5.37
9	83.35 ± 3.63	79.52 ± 1.67	62.33 ± 2.02	60.12 ± 5.85	88.05 ± 5.13	83.38 ± 3.16
5	89.10 ± 3.21	84.42 ± 3.10	70.17 ± 16.11	70.58 ±13.96	92.89 ± 2.30	87.19 ± 1.48
8	81.34 ± 6.94	77.90 ± 8.09	72.16 ± 13.54	67.42 ±10.65	83.18 ± 5.79	79.99 ± 7.62
2	87.41 ± 6.36	84.65 ± 5.99	77.35 ± 10.50	76.72 ±10.99	89.42 ± 5.89	86.24 ± 5.19

TABLE 8.9
MI based BCI systems overview

Advantages	Limitations	Applications
• No external stimulus is required.	• Requires higher training time.	• Controls FES based rehabilitations devices [24-26].
• Feasible for long lasting experiments.	• Needs great amount of focus to perform accurate imagination.	• Controls rehabilitation robotic manipulator [27,28].
• Overall, less fatigue.		
• Causes motor improvement (neuroplasticity).		• Controls prosthetic hand [29].
• Feasible for people with visual or auditory impairment.		

wrist dorsiflexion. Moreover, Irimia et al. [26] conducted rehabilitation therapy sessions for the restoration of paralytic limb movement via RecoveriX system.

8.3.3.2 Case Study for MI-BCI Implementation in Neurorehabilitation: Brain Computer Interface in Cognitive Neurorehabilitation

In this work, a sample-wise adaptive version of the most widely used spatial filter, Common Spatial Patterns (CSP), was implemented using a Recursive Least Squares (RLS) approach [30,31]. It has helped to reduce the training sessions and has shown that it is ideal for dimensionality reduction as well as source identification of MI-based BCI systems. The spatial filter was combined with a Regularized Discriminant Analysis (RDA) classifier to classify the user's intent and a regularized CSP was employed on the shorter training sessions to make it robust.

To test the performance, two different datasets were employed. One was a 4-class MI dataset from the BCI competition IV 2a [32], and the other was our own 3-class MI data recorded from 13 healthy subjects. An online session with real-time feedback was carried out where both adaptive (ACSP) and non-adaptive (CSP) versions of the spatial filters were employed. Results indicated significantly better performances from ACSP: a kappa value of 0.474 was achieved, as opposed to 0.113 from the non-adaptive CSP; an improvement of 4-fold. Overall, the ACSP filter proved to be of significant value for small training sessions, even for more complex tasks such as distinguishing movements from the same limb, which was a step towards personalizing BCI-based stroke rehabilitation methods.

8.3.3.2.1 Methodology and Experimental Setup

- *BCI competition IV-dataset 2a*
  In the BCI competition IV-Dataset 2a [32], the recording was made using 22 Ag/AgCl electrodes with a 3.5 cm distance between them. The monopolar

signals were recorded having the left mastoid as the reference and the right as the ground. The EEG signals were digitized at 250 Hz, bandpass (0.5–100 Hz) filtered, and notch (50 Hz) filtered to suppress the unwanted noises/artifacts and the power-line interference, respectively. Furthermore, three EOG channels were also recorded to monitor the eye movements throughout the experiment. Nine subjects participated in the experiment. It included four MI classes: left hand (class 1), right hand (class 2), feet (class 3) and tongue (class 4). Each session comprised of 6 runs separated by brief breaks and each run included 48 trials (12 for each class). A fixation cross on the computer monitor accompanied with an acoustic warning signal indicated the start of a trial. After 2 s, an arrow (a cue) appears (for 1.25 s) on the screen signaling the subject to start the MI of the particular class among the four classes. After 4 s of MI, the subject is allowed to relax/rest for variable length before the start of the next MI task.

- *Our own dataset*

  This dataset was recorded in our own laboratory using the g.tec EEG system and the 16 electrodes were placed over the motor cortex region along with ground on the forehead and reference electrodes on the left ear lobe.

  The data were collected from 13 healthy subjects of age range between 20 and 31 years (average 26.3), all with normal or corrected vision. For the motor tasks, the same arm (right) was used as the motor disabilities due to stroke are usually one-sided. The three implemented MI classes are: (i) palmar grasp, (ii) pinch, and (iii) elbow flexion. Each session of MI training comprises of 6 runs of 18 trials (6 for each class). In Figure 8.8, the user interface along with the timing information of the experiment are illustrated.

- *Data analysis*

  The signal processing comprised several distinct steps: pre-processing to remove noise and prepare the data, feature extraction to obtain the relevant characteristics of the signal, and finally, the classification to label the

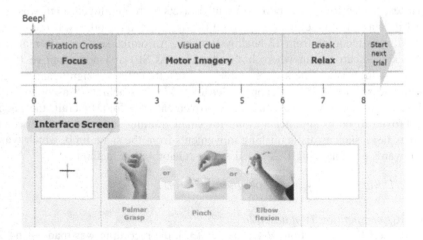

FIGURE 8.8   Interface and timing scheme for a trial

responses. A 4th order Butterworth band-pass (7–30 Hz) filter (zero-phase) was used to remove all the unwanted artifacts and noise from the collected data. Since one of the goals of the work was to determine the feasibility of a system, which was trained on a shorter duration of data, a regularized CSP algorithm with Diagonal Loading (DLCSP) was applied to obtain the filters in that situation. Then, for feature extraction, the ACSP algorithm was developed based on the RLS method. Finally, to classify the extracted features, RDA was implemented.

8.3.3.2.2 Experimental Results

- *Classification performance comparison with BCI competition IV results*

The performance of the developed algorithm was compared with the winner of the BCI competition. In the winning algorithm, the filter bank common spatial patterns (FBCSP) has been used, and the authors have implemented 3 different multiclass extensions [33]. The authors have reported the results in terms of mean kappa value using 10 × 10 – fold cross-validations. The presented study adopted the same strategy to make meaningful comparisons. Table 8.10 shows that the classification performance was consistently lower in the unseen evaluation data. Comparing the algorithm's performances, the FBCSP performed better on average, followed by the ACSP.

- *Classification performance for 3-class MI (own dataset)*

A comparison between the simple CSP and its regularized version, DLCSP, is made to assess whether the use of regularization was necessary for this problem. From

---

TABLE 8.10

Comparison of kappa value of our ACSP algorithm with fixed CSP. The FBCSP's (winner's) performance is also provided in the last column for comparison

Subjects	Fixed CSP	ACSP	FBCSP [33]
1	0.677	0.683	0.676
2	0.363	0.231	0.417
3	0.602	0.677	0.745
4	0.465	0.377	0.481
5	0.246	0.330	0.398
6	0.243	0.366	0.273
7	0.612	0.568	0.773
8	0.749	0.704	0.755
9	0.565	0.771	0.606
Mean	0.502	0.523	0.569
Median	0.565	0.568	0.606

TABLE 8.11

Performance comparison of CSP and DLCSP on the online MI sessions (average maximum kappa values were given as real-time feedback)

Subjects	CSP		DLCSP	
	Fixed	Adaptive	Fixed	Adaptive
1	0.051	0.324	0.075	0.212
2	0.445	0.524	0.052	0.482
3	0.098	0.381	0.083	0.495
4	0.157	0.355	0.045	0.516
5	0.189	0.596	0.208	0.651
6	0.089	0.329	0.104	0.357
7	0.335	0.546	0.05	0.493
8	0.173	0.387	0.130	0.329
9	0.141	0.678	0.049	0.705
10	0.072	0.327	0.077	0.488
11	0.411	0.467	0.103	0.645
12	0.040	0.165	0.300	0.327
13	0.466	0.488	0.190	0.461
Mean	0.205	0.428	0.113	0.474
Median	0.157	0.387	0.083	0.488

Table 8.11, it can be inferred that the regularization was pertinent for the ACSP algorithm for enhancing the performance (the mean kappa value is increased by 0.046 and the median kappa value is increased by 0.101). However, for the fixed CSP, the performance was worse using the regularized version. A comparison of the ACSP vs fixed CSP leads to the conclusion that the former performed significantly better than the latter, both using a simple CSP and its regularized version.

8.3.3.2.3 Case Study Conclusion

This study investigated the feasibility of an MI-BCI system, which could potentially be utilized as an improvement to the present stroke rehabilitation therapies. Furthermore, a strategy to overcome one of the disadvantages of current BCI paradigms, which is the need for long training sessions to calibrate the system's parameters was investigated. Overall, the feasibility of our paradigm was confirmed, and the results suggest that the implemented ACSP filter can be of use towards individualized MI-based BCI systems for stroke rehabilitation. It proved particularly useful when the filter coefficients were obtained on little training data and not in the case when it is trained on large amounts of data. Even though the results were positive, there is nonetheless much room for improvement on the way to practical applicability, namely concerning reducing the number of channels as well as the development of an algorithm, which is unsupervised.

8.4 TYPES OF BCI CONTROLLED MOTION FUNCTIONING UNITS

Different types of functioning/feedback units used in BCI controlled neuroreh-abilitation systems include: (1) functional electric stimulation (FES), (2) robotics assistive unit, and (3) hybrid system with virtual reality (VR) [34]. Based on the BCI paradigms (SSVEP, P300, or MI), once the EEG signals are acquired and processed by the system, the commands are sent to activate the respective functioning unit to assist the patients in performing the rehabilitation exercises.

8.4.1 FUNCTIONAL ELECTRIC STIMULATION (FES)

Neural injuries usually affect the muscle activation and cause the paralysis of certain body areas. To restore the muscle stimulation, the implementation of electrical impulses proves to be an effective approach that activates the nerve endings affected as result of paralysis [35,36]. The FES has been implemented in various medical applications to recover walking, standing, arm reaching, hand grasp, and other neurorehabilitation disorders. Several studies suggest that com-bining rehabilitation strategies with surface FES in the upper limb results in im-proved outcomes in terms of motor function in patients with mild or moderate motor impairment. However, for an efficient FES operation in rehabilitation, the onset time of the therapy and FES dosage should be taken into consideration and must be adjusted with great care. In classical rehabilitation therapies, the application of FES is a passive process, completely independent from brain activities. Whereas, combining the BCI with FES allows the FES system to be activated only when the desired brain areas are active, using a certain threshold. In the BCI-FES system, the FES electrodes are attached on the surface of paralyzed muscles and the electrical stimulation switches ON depending on the selection of the BCI paradigm. For in-stance, in the case of the MI paradigm, the FES device activates once the user imagines performing the desired movement. RecoveriX is such a system, which records EEG data for MI events and provides FES stimulation to specific areas depending on the received imagination inputs. A brief summary of the FES-based BCI systems is presented in Table 8.12.

8.4.2 ROBOTICS ASSISTANCE

In neurorehabilitation, robotics assistance is mainly operated for stroke rehabilita-tion, which combines with BCI to form BCI-Robotics rehabilitation systems. In BCI-Robotics systems, the robotic arm acts as a motion inducing unit that is at-tached to the patient's paretic arm and assists in performing the rehabilitation ex-ercises. In comparison to the conventional rehabilitation therapy, in BCI-Robotics rehab systems, the robotic platform operates autonomously based on the received inputs from the brain signals. For post-stroke rehabilitation, different modes of robotic operations are used, which mainly include passive and assistive mode. The passive robots are used for the patients who are not able to produce even a slight movement on their own and during exercise, the robot performs the entire man-euver. While the assistive robots provide support in rehabilitation therapy to those

TABLE 8.12

FES based BCI systems overview

Advantages	Limitations	Applications
• Coupling of FES with BCI system cause the pairing of cortical and peripheral activities, which improves and strengthens the impaired motor functions and will sustain for a longer period even after the completion of rehab therapy (According to Hebb's principle [37]).	• Useful only for patients having little or moderate motor mobility. • Shows limited effectiveness in terms of selective stimulation for deeper muscles. • Difficult to regulate FES stimulation parameters like current intensity, stimulation timing, duration, etc.	• For neurorehabilitation [38-42].

who already possess minimal movement but cannot execute an action without support. A variety of robotic systems that are adopted in stroke rehabilitation of arms, hands and gait are shown in Figure 8.9. Also, the properties of BCI-Robotics systems are presented in Table 8.13.

8.4.3   VR Based Hybrid Unit

The BCI-Robotics and BCI-FES based rehabilitation systems have delivered promising results; however, these methodologies are not able to introduce an element of "therapy motivation" among the patients. Therefore, with time, patients lose their interest, focus, and enthusiasm to perform the rehabilitation exercises. To overcome this shortcoming and to maximize the effectiveness of rehabilitation, the patients must be provided with some exciting and appealing environments. As a result, augmented and VR technologies have stepped into the neurorehabilitation field. Virtual reality is a 3D virtual environment, which allows a user to experience and interact with a simulated environment in a realistic way. The combination of VR with BCIs in stroke rehabilitation is in the emerging phase, where VR makes a patient feel like a part of a virtual clinical setting. The patient is provided with a thrilling and entertaining task, which causes the activation of more neural circuits and produces an improved motor recovery. Additionally, the performance of the VR-BCI system is further increased by combining with motion controlling units (like FES, haptic, and robotics support), hence, creating a BCI controlled VR-based hybrid system. The list of widely used VR-based neurorehabilitation systems is shown in Figure 8.10 and the characteristics of VR-based hybrid BCI systems are elucidated in Table 8.14.

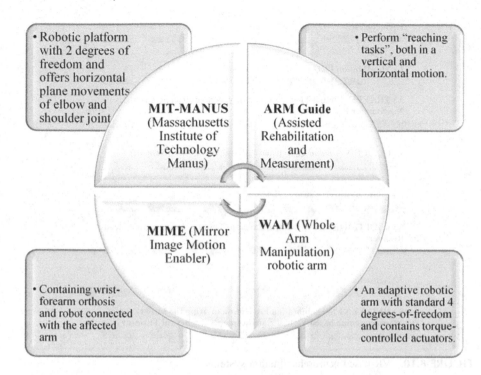

FIGURE 8.9 Robotic systems used in neurorehabilitation

TABLE 8.13
BCI-robotics rehab systems overview

Advantages	Limitations	Applications
• Effective even for patients having "NO" motor function and "ZERO" physical mobility of an affected area (e.g., limb).	• Difficult to design a precise and accurate motion controller to control BCI-Robotics systems in a real-time scenario. • Contains bulky and massive operating setup.	• For neurorehabilitation [43-48].

8.5 NEUROREHABILITATION APPLICATIONS OF BCI SYSTEMS

Currently, BCI systems are widely used in neurorehabilitation applications. These systems facilitate the patients with neural disorder to communicate with their surroundings to perform daily life actions. The detailed neural applications of BCI systems are shown in Table 8.15, which are listed based on the BCI paradigms

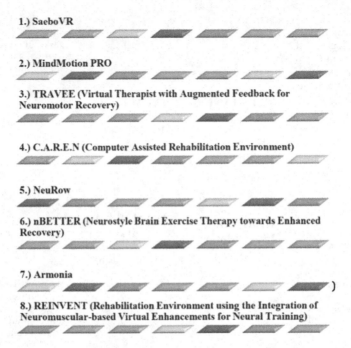

1.) SaeboVR

2.) MindMotion PRO

3.) TRAVEE (Virtual Therapist with Augmented Feedback for Neuromotor Recovery)

4.) C.A.R.E.N (Computer Assisted Rehabilitation Environment)

5.) NeuRow

6.) nBETTER (Neurostyle Brain Exercise Therapy towards Enhanced Recovery)

7.) Armonia

8.) REINVENT (Rehabilitation Environment using the Integration of Neuromuscular-based Virtual Enhancements for Neural Training)

FIGURE 8.10   VR based neurorehabilitation systems

TABLE 8.14
VR based hybrid BCI systems overview

Advantages	Limitations	Applications
• VR provides stimulating, interesting and dynamic environment, thus, supporting the user to carry out long duration rehabilitation sessions. • VR increases the attention span, focus level, and patient's motivation, which enhances the recovery speed. • Provides customized digital environment for every patient. • Can mimic the real-world actions, which are impossible to perform in traditional rehab therapies; for example, road crossing, playing football, etc.	• Low quality VR graphics can produce motion sickness in stroke patients. • Sometimes more practicing sessions are required to make a patient familiar with virtual environment. • Until now, most of the research has been done on stroke patients with small sample size.	• For neurorehabilitation [49-51].

TABLE 8.15
Research studies for different neurorehabilitation systems

Study	BCI paradigms	Motion controlling/ feedback unit	Neurorehabilitation applications
Donchin et al. (2000) [52]	P300	N/A	Operating virtual keyboard
Nijboer et al. (2008) [53]	P300	N/A	For communication of people (BCI speller) with amyotrophic lateral sclerosis (ALS) disorder
Daly et al. (2009) [38]	MI	FES	Rehabilitation of index finger extension
Escolano et al. (2010) [54]	P300	N/A	Controlling of mobile robots by an ALS patient
Gollee et al. (2010) [39]	SSVEP	FES	System feasibility is tested on neurologically intact subjects
Sellers et al. (2014) [55]	P300	N/A	BCI speller for ALS patients
Chen et al. (2014) [56]	SSVEP	N/A	BCI speller
Ang et al. (2015) [43]	MI	Robotics Assistance (MIT-Manus)	Rehabilitation of Shoulder and elbow movement
Chen et al. (2015) [57]	SSVEP	N/A	BCI speller
Xu et al. (2015) [44]	MI	Robotics Assistance (WAM robot arm)	Rehabilitation of upper limb extension/ flexion
Holz et al. (2015) [58]	P300	N/A	Brain painting by a locked-in state patient
Sabathiel et al. (2016) [35]	MI	FES (RecoveriX System)	Rehabilitation of Wrist dorsiflexion
Aydin et al. (2016) [59]	P300	N/A	Internet-based wireless communication between home environment and BCI system for people with neuromuscular diseases
Vourvopoulos et al. (2016) [49]	MI	VR Based Hybrid Unit (NeuRow with vibrotactile feedback)	Exercise containing boat rowing motions from both hands
Arrichiello et al. (2017) [45]	P300	Robotics Assistance	For hand rehabilitation
Zeng et al. (2017) [48]	SSVEP	Robotics Assistance	For ankle rehabilitation
Irimia et al. (2017) [41]	MI	FES (RecoveriX System)	Rehabilitation of right and left hand movements

(Continued)

TABLE 8.15 (Continued)

Study	BCI paradigms	Motion controlling/ feedback unit	Neurorehabilitation applications
Qiu et al. (2018) [40]	MI	FES (RecoveriX System)	Rehabilitation of Left or right wrist dorsiflexion
Li et al. (2018) [41]	P300	FES	Rehabilitation of four fingers (2 fingers of each hand)
Nakanishi et al. (2018) [60]	SSVEP	N/A	BCI speller
Chu et al. (2018) [47]	SSVEP	Robotics Assistance	System feasibility is tested on healthy participants
Lupu et al. (2018) [50]	MI	VR Based Hybrid Unit (TRAVEE system i.e., VR with FES feedback)	Rehabilitation of flexion/extension of hand and fingers
Jessica et al. (2018) [48]	MI	Robotics Assistance (Customized robotic hand orthosis)	Rehabilitation of flexion/extension of fingers
Vourvopoulos et al. (2019) [51]	MI	VR Based Hybrid Unit (REINVENT with vibrotactile feedback)	Rehabilitation of arm movements
Son et al. (2020) [42]	SSVEP	FES	Rehabilitative action observation game (tested on healthy subjects)

(SSVEP, P300, and MI) and motion controlling units (FES, robotics, VR hybrid, and no controlling unit).

8.6 CONCLUSION

In recent years, the development of EEG-based, user-friendly, portable, and non-invasive BCI systems for healthcare applications is a very emerging and dynamic research field. Apart from research purposes, these BCI systems are also used for real-time medical applications like neurorehabilitation, robotics control, wheelchair navigation, etc. However, the effectiveness, reliability, accuracy, and robustness of these systems can further be improved by developing efficient machine learning (ML) and deep learning (DL)-based algorithms. This could decrease the calibration time of the system and increase the overall proficiency of the developed BCI systems. Thus, with time, these BCI systems keep on improving; still, there are some critical concerns that must be addressed:

- Need for completely wireless, portable, and more comfortable EEG headsets that can produce repeatable and precise results in all environments.

- Longer installation time for mounting EEG electrodes. The quality of current dry electrodes should be improved so that they can become a part of every future BCI and speed up the electrode mounting process.
- Development of intelligent algorithms (ML/DL) for accurately processing the brain signals to convert them into control commands for external devices.
- Current BCIs possess low ITRs, which may cause problems for developing systems with minimal processing time.
- BCI illiteracy should be taken into consideration and steps must be taken to overcome this issue. For instance, more training sessions or workshops should be arranged for the patients regarding how to use BCI systems.

With the increasing interest in BCI research among the engineers, clinicians, neuroscientists, and users, it is evident that BCI has a promising future in neurorehabilitation. Even though with the present methodologies, the BCI systems are performing well in healthcare, however, in the coming years, it is expected that the flexible electronics (FE) will play a vital role in designing BCI-based neurorehabilitation systems. Recently, Maiolo et al. [61] have highlighted the advancement of FE in neuroscience for different in-vivo and in-vitro applications. Additionally, an FE-based flexible, portable, and wireless BCI system has been designed for EEG data acquisition by Mahmood et al. and their research findings have been published in *Nature Machine Intelligence* [62]. Therefore, it is highly possible that in the future, FE acts as a neuroscientific tool for developing advanced neurorehabilitation systems and introduces a new innovative dimension within the field of rehabilitation.

REFERENCES

1. Pfurtscheller, G., B. Z. Allison, B. Günther et al. The hybrid BCI. *Frontiers in Neuroscience*. 4, 30, (2010) DOI: 10.3389/fnpro.2010.00003.
2. Wolpaw, J. and E. W. Wolpaw. *Brain-Computer Interfaces: Principles and Practice*. Oxford University Press, Oxford, 2012.
3. Platz, T., C. Eickhof, S. van Kaick et al. Impairment-oriented training or Bobath therapy for severe arm paresis after stroke: a single-blind, multicentre randomized controlled trial. *Clinical Rehabilitation* 19, 7 (2005): 714–724, DOI:10.1191/0269215505cr904oa.
4. Biasiucci, A., R. Leeb, I. Iturrate et al. Brain-actuated functional electrical stimulation elicits lasting arm motor recovery after stroke. *Nature Communications* 9, no. 2421 (2018), DOI:10.1038/s41467-018-04673-z.
5. Young, B.M., Z. Nigogosyan, A. Remsik et al. Changes in functional connectivity correlate with behavioral gains in stroke patients after therapy using a brain-computer interface device. *Frontiers in Neuroengineering*. 7, 25 (2014), DOI:10.3389/fneng.2014.00025.
6. Prasad, G., P. Herman, D. Coyleet al. Applying a brain-computer interface to support motor imagery practice in people with stroke for upper limb recovery: a feasibility study. *Journal of NeuroEngineering and Rehabilitation* 7 60 (2010), DOI:10.1186/1743-0003-7-60.
7. Crosson, B., A. Ford, K.M. McGregor et al. Functional imaging and related techniques: an introduction for rehabilitation researchers. *Journal of Rehabilitation Research and Development*. 47, 2, (2010): pp. vii–xxxiv, DOI:10.1682/jrrd.2010.02.0017.

8. Chen, X., Y. Wang, M. Nakanishi et al. High-speed spelling with a noninvasive brain-computer interface. *Proceedings of the National Academy of Sciences of the United States of America* 112, 44 (2015.): E6058–E6067, DOI: 10.1073/pnas.1508080112.

9. Chiuzbaian, A., J. Jakobsen and S. Puthusserypady. Mind controlled drone: An innovative multiclass SSVEP based brain computer interface. *7th International Winter Conference on Brain-Computer Interface (BCI)*, Gangwon, Korea (South), pp. 1–5, 2019, DOI: 10.1109/IWW-BCI.2019.8737327.

10. Takeshi, S., K. Toshihiro, T. Kouji et al. A BMI-based occupational therapy assist suit: Asynchronous control by SSVEP. *Frontiers in Neuroscience.* 7, (2013) DOI: 10.3389/fnins.2013.00172.

11. Bryan, M., J. Green, M. Chung et al. An adaptive brain-computer interface for humanoid robot control. *11th IEEE-RAS International Conference on Humanoid Robots*, Bled, pp. 199–204, 2011, DOI: 10.1109/Humanoids.2011.6100901.

12. Muller-Putz, G. R. and G. Pfurtscheller. Control of an electrical prosthesis with an SSVEP-based BCI. *IEEE Transactions on Biomedical Engineering.* 55, 1 (2008): 361–364, DOI: 10.1109/TBME.2007.897815.

13. Pfurtscheller, G., T. Solis-Escalante, R. Ortner, P. Linortner and G. R. Muller-Putz. Self-paced operation of an SSVEP-based orthosis with and without an imagery-based "Brain Switch:" A feasibility study towards a hybrid BCI. *IEEE Transactions on Neural Systems and Rehabilitation Engineering.* 18, 4 (2010): 409–414, DOI: 10.1109/TNSRE.2010.2040837.

14. Kwak, N. S., K. R. Müller and S. W. Lee. A lower limb exoskeleton control system based on steady state visual evoked potentials. *Journal of Neural Engineering.* 12, 5 (2015):056009, DOI:10.1088/1741-2560/12/5/056009.

15. Ali, A. and S. Puthusserypady. A 3D learning playground for potential attention training in ADHD: A brain computer interface approach, *37th Annual International Conference of the IEEE Engineering in Medicine and Biology Society (EMBC)*, Milan, pp. 67–70, 2015, DOI: 10.1109/EMBC.2015.7318302.

16. Ordikhani-Seyedlar, M., H. B. D. Sorensen, T. W. Kjaer, H. R. Siebner and S. Puthusserypady. SSVEP-modulation by covert and overt attention: Novel features for BCI in attention neurorehabilitation, *36th Annual International Conference of the IEEE Engineering in Medicine and Biology Society*, Chicago, IL, pp. 5462–5465, 2014, DOI: 10.1109/EMBC.2014.6944862.

17. Farwell, L. A. and E. Donchin. Talking off the top of your head: Toward a mental prosthesis utilizing event-related brain potentials. *Electroencephalography and Clinical Neurophysiology.* 70, 6 (1988): 510–523, DOI: 10.1016/0013-4694(88) 90149-6.

18. Chiou, E. and S. Puthusserypady. Spatial filter feature extraction methods for P300 BCI speller: A comparison. *IEEE International Conference on Systems, Man, and Cybernetics (SMC)*, pp. 003859–003863, 2016, DOI: 10.1109/SMC.2016. 7844836.

19. Iturrate, I., J. M. Antelis, A. Kubler and J. Minguez. A noninvasive brain-actuated wheelchair based on a P300 neurophysiological protocol and automated navigation. *IEEE Transactions on Robotics.* 25, 3 (2009): 614–627, DOI: 10.1109/TRO.2009. 2020347.

20. Bell, C. J., P. Shenoy, R. Chalodhorn and R. P. Rao. Control of a humanoid robot by a noninvasive brain-computer interface in humans. *Journal of Neural Engineering.* 5, 2 (2008): 214–220, DOI:10.1088/1741-2560/5/2/012.

21. Sirvent, J. L., M. José, E. I. Azorín et al. 2010. P300-based brain-computer interface for internet browsing. *Trends in practical applications of agents and multiagent systems.* Springer, Berlin, Heidelberg, pp: 615–622.

22. Blankertz, B., K. Muller, D. J. Krusienski et al. The BCI competition III: Validating alternative approaches to actual BCI problems. *IEEE Transactions on Neural Systems and Rehabilitation Engineering* 14, 2 (2006): 153–159, DOI: 10.1109/TNSRE.2006. 875642.

23. Xiaoqian, M., M. Li, W. Li et al. Progress in EEG-based brain robot interaction systems. *Computational Intelligence and Neuroscience* 2017, (2017): pp. 1–25, DOI: 10. 1155/2017/1742862.

24. Sabathiel, N., D. C. Irimia, B. Z. Allison et al. 2016. Paired associative stimulation with brain-computer interfaces: A new paradigm for stroke rehabilitation. *Foundations of Augmented Cognition: Neuroergonomics and Operational Neuroscience*, ed. D. D. Schmorrow, and C. M. Fidopiastis, 9743, Springer International Publishing, pp. 261–272, DOI: 10.1007/978-3-319-39955-3_25.

25. Cho, W., A. Heilinger, R. Xu et al. Hemiparetic stroke rehabilitation using avatar and electrical stimulation based on non-invasive brain computer interface. *International Journal of Physical Medicine & Rehabilitation* 5, 04 (2017), DOI: 10.4172/2329-9096. 1000411.

26. Irimia, D.C., M. S. Poboroniuc, R. Ortner et al. Preliminary results of testing a BCI-controlled FES system for post-stroke rehabilitation. *Proceedings of the 7th Graz Brain-Computer Interface Conference*, From Vision to Reality. mEDRA, 2017 DOI: 10.3217/978-3-85125-533-1–38.

27. Ang, K. K., C. Guan, K. S. G. Chua et al. Clinical study of neurorehabilitation in stroke using EEG-based motor imagery brain-computer interface with robotic feedback. *Annual International Conference of the IEEE Engineering in Medicine and Biology*, Buenos Aires, pp. 5549–5552, 2010 DOI: 10.1109/IEMBS.2010.5626782.

28. Ang, K. K., C. Guan, K. S. Phua et al. Brain-computer interface-based robotic end effector system for wrist and hand rehabilitation: results of a three-armed randomized controlled trial for chronic stroke. *Frontiers in Neuroengineering.* 7, 30 (2014), DOI:10.3389/fneng.2014.00030.

29. Guger, C., W. Harkam, C. Hertnaes. and G. Pfurtscheller. Prosthetic control by an EEG-based brain-computer interface (BCI), *Proc. AAATE'99*, pp. 590–595, 1999. http://citeseerx.ist.psu.edu/viewdoc/download?doi=10.1.1.467.9453&rep=rep1&type=pdf.

30. Costa, A. P., J. S. Møller, H. K. Iversen. and S. Puthusserypady. Adaptive CSP for user independence in MI-BCI paradigm for upper limb stroke rehabilitation. *IEEE Global Conference on Signal and Information Processing (GlobalSIP)*, pp. 420–423, 2018. DOI: 10.1109/GlobalSIP.2018.8646403.

31. Costa, A. P., J. S. Møller, H. K. Iversen. and S. Puthusserypady. An adaptive CSP filter to investigate user independence in a 3-Class MI-BCI paradigm. *Computers in Biology and Medicine.* 103, (2018): 24–33, DOI: 10.1016/j.compbiomed.2018. 09.021.

32. Brunner, C., R. Leeb, G. R. Muller-Putz et al. BCI competition 2008 – Graz data set A. http://www.bbci.de/competition/iv/desc_2a.pdf. 2020.

33. Ang, K. K., Z. Y. Chin, C. Wang et al. Filter Bank Common Spatial Pattern algorithm on BCI competition IV datasets 2a and 2b. *Frontiers in Neuroengineering* 6, (2012) DOI: 10.3389/fnins.2012.00039.

34. Khan, M.A., R. Das, H.K. Iversen, and S. Puthusserypady. Review on motor imagery based BCI systems for upper limb post-stroke neurorehabilitation: From designing to application, *omputers in Biology and Medicine.* 123, 103843 (2020), (Aug), DOI: 10. 1016/j.compbiomed.2020.103843.

35. Prasad, G., P. Herman, D. Coyle et al. Applying a brain-computer interface to support motor imagery practice in people with stroke for upper limb recovery: a feasibility study. *Journal of NeuroEngineering and Rehabilitation* 7, 60, (2010, Dec 14). doi:10. 1186/1743-0003-7-60

36. Wu, C. Y., P. C. Huang, Y. T. Chen et al. Effects of mirror therapy on motor and sensory recovery in chronic stroke: a randomized controlled trial. *Archives of Physical Medicine and Rehabilitation* 94 6 (2013): pp. 1023–1030, doi:10.1016/j.apmr.2013.02.007

37. Morris, R. G. Hebb, D. O.: The organization of behavior, Wiley, New York, 1949. *Brain Research Bulletin.* 50, 5–6 (1999, Nov.): 437, DOI: 10.1016/S0361-9230(99)00182-3.

38. Daly, J. J., R. Cheng, J. Rogers et al. Feasibility of a new application of noninvasive brain computer interface (BCI): A case study of training for recovery of volitional motor control after stroke. *Journal of Neurologic Physical Therapy.* 33, 4 (2009, Dec.): 203–211, DOI: 10.1097/NPT.0b013e3181c1fc0b.

39. Gollee, H., I. Volosyak, A. J. McLachlan et al. An SSVEP-based brain–computer interface for the control of functional electrical stimulation. *IEEE Transactions on Biomedical Engineering.* 57, 8 (2010, Aug.): 1847–1855, DOI: 10.1109/TBME.2010.2043432.

40. Qiu, Z., S. Chen, I. Daly et al. BCI-based strategies on stroke rehabilitation with avatar and FES feedback. 2018. http://arxiv.org/abs/1805.04986.

41. Li, J., J. Pu, H. Cui et al. An online P300 brain–computer interface based on tactile selective attention of somatosensory electrical stimulation. *Journal of Medical and Biological Engineering.* 39, (2019): pp. 732–738, DOI: 10.1007/s40846-018-0459-x.

42. Son, J. E., H. Choi, H. Lim and J. Ku. Development of a flickering action video based steady state visual evoked potential triggered brain computer interface-functional electrical stimulation for a rehabilitative action observation game. *Technology and Health Care* 28, S1 (2020): 509–519, DOI: 10.3233/THC-209051.

43. Ang, K. K., K. S. G. Chua, K. S. Phua et al. A randomized controlled trial of EEG-based motor imagery brain-computer interface robotic rehabilitation for stroke. *Clinical EEG and Neuroscience* 46, 4 (2015): pp. 310–320, DOI: 10.1177/1550059414522229.

44. Xu, B., A. Song, G. Zhao et al. Robotic neurorehabilitation system design for stroke patients. *Advances in Mechanical Engineering* 7 (2015): pp. 1–12. DOI: 10.1177/1687814015573768.

45. Arrichiello, F., P. D. Lillo, D. Di Vito, G. Antonelli and S. Chiaverini. Assistive robot operated via P300-based brain computer interface, *IEEE International Conference on Robotics and Automation (ICRA)*, Singapore, pp. 6032–6037, 2017. DOI: 10.1109/ICRA.2017.7989714.

46. Zeng, X., G. Zhu, L. Yue et al. A feasibility study of SSVEP-based passive training on an ankle rehabilitation robot. *Journal of Healthcare Engineering* 2017 (2017): pp. 1–9. DOI: 10.1155/2017/6819056.

47. Chu, Y., X. Zhao, Y. Zou, W. Xu and Y. Zhao. Robot-assisted rehabilitation system based on SSVEP brain-computer interface for upper extremity. *IEEE International Conference on Robotics and Biomimetics (ROBIO)*, pp. 1098–1103, 2018. DOI: 10.1109/ROBIO.2018.8664812.

48. Cantillo-Negrete, J., I. Ruben, Carino-Escobar, C-M. Paul et al. Motor imagery-based brain-computer interface coupled to a robotic hand orthosis aimed for neurorehabilitation of stroke patients. *Journal of Healthcare Engineering* 2018 (2018): pp. 1–10. DOI: 10.1155/2018/1624637.

49. Vourvopoulos, A., A. Ferreira and S. Bermúdez i Badia. NeuRow: An immersive VR environment for motor-imagery training with the use of brain-computer interfaces and vibrotactile feedback. Proceedings of the *3rd International Conference on Physiological Computing Systems – Volume 1: PhyCS*, ISBN 978–989-758-197-7, pp. 43–53, 2016. DOI: 10.5220/0005939400430053.

50. Lupu, R. G., D. C. Irimia, F. Ungureanu et al. BCI and FES based therapy for stroke rehabilitation using VR facilities. *Wireless Communications and Mobile Computing* 2018, (2018): pp. 1–8, DOI: 10.1155/2018/4798359.

51. Vourvopoulos A., O. M. Pardo, S. Lefebvre et al. Effects of a brain-computer interface with virtual reality (VR) neurofeedback: A pilot study in chronic stroke patients. *Frontiers in Human Neuroscience.* 13, (2019, June): 210, DOI: 10.3389/fnhum.2019. 00210.

52. Donchin, E., K. M. Spencer and R. Wijesinghe. The mental prosthesis: assessing the speed of a P300-based brain-computer interface, *IEEE Transactions on Rehabilitation Engineering.* 8, 2 (2000, June): 174–179, DOI: 10.1109/86.847808.

53. Nijboer F., E. W. Sellers, J. Mellinger et al. A P300-based brain-computer interface for people with amyotrophic lateral sclerosis. *Clinical Neurophysiology.* 119, 8, (2008): pp.1909–1916, DOI: 10.1016/j.clinph.2008.03.034.

54. Escolano, C., A. R. Murguialday, T. Matuz, N. Birbaumer and J. Minguez. A tele-presence robotic system operated with a P300-based brain-computer interface: Initial tests with ALS patients, *Annual International Conference of the IEEE Engineering in Medicine and Biology*, Buenos Aires, pp. 4476–4480, 2010 DOI: 10.1109/IEMBS. 2010.5626045.

55. Sellers, E. W., D. B. Ryan and C. K. Hauser. Noninvasive brain-computer interface enables communication after brainstem stroke. *Science Translational Medicine.* 6 (2014), DOI: 10.1126/scitranslmed.3007801.

56. Chen, X., Z. Chen, S. Gao and X. Gao. A high-ITR SSVEP-based BCI speller. *Brain-Computer Interfaces* 1, 3–4 (2014, Oct.): 181–191, DOI: 10.1080/2326263X.2014. 944469.

57. Chen, X., Y. Wang, M. Nakanishi et al. High-speed spelling with a noninvasive brain–computer interface. *Proceedings of the National Academy of Sciences* 112, 44 (2015, Nov.): E6058–E6067, DOI: 10.1073/pnas.1508080112.

58. Holz, E. M., L. Botrel, T. Kaufmann and A. Kübler. Long-term independent brain-computer interface home use improves quality of life of a patient in the locked-in state: A case study. *Archives of Physical Medicine and Rehabilitation.* 96, 3 (2015, March): S16–S26, DOI: 10.1016/j.apmr.2014.03.035.

59. Aydin, E.A., Ö. F. Bay and I. Güler. Implementation of an embedded web server application for wireless control of brain computer interface-based home environments. *Journal of Medical Systems.* 40, 27 (2016), DOI: 10.1007/s10916-015-0386-0.

60. Nakanishi, M., Y. Wang, X. Chen, Y. Wang, X. Gao and T. Jung. Enhancing detection of SSVEPs for a high-speed brain speller using task-related component analysis, *IEEE Transactions on Biomedical Engineering.* 65, 1 (2018, Jan.): 104–112, DOI: 10.1109/ TBME.2017.2694818.

61. Maiolo, L., D. Polese and A. ConvertiThe rise of flexible electronics in neuroscience, from materials selection to in vitro and in vivo applications. *Advances in Physics: X.* 4, 1 (2019, Jan.): 1664319, DOI: 10.1080/23746149.2019.1664319.

62. Mahmood, M., D. Mzurikwao, Y. Kim et al. Fully portable and wireless universal brain–machine interfaces enabled by flexible scalp electronics and deep learning algorithm. *Nature Machine Intelligence.* 1, (2019): pp. 412–422, DOI: 10.1038/ s42256-019-0091-7.

9 Scalp EEG Classification Using TQWT-Entropy Features for Epileptic Seizure Detection

Komal Jindal, Rahul Upadhyay, Prabin Kumar Padhy, and Hari Shankar Singh

9.1 INTRODUCTION

Human brain electrical activity varies with various physiological and neurological conditions. Electrical activity of the brain is recorded using multiple electrodes on human brain which is called electroencephalogram (EEG) activity [1]. The EEG activity helps in diagnosing various brain-related disorders viz. epilepsy, Alzheimer, and amyotrophic lateral sclerosis (ALS) [2]. Epileptic seizure is a severe brain illness that can be expressed in terms of transient symptoms of synchronous neuronal activity [3]. It is a group of disorders that affect around 60–65 million people worldwide (1–2% of the total population) [4]. Epileptic seizures disturb the normal neuronal activity pattern that leads to interruption of cognizance, weird response, and muscle fits. It is evident that the early epileptic seizure detection may help in improving the physiological condition of patients by tailored interventions.

Conventionally, neurologists/experts analyze regular EEG time series data for diagnosing various brain-related disorders, which is a time-consuming process. Also, it entails great expertise in reading and understanding the temporal distribution of data. To overcome the drawbacks generated by common visual scanning methods, computer-aided diagnosis (CAD) techniques have been proposed in the literature [5,6]. Such CAD techniques commonly integrate pre-processing, feature extraction, and machine learning steps.

Various time-frequency transforms viz. Stockwell transform (ST) [7], Chirplet transform, and discrete wavelet transform (DWT) are commonly utilized EEG-based time-frequency analysis methods for epilepsy diagnosis. However, many of these transforms have their own limitations [8]. Compared to other time-frequency based methods, many researchers have worked on wavelet based time-frequency decomposition and developed efficient pre-processing and feature extraction methodologies for biomedical applications [9]. Studies carried out on wavelet transform (WT) suggest that the Q-factor value should be low for less oscillatory

221

EEG activity. On the contrary, the Q-factor value should be high for highly os-cillatory physiological activity [10]. However, the limitation of WT lies in its in-capability to tune Q-factor value as per constraints [11]. Also, the selection of an appropriate mother wavelet function is a challenging task.

In addition to conventional WT, rational dilation wavelet transform (RADWT) is also used for signal decomposition; however, it also has the limitation of rational dilation factor and is found to be unsuitable for EEG signal decomposition [12,13]. Considering the limitations of previously used time-frequency transform based methods, Tunable Q Wavelet Transform (TQWT)-based EEG activity decom-position and further feature extraction is proposed in this chapter. The TQWT has the ability to tune Q-factor parameter value in accordance with the input time-domain activity. There is enhancement in the performance of a proposed system by quantitatively capturing the morphological variations [14,15].

In this chapter, TQWT is applied to disintegrate given EEG activity into using sub-bands, initially. Parameters of TQWT were optimized to attain the highest classification results and best representation of the signals. The entropy-based feature set is calculated after decomposing EEG activity into sub-bands. In the present work, four different entropies viz. approximate entropy (A_E), permutation entropy (P_E), Renyi's entropy (R_E), and sample entropy (S_E) are estimated from obtained time-frequency sub-bands. In order to classify non-seizure (normal) and seizure (diseased) activity from given EEG, three classification methods are employed viz. SVM, RF, and ANN. The machine learning techniques are trained and validated on prepared feature vectors. Various parameters of classification algorithms are adjusted to acquire the highest classification performance. The results propounded herein validate the effectiveness of entropies in the automatic epileptic seizure identification. The schematic diagram of the proposed TQWT-based automatic epileptic seizure identification criterion is shown in Figure 9.1. The remaining portion of this chapter is sub-divided as: Section 9.2 defines raw EEG data and TQWT-based EEG signal decomposition techniques. Section 9.3 provides a complete description of entropy-based feature vector extraction and normal and diseased activity classification approaches. The results and discussion section includes detailed results and their expounded significance in Section 9.4. Finally, significant findings of the proposed methodology are wrapped in Section 9.5.

9.2 MATERIAL AND METHODS

9.2.1 EEG DATA

Electroencephalogram records exploited in the present chapter are acquired from the online database of Bonn University [16]. The available data comprised of artifact-free EEG activity in three subsets viz. Z, O, and S, which are recorded under two pathological conditions viz. nonseizure (normal/healthy) and seizure (diseased). Subset O and Z are recorded from subjects extracranially with eyes open and closed settings. Subset S is recorded intracranially from five epileptic subjects during seizure considering all ictal zones. Each dataset consists of 23.6 second-long EEG

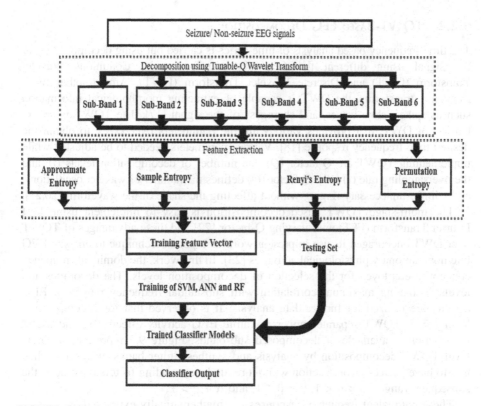

FIGURE 9.1 Schematic diagram of proposed automatic epileptic seizure identification methodology.

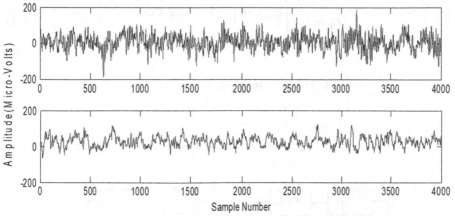

FIGURE 9.2 Exemplary plot of normal and diseased EEG activity.

activity of 100 single channel trials. In order to register ongoing EEG activity, a 128-channel EEG data acquisition system (with sampling rate = 173.61 Hz and resolution = 12-bit) is used in the present work. Figure 9.2 presents an exemplary plot of normal and diseased EEG activity for a single trial.

9.2.2 TQWT-BASED EEG DECOMPOSITION

The time-frequency based analysis of time-series is carried out using decomposition of the signal using different time-frequency transforms viz. Continious Wavelet Transform (CWT) and Discrete Wavelet Transform (DWT). Among other time-frequency transforms, the DWT is capable of extracting morphological information such as spikes, slow waves, and sharpness of the signal [17]. The TQWT is an extension of DWT, that provides various tunable parameters over DWT to obtain the desired time-frequency response [18]. Various parameters needed to be adjusted while implementing TQWT are Q-factor (Q), the number of decomposition levels (j), and the oversampling rate (r) [19]. Q-factor (Q) defines the number of wavelet oscillations, and r limits unnecessary ringing without affecting the shape of the waveform [20,21].

The multi-stage TQWT based decomposition is easy to implement using Fast Fourier Transform (FFT) with varying Q-factor [22] and these advantages of TQWT over DWT encouraged its use in present work as a potent technique to analyze EEG like non-stationary physiological activities [23]. In this work, the dominant frequency concept is employed for the selection of decomposition levels. The decomposition levels (j) having maximum correlation with substantial frequency ranges of EEG activity are utilized for further data analysis. It is observed that for decomposition level $j = 5$, TQWT separates upper rhythmic EEG activity effectively, and useful information is available in decomposed sub-bands. Figure 9.3 represents a single level TQWT decomposition by analysis and synthesis filter banks. It is established that to have perfect reconstruction without redundancy, scaling factors must be in the subsequent ranges: $0 < \alpha < 1$, $0 < \beta \le 1$, and $\alpha + \beta > 1$.

These equivalent frequency responses are mathematically expressed as:

$$H_0^*(\omega) = \begin{cases} \Pi_{m=0}^{j-1} H_0\left(\frac{\omega}{\alpha^m}\right), & |\omega| \le \alpha^j \pi \\ 0, & \alpha^j \pi < |\omega| \le \pi \end{cases} \tag{9.1}$$

$$H_1^*(\omega) = \begin{cases} H_1\left(\frac{\omega}{\alpha^{j-1}}\right) \Pi_{m=0}^{j-2} H_0\left(\frac{\omega}{\alpha^m}\right), & (1-\beta)\alpha^{j-1}\pi \le |\omega| \le \alpha^{j-1}\pi \\ 0, & \text{for other } \omega \in [-\pi, \pi] \end{cases} \tag{9.2}$$

here, Q and r terms can be represented in the form of scaling terms α and β terms as:

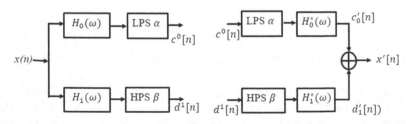

FIGURE 9.3 TQWT signal decomposition using (a) analysis filter and (b) synthesis filter.

$$r = \frac{\beta}{1 - \alpha}, Q = \frac{2 - \beta}{\beta}$$

The plot of TQWT coefficients corresponding to normal and diseased class of EEG activity are presented in Figure 9.4. Figure 9.5 shows the distribution of energy over sample values for decomposed EEG activity. It can be easily deduced from Figure 9.4 that low, as well as high-frequency sub-bands possess some amount of energy for normal and diseased condition. Therefore, all decomposed sub-bands have been considered for estimation of features in the present study. After successfully disintegrating EEG epochs into sub-bands using TQWT, the different types of Eentropies are estimated as features from TQWT sub-bands.

9.3 FEATURE EXTRACTION METHODOLOGY

For automatic epileptic seizure identification, a list of entropy features is extracted, and a brief elucidation of extracted features is given in this part of the chapter. The proposed entropy-based feature set extraction offers the benefits of utilizing important information from estimated time-frequency sub-bands. After decomposing the recorded EEG activity into time-frequency sub-bands, the following four entropy features are estimated and classification is carried out.

9.3.1 APPROXIMATE ENTROPY (A_E) ESTIMATION

Approximate entropy (A_E) proposed by Pincus [24], is a nonlinear parameter estimation which measures regularity of the signal. Approximate entropy (A_E) of a signal $x(n)$; for $1 \leq n \leq N$ may be obtained by following procedure given below. The m-dimensional state space representation is computed from given time series as given in equation (9.3) as below:

$$u_m(n) = \{x(n), x(n + \tau), ..., x(n + (m - 1)\tau)\};$$

$$1 \leq n \leq N - (m - 1)\tau \qquad (9.3)$$

Here, τ denotes delay in time and r represents threshold parameter. The share of $u_m(j)$ within r of $u_m(n)$ vector is given as equation (9.4) below:

$$C_n^m(r) = \frac{1}{N - (m - 1)\tau} \Sigma_{j=1} \theta(r - d[u_m(n), u_m(j)]) \qquad (9.4)$$

$$\theta(x) = \begin{cases} 1, & x > 0 \\ 0, & x \leq 0 \end{cases} \qquad (9.5)$$

where $\theta(x)$ denotes Heaviside function, as given in equation (9.5) and $d[u_m(n), u_m(j)]$ is the Chebyshev's distance, as given in equation (9.6).

(a)

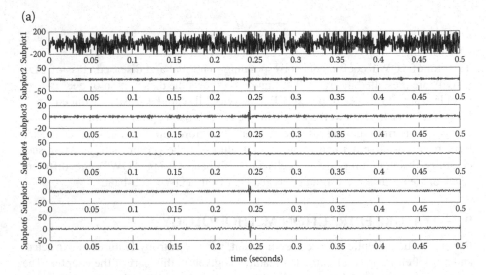

(b)

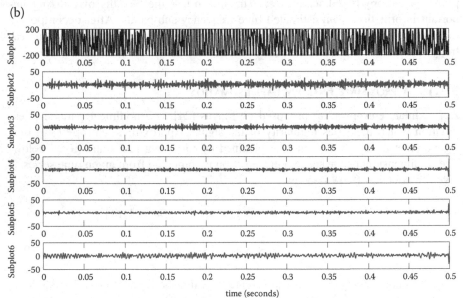

FIGURE 9.4 TQWT coefficient plots of (a) Normal EEG activity and (b) Diseased EEG activity.

$$d\left[u_m(n),\, u_m(j)\right] = \max_{0 \le i \le m}(|x(n+1) - x(j+i)|), \quad n \ge 1,$$
$$j \le N - (m-1)\tau \tag{9.6}$$

The result of logarithmic transformation is given by equation (9.7) [25].

(a)

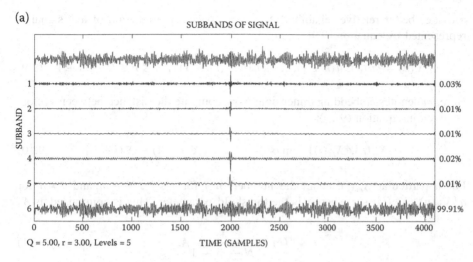

(b)

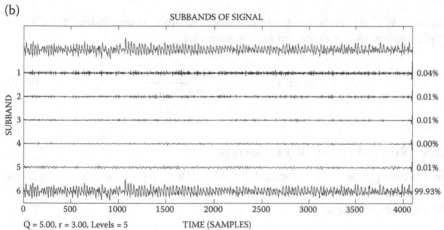

FIGURE 9.5 Energy distribution of TQWT coefficients corresponding to (a) Normal and (b) Diseased EEG activity.

$$\varnothing^m(r) = \frac{1}{N-m+1} \sum_{n=1}^{N-m+1} lnC_n^m(r), \ m \geq 1 \tag{9.7}$$

Finally, approximate entropy is given as:

$$A_E(m, \ r, \ N) = \varnothing^m(r) - \varnothing^{m+1}(r), \ m \geq 1 \tag{9.8}$$

9.3.2 SAMPLE ENTROPY (S_E) ESTIMATION

Sample entropy (S_E) is an extension of A_E, which can quantify the complexity present in the given signal [26]. Unlike A_E, S_E does not depend on data length and provides better relative reliability. The state space representation of any signal is represented by equation (9.9).

$$X(n) = \{u(n), u(n+1), \ldots \ldots, u(n+(m-1))\}, \quad 1 \le n \le N - m + 1 \quad (9.9)$$

Here, m denotes embedding dimension. Now compute the distance between vectors as given in equation (9.10):

$$d[X_m(n), X_m(j)] = \max_{i=0,1,\ldots,m-1} (|X(n+i) - X(j+i)|) \quad (9.10)$$

For a particular $X_m(j)$, count the number of j for $1 \le j \le N - m$ and $j \ne n$ for $d[X_m(n), X_m(j)] \le r$ where r is the threshold parameter. This is epitomized as A_n

$$A_n^m(r) = \frac{1}{N - m - 1} A_n \quad (9.11)$$

Similarly, $A_n^{m+1}(r)$ can be computed corresponding to next data points. Finally, the sample entropy (S_E) is expressed by equation (9.12).

$$S_E(m, r) = -ln \frac{\sum_{n=1}^{N-m} A_n^{(m+1)}(r)}{\sum_{n=1}^{N-m} A_n^{(m)}(r)} \quad (9.12)$$

9.3.3 RENYI'S ENTROPY (R_E) ESTIMATION

Renyi's entropy (R_E) was proposed by Alfred Renyi [27], which is a type of Shannon entropy. The R_E evaluates spectral complexity from a given time-series data and is expressed as:

$$R_E(\gamma) = \frac{1}{1-\gamma} \log\left(\sum_{n=1}^{N} p_n^\gamma \right) \quad (9.13)$$

where order $\gamma > 0$, $\gamma \ne 1$. If $\gamma = 2$ then R_E is known as quadratic R_E and is given as below:

$$R_E = -\log\left(\sum_{k=1}^{N} p_n^2 \right) \quad (9.14)$$

9.3.4 PERMUTATION ENTROPY (P_E) ESTIMATION

Permutation entropy (P_E) was initially suggested by Bandt and Pompe in the year 2002, which is employed to measure randomness of the given time-domain data [28]. The embedding time-domain $X(n)$ is as follows:

$$X(n) = \left[x(n), \, x\left(\frac{n}{\tau}\right), \, \ldots\ldots, \, x\left(\frac{n}{m\tau}\right) \right] \qquad (9.15)$$

where, embedding dimension is presented by m and time delay using τ. For given value of m, there are $m!$ possible permutations. If every permutation is represented as a symbol, then, embedding time domain vector $X(n)$ is denoted by symbol sequence, n, each with probability distribution p_n. Permutation entropy (P_E) is defined by equation (9.16).

$$P_E(m) = -\frac{1}{\ln(m!)} \sum_{n=1}^{N} p_n \ln(p_n) \qquad (9.16)$$

Here, $\frac{1}{\ln(m!)}$ denotes normalization factor with $0 \leq P_E/ln(l!) \leq 1$.

9.4 SOFT COMPUTING TECHNIQUES

In this chapter, three soft computing techniques viz. SVM, ANN, and RF are implemented to train and validate the features extracted from proposed methodology. The classification procedure is implemented using Weka version 3.6.0. Though a number of user-defined classifier parameter optimization are done by recursively performing the classification procedure. In SVM classification, four types of kernels viz. PUK, RBF, polykernel and normalized polykernel are utilized. The results obtained using different parameters of classifiers are shown in results and discussion section next.

9.5 RESULTS AND DISCUSSION

Present work includes 200 trials of normal class EEG signals obtained from ZO dataset, and 100 trials of diseased class EEG signals obtained from S dataset. At first, the recorded activity is disintegrated into six TQWT sub-bands. Various TQWT parameters such as Q, j, and r (as provided in the TQWT description section) are optimized prior to signal decomposition. After decomposition of EEG activity, four entropy features viz. A_E, S_E, R_E, and P_E are estimated from decomposed EEG sub-bands. Further, two types of feature vector sets are prepared encompassing estimated features. The first type of feature set contains single entropy features.

The entropy features of normal and diseased EEG activity are further accumulated to formulate a second feature set. The arranged feature sets are input to three classification models viz. SVM, ANN, and RF for validation purposes. Table 9.1 presents sample feature values estimated from the normal and diseased class of EEG records. It is perceived from Table 9.1 that there exists significant difference in feature values for specific trials of normal and diseased EEG activity. The 10-fold cross-validation approach is followed for the classification of EEG activity using all three classifiers. Figures 9.6–9.9 depict the boxplot of TQWT based A_E, S_E, R_E, and P_E features estimated from normal and diseased classes of EEG records. It is

TABLE 9.1

Sample feature values estimated from normal and diseased classes of EEG records

Entropy	Features						Class
A_E feature	A_E_1	A_E_2	A_E_3	A_E_4	A_E_5	A_E_6	
	1.341326	1.089258	0.963667	1.287686	1.124829	0.875157	N
	1.479413	1.340373	1.207053	1.321679	1.248754	0.823486	N
	1.440961	1.263112	1.100693	1.296211	1.230333	0.81097	N
	1.414553	1.121642	1.141537	1.113019	1.188317	0.211567	D
	1.233727	0.824699	0.852171	0.937962	1.045647	0.166432	D
	1.769493	1.068044	1.025075	1.087998	1.087602	0.236507	D
S_E feature	S_E_1	S_E_2	S_E_3	S_E_4	S_E_5	S_E_6	
	0.24841	0.250336	0.284462	0.208855	0.192001	0.179762	N
	0.273264	0.255582	0.27656	0.24181	0.200938	0.155761	N
	0.280807	0.246982	0.277797	0.242527	0.175519	0.174597	N
	0.322968	0.231059	0.237048	0.279005	0.231192	0.142038	D
	0.287681	0.221831	0.242068	0.299123	0.25383	0.173497	D
	0.358195	0.244214	0.261389	0.301327	0.310539	0.160753	D
R_E feature	R_E_1	R_E_2	R_E_3	R_E_4	R_E_5	R_E_6	
	18.83011	48.07241	45.83892	41.0765	30.34007	48.16334	N
	21.34148	47.68127	48.00255	38.24354	42.30966	47.2872	N
	22.80164	45.81644	53.69389	41.91498	40.53259	51.48352	N
	19.45839	43.17995	41.08300	35.53840	42.02866	42.80719	D
	20.9565	43.7915	35.668990	37.36945	23.85223	40.927924	D
	17.64548	41.76585	43.097272	31.56652	37.16422	40.529672	D
P_E feature	P_E_1	P_E_2	P_E_3	P_E_4	P_E_5	P_E_6	
	0.693146	0.693036	0.692666	0.693017	0.693141	0.693138	N
	0.693142	0.691965	0.692932	0.692785	0.692926	0.693105	N
	0.69307	0.693092	0.692295	0.693127	0.693144	0.693132	N
	0.692997	0.693122	0.69307	0.693144	0.692673	0.692875	D
	0.693139	0.69105	0.692911	0.692544	0.692642	0.691863	D
	0.693146	0.693131	0.693147	0.692811	0.692731	0.693055	D

N: Normal, D: Diseased, A_E_1: Approximate entropy of 1st sub-band, S_E_1: Sample entropy of 1st sub-band, R_E_1: Renyi's entropy of 1st sub-band, P_E_1: Permutation entropy of 1st sub-band.

observed from Figure 9.6 that boxplot of the A_E feature has widespread seizure EEG activity and shows the positively skewed distribution for sub-bands 1, 2, 4, and 5. However, the same is not the case with normal EEG activity. Similar annotations can be made from Figures 9.7 and 9.8. Also, it is perceived from Figure 9.9 that R_E is more negatively skewed in boxplots of normal classes of EEG records as compared to the deseased one.

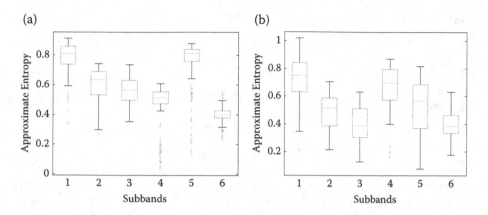

FIGURE 9.6 Boxplot of A_E feature for (a) Normal and (b) Diseased EEG activity.

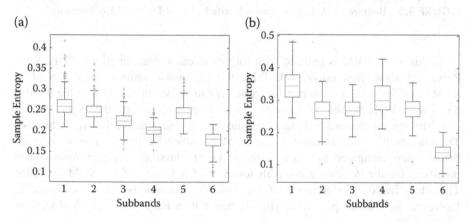

FIGURE 9.7 Boxplot of S_E feature for (a) Normal and (b) Diseased EEG activity.

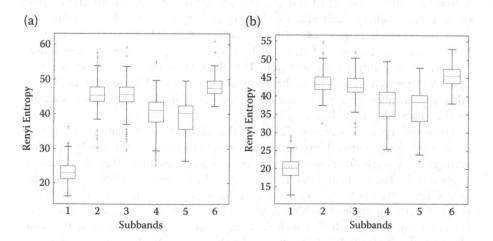

FIGURE 9.8 Boxplot of R_E feature for (a) Normal and (b) Diseased EEG activity.

(a)   (b)

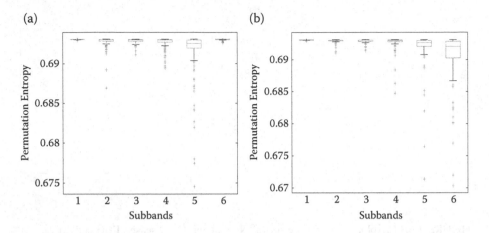

FIGURE 9.9   Boxplot of P_E feature for (a) Normal and (b) Diseased EEG activity.

In this work, SVM is realized with four different kernel functions: PUK, RBF, Poly, and normalized polykernel. Table 9.2 presents classification results of an SVM classifier using four kernel functions. It can be perceived from Table 9.2 that SVM with PUK kernels (Parameters: $\omega = 1$, $\gamma = 1$) attains the highest 100% classification efficiency for 2-class classification problem using the A_E feature set. The classification performance of the SVM classifier for the A_E feature is much better when compared to other features. Least classification performance was measured for the P_E feature using all four kernel functions of the SVM classifier. The classification performance of S_E and R_E features is nearly comparable. However, S_E features performed slightly better than R_E features in SVM classification stage.

Table 9.3 presents mean ± standard deviation parameters of extracted entropy features for binary class of EEG data. Figure 9.10 presents the classification results of all three classifiers obtained using single (1 entropy*6 sub-bands = 6 features) as well as combined entropy (4 entropy*6 sub-bands = 24 features) feature sets. Following the observations of earlier section, SVM with polykernel function is used for combined feature set classification. The observation derived from Figure 9.10 that SVM performance is much better as compared to ANN and RF classifiers. Also, classification results obtained for A_E and combined entropy features are almost comparable using all three classifiers.

However, it is always meaningful to use the least number of features in any type of classification problem. Thereby, it is deduced from Figure 9.5 that only A_E based features are suitable for obtaining good classification results in the seizure identification task. The confusion matrices of SVM (PUK kernel), ANN, and RF classifiers' performances for A_E, S_E, R_E, and P_E features are shown in Tables 9.4–9.7. It is perceived from Tables 9.4–9.7 that the correct identification rate of true negative (i.e., Normal) events is higher than the true positive (Diseased) events. It is concluded from Tables 9.4–9.7 that the SVM (PUK kernel) classifier is capable of

TABLE 9.2

Classification performance of SVM corresponding to various kernels

Kernel	Kernel Parameters	Correct/ Incorrect Classification	A_E	S_E	R_E	P_E
PUK kernel	$\omega = 1\ \gamma = 1$	Correct Classification	300 instances (100%)	295 instances (98.33%)	268 instances (89.33%)	238 instances (79.33%)
		Incorrect Classification	0 instances (0%)	5 instances (1.67%)	32 instances (10.67%)	62 instances (20.667%)
RBF kernel	$\gamma = 0.5$	Correct Classification	298 instances (99.33%)	290 instances (96.67%)	265 instances (88.33%)	217 instances (72.33%)
		Incorrect Classification	2 instances (0.67%)	10 instances (3.33%)	35 instances (11.67%)	83 instances (27.667%)
Poly kernel	Exponent = 2	Correct Classification	299 instances (99.667%)	292 instances (97.33%)	267 instances (89%)	247 instances (82.337%)
		Incorrect Classification	1 instance (0.33%)	8 instances (2.67%)	33 instances (11%)	53 instances (17.667%)

(Continued)

TABLE 9.2 (Continued)

Kernel	Kernel Parameters	Correct/ Incorrect Classification	A_E	S_E	R_E	P_E
Normalized Poly kernel	Exponent = 2	Correct Classification	293 instances (97.667%)	290 instances (96.67%)	248 instances (82.667%)	207 instances (69%)
		Incorrect Classification	7 instances (2.333%)	10 instances (3.33%)	52 instances (17.333%)	93 instances (31%)

TABLE 9.3
(Mean ± standard deviation) values for extracted entropies

Sub-bands	Class	A_E	S_E	R_E	P_E
SB1	Normal	1.417576 ± 0.058449	0.263248 ± 0.034162	24.41239 ± 3.561748	0.693131 ± 2.45305E-05
	Diseased	1.457203 ± 0.183905	0.347878 ± 0.05142	18.3189 ± 3.656673	0.693132 ± 2.36E-05
SB2	Normal	1.261762 ± 0.142664	0.244694 ± 0.023715	45.32462 ± 3.622452	0.692882 ± 0.000596
	Diseased	1.140554 ± 0.139644	0.268569 ± 0.040626	39.70558 ± 2.719214	0.692964 ± 0.000337
SB3	Normal	1.106009 ± 0.116418	0.26361 ± 0.032301	41.1875 ± 4.199042	0.692943 ± 0.000265
	Diseased	1.149855 ± 0.138116	0.270176 ± 0.036086	39.35311 ± 3.811825	0.692959 ± 0.000313
SB4	Normal	1.266274 ± 0.062502	0.225701 ± 0.023313	42.21691 ± 4.560488	0.692792 ± 0.000642
	Diseased	1.164234 ± 0.127998	0.307989 ± 0.050796	39.33653 ± 3.486811	0.692684 ± 0.001219
SB5	Normal	1.16689 ± 0.100608	0.200959 ± 0.016606	40.27368 ± 4.726428	0.691889 ± 0.002569
	Diseased	1.188343 ± 0.113807	0.274075 ± 0.036232	38.15546 ± 4.4556	0.691846 ± 0.003105
SB6	Normal	0.820068 ± 0.127971	0.175491 ± 0.02499	47.57763 ± 3.067692	0.693106 ± 7.42995E-05
	Diseased	0.308808 ± 0.120182	0.138128 ± 0.028014	44.24879 ± 3.615901	0.6904 ± 0.004369

SB1: 1st Sub-band, SB2: 2nd Sub-band, SB3: 3rd Sub-band, SB4: 4th Sub-band, SB5: 5th Sub-band, SB6: 6th Sub-band.

producing most good classification results using A_E features only. The highest classification accuracy results obtained for the A_E feature using ANN and RF classifiers are 99.667% and 98.33%, respectively.

In addition to the confusion matrix, the performance of all three classifier algorithms (using A_F features) is also measured by sensitivity, specificity, F-measure, and precision parameters in Table 9.8. These parameters are computed using equations given next. Here, true positive are values where prediction of classifier is positive and person is diseased. True negative denotes prediction is negative when person is normal. Similarly, false positive denotes the prediction is positive when a person is healthy and false negative denotes the prediction as negative when person is diseased. Results of classification explain the efficacy of the proposed

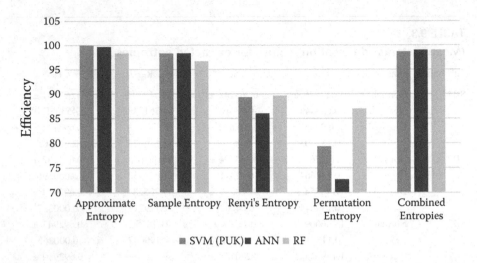

Approximate Entropy, Sample Entropy, Renyi's Entropy, Permutation Entropy, Combined Entropies

■ SVM (PUK) ■ ANN ■ RF

FIGURE 9.10 Classification accuracy corresponding to three classifiers for individual and combined entropy.

TABLE 9.4
Confusion matrix of classifiers' performance for A_E feature

Classifier Type	Normal	Diseased	Class
SVM (PUK Kernel)	200	0	D
	0	100	N
ANN	200	0	D
	1	99	N
RF	199	1	D
	4	96	N

N: Normal, D: Diseased.

TABLE 9.5
Confusion matrix of classifiers' performance for S_E feature

Classifier Type	Normal	Diseased	Class
SVM (PUK Kernel)	200	0	D
	5	95	N
ANN	199	1	D
	4	96	N
RF	199	1	D
	9	91	N

N: Normal, D: Diseased.

TABLE 9.6

Confusion matrix of classifiers' performance for R_E feature

Classifier Type	Normal	Diseased	Class
SVM (PUK Kernel)	191	9	D
	23	77	N
ANN	183	17	D
	25	75	N
RF	189	11	D
	20	80	N

N: Normal, D: Diseased.

TABLE 9.7

Confusion matrix of classifiers' performance for P_E feature

Classifier Type	Normal	Diseased	Class
SVM (PUK Kernel)	199	1	D
	61	39	N
ANN	178	22	D
	38	62	N
RF	188	12	D
	27	73	N

N: Normal, D: Diseased.

TABLE 9.8

SVM, ANN, and RF classifiers performance

Entropy	Classifiers	Sensitivity	Specificity	Precision	F-measure
Approximate entropy	SVM	100%	100%	1.00	1.00
	ANN	100%	99%	0.995	0.998
	RF	97%	99%	0.987	0.987

TQWT-entropy-based methodology in automatic seizure identification tasks. Table 9.9 shows a brief comparison in proposed methodology and previously available work from literature. It can be observed from Table 9.9 that the given criterion performs better than available techniques in automatic seizure identification tasks.

TABLE 9.9

Comparison of the present methodology of automatic seizure detection with previously proposed methods feature sets

Authors	Methodology	Classifier	Accuracy%	Sensitivity%	Specificity%
Ubyeli [28]	Wavelet Coefficient	ANN	94.25	94.50	96
Martis [29,30]	Empirical Mode Decomposition, Hilbert Transform	C4.5 Decision Tree	95.3	98	97
Pachori and Patidar [21]	Empirical Mode Decomposition, Second Order Difference Plot (SODP) based-confidence area measure	LS-SVM	97.75	97.68	98.07
Bhattacharya(a) [31]	Empirical Mode Decomposition	RF	99.4	97.9	99.5
Bhattacharya(b) [32]	TQWT	SVM	98.6	NA	NA
Shanir [33]	Local Binary Pattern (LBP)	k-NN	99.7	99.2	99.8
Acharya [34]	13-Layer deep CNN structure	Convolutional Neural Networks (CNN)	88.7	95	90
Chen [35]	Autoregressive Moving Average (ARMA) Model	SVM	94	99.2	99.8
Gao [36]	A_E and Recurrence Quantification Analysis	Convolutional Neural Networks (CNN)	99.26	98.84	99.35
The proposed work	TQWT, Approximate Entropy	SVM(PUK)	100	100	100

$$Sensitivity = \frac{True\ Positive}{True\ Positive + False\ Negative} \quad (9.17)$$

$$Specificity = \frac{True\ Negative}{True\ Negative + False\ Positive} \quad (9.18)$$

$$Precision = \frac{True\ Positive}{True\ Positive + False\ Positive} \qquad (9.19)$$

$$F1 - Measure = \frac{2 * (Sensitivity * Precision)}{Sensitivity + Precision} \qquad (9.20)$$

9.6 CONCLUSION

The work presented in this chapter aims to propose efficient feature generation and classification methodology for automatic epileptic seizure identification using EEG activity. The TQWT-entropy-based feature generation methodology is proposed for extracting highly discriminable features from two classes (seizure/diseased and nonseizure/normal) of EEG activity. Four entropy features are extracted from six decomposed time-frequency sub-bands, and five feature vectors are obtained with single and accumulated entropy features. Thereafter, three classifier algorithms are implemented for classification of features and validation of the suggested methodology. Multiple experiments are carried out on extracted features to optimize various classifiers' parameters. It is observed in the present study that Q-factor plays an important role in information extraction from any physiological activity. Among all three classifier algorithms, SVM classifier was found as the most suitable classifier algorithm for automated epileptic seizure detection using entropy features. Though classification results attained for different feature vectors (i.e., A_E, S_E, R_E, and combined Entropy features) are very substantial, the approximate entropy (A_E) feature outperforms all other features and produces results with the highest classification efficiency of 100% with the SVM classifier (PUK kernel). Classification results of the proposed work have specified the effectiveness of the proposed TQWT-entropy criterion in automatic epileptic seizure identification tasks. It is specified that the proposed criterion of TQWT-entropy-based methodology is a valuable and potent methodology to identify epileptic seizures utilizing EEG activity.

REFERENCES

1. Kumar, Y., Dewal, M.L. and Anand, R.S. "Epileptic seizure detection using DWT based fuzzy approximate entropy and support vector machine." *Neurocomputing* 133 (2014): 271–279.
2. Mormann, F., Andrzejak, R.G., Elger, C.E. and Lehnertz, K. "Seizure prediction: the long and winding road." *Brain* 130 (2007): 314–333.
3. Jahankhani, P., Kodogiannis, V. and Revett K. "EEG signal classification using wavelet feature extraction and neural networks." *IEEE John Vincent Atanasoff International Symposium on Modern Computing, Los Alamitos, USA, IEEE* (2006): 120–124. doi: 10.1109/JVA.2006.17.
4. Acharya, U.R., Faust, O., Kanatthal, L., Chua, T. and Laxminarayan, S. "Non-linear analysis of EEG signals at various sleep stages." *Computer Methods and Programs in Biomedicine* 80 (2005): 37–45.

5. Dastidar, S. G. and Adeli, H. "Improved spiking neural networks for EEG classification and epilepsy and seizure detection." *Integrated Computer-Aided Engineering* 14, 3 (2007): 187–212.
6. Jindal, K., Upadhyay, R. and Singh, H.S. "Application of tunable-Q wavelet transform based nonlinear features in epileptic seizure detection." *Analog Integrated Circuits and Signal Processing* 100 (2019): 437–452.
7. Chen, Z., Lu, G., Xie, Z. and Shang, W. "A unified framework and method for EEG-based early epileptic seizure detection and epilepsy diagnosis." *IEEE Access* 8 (2020): 20080–20092.
8. Sarabi, M.T., Daliri, M.R. and Niksirat, K.R. "Decoding objects of various categories from electroencephalographic signals using wavelet transform and support vector machine." *Brain Topography* 28 (2015): 33–46.
9. Jindal, K., Upadhyay, R. and Singh, H.S. "Application of hybrid GLCT-PICA denoising method in automated EEG artifact removal." *Biomedical Signal Processing and Control* 60 (2020): 101977.
10. Jindal, K. and Upadhyay, R. "Epileptic seizure detection from EEG signal using flexible analytical wavelet transform." *International Conference on Computer, Communications and Electronics (Comptelix)*, pp. 67–72, 2017.
11. Kumar, M., Pachori, R.B. and Acharya, U.R. "Characterization of coronary artery disease using flexible analytical wavelet transform applied on ECG signals." *Biomedical Signal Processing and Control* 32 (2017): 301–308.
12. Pinnegar, C.R., Khosravani, H. and Federico, P. "Time-frequency phase analysis of ictal EEG recordings with the S-transform." *IEEE Engineering in Medicine and Biology Society* 56, 11 (2009): 2583–2593.
13. Sharma, M. Pachori, R.B. and Acharya, U.R. "A new approach to characterize epileptic seizures using analytic time-frequency flexible wavelet transform and fractal dimension." *Pattern Recognition Letters* 94 (2017): 172–179.
14. Sharma, R. and Pachori, R.B. "Classification of epileptic seizures in EEG signals based on phase space representation of intrinsic mode functions." *Expert System Applications* 42, 3 (2015): 1106–1117.
15. Upadhyay, R., Kankar, P. K. and Padhy, P. K. "A comparative study of feature ranking techniques for epileptic seizure detection using wavelet transform." *Computer and Electrical Engineering* 000 (2016): 1–14.
16. Upadhyay, R., Manglick, A., Reddy, D.K., Padhy. P.K. and Kankar, P. K. "Channel optimization and nonlinear feature extraction for electroencephalogram signals classification." *Computers and Electrical Engineering* 45 (2015): 222–234.
17. Upadhyay, R., Padhy, P.K. and Kankar, P. K. "Application of S-transform for automated detection of vigilance level using EEG signals." *Journal of Biological Systems* 24 (2016): 1–27.
18. EEG time series data (Department of Epileptology University of Bonn). http://www.meb.unibonn.de/epileptologie/science/physik (accessed Oct. 2017).
19. Andrzejak, R.G., Lehnertz, K., Rieke, C., Mormann, F., David, P. and Elger, C.E. "Indications of nonlinear deterministic and finite dimensional structures in time series of brain electrical activity: dependence on recording region and brain state." *Physical Review* 64 (2001): 061907(1–7).
20. Selesnick, I. "Wavelet transform with tunable q-factor." *IEEE Transactions on Signal Processing* 59, 8 (2011): 3560–3575.
21. Patidar, S., Pachori, R.B. and Garg, S. "Detection of septal defects from cardiac sound signals using tunable-Q wavelet transform." *19th IEEE International Conference on Digital Signal Processing*, pp. 580–585, 2014.
22. Schuyler, R., White, A., Staley, K. and Cios, K.J. "Epileptic seizure detection." *IEEE Engineering in Medicine and Biology* 26, 2 (2007): 74–81.

23. Patidar, S. and Pachori, R.B. "Constrained tunable-Q wavelet transform based analysis of cardiac sound signals." *AASRI Conference on Intelligent Systems and Control* 4, pp. 57–63, 2013.
24. Pincus, S. "Approximate entropy (ApEn) as a complexity measure." *American Institute of Physics* 5, 1 (1995): 110–118.
25. Dhavala, S.K., Kumar, G.R. and Rao, K.N. "Training and classification of epilepsy detection using EEG." *International Journal of Advanced Science and Technology* 2 (2013): 9–21.
26. Kumar, A.N., Kumar, K.R. and Venketaraman, V. "Entropy features for focal EEG and non-focal EEG." *Journal of Computational Science* 27 (2018): 440–444.
27. Renyi, A. "On measures of information and entropy." *4th Berkeley Symposium on Mathematical Statistics and Prob*ability 1 (1960): 547–561.
28. Bandt, C. and Pompe, B. "Permutation entropy: a natural complexity measure for time series." *The American Physical Society* 88, 17 (2002): 1–4.
29. Ubyeli, E.D. "Combined neural network model employing wavelet coefficients for EEG signal classification." *Digital Signal Processing* 19, 2 (2009): 297–308.
30. Martis, R.J., Acharya, U.R., Taan, J.H., Petznick, A., Yanti, R., Chua, K.C., Ng, E.Y.K. and Tong, L. "Application of empirical mode decomposition (EMD) for automated detection of epilepsy using EEG signals." *International Journal of Neural Systems* 22, 6 (2012): 1–16.
31. Bhattacharya, A. and Pachori, R.B. "A multivariate approach for patient-specific EEG seizure detection using empirical wavelet transform." *IEEE Transaction on Biomedical Engineering* 64, 9 (2017): 2003–2015.
32. Bhattacharya, A., Pachori, R.B., Upadhyay, A. and Acharya, U.R. "Tunable-Q wavelet transform based multiscale entropy measure for automated classification of epileptic EEG signals." *Applied Sciences* 7, 4 (2017): 385.
33. Shanir, P.P.M., Khan, K.A., Khan Y.U., Farooq, O. and Adeli, H. "Automatic seizure detection based on morphological features using one-dimensional local binary pattern on long term EEG." *Clinical EEG and Neuroscience* 49, 5 (2018): 351–362.
34. Dastidar, S.G., Adeli, H. and Dadmehr N. "Mixed band wavelet-chaos-neural network methodology for epilepsy and epileptic seizure detection." *IEEE Transactions on Biomedical Engineering* 54, 9 (2007): 1545–1551.
35. Chen, Z., Lu, G., Xie, Z. and Shang, W. "A unified framework and method for EEG-based early epileptic seizure detection and epilepsy diagnosis." *IEEE Access* 8 (2020): 20080–20092.
36. Gao, X., Yan, X., Gao, P., Gao, X. and. Zhang, S. "Automatic detection of epileptic seizure based on approximate Entropy, recurrence quantification analysis and convolutional neural networks." *Artificial Intelligence in Medicine* 102 (2020): 101711.

10 An Efficient Single-Trial Classification Approach for Devanagari Script-Based Visual P300 Speller Using Knowledge Distillation and Transfer Learning

Ghanahshyam B. Kshirsagar and Narendra D. Londhe

10.1 INTRODUCTION

Brain machine interface (BMI), also known as brain computer interface (BCI), is primarily designed to provide an external assistive system through the human cognitive ability for those people who have lost their natural neuromuscular control due to severe neural diseases [1-5]. Mainly, this cognitive response is collected from the cortex of the human brain with a process called electro-encephalography (EEG) by placing sensors at the surface of the scalp. Basically, these noninvasive BCI systems are designed for various applications such as control and command [2-4]. These EEG-based BCI systems are mainly categorized into visual, auditory, and somatosensory BCIs based on the type of external stimulus used to generate the command [2,3]. Amongst them, visual P300-based BCI systems gained popularity due to the ease of implementation and less training required to the user [5,6]. Wherein, the event-related potentials (ERPs) are generated with visual tasks using oddball principles [1-8]. Mainly, this generated ERP shows positive amplitude ranging from 250–500 ms [5,6] with the highest value approximately at 300 ms [5,6]; hence, it is called P300 components. However, the inter-subject and intra-subject variability due to factors such as attention, focus, response time, physiological, and psychological conditions may alter the amplitude and its corresponding latency [5].

The first multi-trial visual-based P300 speller was developed for the English language in the late 1980s [9]. Wherein, the 6 × 6 matrix-based row-column (RC) paradigm was designed to provide a visual presentation to the user during the generation of ERP-EEG. Further, researchers have identified the importance of the implementation of visual speller in the native language. In that context, a visual P300 speller had been implemented with 3 to 15 numbers of trials in various languages like Devanagari script [5-8,10,11], Arabic [12], Japanese [13], and Chinese [14]. Generally, implementation of any visual P300 speller includes various steps such as design of a visual stimulus [4], data acquisition [15], feature extraction [16-18] and selection [19,20], and channel selection [10,11], classification of P300 [18-24], and character detection [5-25]. Although each listed component here has its importance in the successful implementation of P300 speller, the detection of P300 plays a vital role, as it yields the accurate detection of the character. Many factors such as subject variability, trial variability, and subject generated noises like eye blinking make the detection of ERP and nonERP highly challenging [5,6]. Therefore, researchers had designed the individual or combined approaches using advanced signal processing, feature extraction, and machine learning for accurate detection of P300 components from the EEG signal. Moreover, most studies had also presented the optimal channel selection based on advanced signal processing techniques [25] or evolutionary optimization [10,11], which aim to minimize the redundant noisy channels to improve the accuracy of P300 detection. In addition to that, few recent studies had also implemented ensemble learning approaches to reduce the false detection rate [6,10,23,26]. Although these conventional approaches had achieved accuracy as high as 96–97%, they are highly feature dependent [7-25]. Therefore, it is required to have expertise skills and prior knowledge of EEG signals to extract efficient features. This makes it less robust which may fail to provide generalize outcomes.

Over the past decade, the focus of the BCI researchers has shifted towards the implementation of efficient deep learning approaches to overcome the problem of feature dependency and variability of channel selection in conventional machine learning [26,27]. Cecotti and Gräser [26] had firstly implemented a convolutional neural network (CNN) and its ensemble variant for the classification of P300. The presented work includes extraction of the temporal features, weight-based feature selection, and redundant channel elimination in a single convolutional network. Further, a group of researchers had presented an improved CNN wherein weight-based feature selection is replaced with group convolution and sub-sampling approach [27]. There is approximately 2-8% improvement in the performance of P300 detection using proposed approach over existing methods. Hence, by considering the ability of automatic feature extraction, we also implemented the customized and fine-tuned Visual Geometry Group network (VGGnet)-based one dimensional (1D) deep CNN (DCNN) for classification in DS-P3S [5-8]. The DCNN [5] provided a huge increment of approximately 11% of accuracy in just three trials than the previous conventional machine-based approaches [10,11] in DS-P3S.

In the above-discussed literature, both states of art machine learning [7-25] or deep learning [5-8,26,27] methods require multiple trials of character flashing to provide a higher detection rate. There is a gradual drop in accuracy of P300 of approximately 8–26% for detection even with deep learning methods. This high trade-off between accuracy and the number of trials to spell a character further leads to a poor information transfer rate (ITR). For that purpose, a single trial-based classification of P300 in DS-P3S was implemented by us in the recent past [6]. In [6], a weighted ensemble (WE) of seven modified DCNNs and a modified character detection algorithm were proposed for the accurate detection of DS characters in a single trial. Although, the WE-DCNN provided high accuracy and the ITR for just a single trial, the DCNN generated numerous trainable parameters. Additionally, the ensemble methods make it more cumbersome which requires high computational capacity and time to handle this burden. Moreover, it also suffers from the problem of high variance due to subject variability.

To handling such problems, compacting the deep models [28,29] and transfer learnings [30,31] had been adopted in other BCI applications. For compressing the deep models, connection-wise pruning, filter wise pruning, and low-rank approximation-based approaches had been proposed in [28]. Concerning that, recently, Lawhren et al. [29] designed a compact CNN model named EEGNet. The main focus of the implemented approach was to reduce the parameters generated in the convolutional layers. Hence, they had used a depth-wise convolution which generates fewer parameters as compared to the standard convolutional layer. Even if this layer-based pruning helped to reduce the trainable parameters, it also compromises accuracy due to dense connectivity of channel-mix convolution. There is a real trade-off between the number of trainable parameters and accuracy [32,33].

To compensate this loss, transferring the learning of the deep model to a compress model called knowledge distillation was proposed in computer vision-based applications [34,35]. The comparable performance achieved by compressed models using knowledge distillation motivated authors to adopt such a technique to design an efficient compact classification model for DS-P3S. In that context, we present a hypothesis that the learning of an efficient shallow model may help to boost the performance of the compact model. Also, it has been proven that the machine or deep learning approaches perform better for maximum trial P300 detection. Therefore, we have also proposed a trial to trial transfer learning in this work. This particular approach will also help to reduce the trial to trial variability. The overall list of proposed hypotheses in this work are as follows:

- Hypothesis 1: The use of channel-wise convolution-based EEGNet will provide the sparse connectivity.
- Hypothesis 2: Transferring the learning of a shallow model via the knowledge distillation approach may strengthen the classification performance of a compact model.
- Hypothesis 3: The use of a weighted-based class balancing approach may reduce the class's unbalancing problem.
- Hypothesis 4: The trail to trail learning transfer may reduce the inter-trial variability.
- Hypothesis 5: The implementation of the subject-wise training of the proposed model may increase the generalization of the model by reducing the variance in the cross-subject analysis.

These proposed hypotheses will provide the following contributions to the visual P300 speller based BCI research; (1) an efficient compact model for single-trial P300 detection, (2) channel-wise convolution to provide sparse connectivity, (3) class weight-based approach to handle the problem of unbalancing in the data and to reduce false detection, (4) knowledge distillation to compensate the loss and reduce the trade-off between accuracy and number of trainable parameters, and (5) transfer learning to handle inter-trial and inter-subject variability.

The proposed hypotheses are evaluated on the same self-generated dataset from [5-8] ERP-EEG recordings of 79 DS characters collected from ten healthy volunteers at the National Institute of Technology Raipur, Chhattisgarh, India. Further, cross-subject and within-subject analysis are also performed to justify the proposed hypotheses.

10.2 METHODOLOGY

This section presents the details of the dataset used in this work, followed by details of the network used for the classification. Further are the mathematical details and explanation of knowledge distillation designed for our application. Lastly, a detail of the transfer learning used in this work is presented. The block diagram of the overall framework is illustrated in Figure 10.1.

10.2.1 THE DATASET

In this work, we have used the same ERP-EEG dataset from our previous work [5,6]. The dataset was recorded using a 16 channel ActiCAP Xpress EEG recording device in lab settings at the National Institute of Technology Raipur, India. Mainly, the EEG signals were recorded from the surface of the scalp by placing the 16 electrodes (FZ, FC1, FC2, C3, CZ, C4, CP5, CP1, CP2, CP6, P3, PZ, P4, O1, OZ, O2) at

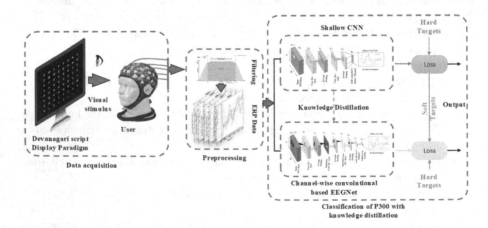

FIGURE 10.1   The block diagram of overall framework used for the classification of P300 in visual DS-P3S.

different locations of the brain such as frontal, central, parietal, and occipital in standard 10–20% EEG montage specially designed to acquire P300 using devices with 16 channels.

For DS-P3S, the visual display paradigm was implemented which contains the 64 characters arranged in the 8 × 8 matrix as shown in Figure 10.2 [5-8]. For recording the ERP-EEG responses, the subjects were given the task of spelling the character performing cognitive task i.e. counting silently on flashing of the target row and target character in which desirable character to spell is placed. Similarly, the spelling task was recorded for 20 words which include 79 characters at the sampling rate of 500 Hz from ten healthy volunteer subjects (male-8, female-2, aged 21–50 years) with normal hearing and vision. The consent of the subjects and ethical clearance from Institute Ethics Committee (IEC), NIT Raipur, had also been obtained. Please refer [5] to further details on the design of the DS paradigm and data acquisition process.

During data acquisition using 8 × 8 matrix based visual paradigm in DS-P3S, for a single character a total of 16 flashes (i.e., 8 rows and 8 columns) are generated in one trial. Wherein, only two have target characters and the rest 14 contains the non-target character. The ERPs corresponding to target and non-target characters are referred to as P300 and nonP300 respectively. Likewise, for 79 characters with 15 trials (i.e., 240 intensifications = 15 trials × 16 flashes), total of 303,360 (i.e., 79 characters × 240 intensifications × 16 channels) ERPs are generated for a single subject. Hence, the total number of ERPs for the dataset of ten subjects becomes 3,033,600. Wherein, each ERP contains a total of 300 samples i.e., 600 ms of data post flashing of target and non-target characters [5-8] (refer [5] for more details). Hence, the dataset becomes $D \in \mathbb{R}^{T \times M}$, where T = 300, and M = 3,033,600 (79 characters × 15 trials × 16 P300 and nonP300 × 16 channels × 10 subjects) for 15 trials and, $D \in \mathbb{R}^{T \times M_1}$, where T = 300, and M_1 = 202,240 (79 characters × 1 trial × 16 P300 and non-P300 × 16 channels × 10 subjects) for single trial. Further, we are rearranging the data in 2D i.e., in spatial-temporal format to extract both temporal and spatial features simultaneously in the same model. Finally, the data became $D \in \mathbb{R}^{T \times N_c \times m}$, where T = 300, N_c = 16 (number of electrodes), and m = 12,640 (79 characters × 1 trial × 16 P300 and nonP300 × 10 subjects).

As discussed earlier, for the spelling of a single character using the RC paradigm, a total of 16 flashes were generated for a single trial, out of which only two flashes contain target character (i.e. P300) and the remaining 14 flashes contain

अ	आ	इ	ई	उ	ऊ	ऋ	ए
ऐ	ओ	औ	अं	अः	क	ख	ग
घ	ङ	च	छ	ज	झ	ञ	ट
ठ	ड	ढ	ण	त	थ	द	ध
न	प	फ	ब	भ	म	य	र
ल	ळ	व	ष	श	स	ह	क्ष
त्र	ज्ञ	श्र	०	१	२	३	४
५	६	७	८	९	#	—	?

FIGURE 10.2 A standard 8 × 8 matrix based visual display paradigm for DS-P3S.

non-target characters (i.e. non-P300). Hence, the ratio of the number of targets and non-target P300 becomes 1:7. This creates main two problems: (1) class unbalancing, and (2) increasing false detection rate as non-P300 may look morphologically similar to P300, which is referred to as error-related potential (ErrP) due to lack of attention during the task of counting. As a result, the overlapping of P300 in the non-P300 zone leads to type I error (i.e., false positive). To handle the effect of this unbalanced data, random under-sampling [5], random oversampling [27], and ensemble learning [6] were adopted in existing studies of visual base P300 spellers. However, these data augmentation approaches have limitations such as, in random oversampling, the addition of artificial P300 to balance with non-P300 in the dataset increased the problem of overfitting. While in the case of random under-sampling, two out of fourteen non-P300 components are selected to balance the dataset. However, this random selection of nonP300 may contain ErrPs, which is the generation of P300 during the flashing of non-target row/column [35-37]. This increases the false detection rate; hence, new data partition-based ensemble learning is presented in [6] to reduce this false detection. However, ensemble learning further increases the computational burden of the system. Therefore, we are adopting a class weight-based approach to balance the dataset. Wherein, the minority class i.e., P300, have assigned higher weights and the majority class i.e., nonP300, with lower weights.

10.2.2 Details of the Proposed Architecture

In this work, we have modified the EEGNet [27] using the filter pruning method [26]. There are two main modifications we have proposed in the existing EEGNet which are; (1) filter pruning, (2) channel-wise convolutional based classification. In filter pruning, instead of selecting the kernel size half the sampling frequency as stated in EEGNet [27], we have selected it as a quarter the sampling frequency, which extracts information above the 4Hz instead of 2Hz [27]. This helped to reduce the number of parameters by half the original at the first layer of convolution. Moreover, we have taken overlapping windowing with the size w = 8 (25ms) in our proposed model. The windowing at rate 25ms acts as a low-pass with a frequency of 40Hz which is the higher frequency limit as all the P300 components are presented below 40Hz. Also, it helps to reduce the training time. Hence, based on this particular approach, we able to capture information between 4–40Hz. In the second modification, as in channel-mix convolution, the network is densely connected which includes both the weaker and stronger channels. The channel(s) with low weight is/are also taking part in the computation, which may not have any contribution to an improvement in learning; rather, they tend to confuse the learning. This leads to two problems; (1) increases the number of trainable parameters, and (2) reducing the network performance. Whereas, in channel-wise convolution, the network will be sparsely connected which makes the weaker channel to zero. Hence, it reduces the trainable parameter as the unwanted channels are eliminated. This will help to avoid unnecessary computation and also boost the classification performance. The pictorial illustration of the channel-wise convolutional based modified EEGNet is as shown in Figure 10.3. The architectural details with its parameters are presented in Table 10.1.

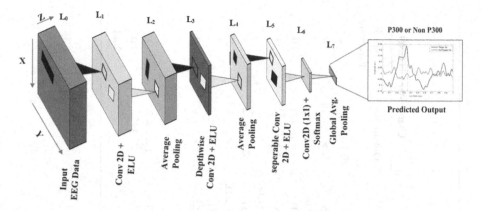

FIGURE 10.3 The pictorial illustration of building blocks of proposed channel-wise modified EEGNet.

10.2.2.1 Block-1 (L_0): Input

As discussed in the dataset section, the data $D \in \mathbb{R}^{X \times Y \times Z}$ in the form of a tensor with order 3 is provided as input ERP-EEG with "X" number of components, "Y" number of channels, and "Z" number of samples as shown in Figure 10.3 and Table 10.1.

10.2.2.2 Block-2 (L_1-L_2): Temporal Information

In L_1, temporal information is computed by performing the convolution of the kernel of size $N = (n, 1)$ with the ERP of size Z where depth $F1 = N_c = 16$, as the number of channels are 16, $n = F_s/4 = 125$ to collect the information above 4Hz, and stride $= 8$ is the windowing size $w = 25$ ms to extract the information below 40Hz. The mathematical representation of convolution operation at L_1 is given here:

$$C^X(j) = f\left(\sum_i^{Nc} \sum_{j=1}^{j \leq X} X_j^X \cdot w_j^X (n, 1) + b_j\right), \tag{10.1}$$

where, $C^X(j)$ is the output of convolution performed over temporal domain i.e. $1 \geq j \leq X$. followed by a sub-sampling layer i.e., average pooling is used at layer L_2 of filter size $(6,1)$ to downsample the sampling frequency approximately to 80Hz. The main advantage of the average pooling over max pooling is it takes the average over the selected size of the kernel. Therefore, other relevant information also extracted which gets neglected using max-pooling.

10.2.2.3 Block-3 (L_3-L_5): Spatial Information

For the computation of the spatial information, a depthwise convolution of size $(1, N_c)$ is used at L_3. As depth-wise convolutions do not provide fully connections with their preceding layer, it helps to reduce the trainable parameters [27] as well as eliminating the lossy channels. The depth D_1 is selected based on the criteria of $D_1 = 2 * F_1$ [27]. Furthermore, to reduce the trainable parameters, the second sub-

TABLE 10.1

The details of the architecture of EEGNet and channel-wise EEGNet

Block No.	Layers	EEGNet Filters	EEGNet Output Size	EEGNet No. of Parameters	Channel-wise EEGNet Filters	Channel-wise EEGNet Output Size	Channel-wise EEGNet No. of Parameters
1	Input	–	300 × 16 X 1	–	–	300 × 16 X 1	–
2	Conv2D +ELU	$F_1 = 16, N = (250,1), S = (1,1)$	51 × 16 × 16	4016	$F_1 = 16, N = (125,1), S = (8,1)$	22 × 16 × 16	2016
	Avg. pooling	$P_1 = (6,1)$	8 × 16 × 16	0	$P_1 = (6,1)$	5 × 16 × 16	0
3	Depthwise Conv2D +ELU	$D_1 = 2, N = (1,16), S = (1,1)$	8 × 1 × 32	544	$D_1 = 2, N = (1,16), S = (1,1)$	5 × 1 × 32	544
	Avg. pooling	$P_2 = (2,1)$	4 × 1 × 32	0	$P_2 = (2,1)$	2 × 1 × 32	0
4	Seperable Conv2D +ELU	$D_2 = 1, N = (1,1), S = (1,1)$	4 × 1 × 1	2144	$D_2 = 1, N = (1,1), S = (1,1)$	1 × 1 × 1	65
	Dropout	p = 0.25	4 × 1 × 1	0	p = 0.25	1 × 1 × 1	0
5	Fully connected	–	–	0	–	–	–
5	Dense	C = 2	2 × 1	258	–	–	–
5	Conv2D+Softmax	$F_3 = 1, N = (1 \times 1)$	–	–	$F_3 = 1, N = (1 \times 1)$	1 × 1 × 2	4
	Global Avg. Pooling	–	–	–	–	2	0
Total number of parameters				6962			2661

sampling layer i.e., average pooling of size (2,1), is added at layer L_4 to down-sample the sampling frequency from 80Hz to approximately 40Hz. Here, we kept the depth parameter D = 1 for our experiment to limit the trainable parameters. Followed by that, a separable convolution of size (1,1) is applied at layer L_6 and used to provide the pointwise learning [27,32] of the feature maps by decoupling the relationship within and between the feature maps. In addition to that, a separable convolution manages to reduce a few parameters.

10.2.2.4   Block-4 (L_6-L_7): Class Prediction

For classification of P300, we have used a channel-wise convolution of size (1×1) with a softmax activation function at layer L_6, which provides the sparse connectivity to the model [32]. Lastly, a global average pooling is used to achieve spatial invariance in feature maps and also reduces their size as it utilizes $1 \times 1 \times d$ instead of h $\times$ w $\times$ d of conventional dense connected layer [32,33].

Activation and regularization: In existing DS-P3S, advanced activation functions like ReLU [5] and leaky ReLU [6] were used to accelerate the training and overcome the dying ReLU problem. However, the main limitation of leaky ReLU is its tendency to become a linear function on differentiation. Moreover, in existing DS-P3S, additional batch normalization was used to provide a covariate shift that also generates few parameters. As our main aim is to reduce the parameters, here we are replacing the leaky ReLU with an exponential linear unit (ELU) [38]. The ELU not only accelerated the training by reducing the distance between the gradientsby providing negative values closer [38]. Moreover, on differentiation, ELU acts as partial linear and nonlinear, unlike leaky ReLU. Therefore, we have used ELU activation at each convolution layer except the classification layer (L_9).

Loss function and optimizer: In this work, the binary cross-entropy loss function is used to calculate the deviation between the predicted and actual class which is expressed as:

$$L = - \sum_i O_i ln(\widehat{O_i}) \tag{10.2}$$

where L is the loss, O_i is the target categories and $(\widehat{O_i})$ is a predicted probability. Further, an adaptive learning approach of a gradient-based optimizer called RmsProp is used to minimize the loss function in equation (10.2) by updating the weights. The main advantage of the RmsProp optimizer is that it uses a moving average of the square gradients of the previous gradient to update the next gradient. The weights are updated by using the following equations:

$$E[g^2]_t = y E[g^2]_{t-1} + (1 - y)g_t^2 \tag{10.3}$$

$$w_{t+1} = w_t - \frac{\eta}{\sqrt{E[g^2]_t + \varepsilon}} \tag{10.4}$$

where y is decay parameter, η is the learning rate, and $E[g^2]_t$ is the moving average of square gradients.

10.2.3 KNOWLEDGE DISTILLATION (TEACHER-STUDENT NETWORK)

In its pioneer study, knowledge distillation (KD) was used to share the learning of ensemble models to a single compact model [34,35]. Hence, by considering its proven outcomes, authors are motivated to design compact CNN models using the KD approach to attend the comparable performance and to compensate for the loss. In view of that, we first propose a teacher-student network-based knowledge distillation approach in this work. The proposed KD is used to share the learning of the shallow model to the proposed compact model. This has been achieved by assigning the class probabilities of the deep model as the soft targets to the compact model during training. Wherein, shallowCNN acts as a teacher network from which logit information is transferred as a soft target to the student network i.e., channel-wise EEGNet during training as shown in Figure 10.4. The student networks learn from both the soft labels and the ground truths. Simultaneously it also understands the data representation and learning ability of the shallowCNN. The detailed mathematical representation of the teacher-student is given as follows.

The objective function can be formulated as:

$$L(z, \hat{z}) = - \sum_c^N z_c \log(\widehat{z_c}) - \alpha. \sum_c^N p_c \log(q_c) \tag{10.5}$$

where z_c and $\widehat{z_c}$ are the true probability and predicted probability of cth class, N is the total number of classes (here N = 2), α is constant to control the contribution between two terms in equation (10.5), p_c and q_c are the soft targets and are expressed as:

$$p_c = \frac{e^{(u_c/T)}}{\sum_b e^{(u_b/T)}}, \text{ and } q_c = \frac{e^{(v_c/T)}}{\sum_b e^{(v_b/T)}} \tag{10.6}$$

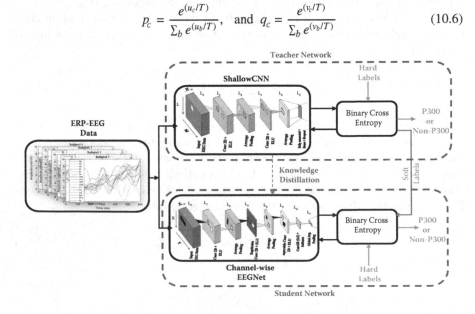

FIGURE 10.4 Pictorial illustration of proposed teacher-student network-based knowledge distillation for designing of a compact classification model.

where T is the temperature which is generally set to 1 and it controls the degree of the softness of the targets; the higher the T, the softer the target. u_c and v_c are the logits of teacher and student model respectively.

Further, the cross-entropy gradient with respect to logits of student model i.e., v_c are solved to obtain final probabilities. The gradient is given as:

$$\frac{\partial C}{\partial v_c} = \frac{1}{T} \left(q_c - P_c \right) = \frac{1}{T} \left(\frac{e^{(u_c/T)}}{\sum_b e^{(u_b/T)}} - \frac{e^{(v_c/T)}}{\sum_b e^{(v_b/T)}} \right) \tag{10.7}$$

Solving equation (10.7) by assuming $\sum_b u_b = \sum_b v_b = 0$,

$$\frac{\partial C}{\partial v_c} \approx \frac{1}{NT^2} \left(q_c - P_c \right) \tag{10.8}$$

where, $\frac{\alpha}{NT^2} = 0.03$ in this work. Lastly, equation (10.8) is solved to get matching logits between shallowCNN and channel-wise EEGNet.

10.3 EXPERIMENTAL SETUP

In this work, we are implementing a list of experiments to evaluate the proposed hypotheses. The experiments are: (1) for hypothesis 1, classification of P300 using shallowCNN, EEGNet, and proposed channel-wise EEGNet; (2) for hypothesis 2, a teacher-student network to share the knowledge of shallowCNN to a proposed compact model; (3) for hypothesis 3, classification of P300 using random un-dersampled data and data with class-weights; and (4) for hypothesis 4, first, classification of P300 is implemented using the data of 15 trials. Further, the optimized weights-based learning is shared to the classification model with single-trial data. Lastly, (5) for hypothesis 5, Leave one subject out (LOSO)-based subject to subject learning transfer is implemented. The details of the transfer learning are given next.

10.3.1 TRANSFER LEARNING

Transfer learning (TL) is primarily proposed to improve the prediction of the target applications by utilizing the learning of similar or different sources [30,31]. Hence, based on the relationships between the target domain and source domain, TL is categorized as domain adaptation [31] and rule adaptation [31]. In domain adaptation-based TL, a single decision rule is used to classify the samples from different domains. Whereas in rule adaptation-based TL, the new decision rule is used in smaller search space to classify the target samples. Here, the part of the learning from the source is utilized to initiate the search space which helps to converge the gradient much faster than normal learning. In this work, for implementing inter-subject TL, we have used domain adaptation. While, for inter-trial TL, we are using rule adaptation TL. The details follow next.

10.3.1.1   Inter-Subject Transfer Learning

In this experiment, leave one subject out-based transfer learning is used. Wherein, one subject acts as a target whereas rest subjects become the source from where the learning is transferred to the target subject [30]. The same process is repeated until every subject becomes a target. This approach is comparatively less computationally costly than the subject adaptation approach wherein the subjects are divided into two sets and forced to converge until the subject gets adopted with the source. This particular approach also has one major limitation that it shifts information during transferring from source to target [30].

10.3.1.2   Inter-Trial Transfer Learning

In the case of inter-trial TL, the experiment with maximum trials i.e. with 15 trials is performed. The model is trained until the termination criteria that is a series of minimum loss with high accuracy of P300 classification. Further, we used this model as a source whose learning is transferred to the target model i.e. experiment with a single trial. The learning of the source is utilized to provide initial search space to the new target model. This particular approach helped not only to improve the learning but also it converges in less time as instead of random initialization and searching for optimal weights the already learned information provides the optimal path for rapid convergence.

10.3.2 TRAINING SETTINGS

In this work, the experiments of the classification of the P300 component using shallowCNN, EEGNet, and the proposed channel-wise EEGNet are implemented using Python with Keras [39] libraries and TensorFlow backend [40]. The selected parameters follow.

Batch size = 50, initial weights and bias for experiments with 15 trials are initialized using the Glorot uniform method [41], where the initial weights for experiments with the single trial are selected via TL, dropout (p) = 0.25 [42], loss = binary cross-entropy (see equation 10.2), optimizer = RmsProp [43], the parameter of RmsProp viz. learning rate η = 0.001, ε = 0.9 with no decay (see equations (10.3) and (10.4), LOSO is used during the experiments with N = 10. Note that both TL i.e., inter-trial and inter-subject, are implemented in single experiments to avoid extra redundant experimentations.

10.4   RESULTS

In this section, we are presenting the cross-subject and within-subject performance analysis for classification of P300 using shallowCNN, EEGNet, and proposed channel-wise EEGNet (CW-EEGNet) with and without knowledge distillation and transfer learning.

10.4.1 SHALLOWCNN

10.4.1.1 Cross-Subject Analysis

Figure 10.5a illustrates the cross-subject analysis of P300 classification using shallowCNN with and without TL in a single trial. It shows that, for shallowCNN, the accuracy achieved are ranging from 83.44% to 93.87% with an average of 88.86% ± 3.20. The data of subject 6 provided the lowest accuracy of 83.44%, whereas, in subject 10 it is highest at 93.87%. Moreover, the other performance parameters such as true positive rate (TPR), true negative rate (TNR), positive predictive value (PPV), and F1-score are also calculated. The range of TPR, TNR, PPV, and F1-score are 82.64% to 93.53% with an average of 88.33%, 84.56% to 93.98% with an average of 89.62%, 81.55% to 93.12% with an average of 88.20%, and 83.57% to 93.75% with an average of 88.97%, respectively.

(a)

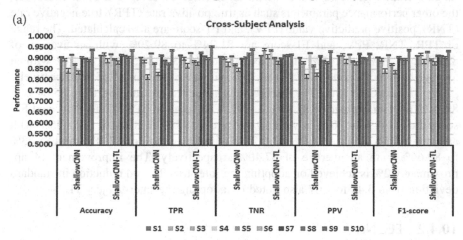

(b)

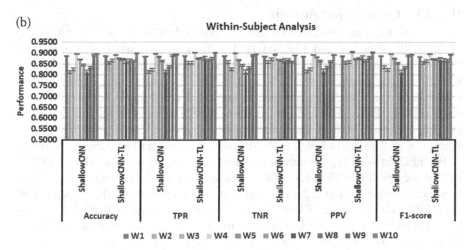

FIGURE 10.5 The results of the classification of P300 using shallowCNN with and without TL; (a) cross-subject analysis, and (b) within-subject analysis.

For shallowCNN with TL, the accuracy achieved are ranging from 87.87% to 93.57% with an average of 90.69% ± 1.64. The lowest accuracy of 87.87% found in the dataset of subject 6 while subject 10 got the highest accuracy of 90.69%. The range of TPR, TNR, PPV, and F1-score are 87.56% to 95.27% with an average of 90.44%, 88.01% to 93.96% with an average of 90.14%, 87.77% to 92.11% with an average of 90.34%, 87.78% to 93.40% with an average of 90.80%, respectively. The improvement of approximately 2% is achieved on adopting the inter-trial TL and reduction in standard deviation from 3.20 to 1.64 also noted on adopting the inter-subject TL.

10.4.1.2 Within-Subject Analysis

Figure 10.5b illustrates the within-subject analysis of P300 classification using shallowCNN with and without TL in a single trial. The accuracy achieved are ranging from 81.11% to 89.65% with an average of 85.65% ± 3.48. Moreover, the other performance parameters such as true positive rate (TPR), true negative rate (TNR), positive predictive value (PPV), and F1-score are also calculated. The range of TPR, TNR, PPV, and F1-score are 81.24% to 89.29% with an average of 85.89%, 81.21% to 89.41% with an average of 86.03%, 81.54% to 89.14% with an average of 85.60%, and 81.22% to 89.30% with an average of 85.55%, respectively.

For shallowCNN with TL, the accuracy achieved are ranging from 85.64% to 89.74% with an average of 87.29% ± 1.07. The range of TPR, TNR, PPV, and F1-score are 85.44% to 90.12% with an average of 87.62%, 85.81% to 88.55% with an average of 87.19%, 85.64% to 90.22% with an average of 87.78%, and 85.63% to 89.66% with an average of 87.40%, respectively. The improvement of approximately 2% is achieved on adopting the inter-trial TL and reduction in standard deviation from 3.48 to 1.07 also noted on adopting the inter-subject TL.

10.4.2 EEGNet

10.4.2.1 Cross-Subject Analysis

Figure 10.6a illustrates the cross-subject analysis of the classification of P300 using EEGNet, EEGNet-TL, and EEGNet-TL-KD in a single trial. It shows that for EEGNet without TL and KD, the accuracy achieved are ranging from 80.92% to 87.69% with an average of 85.05% ± 3.09. The data of subject 3 provided the lowest accuracy of 80.92%, whereas, in subject 2 it is highest i.e., 87.69%. The range of TPR, TNR, PPV, and F1-score are 78.88% to 89.94% with an average of 84.15%, 79.49% to 90.86% with an average of 85.88%, 81.29% to 90.20% with an average of 85.93%, and 81.76% to 88.51% with an average of 84.92%, respectively.

For EEGNet with TL, the accuracy achieved are ranging from 83.41% to 88.98% with an average of 85.88% ± 1.97. The lowest accuracy of 83.41% found in the dataset of subject 3, while subject 2 got the highest accuracy of 88.98%. The range of TPR, TNR, PPV, and F1-score are 83.47% to 89.77% with an average of 86.03%, 82.14% to 90.73% with an average of 85.88%, 81.10% to 88.64% with an average of 85.72%, and 83.31% to 88.62% with an average of 85.90%, respectively. The improvement in accuracy approximately by 1% is achieved on adopting the inter-trial TL with the reduction in standard deviation from 3.09 to 1.97 also noted on adopting the inter-subject TL.

(a)

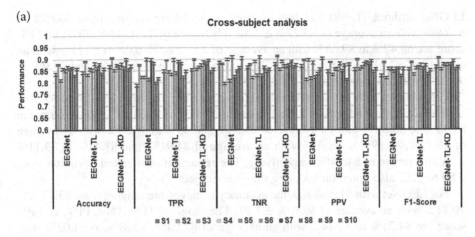

(b)

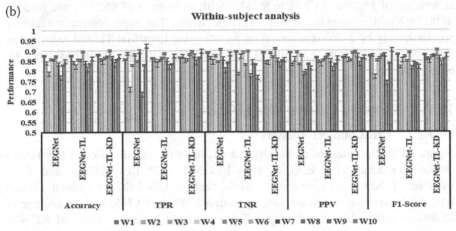

FIGURE 10.6 The results of the classification of P300 using EEGNet with and without TL; (a) cross-subject analysis, and (b) within-subject analysis.

For EEGNet with TL and KD, the accuracy achieved are ranging from 85.21% to 90.41% with an average of 87.23% ± 1.79. The lowest accuracy of 85.21% found in the dataset of subject 3, while subject 2 got the highest accuracy of 90.41%. The range of TPR, TNR, PPV, and F1-score are 84.52% to 89.79% with an average of 87.13%, 85.54% to 91.21% with an average of 87.80%, 85.56% to 89.74% with an average of 87.10%, and 85.60% to 90.47% with an average of 87.44%, respectively. The improvement in accuracy approximately by 2–3% is achieved on adopting the inter-trial TL and reduction in standard deviation from 3.09 to 1.79 also noted on adopting the inter-subject TL along with KD.

10.4.2.2 Within-Subject Analysis

Figure 10.6b illustrates the within-subject analysis of the classification of P300 using EEGNet, EEGNet-TL, and EEGNet-TL-KD in a single trial. It shows that for

EEGNet without TL and KD, the accuracy achieved are ranging from 76.85% to 87.69% with an average of 83.73% ± 3.50. The range of TPR, TNR, PPV, and F1-score are 68.42% to 89.68% with an average of 83.42%, 77.63% to 89.71% with an average of 83.91%, 78.53% to 89.17% with an average of 84.04%, and 73.9% to 90.22% with an average of 84.63%, respectively.

For EEGNet with TL, the accuracy achieved are ranging from 81.01% to 89.55% with an average of 84.96% ± 2.52. The range of TPR, TNR, PPV, and F1-score are 82.11% to 88.51% with an average of 85.35%, 80.33% to 90.55% with an average of 86.11%, 80.89% to 88.01% with an average of 84.91%, and 81.41% to 89.11% with an average of 84.54%, respectively. The reduction in standard deviation from 3.50 to 2.52 also noted on adopting the inter-subject TL.

For EEGNet with TL and KD, the accuracy achieved are ranging from 83.13% to 90.11% with an average of 86.40% ± 1.91. The range of TPR, TNR, PPV, and F1-score are 84.21% to 89.74% with an average of 87.04%, 82.87% to 91.02% with an average of 86.28%, 83.25% to 89.44% with an average of 86.56%, and 83.53% to 90.38% with an average of 86.65%, respectively. The improvement in accuracy approximately by 2–3% is achieved on adopting the inter-trial TL and reduction in standard deviation from 3.50 to 1.91 also noted on adopting the inter-subject TL along with KD.

10.4.3 PROPOSED CHANNEL-WISE EEGNET

10.4.3.1 Cross-Subject Analysis

Figure 10.7a illustrates the cross-subject analysis of the classification of P300 using proposed channel-wise EEGNet (CW-EEGNet), CW-EEGNet-TL, and CW-EEGNet-TL-KD in a single trial. It shows that for CW-EEGNet without TL and KD, the accuracy achieved are ranging from 80.24% to 89.74% with an average of 85.96% ± 2.60. The data of subject 7 provided the lowest accuracy of 80.24%, whereas, in subject 5 it is highest i.e., 89.74%. The range of TPR, TNR, PPV, and F1-score are 80.14% to 88.76% with an average of 84.43%, 80.11% to 90.25% with an average of 84.57%, 80.20% to 88.99% with an average of 84.40%, and 80.27% to 89.24% with an average of 84.54%, respectively.

For CW-EEGNet with TL, the accuracy achieved are ranging from 83.21% to 89.15% with an average of 87.09% ± 1.88. The lowest accuracy of 83.21% found in the dataset of subject 7 while subject 10 got the highest accuracy of 89.15%. The range of TPR, TNR, PPV, and F1-score are 83.41% to 89.45% with an average of 87.28%, 83.11% to 89.85% with an average of 87.66%, 83.47% to 89.74% with an average of 87.12%, and 83.25% to 89.59% with an average of 87.46%, respectively. The improvement in accuracy approximately by 2% is achieved on adopting the inter-trial TL with the reduction in standard deviation from 3.16 to 1.88 also noted on adopting the inter-subject TL.

For CW-EEGNet with TL and KD, the accuracy achieved are ranging from 88.61% to 92.59% with an average of 90.82% ± 1.47. The lowest accuracy of 88.61% found in the dataset of subject 6 while subject 8 got the highest accuracy of 92.59%. The range of TPR, TNR, PPV, and F1-score are 86.98% to 94.40% with an

(a)

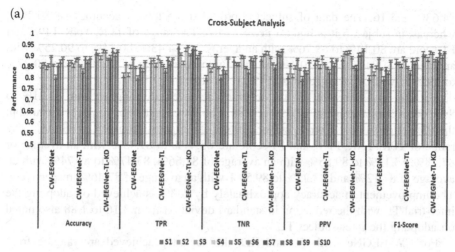

(b)

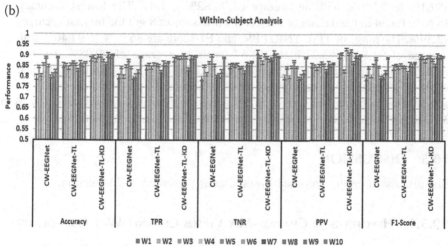

FIGURE 10.7 The results of the classification of P300 using CW-EEGNet with and without TL; (a) cross-subject analysis, and (b) within-subject analysis.

average of 91.84%, 85.27% to 91.86% with an average of 90.08%, 85.89% to 93.37% with an average of 90.19%, and 88.75% to 92.63% with an average of 90.91%, respectively. The improvement in accuracy approximately by 4–5% is achieved on adopting the inter-trial TL and reduction in standard deviation from 2.60 to 1.47 also noted on adopting the inter-subject TL along with KD.

10.4.3.2 Within-Subject Analysis

Figure 10.7b illustrates the within-subject analysis of the classification of P300 using proposed channel-wise EEGNet (CW-EEGNet), CW-EEGNet-TL, and CW-EEGNet-TL-KD in a single trial. It shows that for CW-EEGNet without TL and KD, the accuracy achieved are ranging from 80.24% to 89.74% with an average of

84.63% ± 3.16. The data of subject 7 provided the lowest accuracy of 80.24%, whereas, in subject 5 it is highest i.e., 89.74%. The range of TPR, TNR, PPV, and F1-score are 80.14% to 88.76% with an average of 84.43%, 80.11% to 90.25% with an average of 84.57%, 80.20% to 88.99% with an average of 84.40%, and 80.27% to 89.24% with an average of 84.54%, respectively.

For CW-EEGNet with TL, the accuracy achieved are ranging from 83.21% to 89.15% with an average of 87.09% ± 1.88. The lowest accuracy of 83.21% found in the dataset of subject 7 while subject 10 got the highest accuracy of 89.15%. The range of TPR, TNR, PPV, and F1-score are 83.41% to 89.45% with an average of 87.28%, 83.11% to 89.85% with an average of 87.66%, 83.47% to 89.74% with an average of 87.12%, and 83.25% to 89.59% with an average of 87.46%, respectively. The improvement in accuracy approximately by 2–3% is achieved on adopting the inter-trial TL with the reduction in standard deviation from 3.16 to 1.88 also noted on adopting the inter-subject TL.

For CW-EEGNet with TL and KD, the accuracy achieved are ranging from 88.61% to 92.59% with an average of 90.82% ± 1.47. The lowest accuracy of 88.61% found in the dataset of subject 6 while subject 8 got the highest accuracy of 92.59%. The range of TPR, TNR, PPV, and F1-score are 86.98% to 94.40% with an average of 91.84%, 85.27% to 91.86% with an average of 90.08%, 85.89% to 93.37% with an average of 90.19%, and 88.75% to 92.63% with an average of 90.91%, respectively. The improvement in accuracy approximately by 5–6% is achieved on adopting the inter-trial TL and reduction in standard deviation from 3.16 to 1.47 also noted on adopting the inter-subject TL along with KD.

10.5   DISCUSSION

The discussion on the proposed hypotheses is presented in this section.

10.5.1   HYPOTHESIS 1: CHANNEL-MIX VERSUS CHANNEL-WISE CONVOLUTION

In this sub-section, we are presenting a comparison between the channel-mix convolution and channel-wise convolution for the classification of P300 in DS-P3S. In the channel-mix convolution, the network is densely connected, which includes both the weaker and stronger channels. The channel(s) with low weight is/are also taking part in the computation, which may not have any contribution to the improvement in learning; rather, they tend to confuse the learning. This leads to two problems; (1) it increases the number of trainable parameters, and (2) reduces the network performance. Whereas, in channel-wise convolution, the network will be sparsely connected, which makes the weaker channel to zero. Hence, it reduces the trainable parameter as the unwanted channels eliminate. The same is observed from the Table 10.1, the last dense layer generates 256 trainable parameters; whereas, sparse convolutional layers generated only four trainable parameters. Moreover, the positive increment in the accuracy from 85.05% to 85.96% is achieved for the classification using a channel-wise convolution approach. This ensures that the proposed channel-wise convolution helped to reduce the redundant weaker features that lead to an improvement in the performance. Hence, this satisfies our first hypothesis of utilizing channel-wise convolution over channel-mix to improve the performance with a reduction in trainable parameters.

10.5.2 HYPOTHESIS 2: EFFECT OF KNOWLEDGE DISTILLATION

The comparative analysis of the results of the classification of P300 in a single trial for DS-P3S using deep, shallow, and compact CNN are presented in Table 10.2. The DCNN, M-DCNN, and its ensemble variant, i.e., WE-DCNN, achieved accuracy ranging from 81 to 92.64%, among them WEDCNN had achieved the highest accuracy of 92.64%. However, they are generating 153,730, 153,730, and 1,076,110 (153,730 × 7, where 7 are the number of ensembles) trainable parameters respectively. The numerous parameters increases the computational complexity. Hence, to reduce the computational burden shallowCNN, EEGNet, and CW-EEGNet are implemented which achieved an accuracy of 88.86 ± 3.20, 85.09 ± 2.09, 85.96 ± 2.59 with 27602, 6962, and 2661 the number of trainable parameters, respectively. Although the trainable parameters reduced 5–58 times than existing DCNN [5,6] it also degraded the accuracy by 4–7%. However, in single trial-based approaches, it is imperative to attain high accuracy as the character detection in DS-P3S is based on the maximum intersection of the row-column approach. Therefore, it is not affordable to misclassify single P300s corresponding to either target row or column. Hence, to maintain the trade-off between the trainable parameters and performance, transferring the knowledge from a deep model to a compact is implemented. On adopting the KD with EEGNet and proposed CW-EEGNet, the accuracy of classification has improved to 87.29% and 90.82%, respectively. There is an approximately 2–5% increment in the classification performance achieved with the reduction of the number of trainable parameters by 22–58 times. This ensures the effectiveness of the knowledge distillation for reducing the trade-off between trainable parameters and accuracy.

10.5.3 HYPOTHESIS 3: DATA BALANCING APPROACHES

In this sub-section, the effect of the conventional random under-sampling approach and adopted class-weight based data balancing techniques on the classification performance is analyzed and the results are presented in Table 10.2. In the existing approaches of DS-P3S [5-8], random under-sampling [5] and ensemble-based approach [6,10,23,26] were used to handle data unbalancing problems. In the case of the random under-sampling technique with M-DCNN, approximately 6–7% of the difference between the TPR and TNR were noted. There is approximately a 22% false prediction noted. This must be due to the selection of error-related potentials (ErrPs) during random under-sampling which misleads the classifier. The purpose of solving unbalance becomes unsolved. Hence, the ensemble approach was used in other work. Ensemble learning increases the computational demand and is time-consuming. On the other hand, the minimum difference of approximately 1% was noted in TPR and TNR on adopting the class-weight approach while training the model. This reduces the trade-off between TPR and TNR. This ensures that the effectiveness of the class-weight approach compensates for the effect of ErrPs, as it

TABLE 10.2

The comparative analysis of the classification of P300 in a single trial for DS-P3S using various deep, shallow and compact CNN

Classification Models	# Params	Mean Acc (%) ± SD	TPR (%)	TNR (%)	PPV (%)	F1-score (%)
WEDCNN [6]	153730 * 7	92.64 ± 5.73	92.02	92.17	92.16	92.09
M-DCNN [6]	153730	87.07 ± 5.16	78.30	85.37	84.34	81.21
DCNN [6]	153730	81.84 ± 2.47	87.11	88.35	88.58	87.73
ShallowCNN [26]	27602	88.86 ± 3.20	88.33	89.62	88.20	88.97
ShallowCNN-TL (This work)	27602	90.69 ± 1.64	90.44	91.17	90.34	90.80
EEGNet [29]	6962	85.09 ± 2.09	84.15	86.09	85.93	84.92
EEGNet-TL (This work)	6962	85.88 ± 1.97	86.03	85.88	85.71	85.90
EEGNet- TL-KD (This work)	6962	87.29 ± 1.79	87.13	87.80	87.10	87.44
CW-EEGNet (This work)	2661	85.96 ± 2.59	84.43	84.75	84.40	84.59
CW-EEGNet-TL (This work)	2661	87.09 ± 1.88	87.28	87.66	87.12	87.46
CW-EEGNet-TL-KD (This work)	2661	90.82 ± 1.47	91.84	90.08	90.19	90.91

gets less weight which nullifies its contribution in the learning which improved the positive prediction rate.

10.5.4 Hypotheses 4 & 5: Effect of Transfer Learning

Table 10.3 presents the bias (E) and variance (σ^2) analysis of various classification methods used in this work with TL. Mainly, bias (E) is calculated to ensure the

TABLE 10.3

The bias and variance analysis of different classification models

Methods	W/o TL		W/ TL	
	E	σ^2	E	σ^2
ShallowCNN	11.14	10.26	9.21	2.67
EEGNet	14.91	3.9	14.12	3.4
EEGNet-KD	–	–	12.71	2.87
CW-EEGNet	14.04	6.75	12.91	3.54
CW-EEGNet-KD	–	–	9.18	2.1

effectiveness of inter-trail TL; whereas, variance (σ^2) is calculated to ensure the effectiveness of inter-subject TL. It can be seen from the Table 10.3 that there is approximately a 2% decrement found on adopting TL with shallowCNN. Moreover, approximately 8–9% of the variance was observed on adopting the inter-subject TL. In the case of EEGNet, there is no significant difference noted in the bias and variance, but EEG with KD showed approximately 2% of a reduction in bias with a <1% reduction in variance. Lastly, In CW-EEGNet, approximately 3–5% of reduction in bias was noted on adopting inter-trail TL, while a 2–5% reduction in variance was observed on adopting inter-subject TL. This justifies our hypothesis of using both inter-trail and inter-subject TL for reducing the subject variability and trade-off between the number of trials and accuracy.

10.6 CONCLUSION

In this work, we have implemented an efficient single-trial classification approach for the Devanagari script-based visual P300 speller using knowledge distillation and transfer learning. The proposed channel-wise convolution helped to improve the performance by approximately 1% with a reduction in trainable parameters by 2–3 times. This accomplishes our first hypothesis of the utilization of channel-wise convolution for efficient classification of P300. Moreover, knowledge distillation is implemented for the first time in the classification of P300 in BCI research, to share the learning from shallowCNN model and proposed a compact model to compensate for the loss of information caused due to pruning of training parameters. The positive increment of 2–5% in the accuracy of the classification of P300, with the huge reduction in the number of trainable parameters by 22–58 times on adopting the KD, ensures the effectiveness of KD to maintain the trade-off between the number of parameters and accuracy. This accomplishes our second hypothesis. Also, the class-weight-based data balancing approach is proven better over random under-sampling and ensemble approaches in DS-P3S by reducing the trade-off between TPR and TNR. This accomplishes our third hypothesis. In addition to that, the domain adaptation-based inter-subject TL and rule adaptation-based inter-trial TL helped to reduce the bias and variance by approximately 1–5% and 2–9%, respectively in shallowCNN, EEGNet and proposed CW-EEGNet. This accomplishes our fourth and fifth hypotheses, respectively. These remarkable results, with the compact model for single-trial, will encourage the researchers to implement the BCI systems in mobile devices in the near future.

ACKNOWLEDGMENT

The authors would like to thank all the volunteer subjects who participated and gave their valuable time for data acquisition. Authors acknowledge the Department of Science and Technology, Government of India, for financial support vide Reference No. SR/CSRI/38/2015 (G) under Cognitive Science Research Initiative (CSRI) to carry out this work.

REFERENCES

1. Wolpaw, Jonathan R., Niels Birbaumer, Dennis J. McFarland, Gert Pfurtscheller, and Theresa M. Vaughan. "Brain–computer interfaces for communication and control." *Clinical Neurophysiology* 113, 6 (2002): 767–791.
2. Ramadan, Rabie A., and Athanasios V. Vasilakos. "Brain computer interface: control signals review." *Neurocomputing* 223 (2017): 26–44.
3. Rezeika, Aya, Mihaly Benda, Piotr Stawicki, Felix Gembler, Abdul Saboor, and Ivan Volosyak. "Brain–computer interface spellers: A review." *Brain SCIENCEs* 8, 4 (2018): 57.
4. Abiri, Reza, Soheil Borhani, Eric W. Sellers, Yang Jiang, and Xiaopeng Zhao. "A comprehensive review of EEG-based brain–computer interface paradigms." *Journal of Neural Engineering* 16, 1 (2019): 011001.
5. Kshirsagar, Ghanahshyam B., and Narendra D. Londhe. "Improving performance of Devanagari script input-based P300 speller using deep learning." *IEEE Transactions on Biomedical Engineering* 66, 11 (2018): 2992–3005.
6. Kshirsagar, Ghanahshyam B., and Narendra D. Londhe. "Weighted ensemble of deep convolution neural networks for a single trial character detection in devanagari script based P300 speller." *IEEE Transactions on Cognitive and Developmental Systems* (2019).
7. Kshirsagar, Ghanahshyam B., and Narendra D. Londhe. "Deep convolutional neural network based character detection in Devanagari script input based P300 speller." In *2017 International Conference on Electrical, Electronics, Communication, Computer, and Optimization Techniques (ICEECCOT)*, pp. 507–511. IEEE, 2017.
8. Kshirsagar, Ghanahshyam B., and Narendra D. Londhe. "Performance improvement for devanagari script input based P300 speller." In *2018 5th International Conference on Signal Processing and Integrated Networks (SPIN)*, pp. 142–147. IEEE, 2018.
9. Farwell, Lawrence Ashley, and Emanuel Donchin. "Talking off the top of your head: toward a mental prosthesis utilizing event-related brain potentials." *Electroencephalography and Clinical Neurophysiology* 70, 6 (1988): 510–523.
10. Chaurasiya, Rahul Kumar, Narendra D. Londhe, and Subhojit Ghosh. "Binary DE-based channel selection and weighted ensemble of SVM classification for novel brain–computer interface using Devanagari script-based P300 speller paradigm." *International Journal of Human–Computer Interaction* 32, 11 (2016): 861–877.
11. Chaurasiya, Rahul Kumar, Narendra D. Londhe, and Subhojit Ghosh. "Multi-objective binary DE algorithm for optimizing the performance of Devanagari script-based P300 speller." *Biocybernetics and Biomedical Engineering* 37, 3 (2017): 422–431.
12. Kabbara, Aya, Mahmoud Hassan, Mohamad Khalil, Hassan Eid, and Wassim El-Falou. "An efficient P300-speller for Arabic letters." In *2015 International Conference on Advances in Biomedical Engineering (ICABME)*, pp. 142–145. IEEE, 2015.
13. Yamamoto, Yuya, Tomohiro Yoshikawa, and Takeshi Furuhashi. "Improvement of performance of Japanese P300 speller by using second display." *Journal of Artificial Intelligence and Soft Computing Research* 5, 3 (2015): 221–226.
14. Minett, James W., Hong-Ying Zheng, Manson C.M. Fong, Lin Zhou, Gang Peng, and William S.Y. Wang. "A Chinese text input brain–computer interface based on the P300 speller." *International Journal of Human-Computer Interaction* 28, 7 (2012): 472–483.
15. Salvaris, Mathew, Caterina Cinel, Luca Citi, and Riccardo Poli. "Novel protocols for P300-based brain–computer interfaces." *IEEE Transactions on Neural Systems and Rehabilitation Engineering* 20, 1 (2011): 8–17.
16. Guger, Christoph, Shahab Daban, Eric Sellers, Clemens Holzner, Gunther Krausz, Roberta Carabalona, Furio Gramatica, and Guenter Edlinger. "How many people are able to control a P300-based brain–computer interface (BCI)?." *Neuroscience Letters* 462, 1 (2009): 94–98.

17. González, M. A., E. Garduño, E. Bribiesca, O. Y. Suárez, and V. M. Bañuelos. "P300 detection based on EEG shape features." *Computational and Mathematical Methods* 2016 (2016): 1–14.
18. Turnip, et al. "P300 detection using a multilayer neural network classifier based on adaptive feature extraction." *International Journal of Brain and Cognitive Sciences* 2, 5 (2013): 63–75.
19. Xu, Neng, Xiaorong Gao, Bo Hong, Xiaobo Miao, Shangkai Gao, and Fusheng Yang. "BCI competition 2003-data set IIb: enhancing P300 wave detection using ICA-based subspace projections for BCI applications." *IEEE Transactions on Biomedical Engineering* 51, 6 (2004): 1067–1072.
20. Li, Kun, Ravi Sankar, Yael Arbel, and Emanuel Donchin. "Single trial independent component analysis for P300 BCI system." In *2009 Annual International Conference of the IEEE Engineering in Medicine and Biology Society*, pp. 4035–4038. IEEE, 2009.
21. Kaper, Matthias, Peter Meinicke, Ulf Grossekathoefer, Thomas Lingner, and Helge Ritter. "BCI competition 2003-data set IIb: support vector machines for the P300 speller paradigm." IEEE Transactions on biomedical Engineering 51, 6 (2004): 1073–1076.
22. Thulasidas, Manoj, Cuntai Guan, and Jiankang Wu. "Robust classification of EEG signal for brain-computer interface." *IEEE Transactions on Neural Systems and Rehabilitation Engineering* 14, 1 (2006): 24–29.
23. Rakotomamonjy, Alain, and Vincent Guigue. "BCI competition III: dataset II-ensemble of SVMs for BCI P300 speller." *IEEE Transactions on Biomedical Engineering* 55, 3 (2008): 1147–1154.
24. Lotte, Fabien, Laurent Bougrain, Andrzej Cichocki, Maureen Clerc, Marco Congedo, Alain Rakotomamonjy, and Florian Yger. "A review of classification algorithms for EEG-based brain–computer interfaces: a 10 year update." *Journal of Neural Engineering* 15, 3 (2018): 031005.
25. Bashashati, Ali, Mehrdad Fatourechi, Rabab K. Ward, and Gary E. Birch. "A survey of signal processing algorithms in brain–computer interfaces based on electrical brain signals." *Journal of Neural Engineering* 4, 2 (2007): R32.
26. Cecotti, Hubert, and Axel Graser. "Convolutional neural networks for P300 detection with application to brain-computer interfaces." *IEEE Transactions on Pattern Analysis and Machine Intelligence* 33, 3 (2010): 433–445.
27. Liu, Mingfei, Wei Wu, Zhenghui Gu, Zhuliang Yu, FeiFei Qi, and Yuanqing Li. "Deep learning based on batch normalization for P300 signal detection." *Neurocomputing* 275 (2018): 288–297.
28. Chen, Shi, and Qi Zhao. "Shallowing deep networks: Layer-wise pruning based on feature representations." *IEEE Transactions on Pattern Analysis and Machine Intelligence* 41, 12 (2018): 3048–3056.
29. Lawhern, Vernon J., Amelia J. Solon, Nicholas R. Waytowich, Stephen M. Gordon, Chou P. Hung, and Brent J. Lance. "EEGNet: a compact convolutional neural network for EEG-based brain–computer interfaces." *Journal of Neural Engineering* 15, 5 (2018): 056013.
30. Li, Feng, Yi Xia, Fei Wang, Dengyong Zhang, Xiaoyu Li, and Fan He. "Transfer learning algorithm of P300-EEG signal based on XDAWN spatial filter and Riemannian geometry classifier." *Applied Sciences* 10, 5 (2020): 1804.
31. Jayaram, Vinay, Morteza Alamgir, Yasemin Altun, Bernhard Scholkopf, and Moritz Grosse-Wentrup. "Transfer learning in brain-computer interfaces." *IEEE Computational Intelligence Magazine* 11, 1 (2016): 20–31.
32. Gao, Hongyang, Zhengyang Wang, Lei Cai, and Shuiwang Ji. "ChannelNets: compact and efficient convolutional neural networks via channel-wise convolutions." *IEEE Transactions on Pattern Analysis and Machine Intelligence* (2020).

33. Sakhavi, Siavash, Cuntai Guan, and Shuicheng Yan. "Learning temporal information for brain-computer interface using convolutional neural networks." *IEEE Transactions on Neural Networks and Learning Systems* 29, 11 (2018): 5619–5629.

34. Hinton, Geoffrey, Oriol Vinyals, and Jeff Dean. "Distilling the knowledge in a neural network." arXiv preprint arXiv:1503.02531 (2015).

35. Mirzadeh, Seyed-Iman, Mehrdad Farajtabar, Ang Li, Nir Levine, Akihiro Matsukawa, and Hassan Ghasemzadeh. "Improved knowledge distillation via teacher assistant." arXiv preprint arXiv:1902.03393 (2019).

36. Martens, S. M. M., N. J. Hill, J. Farquhar, and B. Schölkopf. "Overlap and refractory effects in a brain–computer interface speller based on the visual P300 event-related potential." *Journal of Neural Engineering* 6, 2 (2009): 026003.

37. Woldorff, Marty G. "Distortion of ERP averages due to overlap from temporally adjacent ERPs: Analysis and correction." *Psychophysiology* 30, 1 (1993): 98–119.

38. Clevert, Djork-Arné, Thomas Unterthiner, and Sepp Hochreiter. "Fast and accurate deep network learning by exponential linear units (elus)." arXiv preprint arXiv:1511.07289 (2015).

39. Chollet F. 2015. Keras, (www.Keras.io)

40. Abadi M. et al. "TensorFlow: a system for large-scale machine learning." *OSDI* 16 (2016): 265–283.

41. Glorot, Xavier, and Yoshua Bengio. "Understanding the difficulty of training deep feedforward neural networks." In *Proceedings of the Thirteenth International Conference on Artificial Intelligence and Statistics*, pp. 249–256. 2010.

42. Srivastava, Nitish, Geoffrey Hinton, Alex Krizhevsky, Ilya Sutskever, and Ruslan Salakhutdinov. "Dropout: a simple way to prevent neural networks from overfitting." *The Journal of Machine Learning Research* 15, 1 (2014): 1929–1958.

43. Tieleman, Tijmen, and Geoffrey Hinton. "Lecture 6.5-rmsprop: Divide the gradient by a running average of its recent magnitude." *COURSERA: Neural Networks for Machine Learning* 4, 2 (2012): 26–31.

11 Deep Learning Algorithms for Brain Image Analysis

Sai Darahas Akkineni and S. P. K. Karri

11.1 INTRODUCTION

The human brain is the most complex yet powerful system regulating both physiological and psychological aspects of our body. Over the years, several imaging systems (MRI, PET, CT, etc.) in the medical screening pipeline have played a crucial role in understanding and analyzing anomalies associated with the human brain. Such an understanding, however, demands visual analysis of both mono-modal and multi-modal imaging data that burden the experts. The domain of medical image analysis has incepted in the late 20th century, emanating from the advent of processors, with the intent of automating the functional blocks in the diagnosis pipeline. This has, to some extent, reduced the difficulty of studying the intricacies present in the medical imaging data and, further, enhanced the expert's performance. Historically, the automation algorithms in medical image analysis involved the incorporation of rules based on patterns identified by the experts. Such patterns range from the local level features (edges, texture, intensity, etc.) to the global level features (shape, connectivity, etc.). However, the development of such task-specific rules for vast amounts of data had been difficult even with parallel advancements in fields like computer vision, image processing, and statistical signal processing. Moreover, the programming experts needed constant interaction with the domain experts. Hence, researchers began to explore alternate approaches, where these rules can be learned automatically given the data, comprising the expert's annotations. Machine learning (ML) has been a prominent choice in the past two decades for the automation of various pipelines. Modern computer vision algorithms hold ML at its core. A classical supervised ML algorithm can learn from multiple examples, where each example contains features constructed from an image along with the domain expert's annotations. During training, ML formulates a transfer function that can transform the feature space into annotation space or identify subspaces of feature space that attributes to a particular class of labels. The ML algorithm iteratively tweaks the transformation model's parameters such that the estimated annotations (labels) are closer to the expert's annotations on major examples. During testing, such trained transfer function is expected to predict labels of a given image based on its feature vector and this predicted label is required to match the expert's annotation. The construction of these features was considered to be the weakest link in the ML framework as it involves explicit human intervention. Consequently, deep learning (DL) has evolved as a sub-field of ML to automate the construction of these feature quantifiers and has set a benchmark in various image analysis tasks. The choice of employing ML or DL is subjective to the task complexity and availability of data since DL algorithms require huge computing power and a significant amount of data. Hence, DL became popular in current decade even though the theories were laid in the 1970s.

In the past few decades, the processing and diagnosis of several brain diseases have witnessed a significant advancement. The rise of deep learning and artificial intelligence (AI) opened new ways of diagnosing patients for doctors and radiologists. According to [1], the peer-reviewed publications employing deep learning in medical imaging tripled from 2016 to 2017. This year alone there are around 500 such publications. This chapter aims to collate major deep learning algorithms that played a decisive role in functional blocks of brain image analysis such as registration, segmentation, and classification. Additionally, the chapter holds the fundamentals of the artificial neural network (ANN) that is widely employed in deep learning.

11.2   BRAIN IMAGE DATA AND STRATEGIES

The medical image information alters with changes in data acquisition equipment settings, data formats, and patient's involuntary movements during scanning. Such variations impact the image representations and underlying distribution characteristics, hindering the design and performance of the algorithm. Therefore, the standardization of data from single or multiple sources is crucial. Normalization of images can reduce this inconsistency in spatial intensity ranges, thereby improving the performance of the model. Moreover, all the machine learning algorithms prefer the quantized features to follow a normal distribution for standardization. Therefore, scaling and standardization of medical images is a common practice to reduce any dynamic variations.

Volumetric data is common in brain imaging and the 3D volumetric data is formed by stacking 2D slices representing the anatomy of the body. The volumetric nature of the data imposes an additional computational burden so only partial volume is processed at an instance based on the computational complexity of the algorithm and compute capability of the computer. For example, if the data of size $512 \times 512 \times 400$ is beyond the compute capability of the computer, then one approach is training the images patch-wise, where the patches extracted from medical images are fed one after another into the model architecture. Another approach is to train through slice-by-slice 2D analysis. Note that all these methods are subjective to the availability of graphics processing unit (GPU) and Random Access Memory (RAM).

The majority of computer vision algorithms that are driven by deep learning demand an ample amount of data; therefore, the unavailability of large-scale annotated datasets in the medical domain is a major setback. This is essential, as deep learning models are easily prone to overfitting when trained on small datasets.

TABLE 11.1

Popular brain imaging datasets for deep learning

Dataset	Modality	Task
OASIS-3	MRI, PET	Segmentation
BRATS	MRI	Segmentation
OpenNeuro	Multiple	Classification
MSSEG	MRI	Segmentation
ADNI	MRI	Classification
ISLES 2018	MRI	Segmentation
MRBrainS	MRI	Segmentation
iSeg 2017	MRI	Segmentation
ABIDE	MRI	–
IXI	MRI	Segmentation

However, this problem can be mitigated to an extent by increasing the data samples using a technique called "data augmentation." Some general data augmentation techniques include translation, flipping, and rotation. Nevertheless, some large databases are available for various brain imaging tasks, as shown in Table 11.1.

11.3 DEEP NEURAL NETWORKS

A machine learning algorithm should be capable of learning rules based on features so that the corresponding error on unseen data is low reflecting the generalizability of the rules. The performance is primarily subjective to the enriched information encompassed by these features, but the extraction of such feature descriptions on complex data is an escalated burden. The ability to learn these representations in the form of hierarchical abstraction is sought in DL. Deep learning is an emerging sub-field of ML where quantification of features is performed in stages, called layers in the case of neural networks, and each stage emulates a hierarchical abstraction. These algorithms have eliminated the need for explicit feature engineering for various tasks. This ability to learn feature descriptors based on labeled or unlabeled data distinguishes DL from conventional machine learning algorithms.

11.3.1 PERCEPTRON

The neural networks were originally developed to artificially model the biological neurons. The biological neurons are interconnected through a junction called "synapse." The "weights" (or parameters) in a neural network resemble the strength of the synaptic connections present in the neuron. This learning mechanism is largely inspired by Hebb's rule (or *Hebbian Learning*). The strength of this signal decides the net output of the neural networks for a given input. These weights can either be positive (excitatory) or negative (inhibitory). In the same way, higher

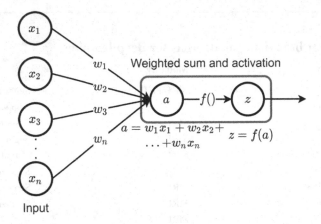

Input

FIGURE 11.1   A graphical representation of perceptron for a given input.

weighted inputs contribute more to the output compared to the less weighted inputs. The weights store the "knowledge base" of the neural network for a given task. The complete architecture is called perceptron. As illustrated in Figure 11.1, the perceptron's output is a weighted linear combination of inputs x_1, x_2, ...,x_n given to an activation function.

$$a = \sum_{i=1}^{n} w_i x_i \tag{11.1}$$

There are several variants of artificial perceptron and the above form is called Rosenblatt's perceptron [2]. Rosenblatt tried to imitate the visual response of human perception based on patterns formed by a matrix of light bulbs using the above neuron model, hence the name perceptron. The current generation perceptron introduced a bias term and the above equation is transformed as shown in equation (11.2). The significance of bias b is to ensure that the neural network produces a non-zero output in case of input absence.

$$a = \sum_{i=1}^{n} w_i x_i + b \tag{11.2}$$

This result is then passed to an activation (or threshold or transfer) function to achieve nonlinearity. If f is an activation function, then the output is given by

$$z = f(a) = f\left(\sum_{i=1}^{n} w_i x_i + b\right) \tag{11.3}$$

The activation function f needs to be monotonically continuous in nature. The selection of the activation function depends upon the problem at hand. Rectified

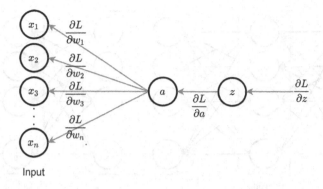

Input

FIGURE 11.2   An illustration of learning mechanism in perceptron.

linear unit (ReLU) is a commonly employed activation function that induces nonlinearity and simultaneously helps in mitigating the vanishing gradient problem. The ReLU can be defined as $\max(0, \text{input})$ that clips off negative values and passes only positive values. The loss function quantifies the disparity between the predicted output ($\hat{z}$) and the actual output (z), represented by the "loss function." This disparity is minimized by adjusting the weights based on the loss function, as shown in Figure 11.2, using a technique called error "backpropagation" [3].

If w_1 is the weight connecting input x_1 and a, then the updated weight w_1 depends upon the weight in the previous iteration, learning rate η, and the extent of contribution of weight to the loss as shown below

$$w_1 = w_1 - \eta \frac{\partial L}{\partial w_1} \tag{11.4}$$

$\frac{\partial L}{\partial w_1}$ is computed using the chain rule

$$\frac{\partial L}{\partial w_1} = \frac{\partial L}{\partial z} \cdot \frac{\partial z}{\partial w_1} = \frac{\partial L}{\partial z} \cdot \frac{\partial z}{\partial a} \cdot \frac{\partial a}{\partial w_1}$$

Though the perceptron was able to emulate the learning mechanism of the brain to some extent, it failed to learn rules for more complex tasks. For this reason, to learn more complex features, many perceptrons are interconnected in the form of a network, known as a feedforward neural network.

11.3.2   FEEDFORWARD NEURAL NETWORKS

The input data in feedforward neural networks (shown in Figure 11.3) is transformed across a series of layers to get closer and closer to the expected output. A set of input data samples together is called a "batch." Batch processing allows parallel computation on GPUs. Depending upon the configuration of the GPU, batches of data are retrieved from the disk and stored in the GPU memory for further computation. In a feedforward neural network, the whole process of the weighted sum

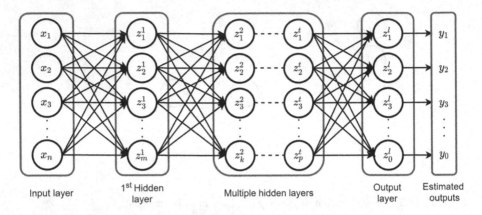

FIGURE 11.3 Feedforward neural networks.

of the previous layer's output and transforming based on activation function across layers resulting in an output is called "forward propagation." Activation function at all layers need not be the same, but uniformity is maintained across hidden layers except for the output layer. In the case of regression, the tanh function is employed at the output layer and for classification, the sigmoid or softmax function is preferred. The weights of feedforward neural networks are updated during the training based on error backpropagation [3], and the amount of weight to be updated is defined by the optimization algorithm. Some common optimization algorithms include stochastic gradient descent, Adam, etc. The weights are updated based on the magnitude and sign of the loss derivative with respect to weight. A hyperparameter η, also called a "learning rate," decides how aggressively the neural network can correct its weights i.e., a higher learning rate implies faster update. However, a higher learning rate does not guarantee convergence. Hence, advanced optimizers are employed, such as Adam, that can adapt to the learning rate by tracking error. The phenomenon, where the neural network estimates labels accurately for the training examples but is unable to generalize well for the unseen or testing data; this is called "overfitting." This is usually the case when the training loss keeps reducing and the validation loss keeps escalating after initially reducing for some batches, forming a V-curve. One way to prevent the model from overfitting is by appending a "regularization" term with the Lagrangian multiplier to the loss function.

Backpropagation in deep neural networks is similar to perceptron, except that the error is propagated across several layers as shown in Figure 11.4.

Let w_{p0} be the weight connecting z_p^t perceptron and z_0^l perceptron. Based on the update rule, fine-tuning the weight w_{p0} involves the derivative $\frac{\partial L}{\partial w_{p0}}$ given by the chain rule

$$\frac{\partial L}{\partial w_{p0}} = \frac{\partial L}{\partial y_0} \cdot \frac{\partial y_0}{\partial w_{p0}} = \frac{\partial L}{\partial y_0} \cdot \frac{\partial y_0}{\partial z_0^l} \cdot \frac{\partial z_0^l}{\partial w_{p0}}$$

One complete iteration over all the training data is called an "epoch." After multiple epochs, the weight update becomes negligible, as the change in loss tends towards

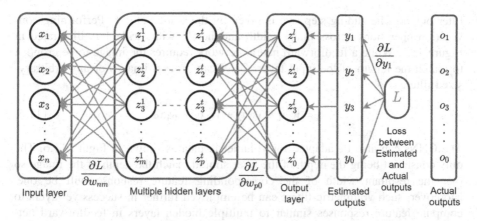

FIGURE 11.4 Backpropagation in feedforward neural networks.

zero, and the network is said to have reached convergence. The number of epochs ranges from 100 to several thousand. Rather than training the network with randomly initialized weights, in practice, weights from a pre-trained model that are trained on a similar task are employed as initial weights. Such a training mechanism is called "transfer learning" since it reduces the compute complexity and convergence time.

11.3.3 CONVOLUTIONAL NEURAL NETWORKS

LeCun [4] demonstrated a convolutional neural network (CNN), with the capability of error backpropagation, for a character identification task. The convolutional neural networks resemble feedforward neural networks, discussed earlier, except the linear combination here is done using a convolution operation. The convolution operation has demonstrated to be more efficient on data containing images. CNNs consist of successively connected convolutional and pooling layers. The weights in a CNN are represented as "filters" (or kernel). Activation maps, considered as features, are computed by sliding the filter over the image or the previous layer's

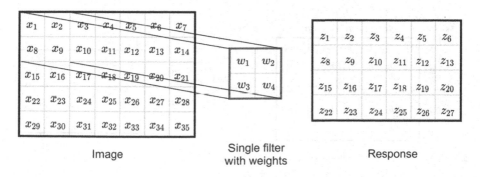

FIGURE 11.5 Convolution operation of an image with a single filter.

filter output. The sliding step size is given by the stride value S. Performing convolution operations across image width and height with stride 1 is illustrated in Figure 11.5. While a feedforward neural network requires the image to be cropped to match the length of the input layer, CNN can process images of any arbitrary-sized filter.

$$z_1 = w_1 x_1 + w_2 x_2 + w_3 x_8 + w_4 x_9 \qquad (11.5)$$

The CNNs can also be adapted for volumetric data as shown in Figure 11.6. The only constraint being the depth of the filter should match the depth of the image so that the resultant width of the corresponding feature response will be one. Moreover, such volumetric filters can be employed further in successive layers to compute feature responses similar to multiple hidden layers in feedforward networks. Such consecutive processing of feature responses with filters constitutes the hierarchical abstraction in CNNs. The spatial size of features is preserved by adding zeros (or any user-defined value) around the input volume, termed as "padding." When an input volume of dimensions $W \times H$ is convolved with a filter of size f and padding p, the output size $W' \times H'$ is given by the equations

$$W' = \frac{W - f + 2p}{S} + 1 \quad H' = \frac{H - f + 2p}{S} + 1 \qquad (11.6)$$

In general, for a stride value 1, the padding size is measured using the equation, $p = \frac{f-1}{2}$. This ensures same width and height across both input and output volumes. The weights associated with filters detect features such as edges and other important characteristics of the image. Several activation maps (shown in Figure 11.6), formed using different CNN filters in a given layer, are stacked together to form a "feature map," which in turn acts as the input volume to subsequent CNN layers. Each element of the feature map is computed from a local region of the input volume, a property called "local connectivity." Another important characteristic of convolutional neural networks is "parameter sharing." This significantly reduces the

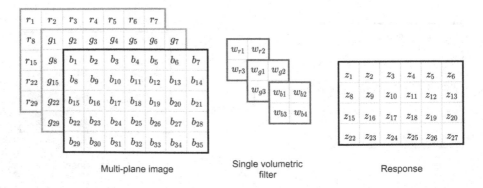

Multi-plane image   Single volumetric filter   Response

FIGURE 11.6 Convolution operation of an image with a single volumetric filter.

number of parameters assuming that the images are translationally invariant i.e., the output of kernel does not change with location of an object in the image.

Feature maps are computed through a pooling operation with a stride to increase the receptive field of CNNs and reduce the computational burden of successive CNN layers. As the input volume passes through each layer, the pooling identifies the dominant response within a neighborhood, and striding downsamples the response. Note that pooling without stride doesn't reduce the size. "Downsampling" lowers its resolution promoting multi-resolution learning. This has proven to increase the performance of CNNs by learning more complex features [5]. However, recent models replaced the pooling layer with strided convolution. A local response normalization layer [6] that prevents the inputs from saturating can be added before applying the activation function. However, these layers are replaced with more sophisticated "batch normalization" [7] layers that emulate a similar outcome.

The process of reversing the convolution operation, intuitively called "deconvolution" (or transposed convolution), is employed to upscale a feature response in contrast to conventional methods like bilinear interpolation that induce undesirable blur. The weights in transposed convolution aids in learning rules for upscaling feature responses subjective to the task. As shown in Figure 11.7, transposed convolution has its own weights that are multiplied element-wise, at each pixel, with the input. The cumulative sum of each result gives the resultant response of transposed convolution. Similar to convolution, these weights are updated during backpropagation. There is another operation called "upsampling," which performs a similar operation.

11.4 IMAGE REGISTRATION

The process of spatially transforming a "floating" (or moving or source or warped) image to align with the "fixed" (or target or reference) image is called registration. The primary goal of registration is to eliminate the deformation artifacts and compensate for the influence on data, caused during the data acquisition process. This transformation can be among two or more subjects of the same modality (inter-subject) or different modalities of the same subject (intra-subject) etc.

Registration can be carried out by different techniques, however, three important factors that need to be considered for any image registration task are the selection of transformation model, similarity metric, and optimization method. An appropriate transformation model should be chosen to accurately

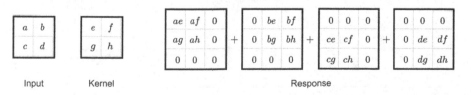

FIGURE 11.7   Transposed convolution.

characterize the geometric deformation between fixed and floating images. Based on the transformation model employed, registration tasks are classified into rigid models and deformation (nonrigid) models. The number of degrees of freedom is the main characteristic that differentiates these models from each other. In employing deep learning methods for the image registration task, the similarity metric acts as an evaluation metric that is optimized while training. Mutual information (MI), derived from "information theory," is a metric to measure the similarity between fixed and floating images. Other similarity metrics like normalized mutual information (NMI), sum of squared differences (SSD), cross-correlation (CC), and normalized cross-correlation (NCC) are also employed in image registration. The transformation parameters are updated to minimize the dissimilarity between the fixed and floating images.

Two strategies successfully employed in literature for image registration using deep learning are (1) learning similarity metric, and (2) estimating transformation parameters.

11.4.1 RIGID REGISTRATION

In rigid registration, the input images that need to be registered are considered as rigid bodies, which can be spatially transformed into each other. The objects in the images are assumed to be nondeformable. In the case of affine transformation, the transformation matrix of size 3×3 for image and 4×4 for volume holds parameters of translation, rotation, and scaling across all dimensions. The projective transformation has two additional parameters in the matrix for the image.

As illustrated in Figure 11.8, concatenated fixed (reference) and floating (deformed) images act as input to the CNN. By the inherent nature of CNNs, more complex features are learned with the increase in the number of layers and stored in a latent space representation. The features in latent space are decoded to predict the transformation parameters. These estimated parameters during the training are used to spatially transform the floating image to the registered image using an image resampler such as spatial transformer networks. If there is any discrepancy in the transformation, it is backpropagated as loss, correcting the weights in the network. A deep learning framework for unsupervised image registration is shown in Figure 11.9. In this case, the extracted features from the images are fed to CNN to estimate the transform parameters. The registered image is juxtaposed with the fixed image using a similarity metric, and the error is backpropagated to the network.

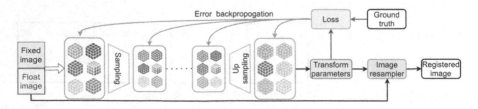

FIGURE 11.8   A supervised framework for image registration using deep learning.

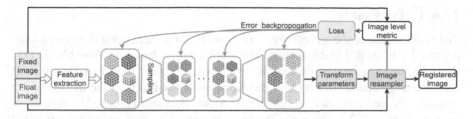

FIGURE 11.9   An unsupervised framework for image registration using deep learning.

11.4.2 DEFORMABLE REGISTRATION

The rigid models are the best linear approximations of physical bodies, but they are not applicable for nonlinear objects where significant deformation is typical. The term "deformable" is derived from the elastic theory, which means changing of shape over time. A fully convolutional neural network was trained in [8] to predict the deformable field, used for learning transformation parameters. The dataset used consists of 2D/3D inter-subject brain MR volumes.[1] As discussed earlier, the lack of enough annotated data is the primary challenge for employing deep learning algorithms in medical image analysis. Reference [9] presented an automatic training set generation method using the ADNI dataset.[2] The model architecture is based on GoogleNet [10]. The network learns all possible deformations for accurate ground truth generation. Given the lack of annotated data for medical imaging tasks, unsupervised learning has been widely adopted in deformable registration. VoxelMorph [11] is an unsupervised learning technique for estimating the transformation parameters. The network is similar to the UNet [12] configuration but with skip connections. The model formulates a deformation field to interpret the discrepancies between the input images. The deformation field directly maps the floating image to the fixed image using a spatial transformer network [13]. The Mean Square Error (MSE) is the most commonly employed loss function to compare the images for intensity variations. Along with the conventional loss function, an unsupervised loss function was introduced to account for the computation of errors in registration of input volumes in addition to the regularization term that avoids overfitting.

Generative adversarial network (GAN), since its inception in 2014, has been widely used in various supervised and unsupervised applications [14]. It comprises two deep learning models, namely generator and discriminator. During training, both models try to compete and outperform one another, but indirectly compliments each other's performance. The generator will try to deceive the discriminator by producing fake images and the discriminator will in turn learn to discriminate the real from fake. The generator parameters are held constant when the discriminator is allowed for training and vice versa until the model converges. Reference [15] trained a GAN architecture with a discriminator to assess the registration alignment. The dissimilarity between the floating and fixed volumes was measured using binary cross-entropy.

11.4.3 EXPERIMENTS

The performance of the unsupervised framework for image registration using deep learning[3] is evaluated in this section. The architecture is based on VoxelMorph [11] that uses an unsupervised framework as shown in Figure 11.9. Popular tools for deep learning namely TensorFlow and Keras were used to train the model, which estimates the deformation field between fixed and floating volumes. The data holds images of shape 192×160 each. The brain images were first intensity-normalized and skull-stripped with FreeSurfer.[4] The network was built on top of UNet along with a spatial transformer network. The predicted deformation field directly maps the floating image to the fixed image using the spatial transformer network. The model was trained with a batch size of eight and up to ten epochs. The results, shown in Figure 11.10, demonstrates how each pixel is deformed based on the deformation field so that the floating image matches the fixed image.

11.4.3.1 Impact of Loss Function

Adding a smoothing function can penalize the local variations in the deformation field. Therefore, the network was trained appending smooth loss function for more accurate results as shown in Figure 11.11.

In an n-D domain $\Omega \subset \mathbb{R}$, if f, m are the fixed and floating image, p is a voxel, and ϕ is the deformation field given by $\phi = Id + u$ [11], then the resultant loss is given by

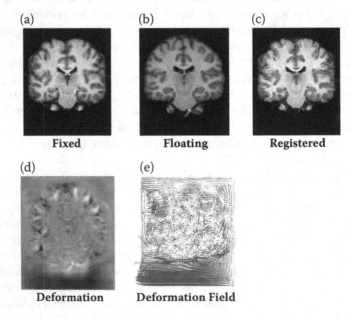

FIGURE 11.10 Results of deep learning deformable image registration using VoxelMorph. From left to right: input fixed MRI in (a), input floating MRI in (b), registered image in (c), deformation between fixed and floating images in (d), and the deformation field in (e).

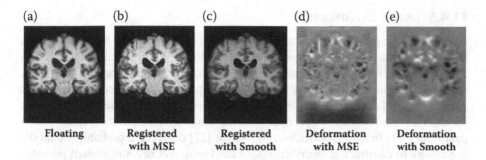

(a)   (b)   (c)   (d)   (e)

| Floating | Registered with MSE | Registered with Smooth | Deformation with MSE | Deformation with Smooth |

FIGURE 11.11 Comparing the effect of the loss function in deep learning-based deformable image registration using VoxelMorph. From left to right: input floating in (a), registered image using only MSE loss function in (b), registered image with addition of smooth loss function in (c), deformation with MSE loss function in (d), and deformation with the addition of smooth loss function in (e).

$$L(f, m, \phi) = L_{\text{sim}}(f, m°\phi) + \lambda L_{\text{smooth}}(\phi) \qquad (11.7)$$

$$L_{\text{sim}}(f, m, \phi) = \frac{1}{|\Omega|} \sum_{p \in \Omega} [f(p) - [m°\phi](p)]^2 \qquad (11.8)$$

$$L_{\text{smooth}} = \sum_{p \in \Omega} \|\nabla u(p)\|^2 \qquad (11.9)$$

11.4.4 MULTIMODAL REGISTRATION

Each modality of the brain provides unique information for analysis. Therefore, combining such information from different modalities is useful for a more accurate diagnosis of the subject. Hence, multimodal registration is also known as "coregistration." In multimodal registration, the fixed and floating images are of different modalities (CT, MR T1, MR T2, PET, etc.). Reference [16] proposed a CNN architecture with multi-layer perceptron network for learning transformation parameters between T1 and T2 weighted MR scans of the brain. A similarity metric learning using deep learning was presented in [17] with gradient descent optimization. It was one of the first intensity-based multimodal registration. A deep similarity learning method was proposed in [18] using a stacked denoising encoder [19]. A binary classifier was trained to learn the alignment of CT and MR head image patches. An unsupervised method was presented in [20] using a similar dataset, comprising MR and US scans of the brain. The loss function was composed of L2 distance along with an image gradient incorporating both pixel intensity and gradient information into the model.

11.4.5 ATLAS CONSTRUCTION

One of the key goals in neuroimaging research is to understand the relationships between brain structures and corresponding functions [21]. The brain atlas acts as a 3D coordinate reference system having canonical representations of the brain anatomy. Various factors including genetics, age, and gender contribute to the construction of large population-based atlases. These atlases are intended to provide an accurate comprehensive description of the brain by incorporating multi-modal data from PET, functional MRI, etc. Reference [22] designed a probabilistic model framework to construct deformable templates. The neural network trained provides an efficient alignment of images to these templates. A deep residual regression network was proposed in [23] using a bi-variant geodesic distance-based loss function that learns to register the input volumes and then a correction network facilitates a forward propagation through the network.

11.5 IMAGE SEGMENTATION

The need for automated segmentation techniques for more accurate diagnosis has led to the development of various deep learning methods for the segmentation of medical images. Segmentation algorithms essentially delineate regions of interest of an image from the background. Initially, the image is segmented into regions of interest (organ, tissue, etc.) which are then assigned with a label. The segmentation methods for medical images operate on intensity, frequency, texture, structural, and morphological variations in the image. In deep learning, segmentation is carried out at various resolutions with lower resolutions (edges) contributing features to the higher resolutions (regions). The idea of segmentation varies with the type of data and subject under consideration. However, the main purpose remains to analyze a group of pixels or voxels and discriminate them based on subjective characteristics.

A considerable amount of current research for medical image segmentation was anchored around employing deep learning algorithms. Before the advent of deep learning, many conventional techniques such as regions growing, graph-cut, clustering, and random forests replete the literature for medical segmentation. Nevertheless, deep learning algorithms have consistently outperformed these conventional techniques at different levels.

The majority of deep learning-based segmentation algorithms employ encoder-decoder model architecture, shown in Figure 11.12. These are fully convolutional neural (FCN) networks with successive encoder and decoder architecture. The input volume is transformed to a "latent space" by the encoder part, while the decoder part rescales the latent space features to the size of the input volume. In the encoder, after convolution, the spatial size of the feature maps is reduced with successive pooling and stride operations. On the other hand, the decoder employs a series of transposed convolutions with convolutions retrieving to the same size as input from the latent space. However, it is recommended to store the encoder architecture's max-pooling indices to accurately retrace back the high frequency features from latent space. One popular encoder-decoder model for semantic segmentation is SegNet [24], shown in Figure 11.13. The encoder network resembles the primitive

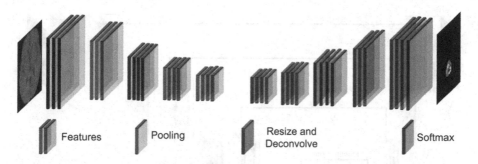

FIGURE 11.12   A schematic diagram of encoder-decoder architecture.

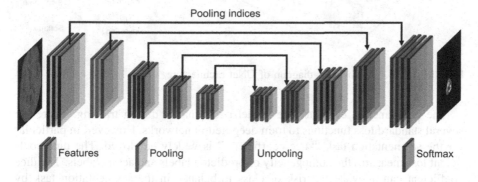

FIGURE 11.13   A schematic diagram of SegNet architecture.

deep learning architecture VGG16 [25]. The decoder, on the other hand, upsamples its feature maps based on the stored max-pooling indices at every downsampling layer of the encoder. The indices incorporate boundary details that are lost during max-pooling operation. The output layer is softmax since the architecture is trained for multi-class segmentation.

Among various deep learning architectures proposed for medical image segmentation, UNet [12] stands out. UNet is a prominent semantic segmentation architecture with downsampling and upsampling layers as shown in Figure 11.14. The learned representations in the latent space along with "long skip connections" form the basis of this architecture. These skip connections act as identity mapping between the upsampling and downsampling layers preserving spatial information across the network. This prevents the model from underfitting providing a direct path for gradient flow. The essence of skip connections (both short and long) in fully convolutional networks was investigated in [26]. The output is then passed into a softmax activation function and the network was trained with a cross-entropy loss function. The loss function is modified such that more weightage is given to misclassification along object boundaries. Several variants of UNet were introduced in the literature. In [27], for example, they extended the UNet architecture for volumetric data by performing 3D convolution operations with a dice coefficient as the loss function.

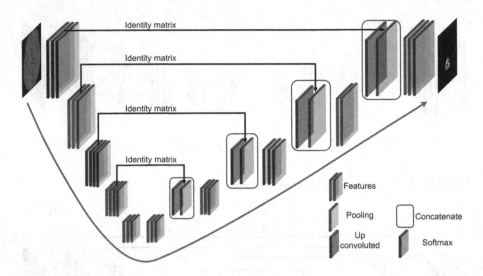

Features

Pooling

Concatenate

Up convoluted

Softmax

FIGURE 11.14   A schematic diagram of UNet architecture.

The loss function evaluates the model performance during training. There are several standard loss functions to train deep neural networks. However, in particular for the segmentation task, "dice coefficient," is widely employed. The dice coefficient loss measures the homogeneity of predicted labels and actual labels. The dice coefficient can alleviate the risk of class imbalance in the segmentation task by penalizing the false positives. There are two implementations of dice coefficient loss – binary and multi-class [28]. The generalized form of dice loss is shown here:

$$\text{Dice Loss} = 1 - 2\frac{\sum_{j=0}^{M} w_j \sum_{i=0}^{N} r_{ij}p_{ij}}{\sum_{j=0}^{M} w_j \sum_{i=0}^{N} r_{ij} + p_{ij}} \qquad (11.10)$$

where w_j represents weight assigned to the class j, p_i is the output of sigmoid or softmax activation function, and r_i represents the corresponding ground truth.

Another popular metric for segmentation tasks is "jaccard similarity index." It prevents the model from under and over-segmentation. A better balance between precision and recall can be achieved by "tversky loss" [29], compared to the dice coefficient, ensuring better performance on class imbalanced images. The same functions can also be used as evaluation metrics.

11.5.1   ISCHEMIC STROKE LESION SEGMENTATION

The obstruction of blood flow causes a stroke, so an automated segmentation model capable of identifying the early phases will improve the survivability of the patient. Ischemic stroke lesion segmentation (ISLES) data[5] comprises MRI diffusion-weighted imaging (DWI) and CT perfusions (CTP) of 63 subjects. The testing dataset includes 40 stroke subjects, primarily used for the evaluation of the trained model. A CNN architecture was proposed for stroke segmentation using encoder-decoder architecture [30]. In the challenges of 2016 and 2017, an ensemble of multi-scale networks was proposed [31]. More recently, [32] presented a fully convolutional neural network based on PSPNet that exploits the advantage of pyramid pooling to provide global and local contextual information. The model was trained using the focal loss to enforce the model to learn more complex features.

11.5.2 BRAIN TUMOR SEGMENTATION

Medical image computing and computer-assisted intervention (MICCAI) organizes various international challenges annually, extending across pathologies such as skin, kidney, brain, etc. The brain tumor segmentation data[6] consists of four multimodal scans of 335 patients. The volume data is a stack of 155 slices. The four-pulse sequences include T1, FLAIR, T2, and T1-contrasted each exploiting the distinct physiological aspects of various tissue types, promoting disparity between the individual classes. All images are skull stripped. These pulse sequences come with 5-class segmentation ground truth, one for each patient. The labels in the provided data are enhancing tumor (ET), edema (ED), necrotic (NCR) and nonenhancing (NET), and background.

An architecture with conditional random fields (CRFs) appended to the last layer of fully convolutional networks (FCNs) was designed to attain a crisp delineated segmentation [33]. This model was trained using 2D images patch-wise. In the 2017 challenge, a cascaded convolutional neural network [34] was proposed where each tumor sub-regions is trained with each network taking input from the previous network. All three networks have a similar structure comprised of an encoder part followed by a decoder part. In the same year, [35] trained an ensemble of models for brain tumor segmentation. They used a batch size of 8 and $64 \times 64 \times 64$ cropped region for computation. Their method outperformed all the other architectures in the challenge. In 2018, [36] trained a rather computationally intensive architecture with a crop size $160 \times 192 \times 128$ compromising on the batch size to be 1. This architecture was based on the variational autoencoder [37], providing regularization to the shared encoder part that is learned only during training. Reference [38] is a variant of UNet with slight modifications and was trained on BRATS 2018 dataset.

11.5.3 MULTIPLE SCLEROSIS LESION SEGMENTATION

Regressing of the myelin shield around axons leads to multiple sclerosis (MS). Estimating the extent of growth can help in the early treatment of the disease. The MS lesions can be detected using T1-weighted and T2-weighted MRI sequences. Lesion segmentation needs features from both local and global context to perform accurate segmentation. Reference [39] used UNet-like architecture to segment white matter lesions. They replaced the 2D convolutions in UNet architecture with 3D and reduced the skip connections to one. One challenge faced during lesion segmentation is class imbalance because the majority of voxels come under normal class. Reference [39] tackled this problem by designing a loss function that includes both sensitivity and specificity. A less susceptible model to class imbalance was achieved by assigning a larger weight to the specificity.

11.5.4 Hippocampus Segmentation

Multiple brain anomalies such as Alzheimer's can be studied using the hippocampus. The volume of the hippocampus in the brain determines the extent of dementia in Alzheimer's type. Reference [40] proposed an unsupervised deep learning model to learn from image patches taken from 7.0 T MRI images. Independent subspace analysis (ISA) based on two-layer stacked CNN was used for segmenting the hippocampus. A deep learning model was proposed in [41] based on a stacked autoencoder [19]. The MRI data contains T1- and T2-weighted sequences of the infant's brain. The network employs an encoder-decoder model learning latent representation in the input volumes. The patch size was fixed to $11 \times 11 \times 11$ for limiting the computational time.

11.5.5 Experiments

Two deep learning-based image segmentation models were evaluated in this section.

Among the many types of brain tumors, lower-grade gliomas (LGG) are the most common and lethal, thus, require an early diagnosis for the survival of the patient. A UNet based architecture with the addition of batch normalization was trained for segmenting LGG. The dataset comprises FLAIR sequence brain volumes of 110 patients.[7] The network was implemented using PyTorch, an open-source deep learning framework. The results are as shown in Figure 11.15.[8] All the images were scaled, normalized, and skull-stripped for pre-processing. To mitigate the class imbalance problem, an oversampling based data augmentation method was employed. To further improve the performance, the false positives across all three dimensions were removed using 6-connected pixels. Only the pixels contributing to the largest volume were retained in the final segmentation mask.

A cascaded fully convolutional neural network [34] was trained on a dataset comprising multi-modal information from T1, T1-weighted, T2-weighted, and FLAIR MRI sequences of the brain.[9] Each network hierarchically segments the brain MRI into three classes. Thus, the multi-class segmentation is considered as a binary segmentation problem with three architectures. A hierarchical segmentation process is employed, where the whole tumor is first extracted then the segmentation of enhancing tumor followed by tumor core. This way of hierarchically segmenting the image successively using one on top of another is called "over-segmentation." The receptive field of each network decreases such that the network trained for the whole tumor has 217×217 and the network for enhancing tumor has 113×113. The network employs 3D dilated convolutions of size 3×3 and several 1×1 convolutions. Each layer has a batch normalization operation to avoid the "exploding gradient problem." Residual connections were added to enhance the model's performance. The results are shown in Figure 11.16.

(a)   (b)   (c)

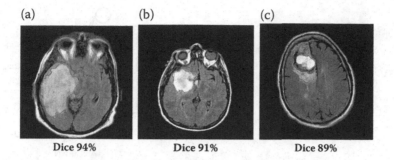

Dice 94%   Dice 91%   Dice 89%

FIGURE 11.15   Results of gliomas tumor segmentation [42] on different scans with corresponding dice score to depict the performance under different scenarios. From left to right dice similarity coefficient of 94%, 91%, and 89% for (a), (b), and (c) respectively.

(a)   (b)

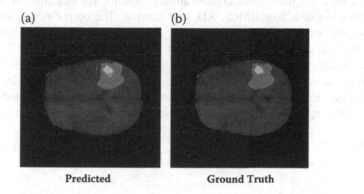

Predicted   Ground Truth

FIGURE 11.16   Results of deep learning-based brain tumor segmentation. Here (a) is the predicted segmentation corresponding to the ground truth in (b). The network was trained hierarchically inspired by the architecture in [34] and using NiftyNet [43], an open-source deep learning framework.

11.6   IMAGE CLASSIFICATION

The detection of abnormality and assigning a particular class to it is the fundamental task of prescreening systems to reduce the workload and prioritize the work of the expert. The typical configuration of CNN for an image classification task is as shown in Figure 11.17.

The "sigmoid" activation function is used at the output layer in case of multi-label classification problems that have more than one label for each sample, producing 0 or 1 as output. Note that the sum of these outputs might not be equal to 1 except in the case, where there are only two classes. Another activation function to note is "softmax," given by the equation

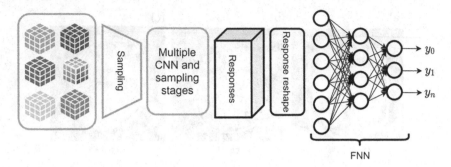

FIGURE 11.17 The architecture of CNN for an image classification task.

$$f(y_i) = \frac{\exp(y_i)}{\Sigma_j \exp(y_j)} \qquad (11.11)$$

This is used for multi-class classification problems, for example, in Alzheimer's classification with labels MCI, AD, and normal. The output of the softmax activation function will always sum up to 1. All the classes should be independent of each other to apply softmax as an output activation function.

Several loss functions that are specific to segmentation were discussed in the previous section. Few loss functions are generally applicable for any binary and multi-class problem. The binary cross-entropy (BCE) between predicted label $\hat{y}$ and actual label y, as shown below, is suitable for a two-class classification task.

$$BCE = -\frac{1}{N} \sum_{i=0}^{N} y_i. \, log\,(\hat{y_i}) + (1 - y_i). \, log\,(1 - \hat{y_i}) \qquad (11.12)$$

This can be generalized for an M-class classification problem, called categorical cross-entropy (CCE), as shown below

$$CCE = -\frac{1}{N} \sum_{i=1}^{N} \sum_{j=1}^{M} y_{ij}. \, log\,(\hat{y}_{ij}) \qquad (11.13)$$

A powerful extension of this is weighted cross-entropy (WCE) that is explicitly used when there is a class imbalance in the dataset is shown here:

$$WCE = -\frac{1}{N} \sum_{i=1}^{N} \sum_{j=1}^{M} w_j y_{ij} \, log\,(\hat{y}_{ij}) \qquad (11.14)$$

Note that for multi-class classification problems, the output labels need to be "one-hot encoded" before computation.

11.6.1 SCHIZOPHRENIA DIAGNOSIS

Schizophrenia is a mental disorder of the brain that results in hallucinations, delusions, or some similar abnormal behavior in individuals. This is still an area of active research, and many diagnostic tools were being developed to accurately find reliable discriminating features of schizophrenia in brain imaging studies. The challenge has been the heterogeneous nature of schizophrenic patients due to various other mental disorders. Some popular databases for schizophrenia diagnosis are Northwestern University Schizophrenia Data and Software Tool (NUSDAST), BrainGluSchi, and the Center of Biomedical Research Excellence (COBRE).[10] Multiple deep learning algorithms were developed alongside having high specificity and sensitivity to automate the schizophrenia clinical diagnosis. A discriminator auto-encoder neural network was proposed with a sparsity constraint [44]. Their work obtained an accuracy of approximately 85% on classifying schizophrenic patients from healthy ones. The discriminator autoencoder neural network was trained on multi-atlas fcMRI data with 474 schizophrenic patients.

11.6.2 DIAGNOSIS OF ALZHEIMER DISEASE

Alzheimer's disease (AD) is caused by the prolonged degeneration of nerve cells. Delayed treatment may lead to cases of dementia and other cognitive problems. Identification of prodromal mild cognitive impairment (MCI) stage improves the chances for AD treatment and is, therefore, the focus of most researchers. Magnetic resonance imaging (MRI) and PET scans are usually preferred for examining Alzheimer's conditions in the brain. Reference [45] trained a stacked autoencoder [19] in an unsupervised manner with concatenated MRI and PET scans as input. The model happened to be a classification problem with labels: AD, NC, cMCI, and ncMCI. The model was evaluated using both unimodal (MRI) and multimodal (MRI and PET) datasets. Their deep learning method outperformed SVM-based methods for both binary and multi-class. Few works are based on predicting the probability of AD after MCI. A deep neural network was proposed called a Multi-Structure Point Network (MSPNet) [46], inspired by PointNet [47], to directly access point clouds. The network analyzes multiple structures simultaneously mapping the data to a canonical space using spatial transformer networks. A 3D auto-encoder architecture for classifying AD subjects was proposed in [48]. They reached a classification accuracy of about 99% on the ADNI dataset by exploiting pre-trained models using transfer learning. The pre-trained model was trained further using a dementia dataset. A three-class binary classification problem was proposed in [49] with labels AD, HC, and MCI. The network was based on stacked autoencoder [19] architecture trained three times for each label independently. This model achieved an accuracy of 85.0% for MCI, 75.8% for MCI converter, and 95.9% for AD.

11.7 CONCLUSION

Deep learning algorithms played a crucial role in the advancement of automated visual screening and analysis of brain images, on par with radiologists. This chapter discussed various important algorithms in the field of brain image analysis. Such algorithms act as tools for laying down foundations of qualitative and quantitative rules to model brain functionality. Current generation deep learning algorithms majorly focused on encoder-decoder architectures to extract the crucial features by constructing an effective latent space. The introduction of GAN caused a paradigm shift by achieving promising results for various supervised and unsupervised tasks. However, training such models need substantial in-depth knowledge. Explainable AI (XAI) is another subfield receiving major thrust, as rules learned by deep learning models are not adequately interpretable by doctors or programming experts. However, the efficacy of deep learning algorithms has boosted confidence in the medical community, and currently, multiple algorithms are being employed at the prescreening stage of diagnosis. All these methods go hand in hand with doctors and radiologists to improve the diagnosis of the patients. Moreover, they lay the foundations for better understanding and modeling of the human brain and its behavior.

NOTES

1 https://www.oasis-brains.org/
2 http://adni.loni.usc.edu/
3 https://github.com/voxelmorph/voxelmorph
4 https://surfer.nmr.mgh.harvard.edu/
5 http://www.isles-challenge.org/
6 http://braintumorsegmentation.org/
7 Available at https://wiki.cancerimagingarchive.net/
8 https://github.com/mateuszbuda/brain-segmentation-pytorch
9 https://github.com/taigw/brats17
10 All datasets are available at http://schizconnect.org/

REFERENCES

1. Sahiner, Berkman, Aria Pezeshk, Lubomir M. Hadjiiski, Xiaosong Wang, Karen Drukker, Kenny H. Cha, Ronald M. Summers, and Maryellen L. Giger. "Deep learning in medical imaging and radiation therapy." *Medical Physics* 46, 1 (2019): e1–e36.
2. Rosenblatt, F. "The perceptron: a probabilistic model for information storage and organization in the brain." *Psychological Review* 65, 6 (1958): 386.
3. Rumelhart, David E., Geoffrey E. Hinton, and Ronald J. Williams. "Learning representations by back-propagating errors." *Nature* 323, 6088 (1986): 533–536.
4. LeCun, Yann, Léon Bottou, Yoshua Bengio, and Patrick Haffner. "Gradient-based learning applied to document recognition." *Proceedings of the IEEE* 86, 11 (1998): 2278–2324. IEEE.
5. Burt, Peter J., and Edward H. Adelson. "The Laplacian pyramid as a compact image code." *IEEE Transactions on Communications* 31, 4 (1983): 532–540.
6. Krizhevsky, Alex, Ilya Sutskever, and Geoffrey E. Hinton. "ImageNet classification with deep convolutional neural networks." *Communications of the ACM* 60, 6 (2017): 84–90.
7. Ioffe, Sergey, and Christian Szegedy. "Batch normalization: accelerating deep network training by reducing internal covariate shift." In *Proceedings of International Conference on Machine Learning, ICML*, pp. 448–456. 2015. http://citeseerx.ist.psu.edu/viewdoc/summary?doi=10.1.1.697.5768.

8. Yang, Xiao, Roland Kwitt, and Marc Niethammer. "Fast predictive image registration." In *Deep Learning and Data Labeling for Medical Applications*, pp. 48–57. Springer, Cham, 2016.

9. Ito, Masato, and Fumihiko, I. "An automated method for generating training sets for deep learning based image registration." In *5th International Conference on Bioimaging, Proceedings of 11th International Joint Conference on Biomedical Engineering Systems and Technologies*. 2018.

10. Szegedy, Christian, Wei Liu, Yangqing Jia, Pierre Sermanet, Scott Reed, Dragomir Anguelov, Dumitru Erhan, Vincent Vanhoucke, and Andrew Rabinovich. "Going deeper with convolutions." In *Proceedings of the IEEE Conference on Computer Vision and Pattern Recognition*, pp. 1–9. 2015.

11. Balakrishnan, Guha, Amy Zhao, Mert R. Sabuncu, John Guttag, and Adrian V. Dalca. "VoxelMorph: A learning framework for deformable medical image registration." *IEEE Transactions on Medical Imaging* 38, 8 (2019): 1788–1800.

12. Ronneberger, Olaf, Philipp Fischer, and Thomas Brox. "U-Net: convolutional networks for biomedical image segmentation." In *International Conference on Medical Image Computing and Computer-Assisted Intervention*, pp. 234–241. Springer, Cham, 2015.

13. Jaderberg, Max, Karen Simonyan, Andrew Zisserman, and Koray Kavukcuoglu. "Spatial transformer networks." In *Advances in Neural Information Processing Systems*, pp. 2017–2025, 2015.

14. Goodfellow, Ian J., Jean Pouget-Abadie, Mehdi Mirza, Bing Xu, David Warde-Farley, Sherjil Ozair, Aaron Courville, and Yoshua Bengio. "Generative adversarial nets." In *Advances in Neural Information Processing Systems*, pp. 2672–2680. 2014.

15. Fan, Jingfan, Xiaohuan Cao, Zhong Xue, Pew Thian Yap, and Dinggang Shen. "Adversarial similarity network for evaluating image alignment in deep learning based registration." In *International Conference on Medical Image Computing and Computer-Assisted Intervention*, pp. 739–746. Springer, Cham, 2018.

16. Wu, Shuang, Sravanthi Bondugula, Florian Luisier, Xiaodan Zhuang, and Pradeep Natarajan. "Zero-shot event detection using multi-modal fusion of weakly supervised concepts." In *Proceedings of the IEEE Conference on Computer Vision and Pattern Recognition, CVPR*, pp. 2665–2672. 2014.

17. Simonovsky, Martin, Benjamín Gutiérrez-Becker, Diana Mateus, Nassir Navab, and Nikos Komodakis. "A deep metric for multimodal registration." In *International Conference on Medical Image Computing and Computer-Assisted Intervention*, pp. 10–18. Springer, Cham, 2016.

18. Cheng, Xi, Li Zhang, and Yefeng Zheng. "Deep similarity learning for multimodal medical images." *Computer Methods in Biomechanics and Biomedical Engineering: Imaging and Visualization* 6, 3 (2018): 248–252.

19. Vincent, Pascal, Hugo Larochelle, Isabelle Lajoie, Yoshua Bengio, and Pierre Antoine Manzagol. "Stacked denoising autoencoders: learning useful representations in a deep network with a local denoising criterion." *Journal of Machine Learning Research* 11 (2010): 3371–3408.

20. Sun, Li, and Songtao Zhang. "Deformable MRI-ultrasound registration using 3D convolutional neural network." In *Simulation, Image Processing, and Ultrasound Systems for Assisted Diagnosis and Navigation*, pp. 152–158. Springer, Cham, 2018.

21. Toga, Arthur W., Paul M. Thompson, Susumu Mori, Katrin Amunts, and Karl Zilles. "Towards multimodal atlases of the human brain." *Nature Reviews Neuroscience* 7, 12 (2006): 952–966.

22. Dalca, Adrian V., Marianne Rakic, John Guttag, and Mert R. Sabuncu. "Learning Conditional deformable templates with convolutional networks." In *Advances in Neural Information Processing Systems*, pp. 806–818. 2019.

23. Salehi, Seyed, Sadegh Mohseni, Shadab Khan, Deniz Erdogmus, and Ali Gholipour. "Real-time deep registration with geodesic loss." *ArXiv: Computer Vision and Pattern Recognition*, 2018.

24. Badrinarayanan, Vijay, Alex Kendall, and Roberto Cipolla. "SegNet: a deep convolutional encoder-decoder architecture for image segmentation." *IEEE Transactions on Pattern Analysis and Machine Intelligence* 39, 12 (2017): 2481–2495.

25. Simonyan, Karen, and Andrew Zisserman. "Very deep convolutional networks for large-scale image recognition." In *Proceeding of International Conference on Learning Representations, ICLR*, pp. 1–14. 2015.

26. Drozdzal, Michal, Eugene Vorontsov, Gabriel Chartrand, Samuel Kadoury, and Chris Pal. "The importance of skip connections in biomedical image segmentation." In *Deep Learning and Data Labeling for Medical Applications*, pp. 179–187. Springer, Cham, 2016.

27. Milletari, Fausto, Nassir Navab, and Seyed Ahmad Ahmadi. "V-Net: fully convolutional neural networks for volumetric medical image segmentation." In *Proceedings of 4th International Conference on 3D Vision, 3DV*, pp. 565–571. IEEE, 2016.

28. Sudre, Carole H., Wenqi Li, Tom Vercauteren, Sebastien Ourselin, and M. Jorge Cardoso. "Generalised dice overlap as a deep learning loss function for highly unbalanced segmentations." In *Deep Learning in Medical Image Analysis and Multimodal Learning for Clinical Decision Support*, pp. 240–248. Springer, Cham, 2017.

29. Salehi, Seyed, Sadegh Mohseni, Deniz Erdogmus, and Ali Gholipour. "tversky loss function for image segmentation using 3D fully convolutional deep networks." In *International Workshop on Machine Learning in Medical Imaging*, pp. 379–387. Springer, Cham, 2017.

30. Nielsen, Anne, Mikkel Bo Hansen, Anna Tietze, and Kim Mouridsen. "Prediction of tissue outcome and assessment of treatment effect in acute ischemic stroke using deep learning." *Stroke* 49, 6 (2018): 1394–1401.

31. Choi, Youngwon, Yongchan Kwon, Hanbyul Lee, Beom Joon Kim, Myunghee Cho Paik, and Joong Ho Won. "Ensemble of deep convolutional neural networks for prognosis of ischemic stroke." In *International Workshop on Brainlesion: Glioma, Multiple Sclerosis, Stroke and Traumatic Brain Injuries*. Springer, Cham, 2016.

32. Abulnaga, S. Mazdak, and Jonathan Rubin. "Ischemic stroke lesion segmentation in CT perfusion scans using pyramid pooling and focal loss." In *International MICCAI Brainlesion Workshop*, pp. 352–363. Springer, Cham, 2018.

33. Zhao, Xiaomei, Yihong Wu, Guidong Song, Zhenye Li, Yazhuo Zhang, and Yong Fan. "A deep learning model integrating FCNNs and CRFs for brain tumor segmentation." *Medical Image Analysis* 43 (2018): 98–111.

34. Wang, Guotai, Wenqi Li, Sébastien Ourselin, and Tom Vercauteren. "Automatic brain tumor segmentation using cascaded anisotropic convolutional neural networks." In *International MICCAI Brainlesion Workshop*, pp. 178–190. Springer, Cham, 2017.

35. Kamnitsas, K., W. Bai, E. Ferrante, S. McDonagh, M. Sinclair, N. Pawlowski, M. Rajchl, et al. "Ensembles of multiple models and architectures for robust brain tumour segmentation." In *International MICCAI Brainlesion Workshop*, pp. 450–462. Springer, Cham, 2017.

36. Myronenko, Andriy. "3D MRI brain tumor segmentation using autoencoder regularization." In *International MICCAI Brainlesion Workshop*, pp. 311–320. Springer, Cham, 2018.

37. Kingma, Diederik P., and Max Welling. "Auto-encoding variational bayes." In *Proceeding of International Conference on Learning Representations*. 2014.

38. Isensee, Fabian, Philipp Kickingereder, Wolfgang Wick, Martin Bendszus, and Klaus H. Maier-Hein. "No new-net." In *International MICCAI Brainlesion Workshop*, pp. 234–244. Springer, Cham, 2018.

39. T. Brosch, Tang L.Y.W., Yoo Y., Li D.K.B., Traboulsee A., and Tam R. "Deep 3D convolutional encoder networks with shortcuts for multiscale feature integration applied to multiple sclerosis lesion segmentation." *IEEE Transactions on Medical Imaging* 35, 5 (2016): 1229–1239.

40. Kim, Minjeong, Guorong Wu, and Dinggang Shen. "Unsupervised deep learning for hippocampus segmentation in 7.0 Tesla MR images." In *International Workshop on Machine Learning in Medical Imaging*, pp. 1–8. Springer, Cham, 2013.

41. Guo, Yanrong, Guorong Wu, Leah A. Commander, Stephanie Szary, Valerie Jewells, Weili Lin, and Dinggang Shent. "Segmenting hippocampus from infant brains by sparse patch matching with deep-learned features." In *International Conference on Medical Image Computing and Computer-Assisted Intervention*, pp. 308–315. Springer, Cham, 2014.

42. Buda, Mateusz, Ashirbani Saha, and Maciej A. Mazurowski. "Association of genomic subtypes of lower-grade gliomas with shape features automatically extracted by a deep learning algorithm." *Computers in Biology and Medicine* 109 (2019): 218–225.

43. Gibson, Eli, Wenqi Li, Carole Sudre, Lucas Fidon, Dzhoshkun I. Shakir, Guotai Wang, Zach Eaton-Rosen, et al. "NiftyNet: a deep-learning platform for medical imaging." *Computer Methods and Programs in Biomedicine* 158 (2018): 113–122.

44. Zeng, Ling Li, Huaning Wang, Panpan Hu, Bo Yang, Weidan Pu, Hui Shen, Xingui Chen, et al. "Multi-site diagnostic classification of schizophrenia using discriminant deep learning with functional connectivity MRI." *EBioMedicine* 30 (2018): 74–85.

45. Suk, Heung I. L., Seong Whan Lee, and Dinggang Shen. "Latent feature representation with stacked auto-encoder for AD/MCI DIAGNOSis." *Brain Structure and Function* 220, 2 (2015): 841–859.

46. Gutiérrez-Becker, Benjamín, and Christian Wachinger. "Deep multi-structural shape analysis: application to neuroanatomy." In *International Conference on Medical Image Computing and Computer-Assisted Intervention*, pp. 523–531. Springer, Cham, 2018.

47. Qi, Charles R., Hao Su, Kaichun Mo, and Leonidas J. Guibas. "PointNet: deep learning on point sets for 3D classification and segmentation." In *Proceedings of the IEEE Conference on Computer Vision and Pattern Recognition, CVPR*, pp. 77–85. 2017.

48. Asl, Ehsan Hosseini, Mohammed Ghazal, Ali Mahmoud, Ali Aslantas, Ahmed Shalaby, Manual Casanova, Gregory Barnes, Georgy Gimel'farb, Robert Keynton, and Ayman El Baz. "Alzheimer's disease diagnostics by a 3D deeply supervised adaptable convolutional network." *Frontiers in Bioscience* 23, (2018): 584–596.

49. Suk, Heung Il, and Dinggang Shen. "Deep learning-based feature representation for AD/MCI classification." In *International Conference on Medical Image Computing and Computer-Assisted Intervention*, pp. 583–590. Springer, Berlin, Heidelberg, 2013.

12 Evolutionary Optimization-Based Two-Dimensional Elliptical FIR Filters for Skull Stripping in Brain Imaging and Disorder Detection

Savita Srivastava, Atul Kumar Dwivedi, and Deepak Nagaria

12.1 INTRODUCTION

Medical resonance imaging (MRI) is widely used in the medical field for the studies of brain. It produces the 2D scan of brain image which give information about the anatomical structure of soft tissues. These 2D scans are produce by the used of radio wave propagation within a magnetic field which produces signal along the human organ. Conventionally, MRIs of the brain are interpreted by radiologists qualitatively and visually. The major advantage of an MRI is high spatial resolution that allows quantitative clinical studies and also gives the detailed information on the brain tissues (anatomical structure). However, various MRI scan techniques consume much time in image segmentation and has too large of manual localization. So to overcome these drawbacks, computer-aided design has been developed, which increases the reliability, accuracy, and diagnosis time. In the localization of a brain tumor, image pre-processing is done for eliminating the noncerebral part. This technique is called skull stripping. Various image processing approaches are required before exploring the brain images. Image processing has several methods that are germain to a wide range of applications. Among these methods, segmentation is an important and crucial process in medical image processing and analysis. There are several algorithms being proposed in the medical image segmentation field. Algorithms with the silver standard mask method that reduces the cost of manual segmentation have been proposed for skull stripping in [1]. Brain mask methods which are relatively more complex

293

with possibility of brain tissue erosion have been discussed in [2]. In [3], a 3D unit based on deep neural network applied on publically available datasets has been proposed for skull stripping. Although the studies of these methods are efficient and accurate for skull stripping, they still need improvement for quality assurance of the skull-stripping method [4]. After the skull-stripping method, the next method for a brain tumor is image segmentation [5]. The methods of image segmentation can be broadly divided into three parts, i.e., basic, discriminative, and generative. Basic methods includes edge-based, region growing, thresholding, and texture-based. Discriminative methods involve clustering techniques and supervised methods like artificial neural networks and support vector machines. Thresholding is a low complexity approach for which Bernsen [6] and Otsu [7] commonly used algorithms. In [8], a biologically inspired Berkely wavelet transformer and support vector machine-based brain tumor detection techniques have been reported. Recently, various automated medical image segmentation techniques for automatic brain tumor localization with the help of multilevel thresholding and absolute intensity difference have been reported [5]. The main aim of brain tumor segmentation is to provide optimum thresholding. In this regard, an evolutionary optimization approach using multilevel thresholding has been used for brain tumor segmentation [9]. In [10,11], particle swarm optimization (PSO) has been used for the optimizing threshold. A hybrid PSO has been used for selecting an optimum multilevel threshold. Ant colony optimization (ACO) has been used for brain tumor segmentation. The proposed techniques are based on advantages of textural features. The ACO-based techniques have shown better performance over ABC, PSO, and K-, which means based techniques for multilevel thresholding.

Various evolutionary optimization algorithms for the design of digital filters have been reported in literature. An evolutionary algorithm is characterized by representation of parameters such as population size, the fitness of population, variation operators (exploration capability), and selection of individuals (exploitation capability). Many efforts have been made to have a proper moderation in exploration and exploitation problems. In order to overcome this, in this chapter, quantum inspired ABC algorithm has been proposed. The quantum-inspired ABC (QABC) is built upon the principle of Q-bits. Q-bit, which is specified by Q-bit strings, is defined as the smallest unit of representing information. The property of a Q-bit individual has a binary solution (linear superposition) in each state, probably. Therefore, the representation Q-bit shows better characteristics of population diversity over the other representations. Initially, QABC can reflect various diverse entities, since a Q-bit entity shows linear superposition with the same probability for all possible states. Also a Q-gate is viewed as a QABC variation operator to move the population towards optimal solutions and inevitably towards a single state. When each Q-bit reaches either 1 or 0, the individual Q-bit converges into a single state and the property of diversity gradually disappears. By this inherent mechanism, QABC can be used in moderation in exploration and exploitation problems.

12.2 PRE-PROCESSING

This chapter clearly analyzes the subject of pre-processing and its methods that are essentially required in the MRI segmentation. The brain image requires careful consideration during inspection or diagnosis because all the needful information about the brain is mapped into the intensity variation [12]. So we require pre-processing methods to eliminate the unwanted marks and labels present in the image. Pre-processing methods improve the image quality. This section discusses various pre-processing methods, such as removing the un-related parts from the background of the MRI brain images which improves image quality.

12.2.1 IMAGE ENHANCEMENT

Image enhancement improves the image quality by reducing the blurring, increasing contrast, and removing unwanted images. Here, filters are used mainly to suppress the low frequencies, i.e., detecting edges or enhancing the image, or high frequencies i.e., image smoothing [13]. Image enhancement and restoration techniques are illustrated in the frequency domain and spatial domain. However, convolution in time domain and spatial domain is multiplied in the frequency domain. Using a convolution mask over an image is much simpler and faster than the Fourier transform. So, the spatial filtering technique is discussed here. The captured images may have noise which may not provide the desired images required for analysis. Moreover, images which have some quality that are acceptable may need to be emphasized and highlighted [14].

Spatial processing is divided into two parts: mask processing and point processing. The mask processing has pixels of a neighborhood mask in a circle or square, which tends to generate the pixel in enhanced image coordinates. On the other hand, point processing in the images deals with the independent transformation of individual pixels of other pixels.

12.2.2 IMAGE DENOISE

This section takes pre-processing technique with denoising method in MRI. MRI is a commanding. At some stage of diagnostic technique, during image acquisition the integrated noise corrupts the computer aided examination and human interpretation of the images. The time average of image sequences intended to Increasing Signal to Noise Ratio (SNR) will end in additional acquisition time and will be significantly reduce a temporary solution [15]. Consequently, de-noising should be done for more precise diagnosis and fto enchance the image quality. Noise processing in images is influenced through data transmission media, discrete sources of radiation, and image quantization. The noise characteristic is dependent on its source, as is the operator that trims the impact down. It is a major task to resist the inevitable fuzziness of finer features carried out in high frequency modes. The most common type of noises found in medical images is Gaussian, salt and pepper, and shot and speckle [16]. In Gaussian noise, pixels of each image usually shows small variations from its original value. Salt and pepper noise affects images in situations when a faulty switching transition takes place. Short noise affects the lighter image section. Speckle noise affects the quality of radar images, which in turn reduces the active and synthetic apertures.

12.2.3 SKULL STRIPPING

Skull stripping is crucial pre-processing step in brain tumor segmentation. The standard skull-stripping methods can be classified as manual marking based (gold standard), intensity variation based, morphology (texture), map based, and hybrid methods. The manual skull stripping is conducted by analysts with efficient and précised results. Because of its accuracy, this method is also called gold standard. This method is time consuming as it takes a hours for each brain image segmentation. The second method is intensity based [17], these are less robust, faster, and very sensitive to small changes in noise, artefacts, and contrast of image. Methods that use image morphology are also fast, but based on experimentally computed parameters and mathematical morphological computation related to image shape and size. Changeable surface methods are a special category of skull-stripping methods in which balloon-like standard templates deform to take the shape of the brain. The standard templates can be suitable for both the exterior and interior skull boundaries.

12.3 FILTER DESIGN FOR IMAGE ENHANCEMENT (FORMULATION OF OBJECTIVES)

Generally, image enhancement highlights the specific features of an image by altering the original digital values. The classical approach for image enhancement is histogram equalization. It performs better for an ordinary image [18]. Histogram equalization is defined as transformation mapping of each input image pixel into the corresponding image pixel of processed output. Histogram equalization and their complex methods are used to measure contrast enhancement of images whose techniques are discussed next:

For a given image S, the probability density function p (S_j) is defined as

$$p(S_j) = \frac{m^j}{m} \qquad (12.1)$$

where m represents total number of samples in the input image, m^j represents the number of times the level (S_j) shown in the input image S.

Based on the Probability Density Function (PDF), the Cumulative Distribution Function (CDF) is expressed as

$$c(S) = \sum_{i=0}^{j} s_i \qquad (12.2)$$

where $Sj = s$, for $j = 0...1..L_1$ and $c(S_{L-1}) = 1$. By using CDF, histogram equalization mapped the input image into the entire dynamic range, (S_0, S_{L-1}). So, based on the CDF the transform function f(S) is defined as

$$f(S) = S_0 + (S_{L-1} - S_O)c(S) \qquad (12.3)$$

The output of the histogram equalization can be written as,

$$z(S) = f(S) \qquad (12.4)$$

$$= f(S(k, i)|^{\forall} S(k, i)^{\in}X \qquad (12.5)$$

The histogram equalization shows better performance in contrast enhancing by introducing significant improvement in the brightness of an image.

12.4 FILTER DESIGN FOR IMAGE DENOISING (FORMULATION OF OBJECTIVES)

Image noise is random variations in the images color produced by medical devices. Generally image noises are considered an unwanted product at the time of image acquisition. Image de-noising is defined as a process to remove noise from the images. In the 2D FIR filter design, the input and output relations of the images is given as follows:

$$z(k, i) = \sum_{p=0}^{M_1-1} \sum_{q=0}^{M_2-1} x(p, q)s(k - p, i - q) \qquad (12.6)$$

where $s(k, i)$ represents input image, $z(k, i)$ represents output image, $x(p, q)$ represents the coefficients, and M_1 and M_2 represents the 2D FIR filter order. The aim of this process is to minimize the Mean Square Error (MSE), which is expressed as

$$z(k, i) = \frac{1}{N_1 N_2} \sum_{p=0}^{M_1-1} \sum_{q=0}^{M_2-1} x(p, q)s(k - p, i - q) \qquad (12.7)$$

where N_1 and N_2 are the input images size.

12.5 FILTER DESIGN FOR SKULL STRIPPING (FORMULATION OF OBJECTIVES)

Skull stripping is the removal of unwanted image portions from a scanned image to have the image required for tissue detection [19]. In this work, the image is passed through 2D Finite impulse response filters in two stages to extract the brain tumor. The desired response of the skull stripping filter is given as

$$D_{ss}(k, i) = \sum_{\alpha=-\infty}^{\infty} \sum_{z=-\infty}^{\infty} h_e(\alpha, z)s(k - \alpha, i - z) \qquad (12.8)$$

where $h_e(\alpha, z)$ are elliptical kernel filter coefficients to be optimized. The resultant image after skull stripping $D_{ss}(k, i)$, is passed through an adaptive filter for segmentation of the brain tumor. The resultant image $D_t(k, i)$ is given by

$$D_{ss}(k, i) = \sum_{\alpha=-\infty}^{\infty} \sum_{z=-\infty}^{\infty} h_{bf}(\alpha, z) D_{ss}(k - \alpha, \ i - z) \qquad (12.9)$$

where h_{bf} is a 2Dl adaptive filter for tumor segmentation. The tumor area is calculated from the segmented image using a binarization method. A binary image can be represented as sum of total white and black pixels. In order to calculate the area of a total number of white pixels in an image, is calculated

$$P = \sum_{w=0}^{P_w} \sum_{h=0}^{P_h} f_t(w, h) \qquad (12.10)$$

where w is width, h is height, P_w is number of width pixels, P_h is number of height pixels, $f_t(w, h)$ is a function of tumor image $D_t(k, i)$ which has value 1 for white pixel and 0 for black pixel. As we know, one pixel corresponds to 0.264 mm. The area in cm is calculated by

$$A = [0.0264\sqrt{P}]^2 \qquad (12.11)$$

The error between the desired areas, which is obtained using manual segmentation known as ground truth, is given as

$$E_A = [A_d - A]^2 \qquad (12.12)$$

After solving equation equation (12.12) the optimum solution for skull-stripping kernel and adaptive filter can be obtained.

12.6   ABC ALGORITHM

The ABC (artificial bee colony) algorithm is swarm intelligence-based evolutionary algorithm which mimics the honey bees' behavior for searching food sources [20]. This algorithm has better efficiency and accuracy for the multidimensional problems. The artificial bees' colony has three different types of bees in hives that play important role in the search of food: scout bees, employed bees, and onlooker bees. The employed and onlooker bees are of the same number in the colony and equal to the number of food sources in the beehive [21]. The efficient solution of the optimization problem according to the location of each food source and the fitness value is its nectar amount. In this algorithm, a scout bee randomly generates the initial position of the swarm and assigns each employed bee to a food source as

$$s_{ki} = s_k^{min.} + r(s_k^{max.} - s_k^{min.}) \qquad (12.13)$$

where, $s_k^{max.}$ and $s_k^{min.}$ are the max. and min. values of the ith dimension, respectively, and r is a random number within range [0,1]. At each iteration, the employed bee randomly selects a food source and locates a new food source s_i given as

$$x_{i,d} = s_{i,d} + \alpha_{i,d}(s_{i,d} - s_{w,d}) \tag{12.14}$$

where $\alpha_{i,d}$ represents s random number within [−1,1]. $s_{i,d}$ is the i_{th} position of the food source in the d_{th} dimension, and x_i represents the new food source position in "d" dimension. The nectar amount is determined for the new food source x_i. If x_i has a nectar amount, then the current food source s_i will be updated.

$$D_{it} = \begin{cases} x_i \, (v + 1) & \textit{if fit } s_i(v) < \textit{fit } x_i(v + 1) \\ s_i \, (v) \; \textit{if fit } s_i(v) \geq \textit{fit } x_i(v + 1) \end{cases} \tag{12.15}$$

The honey bee colony has only one scout bee. So the employed bee, whose source of food has been stranded, has to behave as a scout bee and find a new food source by conducting random searches [22]. After completing all the searching processes by the employed bee, the nectar amount's information with food source positions has been gathered with onlooker bees. Each onlooker bee, based on their probability value, selects a food source and searches a new food source correspondent to the selected food source. The probability of the food source is determined as follows:

$$P_i = \frac{\text{fit } n_k}{\sum_{i=1}^{N} \text{fit } n_i} \tag{12.16}$$

where, fit n_k represents a food source's fitness value and N is the number of the colony size.

12.7 QABC ALGORITHM

In a digital computer, the bit is the smallest unit of information with values 0 or 1 at certain intervals of time; whereas, a quantum bit (Q-bit) in quantum computing is defined as smallest unit of information which lies in states of either 0, 1, or a combination of both at the equal time interval [23]. A Q-bit is presented in paired numbers (β, α), where $|\beta|^2$ shows the finding of Q-bit in state 0 and 1 probabilistically. The Q-bit state is represented as follows:

$$|\varnothing + \beta|0 + \alpha|1 \tag{12.17}$$

Each Q-bit in quantum computing must satisfy the following normalization equation:

$$|\beta|^2 + |\alpha|^2 = 1 \tag{12.18}$$

In quantum computing, n Q-bits represent the sequence of an individual q as follows:

$$q = [q_1, q_2 \ldots \ldots q_N] = \begin{bmatrix} \beta_1 & \ldots \ldots & \beta_m \\ \alpha_1 & \ldots \ldots & \alpha_m \end{bmatrix} \qquad (12.19)$$

The observation of the Q-bit process is performed as follows: if rand $(0, 1) < (\beta_q)^2$ then $f_q = 0$, else $f_q = 1$. In order to update the Q-bit values for each individual, a sequence of quantum operations has been applied [24]. Q-gate is one of the quantum operations to update Q-bits. In most of the studies, the rotation of Q-gate is more than the other Q-gates. The rotation Q-gate $G(\Delta\emptyset_q)$ is defined as follows:

$$G(\Delta\emptyset_q) = \begin{bmatrix} \cos(\Delta\emptyset_q) & -\sin(\Delta\emptyset_q) \\ \sin(\Delta\emptyset_q) & \cos(\Delta\emptyset_q) \end{bmatrix} \qquad (12.20)$$

where $\emptyset$ represents the rotation angle towards either 0 or 1 of Q-bit state. The Q-bit state at time "t" is represented as follows:

$$\begin{bmatrix} \beta_q(v+1) \\ \alpha_q(v+1) \end{bmatrix} = G(\Delta\emptyset_q) \begin{bmatrix} \beta_q(v) \\ \alpha_q(v) \end{bmatrix} \qquad (12.21)$$

12.8 SKULL STRIPPING AND BRAIN TUMOR LOCALIZATION ARCHITECTURE

The complete process of the localization of a brain tumor is completed in five stages.

Stage 1 – Pre-Processing: This step is to make images suitable for analysis and imaging modalities. This process also improves features of images. In the pre-processing stage, the image is passed through an image de-noising filter. The enhanced and de-noised image is forwarded to stage 2 for skull stripping.

Stage 2 – Skull Stripping: In an MRI, some nonbrain tissues present are removed using skull stripping. Removing skull tissues is a very exhaustive, time-consuming, manual operation. Manual annotation based methods are accurate. If accuracy is sacrificed, an approximately accurate approach using artificial intelligence (AI) can be devised. Artificial intelligence based methods are automated and faster in comparison to manual annotation based methods. Artificial intelligence techniques, like deep learning, require very large amounts of data for training. In this work, a recently developed ABC optimization algorithm is used for performing the task of skull stripping. The proposed algorithm can work on a single image. This does not require a large database for training and testing. The skull-stripping process is based on a design given by dynamic elliptical kernels. After skull stripping, the next step is segmentation.

Stage 3 – Segmentation: The most important stage of brain tumor extraction is tumor segmentation from a skull-stripped image. The descrimative methods like k means clustering, and others have used recently developed evolutionary optimization techniques to improve segmentation quality in brain tumor detection and localization. In the proposed work, an error sensitive FIR filter has been used for segmentation. The filter takes feedback from the output of the segmentation. The iterative processes, with the help of QABC optimization, adaptively change coefficients of the filter to provide the desired segmentation. The coefficient of filter changes according to the MRI of reference. A result obtained has been outlined later in this chapter.

Stage 4 – Localization: After segmentation of tumor, tumor location is also important. In this work, location information of tumor has been evaluated using pixel values.

Stage 5 – Post Segmentation Analysis: After localizing the image location, which is in pixel values, to be converted in measurable units like cm and mm. A number of images are tested using the proposed mythology. These five images have been presented in the Results and Discussion section.

12.9   RESULTS AND DISCUSSION

In order to test the efficiency of a proposed approach, standard size brain MRIs are considered for experimentation is 256×256 (Figure 12.1).

The efficiency of the proposed approach is tested in three stages. In the first stage the technique is tested for skull stripping. The optimized parameters for skull stripping have been recorded. In the second stage, the technique is tested for image segmentation. The process of image segmentation for brain tumor segmentation is performed with the help of an adaptive FIR filter. In the last stage, brain tumor

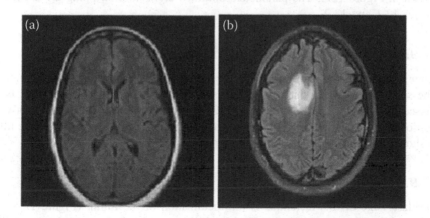

FIGURE 12.1   MRI of brain (a) without tumor and (b) MRI of brain with tumor

TABLE 12.1

Best image parameters with image area using proposed antlion algorithm

Image No:	Optimized Kernel for Skull Stripping			Proposed Method	
	a	b	Tumor Area in cm^2 (Ground Truth)	Optimum Threshold	Tumor Area in cm^2
Im_1	1.0020	0.4524	154.5	0.63000	154.7945
Im_2	0.6211	0.7053	28.00	0.35600	27.9003
Im_3	0.8194	0.7957	42.00	0.67451	41.9100
Im_4	0.7550	0.5198	59.00	0.6992	58.9591
Im_5	0.8199	0.6389	40.00	0.3844	39.7007

localization is performed by using an eight point analyses. All the simulations and filter designs has been executed using a Microsoft Windows 7 operating systems Intel(R) Core(TM) i3-6006U processor with 8 GB RAM with MATLAB® R16b. A number of pilot experiments have been performed to set the parameter of the ABC population size = 25, iteration 200, and upper bound and lower bound = [−1, 1].

12.9.1 EXAMPLES OF SKULL STRIPPING

A number of images have been selected for experimentation of skull stripping. The axis of the elliptical kernel used for skull stripping has been adaptively optimized. The optimized parameters are shown in Table 12.1. The results of five total images are shown in the table. The evolutionary optimization based skull stripping has been performed using the elliptical kernel. Images resulting after skull stripping are shown in Figure 12.2. The parameters obtained after skull stripping are shown in Tables 12.1 and 12.2.

12.9.2 EXAMPLES OF TUMOR SEGMENTATION

After completing the skull stripping, the next stage is brain tumor segmentation. The same five images that have been used for skull stripping have, again, been passed through 2D adaptive filters. This 2D filter is not fixed. The filter adaptively improves segmentation of brain tumor. The frequency response of the adaptive filter is shown in Figure 12.3.

12.9.3 TUMOR LOCALIZATION

The last stage of this technique is the localization of the tumor (Figure 12.4 and Table 12.3). The algorithm used for identifying positions of tumors has been discussed earlier.

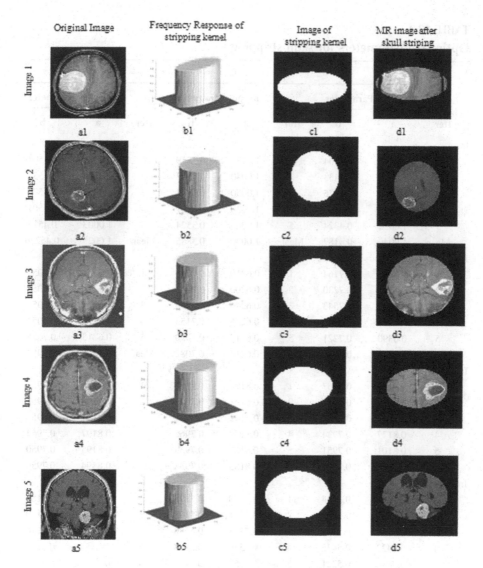

FIGURE 12.2   Images after skull stripping kernel and adaptive thresholding

12.10   CONCLUSION

This chapter provides the application of evolutionary optimization in brain image processing. Various aspects of pre-processing, like image de-noising and skull stripping using the 2D FIR filter design, are covered like amplitude response, phase response, group delay, and power consumption. A novel quantum computation-based version of ABC algorithm is proposed, which is computationally efficient as compared to classical ABC and its improved versions.

TABLE 12.2

Optimized parameters for skull stripping

| | GA | | | PSO | | | QABC | | |
| | Kernel Parameter | | | Kernel Parameter | | | Kernel Parameter | | |
Iter	a	b	Iter	a	b	Iter	a	b
Im_1								
1	1.0064	0.4104	1	1.0030	0.3530	1	1.0062	0.4504
2	1.0033	0.4433	2	1.0040	0.5532	2	1.0030	0.4533
3	1.0051	0.4576	3	1.0050	0.1342	3	1.0050	0.4576
4	1.0021	0.3501	4	1.0030	0.5501	4	1.0001	0.4501
5	1.0032	0.4324	5	1.0003	0.3524	5	1.0003	0.4524
Mean	1.0040	0.4187	Mean	1.0030	0.3885	Mean	1.0029	0.45276
Im_2								
1	0.6233	0.7164	1	0.6210	0.7153	1	0.6201	0.7050
2	0.6221	0.7230	2	0.6200	0.7003	2	0.6210	0.7057
3	0.6233	0.7543	3	0.6206	0.7050	3	0.6209	0.7052
4	0.6254	0.7765	4	0.6255	0.7153	4	0.6210	0.7054
5	0.6390	0.7221	5	0.6213	0.7050	5	0.6213	0.7055
Mean	0.6266	0.7385	Mean	0.6217	0.7082	Mean	0.6209	0.7054
Im_3								
1	0.8172	0.7967	1	0.8198	0.7956	1	0.8190	0.7952
2	0.8184	0.7971	2	0.8191	0.7947	2	0.8198	0.7963
3	0.8190	0.7986	3	0.8192	0.7961	3	0.8191	0.7951
4	0.8177	0.7934	4	0.8172	0.7965	4	0.8197	0.7964
5	0.8101	0.7951	5	0.8162	0.7939	5	0.8195	0.7950
Mean	0.8165	0.7962	Mean	0.8183	0.7954	Mean	0.8194	0.7956
Im_4								
1	0.7320	0.5104	1	0.7320	0.5198	1	0.7540	0.5181
2	0.7410	0.5213	2	0.7151	0.5198	2	0.7565	0.5170
3	0.7331	0.5034	3	0.7328	0.5198	3	0.7535	0.5176
4	0.7422	0.5435	4	0.7543	0.5198	4	0.7550	0.5188
5	0.7650	0.5221	5	0.7553	0.5188	5	0.7555	0.5198
Mean	0.7427	0.5201	Mean	0.7379	0.5196	Mean	0.7549	0.5183
Im_5								
1	0.8181	0.6351	1	0.8181	0.6354	1	0.8188	0.6377
2	0.8198	0.6357	2	0.8175	0.6352	2	0.8176	0.6373
3	0.8187	0.6363	3	0.8169	0.6362	3	0.8132	0.6376
4	0.8177	0.6371	4	0.8175	0.6377	4	0.8121	0.6386
5	0.8189	0.6377	5	0.8196	0.6314	5	0.8155	0.6381
Mean	0.8186	0.6364	Mean	0.8179	0.6352	Mean	0.8154	0.6379

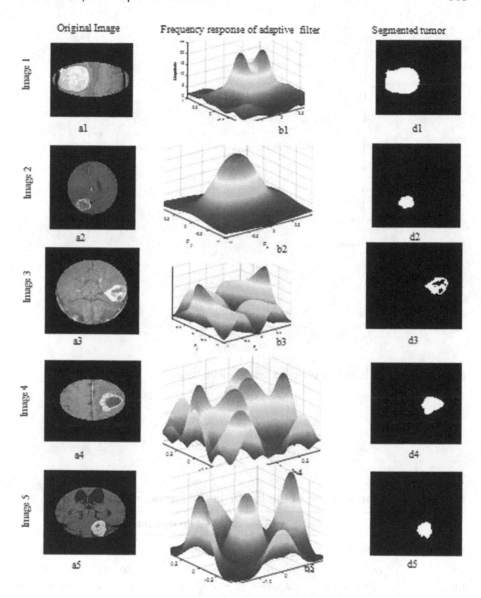

FIGURE 12.3 Images after skull stripping kernel and adaptive thresholding

Designed filters are compared with the other state of the art algorithms. Filter designs are validated by using FPGA Virtex-7. The results obtained using hardware are compared to simulation results. The case studies of skull stripping using 2D filters for brain tumor image processing have been considered.

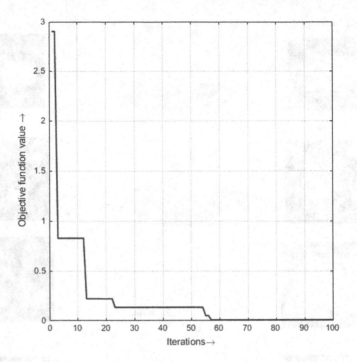

FIGURE 12.4   Reduction in objective function with iterations

TABLE 12.3

Calculation of the location of the tumor in the considered images

	Images considered for segmentation				
Location	Im_1	Im_2	Im_3	Im_4	Im_5
TP	069, 062	161, 106	106, 195	109, 172	152, 154
BP	129, 063	198, 093	155, 197	164, 164	198, 154
LP	105, 025	180, 081	129, 161	138, 147	172, 131
RP	093, 098	178, 126	119, 219	131, 209	174, 170
LTP	087, 044	171, 094	118, 178	124, 160	162, 143
RTP	081, 080	170, 116	113, 207	120, 191	163, 162
LBP	117, 044	189, 087	142, 179	151, 156	185, 143
RBP	111, 081	188, 110	137, 208	148, 187	186, 162

REFERENCES

1. P. Kalavathi and V.B. Surya Prasath. Methods on skull stripping of mri head scan images – a review. *Journal of Digital Imaging* 29, 3 (2016): 365–379.
2. Suresh A. Sadananthan, Weili Zheng, Michael W.L. Chee, and Vitali Zagorodnov. Skull stripping using graph cuts. *NeuroImage* 49, 1 (2010): 225–239.
3. Hyunho Hwang, Hafiz Zia Ur Rehman, and Sungon Lee. 3d u-net for skull stripping in brain mri. *Applied Sciences* 9, 3 (2019): 569.
4. Abigail B. Waters, Ryan A. Mace, Kayle S. Sawyer, and David A. Gansler. Identifying errors in freesurfer automated skull stripping and the incremental utility of manual intervention. *Brain Imaging and Behavior* 13, 5 (2019): 1281–1291.
5. Sanjay Agrawal, Rutuparna Panda, Leena Samantaray, and Ajith Abraham. A novel automated absolute intensity difference based technique for optimal mr brain image thresholding. *Journal of King Saud University-Computer and Information Sciences*, 2017.
6. John Bernsen. Dynamic thresholding of gray-level images. *In Proc. Eighth Int'l conf. Pattern Recognition*, Paris, 1986.
7. Nobuyuki Otsu. A threshold selection method from gray-level histograms. *IEEE Transactions on Systems, Man, and Cybernetics* 9, 1 (1979): 62–66.
8. Nilesh Bhaskarrao Bahadure, Arun Kumar Ray, and Har Pal Thethi. Image analysis for mri based brain tumor detection and feature extraction using biologically inspired bwt and svm. *International Journal of Biomedical Imaging* 2017, 2017.
9. Subhashis Banerjee, Sushmita Mitra, and B Uma Shankar. Single seed delineation of brain tumor using multi-thresholding. *Information Sciences* 330 (2016): 88–103.
10. Yong Zhao, Zongde Fang, Kanwei Wang, and Hui Pang. Multilevel minimum cross entropy threshold selection based on quantum particle swarm optimization. In *Eighth ACIS International Conference on Software Engineering, Artificial Intelligence, Networking, and Parallel/Distributed Computing (SNPD 2007)*, volume 2, pp. 65–69. IEEE.
11. Bahar Khorram and Mehran Yazdi. A new optimized thresholding method using ant colony algorithm for mr brain image segmentation. *Journal of Digital Imaging* 32, 1 (2019): 162–174.
12. B. Venkateswara Reddy, P. Bhaskara Reddy, P. Satish Kumar, and S. Siva Reddy. Developing an approach to brain mri image preprocessing for tumor detection. *International Journal of Research* 1, 6 (2014): 725–731.
13. S. Rajeshwari and T. Sree Sharmila. Efficient quality analysis of mri image using preprocessing techniques, 2013.
14. D. Arun Kumar. A new method on brain mri image preprocessing for tumor detection. *International Journal of Engineering, Technology, Science and Research* 1 (2015): 40–44.
15. E. Ben George and M. Karnan. Mri brain image enhancement using filtering techniques. *International Journal of Computer Science & Engineering Technology (IJCSET)* 3, 9 (2012): 399–403.
16. M. Usman Akram and Anam Usman. Computer aided system for brain tumor detection and segmentation. In *International Conference on Computer Networks and Information Technology*, pp. 299–302. IEEE, 2011.
17. David W. Shattuck, Stephanie R. Sandor-Leahy, Kirt A. Schaper, David A. Rottenberg, and Richard M. Leahy. Magnetic resonance image tissue classification using a partial volume model. *NeuroImage* 13, 5 (2001): 856–876.
18. Prem Natarajan, Nikhil Krishnan, Natasha Sandeep Kenkre, Shraiya Nancy, and Bhuvanesh Pratap Singh. Tumor detection using threshold operation in mri brain images. In 2012 IEEE *International Conference on Computational Intelligence and Computing Research*, pp. 1–4. IEEE, 2012.

19. Florent Ségonne, Anders M. Dale, Evelina Busa, Maureen Glessner, David Salat, Horst K. Hahn, and Bruce Fischl. A hybrid approach to the skull stripping problem in MRI. *Neuroimage* 22, 3 (2004): 1060–1075.

20. Bahriye Akay and Dervis Karaboga. A modified artificial bee colony algorithm for real-parameter optimization. *Information Sciences*, 192 (2012): 120–142.

21. Guopu Zhu and Sam Kwong. Gbest-guided artificial bee colony algorithm for numerical function optimization. *Applied Mathematics and Computation* 217, 7 (2010): 3166–3173.

22. Jia Chen, Weiyu Yu, Jing Tian, Li Chen, and Zhili Zhou. Image contrast enhancement using an artificial bee colony algorithm. *Swarm and Evolutionary Computation* 38 (2018): 287–294.

23. Xiaohui Yuan, Pengtao Wang, Yanbin Yuan, Yuehua Huang, and Xiaopan Zhang. A new quantum inspired chaotic artificial bee colony algorithm for optimal power flow problem. *Energy Conversion and Management* 100 (2015): 1–9.

24. Fengcai Huo, Yang Liu, Di Wang, and Baoxiang Sun. Bloch quantum artificial bee colony algorithm and its application in image threshold segmentation. *Signal, Image and Video Processing* 11, 8 (2017): 1585–1592.

13 EEG-Based Neurofeedback Game for Focus Level Enhancement

Humaira Nisar, Han Shen Chong, Saeed Mian Qaisar, Yeap Kim Ho, and Chuang Huei Gau

13.1 INTRODUCTION

With the improvement in healthcare in recent times a significant increase in life expectancy has been observed. Although this is a positive outcome of advanced medicine and healthcare, an increase in age-related cognitive decline has also been observed. Some examples of age related cognitive decline are slower processing speed, deficit in inhibitory processing, decline in executive functions such as cognitive flexibility, attention, and working memory [1]. In addition to the cognitive decline observed in aging populations, behavioral disorders and psychological symptoms also result in cognitive decline in otherwise non-aging population. Daily stress in an otherwise healthy population has also been associated with reduction in attentional resources. Hence, there should be a mechanism to counter the effect of cognitive decline. This need for improvement in the overall well-being of the human population has given rise to different types of therapies, one of which is electroencephalography (EEG)-based neurofeedback (NF) [2].

Electroencephalography is an electrophysiological method which is used to record the electrical activity of the brain [3]. Electroencephalography is acquired by placing electrodes on the scalp of the subject to record the voltage fluctuations due to the ionic activity of the neurons in the brain. The first human EEG was recorded in 1924 by German physiologist and psychiatrist Hans Berger [3]. Over the years, EEG has evolved into a relatively stable and reliable technology. For example, quantitative EEG (qEEG) is increasingly used in brain studies [4] for the diagnosis of mental illness such as attention deficit hyperactivity disorder (ADHD), sleep disorder, epilepsy, stress [5]. The qEEG uses modern computerized algorithms to perform time-series, frequency domain, and statistical analyses on raw EEG data. Hence, qEEG may act as a guide to help healthcare providers to diagnose mental illnesses and behavioral disorders more accurately and devise a suitable therapy for the patients [4].

According to *Psychology Today* [6], therapeutic interventions are often used to enhance the well-being of subjects needing support, but either rejects it, is reluctant to ask for it, or is unable to accept assistance. Therapeutic interventions usually involve some form of activities such as games (video games, 2D/3D), music, or drama. The therapeutic intervention involving the application of EEG technology is known as neurofeedback (NF) training. Self-regulation plays an important role in enhancing the performance of individuals. Neurofeedback is a promising non-invasive approach for improving human brain frequency rhythms through self-regulation of brain activity.

Hence, we can say that NF is a brainwave training technique to enhance performance in healthy subjects, aging populations, as well as subjects under clinical conditions. In healthy subjects, it may enhance the existing faculties of human beings to make them more productive. In aging populations, it can help to improve cognitive decline; whereas, it has shown improvement in clinical conditions such as ADHD [7], autism spectrum disorder [8], depression [9], stress [10,11], and epilepsy [12]; improvement of cognition (working memory) in aging adults [1], brain injury [13], trauma [14], post-traumatic stress disorder [15], and insomnia or disrupted sleep habits [16].

In NF, the electrophysiological state of the subject is displayed on a computer screen in the form of a bar chart and then the subject is encouraged to improve the desired activity [1]. In order to perform NF training, it is necessary that there is an interface between the brain and the computer system; hence, the term brain computer interface (BCI) can be referred to here. In the following sections, we will discuss the relationship between BCI and NF.

13.1.1 BRAIN COMPUTER INTERFACE AND NEUROFEEDBACK

Brain computer interface (BCI) works as a control and communication channel between the brain and the computer. The subject uses his brainwaves to communicate with the computer rather than using typical input devices such as a mouse and a keyboard. The BCI usually consists of a brainwave acquisition device such as an EEG headset and a computer. The EEG headset acquires the brainwaves of the user; these brain signals are transmitted to the computer that processes these signals and translates them into a useful form that can be used to control the output device [17]. Figure 13.1 shows a typical representation of a BCI. The BCI is the building block of NF system.

In NF training, the users get the response or feedback about their brain activity in real time from a computer-based system, usually a BCI which assesses the brain activity of a subject [6]. Sound or visual signals are used by the system to retrain or reorganize the subject's brain activities. The subject thus learns to control and enhance his brain activity by participating in this process; the brain abilities can be enhanced over a number of training sessions. This is thought to relieve the effects of numerous neurological and mental health disorders. Hence, NF can also be considered as an alternative way of treatment or therapy.

In an NF session, the therapist will attach the electrodes to the scalp of the subject to collect the subject's brainwaves. The brainwaves are then fed to a computer that can process and analyze the collected brainwaves. After analyzing the

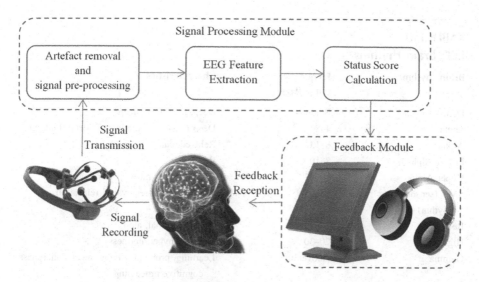

FIGURE 13.1   Representation of a BCI-based NF system.

brain activity, the software will then provide feedback in real time about the brain activity of the subject e.g., for alpha protocol it will inform whether alpha band power is increasing or decreasing by displaying a bar graph in real time. After analyzing the brain activity and providing feedback, the computer will then use predefined programs such as video games to help the subjects to reorganize or retrain their brain activities to a desirable pattern. The NF sessions are not regarded as treatment, but instead as a means of controlling or manipulating brain activity in a healthy way. This is achieved through routine training activities using computerized neurofeedback software that aids the central nervous system to reorganize and regulate the brainwaves.

The NF sessions are carried out periodically once or twice a week, maybe lasting a total of 20 weeks. Some subjects may require fewer sessions while others may need more. In terms of duration, better and long lasting results are observed with ten NF training sessions or more on average [18]. However the number of sessions and the duration may vary from one individual to another.

13.1.2   TYPES OF NF AND BRAIN RHYTHMS

The NF training design protocol is based on EEG/brain rhythms. Different brain rhythms are associated with different functions as given in the Table 13.1. It should be noted here that there is a slight difference in the range of frequencies for brain rhythms reported in the literature. Hence, based on these brain rhythms, the NF treatment mainly focuses on the delta, theta, alpha, beta, and gamma treatment protocol. In addition, sometimes a combination of different rhythms such as the alpha/theta ratio or beta/theta ratio are also observed [19,20]. The most commonly used NF is the frequency or power NF. In this technique, the amplitude of specific brain waves in specific brain locations are changed using feedback from the surface electrodes [19].

TABLE 13.1

EEG brain rhythms

Brain rhythm	Frequency range (Hz)	Characteristics
Delta	Below 4	Deep, dreamless sleep
Theta	4–8	Deep relaxation, meditation, deep thinking
Alpha	8–13	Relaxed, calm, not thinking
Lower Alpha	8–10	Recalling
Upper Alpha	10–13	Optimized cognitive performance
SMR (sensorimotor rhythm)	13–15	Mental alertness, physical relaxation
Beta	13–30	Awake, normal, alert
High Beta	20–30	Anxiety, hyper-alertness
Gamma	Above 30	Learning, problem solving, mental sharpness, cognitive processing

Many studies focus on alpha protocol in a population considered healthy. Alpha waves play a role in the mental state and cognitive performance of the subjects [21,22]. Based on literature review, it is found that alpha training had positive outcome in healthy populations [23]. In another study when the participants were able to modulate their upper-alpha, they performed better in working memory tasks, thus improving the cognitive performance by using NF protocol [1]. Alpha rhythm is also used in the process of relaxation. Hence, alpha NF training is commonly used for inducing relaxation and reducing stress and anxiety in the frequency range 7–10Hz [17]. Theta rhythm (4–8Hz) is also related to cognitive performance specifically during memory tasks. Enhanced theta activity is related to memory encoding and retrieval [1]. Beta rhythm is associated with the awake, normal, alert, and conscious states. Thus, in order to focus and solve problems, beta waves play an important role. Hence, beta NF training is used to improve focus and attention (12–14Hz). An improvement in this frequency range may result in improved cognitive processing [19].

Hence, we may say that the alpha band is associated with relaxation; if a subject is in a relaxed state, the alpha band power will be high. This means that a person in a focused state will not have a low alpha band power, but high beta band power, as the beta band is mainly related to focus and attention. Therefore, in this work we are planning to use the information related to alpha and beta band powers to develop a method for enhancing focus level.

13.1.3 EEG-BASED GAMES

Computerized EEG-based games are video games designed for NF sessions, where the subjects are expected to play/control the various elements in the game by thinking (generating specific EEG signals and extracting useful features from them) without using the conventional input devices such as the keyboard or the mouse. With a suitable game protocol and game play mechanism, the EEG-based games may enhance the brain activity of the subjects/players.

Video games used for NF training are directly inspired from traditional games and are often used for cognitive intervention (attention, working memory, inhibitive intervention). However, unlike normal video games, the main feature of EEG-based NF games is that these employ a closed loop structure based on four compulsory modules: data acquisition, processing, signal generation for control purposes, and gaming interface, as shown in the Figure 13.1. In these games, game elements (GE) play an important role. Game elements are a set of video game components which may include patterns, objects, principles, models, or methods. The most frequently used GEs (in descending order) by cognitive outcomes are: score system, narrative context, time pressure, reward system, win/loose, avatar/character, and multiplayers [24]. While playing computer games, positive feedback messages (which are considered GE) can promote the confidence level. Another possible example is the availability of tutorials to introduce game mechanics that are initially beyond the new user's understanding. Lumsden et al. reported that subjects with ADHD are very responsive to immediate feedback. Hence, rewards and feedback of GEs are very suitable for subjects suffering from ADHD [25]. A brief overview of EEG-based games that enhance the focus level will be given in the following section.

There are many games available in the literature to enhance the attention level. These games use different protocols, e.g., archery games use alpha protocol (using alpha power) [26], or a ball driving game in [27] uses theta and beta protocol (using a ratio of theta to beta band power). The researchers in *Refill*, the matrix game [28], used the sample entropy feature to quantify the FL.

The EEG-based BCI archery game was proposed by Liao et al. [26]. In the archery game, the player has to make a shot at the target located at the center of the screen. The FL is displayed with the help of a bar on the right side of the screen; the score is displayed at the top right. The distance between the center of the target and the arrow on the target determines the FL of the player. Hence, the FL of the player is the main controller of the game. The player has 10 seconds to complete a shot, and the total score is calculated after ten shots are completed. In this game the FL detection algorithm has three steps: artifact removal, focus feature extraction, and FL value determination. The alpha band power is used as an indicator of FL. Studies show that the alpha band power decreases as a user's mental state moves from an unfocused state to a focused state. Therefore, the focus feature (FF) is defined as the inverse of the average alpha rhythm.

Another group of researchers designed a game called *Refill the Matrix* [28]. The game requires the subjects to focus on a set of numbers that are displayed in the form of a 3 × 3 matrix on the computer screen, memorize them, and then to correctly refill the matrix. The subject can correctly refill the matrix only if the subject's attention level exceeds a certain threshold. The FL which acts as the control parameter in this game is continuously displayed in the form of a progress bar in the graphical user interface (GUI) of the game which provides the feedback to the player. The focus level in the form of a progress bar motivates the player to focus and reach a value high enough to exceed the threshold. The FL of the subject in the *Refill the Matrix* EEG game is measured by estimating the sample entropy. Studies show that the EEG signals of a person in an attentive state are more complicated than in the inattentive state. Thus, the entropy of the EEG signal in attentive states is higher than inattentive states. Hence, the FL is quantified using the sample entropy (SampEn) feature, by averaging the values obtained from all channels.

In both games FL is used as the control parameter to trigger certain mechanics in the game. For example, the accuracy of the arrows in the archery EEG game is proportional to the FL of the subjects, while the subjects of the R*efill the Matrix* game requires them to reach a threshold FL in order to fill in the answers in the matrix. Thus, in order to improve the FL of the subjects, a game play mechanics in which the subjects use the FL to control the game must be developed. Hence, it is concluded that there are different ways to enhance the FL.

13.2 NEUROFEEDBACK GAME DESIGN

To increase the FL of the participants, a car driving game is designed for NF training. In this game a car is driven in a virtual environment. The game provides a pleasing as well as challenging atmosphere, in which the participants compete against time to reach the finish line as fast as possible. Research on GUI has shown that the participants of a game feel better when there are many features in the game. However, if a computer game is developed using EEG signals alone then it may result in limited interaction, as it is difficult to classify large numbers of EEG signals. This means that the participants cannot control as many features as they like and may not feel a good degree of engagement [25]. That's why when EEG signals are combined with traditional interaction elements, the participants feel a higher level of involvement in the games. The EEG signals received from the BCI device are used to regulate the game properties.

In car racing games, different parameters considered important can affect the performance. For example, parameters related to the car drive, i.e., steering quality, maximum speed and acceleration, engine power and torque, braking quality; and outside parameters, i.e., road condition, road surroundings, weather condition, and color of car. Some of these parameters are affective in nature such as the beauty of the surroundings, car color, and weather, where a change in these parameters may have positive effects.

13.2.1 SYSTEM FRAMEWORK

The BCI for this project was developed with the EMOTIV Insight headset [29] and a desktop computer (Intel Core i5-8400 CPU @ 2.80GHz, Nvidia GTX 1050 Ti, 16 GB RAM, Windows 10–64 Bit Home Edition). The EMOTIV Insight headset is connected to the desktop computer with the wireless dongle. In order to connect the EMOTIV headset to the desktop, the EMOTIV App, EMOTIV BCI, and EMOTIV Pro software are required which are freely available from the official EMOTIV website. The EMOTIV App version 2.4.1.90 is used for this project.

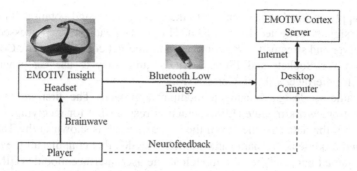

FIGURE 13.2 The general framework of the BCI-based NF game.

The framework of the BCI-based NF game system is shown in the Figure 13.2. The EMOTIV Insight headset collects the EEG signal from the subject and feeds it to the computer via Bluetooth low energy connection. The recorded signals are sent from the computer to the EMOTIV Cortex server for processing. During the signal processing, artifacts in the signals are removed automatically. Then the signals are decomposed to different frequency band and the fast Fourier transform (FFT) is applied to the signals to calculate the average power of each frequency band. The processed signals are then packaged in the form of the JavaScript object notation (JSON) format and then sent back to the computer to provide feedback to the subject, forming a complete neurofeedback loop.

13.2.2 EEG DATA ACQUISITION MODULE

The EMOTIV Insight headset is used for data acquisition. It is a low cost non-invasive EEG recording headset that consists of five channels of EEG data located at AF3, AF4, T7, T8, and Pz [30]. The location of electrodes follows the international 10–20 system of electrode placement. The internal sampling rate is 2048Hz which is then down-sampled to 128Hz per channel and the data is sent to a computer via a Bluetooth device. The available frequency range is 0.5–43Hz. The signal is filtered through a built in digital 5th order Sinc filter.

The availability of a low-priced EEG headset and associated software development kit (SDK) to develop the games based on EEG signals is the most important reason to use this device in this research. Although the channels in this headset are very low, research shows that this EEG headset has the capability to measure attention levels [26,28].

13.2.3 EEG GAME DESIGN WITH UNITY 3D

The game engine known as Unity3D [30,31] is used to design and develop car racing games. There are many game engines available such as Unreal Engine and Godot Engine; however, Unity3D is chosen for this project because Unity3D uses the C# programming language which is highly compatible with the Cortex application programming interface (API) provided by EMOTIV. Cortex API is used to develop applications that can connect to the cortex server and obtain EEG data. All the EEG signals collected by the EMOTIV EEG headset are processed by the Cortex server and streamed to the computer via internet connection. The Cortex API is built on WebSockets and JSON, so it is quite easy to use C# programming language to interface with the Cortex API.

The game is designed using a modular approach. The first module is the EMOTIV framework module (EFM) which is responsible for receiving, decoding, and handling the data streamed from the Cortex server as shown in the Table 13.2. The second module is the main game module (MGM) that contains all the codes for the main game logic, and the third module is the user interface module (UIM) which is used for displaying information and navigating the game. The UIM contains UI elements such as menus, buttons, and heads-up display (HUD). The menus and buttons were created for navigation purposes, while the HUD was created to display important information during game play.

13.2.4   THE CAR DRIVING GAME

The game consists of a main menu, three different stages, a pause menu, and various other functions. The game runs on the Windows platform and requires a keyboard, a mouse, and an EEG headset to be played. When the player clicks on the Start button in the main menu, the player will be redirected to the track selection panel. In the track selection panel, the player can choose the track. The Training Ground Track is an empty space suitable for training purposes, whereas the Sprint Track and the Drift Track are used for NF training sessions.

13.2.4.1   The EEG Headset Panel

In the EEG headset panel the player can connect the game to the EEG headset and the Cortex server as shown in the Figure 13.3a. Information such as the status of the headset, battery level, contact quality, steering position, mental command, focus level, alpha band power, and beta band power are displayed in the EEG headset panel once the game is connected to the Cortex server. The player can control the

---

TABLE 13.2
Data retrieved by the EFM

Data	Usage
Mental commands	Move the car forward or backward
Headset status	The connection status of the headset
Battery level	The battery level of the connected EEG headset
Contact quality	The contact quality of the connected EEG headset
Alpha band power	To determine the FL of the player
Beta band power	To determine the FL of the player
Magnetometer X-axis value	To determine the steering position according to the position of the head

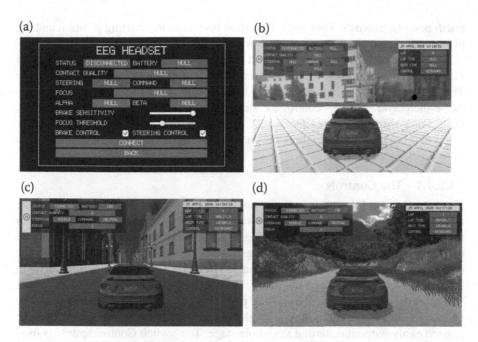

FIGURE 13.3   (a) The EEG headset panel. (b) Training Ground stage, (c) the Sprint Track stage, (d) the Drift Track stage.

brake sensitivity and the threshold focus as well as enabling or disabling the FL brake control and the steering control. The player can also customize the paint color of the car in the car paint panel.

13.2.4.2   The Stages

The game is designed in a virtual environment which is pleasing to the participants. There are three stages built for the NF training sessions, (refer to the Figure 13.3b–d).

Throughout the game play, the scores and FL of the player is shown on the HUD (refer to the Figure 13.3b–d). Various other useful information such as the connection status, contact quality, battery level of the EEG headset, steering position, current mental command, date, time, lap time, and best time as well as the current active control are all available on the HUD. All of this information acts as the feedback for the players during the game play, forming the complete NF loop.

The Training Ground is only developed for testing and is not used in actual game playing. The Sprint Track stage is set in a straight road between block of buildings. It is also decorated with street lights and an evening "skybox". A skybox is a method to make the stage look bigger than it is by building a cuboid which contains the images of distant objects such as the mountains and the sky. In the Sprint Track stage, the player will have to reach the finish point as soon as possible to get a high score. In the Sprint Track stage, the steering control is disabled so the player can only move the car forward or backward. The time taken by the player to reach the finish point is recorded. Then the car position is reset to the starting position and the player will repeat the lap two more times.

The Drift Track stage is set in a forest environment. It is decorated with trees and plants as well as a skybox with mountains. The Drift Track stage has a curvy track. The Drift Track has a higher difficulty level as compared to the Sprint Track because the player needs to control the steering of the car to turn left or right. The Drift Track shares the same mechanics with the Sprint Track except that the car position is not reset upon reaching the end point, since the Drift Track is in the form of a closed loop.

13.2.4.3 The Controls

The list of available controls is shown in Table 13.3. It can be observed that some of the controls are keyboard exclusive; whereas, others can be controlled using both the EEG headset and keyboard. The Toggle Light control is used to switch on and off the lights of the car. The Reset Lap control will reset the car position to the starting point and reset the current lap time. The Reset Lap control is introduced to help the player reset the lap if the car is stuck or trapped. The Reset Session control will reset the car position to the starting point, the current lap time, and also the lap count. The Reset Session button is implemented so that the player can restart the session easily without restarting the whole stage. The Switch Control feature is used to switch the control between the keyboard and the EEG headset.

13.2.5 COMPUTATION OF FL AND SCORES

13.2.5.1 Computation of FL

The FL is calculated using the inverse of the alpha band power and the beta band power retrieved from the EMOTIV framework module (EFM) from the Cortex server. The calculations for the computation of FL are shown in equations (13.1) to (13.8).

TABLE 13.3
List of controls in the car driving game

Keyboard	EEG Headset	Controls
Up Arrow	Push	Forward
Down Arrow	Pull	Backward
Left Arrow	Magnetometer	Left
Right Arrow	Magnetometer	Right
F	Null	Toggle light
R	Null	Reset lap
T	Null	Reset session
M	Null	Switch control

$$P_{\alpha n} = [P_{\alpha 1}, \ P_{\alpha 2} \ldots \ P_{\alpha 5}], \ P_{\beta n} = \left[P_{\beta 1}, \ P_{\beta 2} \ldots \ P_{\beta 5} \right] \tag{13.1}$$

$$P_{\alpha} = \frac{1}{n} \Sigma_{n=0}^{5} P_{\alpha n}$$

$$P_{\beta} = \frac{1}{n} \sum_{n=0}^{5} P_{\beta n} \tag{13.2}$$

where P_{α} and P_{β} are the average power in the alpha and beta bands, respectively, and n is the number of channels (n is equal to 5 for EMOTIV Insight). The average P_{α} and P_{β} values are displayed in the EEG headset panel for information. Equations (13.3) and (13.4) are used to determine the R_{α} and R_{β}, the inverse of the average alpha and beta band power, respectively.

$$R_{\alpha} = \frac{1}{n} \Sigma_{n=0}^{5} \frac{1}{P_{\alpha n}} \tag{13.3}$$

$$R_{\beta} = \frac{1}{n} \Sigma_{n=0}^{5} \frac{1}{P_{\beta n}} \tag{13.4}$$

Equations (13.5) and (13.6) are used to measure FL. Equation (13.5) shows that if the average inverse alpha band power is greater than 1.0, the FL will be 100, else the FL will be $100R_{\alpha}$. It means that the higher the average alpha band power, the lower the FL. Equation (13.6) shows, if the value of one minus the average inverse beta band power is less than 0, the FL will be zero, else the FL will be $100R_{\beta}$. The higher the average beta band power, the smaller the average inverse beta band power and the value of one minus the average inverse of beta band power will be higher. In other words, the higher the beta band power, the higher the FL of the subject. Equation (13.7) gives the average FL, $FL_{average}$, which is used to control the brakes of the car. If the $FL_{average}$ drops below the threshold FL, the brake will be activated and the car will be slowed down. Equation (13.8) is used to compute the average FL throughout the NF session, where N is the total number of sessions.

$$FL(R_{\alpha}) = \begin{cases} 100, & R_{\alpha} \geq 1.0 \\ 100R_{\alpha}, & R_{\alpha} < 1.0 \end{cases} \tag{13.5}$$

$$FL(R_{\beta}) = \begin{cases} 0, & 1 - R_{\beta} \leq 0.0 \\ 100R_{\beta}, & 1 - R_{\beta} > 1.0 \end{cases} \tag{13.6}$$

$$FL_{average} = \frac{FL(R_{\alpha}) + FL(R_{\beta})}{2} \tag{13.7}$$

$$FL_{session} = \frac{FL_{average1} + FL_{average2} \cdots + FL_{averageN}}{N} \qquad (13.8)$$

13.2.5.2 Computation of Scores

The scores for the Sprint and Drift Track stages are computed from the best time recorded during the playing session. The maximum score for the Sprint and Drift Track is set to 100; whereas, the minimum score is set to 0.

$$Sc_{maxSprint} = 100, \; Sc_{maxDrift} = 100 \; Sc_{minSprint} = 0, \; Sc_{minDrift} = 0$$

where S_c stands for score.

The best time, T_{best}, is recorded in deciseconds. The maximum time, T_{max} estimated for both tracks are 10 minutes which is equivalent to 6,000 deciseconds. The expected minimum time, T_{min}, in which a player can complete one lap, is set to 15 seconds or 150 deciseconds for the Sprint Track and 40 seconds or 400 deciseconds for the Drift Track. The scores for both tracks will be 100 if the player manages to finish a lap in a time shorter or equal to the expected minimum time and 0 if the player finishes a lap in a time longer than the expected maximum time. The relationship between the scores and the best time is assumed to be linearly proportional. Equations (13.9) and (13.10) are derived based on these assumptions. The formulas for the computation of the scores for the Sprint Track and the Drift Track are shown in equations (13.9) and (13.10), respectively.

$$T_{maxSprint} = 6000, \; T_{maxDrift} = 6000$$

$$T_{minSprint} = 150, \; T_{minDrift} = 400$$

For $\frac{T_{best}}{10} < T_{min}$:

$$Sc_{Sprint}(T_{best}) = 100$$
$$Sc_{Drift}(T_{best}) = 100$$

For $\frac{T_{best}}{10} \geq T_{min}$:

$$\frac{Sc_{max} - Sc_{min}}{T_{min} - T_{max}} = \frac{Sc(T_{best}) - Sc_{min}}{T_{best} - T_{max}}$$
$$Sc_{Sprint}(T_{best}) = -\frac{2}{117}T_{best} + \frac{4000}{39}$$
$$Sc_{Drift}(T_{best}) = -\frac{1}{56}T_{best} + \frac{750}{7}$$

For $\frac{T_{best}}{10} > T_{max}$:

$$Sc_{Sprint}(T_{best}) = 0 \quad Sc_{Drift}(T_{best}) = 0$$

$$Sc_{Sprint}(T_{best}) = \begin{cases} 100, & \frac{T_{best}}{10} < 15 \\ -\frac{2}{117}T_{best} + \frac{4000}{39}, & \frac{T_{best}}{10} \geq 15 \\ 0, & \frac{T_{best}}{10} \geq 600 \end{cases} \quad (13.9)$$

$$Sc_{Drift}(T_{best}) = \begin{cases} 100, & \frac{T_{best}}{10} < 40 \\ -\frac{1}{56}T_{best} + \frac{750}{7}, & \frac{T_{best}}{10} \geq 40 \\ 0, & \frac{T_{best}}{10} \geq 600 \end{cases} \quad (13.10)$$

13.3   NEUROFEEDBACK SESSION

13.3.1   SUBJECTS

Ten healthy subjects (5 males, 5 females) with an age ranging from 15 to 78 years (mean: $38.6 \pm$ standard deviation: 20.16) participated in the study. Informed consent was obtained from the participants.

For all subjects, the complete flow of the NF training game session is shown in Figure 13.4. Before the training session the subjects are briefed about the procedure in detail.

13.3.2   MENTAL COMMAND TRAINING

During the mental command training session, the player needs to actively think or imagine an idea. The GUI of EMOTIV BCI will display a box to help the player visualize the idea as shown in the Figure 13.5. For example, if the player is training the "Push" command, the box will move further away from the player as if the player is actually pushing the box away. This will create a unique brain signal with the signature of the PUSH command [32,33]. The EMOTIV BCI software makes use of this phenomenon to extract the features for this training. Later when the player thinks that he is PUSHing, while wearing the EEG Headset, the system will compare this signal with the stored signal. If the signal matches then the command will be triggered. The triggered command will be captured by the Cortex server and streamed to the data stream as a message. The EFM will then receive the message and convert it into a signal to trigger the event in the game to move the car forward. For this game, only two mental commands are used which are the PUSH command

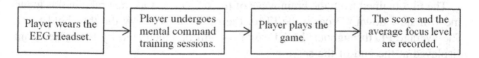

FIGURE 13.4   The flow of the NF session.

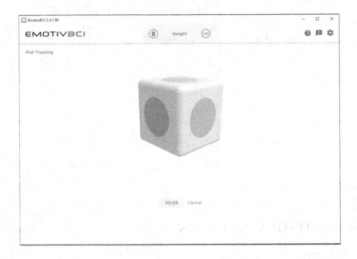

FIGURE 13.5   Mental command training session with EMOTIV BCI.

and the PULL command as mentioned in the Table 13.2. The PUSH command is associated with the forward action of the car while the PULL command is associated with the backward movement of the car. The steering of the car is controlled by the head position of the player. If the player tilts the head towards the left, the car will turn left and if the player tilts the head towards RIGHT then car will turn right. The steering control makes use of the magnetometer in the EEG headset to obtain the current position of the player's head.

13.3.3   NEUROFEEDBACK SESSIONS THROUGH GAME PLAYING

During the actual NF training sessions, the subjects drive the car with their brain waves in the Sprint and Drift stages. Every subject played three sessions each for both stages for three consecutive days. In every session the subjects completed three laps, thus a total of nine laps for each stage. The shortest time taken to complete a lap out of three laps will be recorded and the score of the subject will be computed according to the recorded time at the end of the session. The speed of the car is controlled by the FL of the subject obtained by the brain wave data of the subject during game play. If the FL of the subject is high, the speed of the car will also be high and, hence, it will take a short time to complete a lap. A shorter time will give rise to a higher score and, thus, the score can be used to represent and measure the FL of the subject.

The FL obtained from the brain wave of the subject acts as the brake in this game and will slow down the car if the FL of the player falls below the threshold level. The average FL throughout the NF sessions will be calculated by the system and displayed at the end of the session.

13.4   RESULTS AND DISCUSSION

In this section we will discuss the performance of the subjects in terms of their scores and FL obtained. It is observed that all subjects performance in terms of scores, and the FL has been enhanced across the three sessions in both Sprint and Drift stages. Tables 13.4 and 13.5 and Figures 13.6 and 13.7 show the scores and FL of the subjects in the Sprint and Drift Track stage, respectively. It is observed that the average overall score in the Sprint stage is higher than the Drift stage, as Sprint stage is easy to maneuver. The game play mechanics in the Sprint Track stage is much simpler than the Drift Track stage. The player only needs to move the car forward in the Sprint Track stage while the player needs to control the steering of the car by tilting the head in the Drift Track stage, as well as moving the car forward. This brings to the second observation that the overall average FL achieved in the Sprint stage is much less than the Drift stage, as in Drift stage the subjects have to focus more to achieve a similar score as in the Sprint stage as the difficulty of the level is higher. Average difference in scores and FL for the Drift stage is higher than the Sprint stage, which shows that higher the difficulty level in a NF session better will be the improvement achieved. It can be said that, the higher the difficulty of a stage, the higher the FLs of the players.

13.4.1   EFFECT OF AGE OF THE PARTICIPANTS

It is also observed from Tables 13.3 and 13.4 that the scores and FL are inversely proportional to the age of the participants; as the age increases, the scores and FL decrease for both male and female participants as clearly shown in the Figures 13.8 and 13.9.

Hence, to increase the performance of the older adults, they were asked to train themselves so their FL increases by 10%. The four subjects (age above 40 years, 2 males and 2 females) were asked to go through the same NF training sessions daily until their FL is improved by at least 10%. Table 13.6 shows the days taken to improve the FL by 10%. Again, these results show that for older adults more NF sessions are required to increase the FL to a desired value. But the positive aspect is that they are able to achieve the target although in more sessions.

Lastly from Figures 13.10 and 13.11, it can be seen that the score and FL differences across sessions decrease with the increase in the age of the participants. The score differences and the FLs differences are obtained by using the score and FLs of the third NF session minus the score and the FLs of the first NF session in Tables 13.4 and 13.5. The results may indicate that the effectiveness of the NF session decreases with the increase in the age of participants.

13.4.2   EFFECT OF GENDER OF THE PARTICIPANTS

Table 13.7 gives a comparison of the effect of gender on scores and FL in the Sprint and Drift stages. It is observed that the scores and FL of males are better than females. However, another important observation is that females maintain their scores in both stages and the FL slightly increased in the Drift stage. This is in

TABLE 13.4

The scores and FL of the subjects in the Sprint track

Subject	Age	Gender	Score			Score Average	Score Difference (3-1)	FL			FL Average	FL Difference (3-1)
			1	2	3			1	2	3		
A	16	F	76	89	90	85	14	69	72	85	76	16
B	21	F	60	65	69	65	9	60	81	85	76	25
C	33	F	32	36	37	35	5	25	30	31	29	6
D	52	F	25	29	26	27	1	20	25	23	23	3
E	60	F	20	22	21	21	1	15	20	19	18	4
F	15	M	75	82	92	83	17	60	72	74	69	14
G	20	M	70	82	82	78	12	67	69	75	71	8
H	28	M	55	56	64	59	9	48	52	53	51	5
I	45	M	30	39	35	35	5	27	29	30	29	3
J	78	M	25	26	27	26	2	20	18	21	20	1
Overall Average						51	7.5				46	8.5

TABLE 13.5
The scores and FL of the subjects in the Drift track

Subject	Age	Gender	Score			Score Average	Score Difference (3-1)	FL			FL Average	FL Difference (3-1)
			1	2	3			1	2	3		
A	16	F	65	79	81	75	16	70	78	89	79	19
B	21	F	72	86	94	84	22	65	89	95	83	30
C	33	F	29	30	38	33	9	33	36	45	38	12
D	52	F	23	21	26	24	3	26	27	30	28	4
E	60	F	15	16	16	16	1	16	19	20	19	4
F	15	M	70	79	92	81	22	80	82	96	86	16
G	20	M	65	71	82	73	17	80	80	91	84	11
H	28	M	37	46	50	45	13	60	65	66	64	6
I	45	M	25	28	31	28	6	45	48	49	48	4
J	78	M	27	26	28	27	1	26	25	27	26	1
Overall Average						49	11				56	10.7

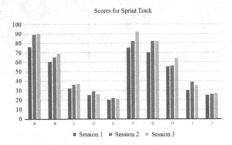
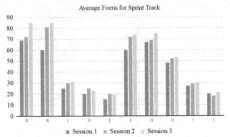

FIGURE 13.6   Scores and FL for Sprint track.

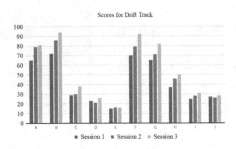
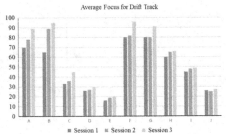

FIGURE 13.7   Scores and FL for Drift track.

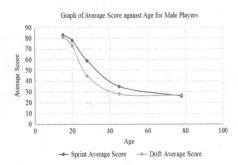
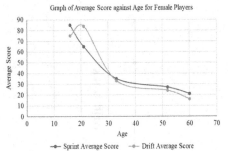

FIGURE 13.8   Average score versus age for male and female participants.

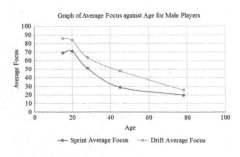
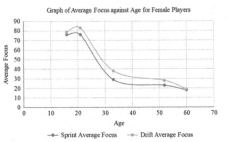

FIGURE 13.9   Average FL versus age for male and female participants.

TABLE 13.6
Improvement in FL by 10%

Person	Age	Gender	Days Taken
D	52	F	3
E	60	F	5
I	45	M	4
J	78	M	6

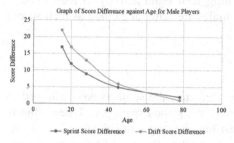 

FIGURE 13.10   Score difference versus age for male and female participants.

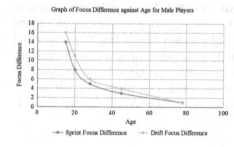 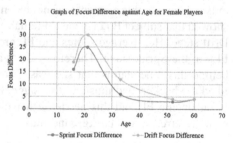

FIGURE 13.11   Focus difference versus age for male and female participants.

TABLE 13.7
The scores and FL of the subjects in the Sprint track stage

Gender	Sprint stage Score/score difference	FL/FL difference	Drift stage Score/score difference	FL/FL difference
Females average	46.6/6	44.4/10.8	46.4/10.2	49.4/13.8
Males average	56.2/9	48.0/6.2	50.8/11.8	61.6/7.6

contrary with the male performance, which shows that with increase in difficulty level their score decreased, whereas their FL increased much higher as compared to the females. This may be due to the reason that with higher difficulty levels, males have to focus more than females.

It is also observed that the core and FL difference improves in both genders from the Sprint to Drift stage. However, if we compare males with females, improvement in FL across sessions is more achieved in females as compared to male participants, while males are better in getting higher score difference across sessions.

Figures 13.10 and 13.11 show the scores and FL differences across sessions versus age for male and female participants. As expected, the scores and FL differences increase from the Sprint to Drift stage in all cases. From these figures it is observed that females are better in retraining their brain activity as their FL difference is higher than the males; although males are better at gaming as their scores and score differences are better.

13.4.3 EFFECT OF GAME ELEMENTS

In order to investigate the effect of game elements, the subjects were allowed to choose the color of the car to further improve the game experience. Three subjects played the game with their favorite and least favorite choice of car color. The results are shown in the Table 13.8. It can be seen that color effects the FLs of the players, as the scores and FL show a significant increase for favorite car color.

Another game element that affected the results was the presence of background music, however this element was not extensively tested. The investigation of results showed that subject B (21-year old female) has shown very good performance in the Drift stage. Her average scores and FL are significantly higher than her scores and FLs in the Sprint stage. Therefore, she was interviewed to investigate the reasons behind this. She claims that she was more focused in the Drift Track because she liked the background music in this stage. Hence, music may play an important role in enhancing FL and this needs further investigation, as none of the other participants referred to the background music.

TABLE 13.8
The score and FL of the players for cars of different colors

| | | Session | | | | | |
| | | Fav. Color | | Least Fav. Color | | Difference | |
`Subject	Age	Score	FL	Score	FL	Score	FL
1	24	70	67	65	60	−5	−7
2	24	65	59	66	60	+1	+1
3	24	81	71	62	57	−19	−14
Average		72	66	64	59		

From these results we conclude that NF training has a positive effect and can improve the FL of the participants. However, the number of sessions required by the participants may vary depending on the gender and age of the participants. In addition, adding game elements like color and music may further enhance the FL. Based on this pilot study, we can say that EEG-based NF training/therapy may be considered as a promising candidate for improving the FL of subjects in a wide age group ranging from teen agers to older adults around 80 years of age. However, the number of sessions required will vary for different age groups.

13.5 CONCLUSION AND FUTURE RECOMMENDATIONS

This chapter proposes a neurofeedback car racing game-based intervention for enhancing FL of participants belonging to agerange from 15 to 78 years. In this pilot study, the experimental analysis of ten healthy subjects was performed. The results show significant improvement in game scores and FL. More extensive analysis with a bigger sample size in every age group is required to explore the effectiveness of this intervention.

From the experiments we have come to a few conclusions. First, the FL of the subjects improves as the difficulty of the game increases. Second, the FL of the subjects is highly dependent on the age of the subjects, i.e., FL is inversely proportional to the age of the participants, as the age increases, FL decreases. The effectiveness of the NF sessions also decreases with the increase in the age of the participant. Hence, more NF sessions will be required by older participants. Third, game elements such as color of the car and music may affect the FL of the players positively. However, more extensive experiments with bigger sample sizes are needed to establish the impact of these elements.

There are some weaknesses in the study. First of all, the EMOTIV Insight headset requires a very stable and high-speed internet for streaming the recorded EEG signals to the Cortex derver via the internet for processing. The latency of the network will also affect the accuracy of the data because the main game module (MGM) and the emotive framework module (EFM), which is responsible for handling the received message from the Cortex server, is running concurrently. If the signal from the EEG headset lags behind the game loop, the data recorded will be inaccurate. Second, the sample size in this experiment is small because of the constraints of social distancing due to Covid-19. The equipment needs through cleaning between sessions so it was not possible to gather data from many participants. In addition, it was also not easy to hire participants under the current social scenario. In spite of small sample size, this pilot study shows promising results, and we plan to elaborate this study in the future for the health and well-being of the community.

ACKNOWLEDGMENT

This work is financially supported by Universiti Tunku Abdul Rahman Research Fund (UTARRF) Grant No. IPSR/RMC/UTARRF/2020-C2/H01 and Excellent Research Centre Award Fund, Centre for Healthcare, Science and Technology, Universiti Tunku Abdul Rahman, Malaysia.

REFERENCES

1. Reis, J., Portugal, A.M., Fernandes, L., Afonso, N., Pereira, M., Sousa, N. and Dias, N.S. An alpha and theta intensive and short neurofeedback protocol for healthy aging working-memory training. *Frontiers in Aging Neuroscience* 8 (2016): 157.
2. Scott, S.B., Graham-Engeland, J.E., Engeland, C.G., Smyth, J.M., Almeida, D.M., Katz, M.J., Lipton, R.B., Mogle, J.A., Munoz, E., Ram, N. and Sliwinski, M.J. The effects of stress on cognitive aging, physiology and emotion (ESCAPE) project. *BMC Psychiatry* 15, 1 (2015): 1–14.
3. Nisar, H., Ho, Y.K., Kamel, N. and Malik, A.S. Introduction to EEG and ERP signals. *EEG/ERP Analysis: Methods and Applications* (2014): 12–20. DOI: 10.1201/B17605.
4. Billeci, L., Sicca, F., Maharatna, K., Apicella, F., Narzisi, A., Campatelli, G., Calderoni, S., Pioggia, G. and Muratori, F. On the application of quantitative EEG for characterizing autistic brain: a systematic review. *Frontiers in Human Neuroscience* 7 (2013): 442.
5. Nawaz, Rab, Jian Tong Ng, Humaira Nisar, and Yap Vooi Voon. "Can background music help to relieve stress? An EEG analysis." In *2019 IEEE International Conference on Signal and Image Processing Applications (ICSIPA)*, pp. 68–72. IEEE, 2019.
6. Psychology Today, 2020. Therapeutic Intervention. https://www.psychologytoday.com/intl/therapy-types/therapeutic-intervention
7. Johnstone, S.J., Roodenrys, S.J., Johnson, K., Bonfield, R. and Bennett, S.J. Game-based combined cognitive and neurofeedback training using Focus Pocus reduces symptom severity in children with diagnosed AD/HD and subclinical AD/HD. *International Journal of Psychophysiology* 116 (2017): 32–44.
8. Coben, R., Linden, M. and Myers, T.E. Neurofeedback for autistic spectrum disorder: a review of the literature. *Applied Psychophysiology and Biofeedback* 35, 1 (2010): 83.
9. Hammond, D.C. Neurofeedback treatment of depression and anxiety. *Journal of Adult Development* 12, 2–3 (2005): 131–137.
10. Nawaz, R., Nisar, H. and Voon, Y.V. The effect of music on human brain; frequency domain and time series analysis using electroencephalogram. *IEEE Access* 6 (2018): 45191–45205.
11. Nawaz, R., Ng, J.T., Nisar, H. and Voon, Y.V. Can background music help to relieve stress? An EEG analysis. In *2019 IEEE International Conference on Signal and Image Processing Applications (ICSIPA)* (pp. 68–72). IEEE, 2019 September.
12. Egner, T. and Sterman, M.B. Neurofeedback treatment of epilepsy: from basic rationale to practical application. *Expert Review of Neurotherapeutics* 6, 2 (2006): 247–257.
13. Robbins, Erin Paige. "Effects of neurofeedback therapy on patients with traumatic brain injuries." (2017).
14. Fisher, Sebern F. "Neurofeedback and developmental trauma: a personal story." *Neurofeedback: The First Fifty Years* (2019).
15. Gapen, Mark, Bessel A. van der Kolk, Ed Hamlin, Laurence Hirshberg, Michael Suvak, and Joseph Spinazzola. "A pilot study of neurofeedback for chronic PTSD." *Applied Psychophysiology and Biofeedback* 41, 3 (2016): 251–261.
16. Cortoos, Aisha, Elke De Valck, Martijn Arns, Marinus H.M. Breteler, and Raymond Cluydts. "An exploratory study on the effects of tele-neurofeedback and tele-biofeedback on objective and subjective sleep in patients with primary insomnia." *Applied Psychophysiology and Biofeedback* 35, 2 (2010): 125–134.
17. Nisar, Humaira, Hong-Way Khow, and Kim Ho Yeap. "Brain-computer interface: controlling a robotic arm using facial expressions." *Turkish Journal of Electrical Engineering & Computer Sciences* 26, 2 (2018): 707–720.
18. Lecomte Gael, Juhel, Jacques. "The effects of neurofeedback training on memory performance in elderly subjects." *Psychology* 2, 08 (2011): 846.

19. Marzbani, H., H. Marateb, and M. Mansourian. "Methodological note: neu-rofeedback: a comprehensive review on system design, methodology and clinical applications." *Basic and Clinical Neuroscience* 7, 2 (2016): 143–158. DOI: 10.15412/J.BCN.03070208.

20. Dempster, Tammy. "An investigation into the optimum training paradigm for alpha electroencephalographic biofeedback." PhD diss., Canterbury Christ Church University, 2012.

21. Klimesch, W., Schack, B. and Sauseng, P. The functional significance of theta and upper alpha oscillations. *Experimental Psychology* 52, 2 (2005): 99–108.

22. Zoefel, B., Huster, R.J. and Herrmann, C.S. Neurofeedback training of the upper alpha frequency band in EEG improves cognitive performance. *Neuroimage* 54, 2 (2011): 1427–1431.

23. Cheah, Kit Hwa, Humaira Nisar, Vooi Voon Yap, and Chen-Yi Lee. "Convolutional neural networks for classification of music-listening EEG: Comparing 1D convolutional kernels with 2D kernels and cerebral laterality of musical influence." *Neural Computing and Applications* 32, 13 (2020): 8867–8891.

24. Ferreira-Brito, F., Fialho, M., Virgolino, A., Neves, I., Miranda, A.C., Sousa-Santos, N., Caneiras, C., Carriço, L., Verdelho, A. and Santos, O. Game-based interventions for neuropsychological assessment, training and rehabilitation: Which game-elements to use? A systematic review. *Journal of Biomedical Informatics* 98 (2019): 103287.

25. Lumsden, J., Edwards, E.A., Lawrence, N.S., Coyle, D. and Munafò, M.R. Gamification of cognitive assessment and cognitive training: a systematic review of applications and efficacy. *JMIR Serious Games* 4, 2 (2016): e11.

26. Liao, Lun-De, Chen, Chi-Yu, Wang, I-Jan, Chen, Sheng-Fu, Li, Shih-Yu, Chen, Bo Wei, Chang, Jyh-Yeong & Lin, Chin-Teng. Gaming control using a wearable and wireless EEG-based brain-computer interface device with novel dry foam-based sensors. *Journal of Neuroengineering and Rehabilitation*, [e-journal] 9, 5 (2012). https://doi.org/10.1186/1743-0003-9-5.

27. Shenjie, Sun, Kavitha P. Thomas, and A.P. Vinod. "Two player EEG-based neuro-feedback ball game for attention enhancement." In *2014 IEEE International Conference on Systems, Man, And Cybernetics (SMC)*, pp. 3150–3155. IEEE, 2014.

28. Thomas, K.P., Vinod, A.P. and Guan, C. Design of an online EEG based neurofeed-back game for enhancing attention and memory. In *2013 35th Annual International Conference of the IEEE Engineering in Medicine and Biology Society (EMBC)* (pp. 433–436). IEEE, 2013, July.

29. EMOTIV, 2020. Insight Brainwear® 5 Channel Wireless EEG Headset https://www.emotiv.com/insight/

30. https://www.emotiv.com/comparison/

31. https://unity.com

32. Nisar, Humaira, Hari Chand Balasubramaniam, and Aamir Saeed Malik. "Brain computer interface for operating a robot." In *AIP Conference Proceedings*, 1559, 1, pp. 37–46. American Institute of Physics, 2013.

33. Nisar, H., Q. W. Yeoh, H. C. Balasubramanium, W. T. Wei, and Aamir Saeed Malik. "Analysis of brain activity while performing cognitive actions to control a car." In *The 15th International Conference on Biomedical Engineering*, pp. 947–950. Springer, Cham, 2014.

14 Detecting K-Complexes in Brain Signals Using WSST2-DETOKS

Zahra Ghanbari and Mohammad Hassan Moradi

14.1 INTRODUCTION

Quality of sleep can affect mental and physical performance directly. Appropriate sleep can provide proper learning, memory consolidation, and insight formation [1-3]. Regarding physical performance, ingesting too many calories in people with poor sleep quality is reported [4]. Insufficient sleep, insomnia, and other sleep disorders are considerable problems of our stressful lifestyles [5]. Polysomnography (PSG) is used for the purpose of studying the quality of sleep and diagnosing sleep disorders. Polysomnography is composed of several parameters. In its simplest form, it consists of an electroencephalogram (EEG), electrooculogram (EOG), and electromyogram (EMG) [6]. Studying the aforementioned signals, especially EEG, provides worthy insights into micro- and macrostructures of sleep. Macrostructures of sleep include five major stages: W, N-1, N-2, N-3, and REM (rapid eye movement) [7]. Relaxed wakefulness, stage W, is called the period of pre-sleep drowsiness. At light sleep in stage N-1, slow eye movements can be detected as well as brain waves of mixed frequencies with low amplitudes. While the body prepares for deep sleep, stage N-2 starts; it comes after stage N-1. At stage N-2 eye movements stop. Moreover, brain waves are slowing down and represent occasional bursts of rapid brain waves. Deep sleep, stage N-3, is accompanied by tremendously slow brain waves. Moreover, in this stage, slower, deeper, more rhythmic breathing is observed in addition to the absence of muscle activity. In addition to the above stages, we have REM stage. Eyes move in various directions rapidly, muscles become temporarily paralyzed, and the breathing increases [7].

Despite macrostructures, sleep microstructure is associated with the mixture of background oscillatory activity and transient events in EEG. Actually, six waveforms in EEG are of great importance: theta rhythms, alpha rhythms, sleep spindle, K-complex, slow wave activity, and tooth waves.

K-complex is one of the most underlying micro-events in the sleep EEG, which was introduced around 80 years ago. It is known as the largest grapho-element in the EEG signal. K-complex, according to the American Academy of Sleep Medicine (AASM) is a "well delineated negative sharp wave immediately followed by a positive component standing out from the background EEG, with total duration

≥500 ms, usually maximal in amplitude over the frontal regions" [8]. A duration of 500 ms to 1,500 ms is usually considered for K-complex patterns. However, a maximum duration of 1,000 ms to 3,000 ms is imposed for it. The K-complex pattern has a crucial role in scoring sleep stages. Moreover, it has a sleep protection role; i.e., preventing brain form awaking in response to sensory inputs recognized harmless, while sleeping. In addition, K-complex serves as a predecessor of the slow wave activity which has a reactive homeostatic function in the brain. From a practical perspective, K-complex is important in studying the functional role of sleep as well as diagnosing sleep disorders. In addition, K-complex alongside sleep spindle are hallmarks in the second stage of the nonrapid eye movement (NREM) sleep [9,10]. Therefore, precise identification of K-complexes is essential for reliable projection of the sleep macrostructure and then for the analysis of sleep quality.

Studying K-complex is of great importance both in children and adult sleep studies. Moreover, it is important in diagnosing cognitive and neuro-physiologic disorders. Thus, reliable methods for detection and analysis of K-complex are essential for both research and clinical applications [11,12]. Correlations between some sleep disorders including apnea, insomnia, and the number of K-complexes are reported [13]. As K-complex and slow wave activity share similarities, it is crucial in memory consolidation [14].

K-complex is a much studied topic in current sleep medicine and neuroscience. Many efforts have been made to decode information embedded in this pattern and its relation to diverse sleep disorders [15]. Many methods are used in automatic detection and classification of the K-complex pattern. In a classification problem, the EEG signal is segmented into fixed-length parts, and what should be done is to determine whether each segment contains the K-complex or not. Approaches include the support vector machine, neural networks, and logistic regression [9,16] are used. For the detection purpose, however, an EEG signal is used in its unsegmented form. The output will be a set of segments detected as K-complexes. Obtained segments are of different lengths. Methods used for detection include: likelihood threshold [17], wavelet transform [18,19], a combination of wavelet transform and Teager energy operator [20], a combination of morphological analysis and tunable Q-factor wavelet transform [12], short term event extraction based on non-linear filtering [21], switching multiple models [22], a combination of singular value decomposition (SVD), variation mode decomposition and discrete wavelet transform [23], deep, and fuzzy neural networks [24], and the multi-taper-based method [10]. Parekh et al. have proposed a nonlinear model for EEG signal which models EEG as a transient, a low frequency, and an oscillatory component. These components are estimated using a fast nonlinear optimization algorithm. The low frequency component is used to detect K-complex. The approach is called detection of K-complexes and sleep spindles (DETOKS) [25]. In our previous work, we proposed using a synchro-squeezing wavelet transform for K-complex detection. A synchro-squeezing wavelet transform is an empirical mode decomposition (EMD) approach that is a combination of wavelet transform and reallocation approaches [26]. It was used in biomedical applications previously [27]. We proposed a modified version of DETOKS. In our proposed method, DETOKS is enriched using synchro-squeezing wavelet transform, which results in superior performance [28,29]. In this chapter, we are going to modify our proposed method by using second-order synchro-squeezing wavelet transform, proposed by Pham and Meignen in 2018 [30].

The rest of this chapter is organized as follows: synchro-squeezed wavelet transform is discussed in Section 14.2. Section 14.3 is dedicated to second order wavelet based SST (WSST2). In Section 14.4, DETOKS is introduced briefly. Our proposed method for K-complex detection (WSST2-DETOKS) is illustrated in Section 14.5. Section 14.6 is concentrated on the data which is used in this study. Moreover, it contains our proposed scoring method in the case of the existence of different annotations made by two experts. Results are reported in Section 14.7. Finally, Section 14.8 is dedicated to the conclusion.

14.2   SYNCHRO-SQUEEZED WAVELET TRANSFORM

Synchro-squeezed wavelet transform was proposed in 2011 by Daubechies et al. [26]. Synchro-squeezing can be considered as a special case of re-allocation approaches. Given a time-frequency map, $R(t, \omega)$, re-allocation methods try to sharpen it via allocating its values to a different set of points, $R(t', \omega')$. Such an allocation is specified by the local behavior of $R(t, \omega)$ around point (t, ω). In the following, synchro-squeezing is explained. For a given signal, s, continuous wavelet transform is defined as:

$$W_s = \int s(t) a^{-\frac{1}{2}} \overline{\psi\left(\frac{t-b}{a}\right)} dt \qquad (14.1)$$

where ψ is a wavelet chosen approximately. It reallocates $W_s(a, b)$ so that a concentrated time-frequency representation can be obtained. Then, instantaneous frequency lines can be extracted.

The wavelet-based synchro-squeezing transform (WSST) was primarily introduced for auditory signals analysis [31]. Signals that comprise constituent components, which have time-varying oscillatory characteristics, can be written as:

$$s(t) = \sum_{k=1}^{K} s_k(t) \qquad (14.2)$$

where $s_k(t)$ is a Fourier-like oscillatory component. It is a mono-component asymptotic $AM - FM$ signal and

$$s_k(t) = A_k(t)\cos(\varphi_k(t)) \qquad (14.3)$$

where $A_k(t)$ stands for the instantaneous amplitude and $\varphi_k(t)$ represents the instantaneous phase. Therefore, the instantaneous frequency is:

$$f_{inst}(t) = d\varphi_k(t)/dt \qquad (14.4)$$

One may summarize computing WSST in the following steps:

1. Calculating the complex continuous wavelet transform (CWT). For a given $s(t)$, CWT is defined as follows:

$$W_s(a, b) = \int s(t) a^{-\frac{1}{2}} \overline{\psi\left(\frac{t-b}{a}\right)} d \tag{14.5}$$

The mother wavelet, ψ, should satisfy the following condition for any ξ value:

$$\int_0^\infty \frac{1}{\xi} |\psi(\xi)|^2 d\xi < \infty \tag{14.6}$$

If the condition $\hat{\psi}(\xi)$ holds for $\xi < 0$, $\psi(\xi)$ is analytic. $\psi(t)$ can be defined as:

$$\psi(t) = g(t) e^{j\omega_0 t} \tag{14.7}$$

where ω_0 represents the central angular frequency of the wavelet, and $g(t)$ stands for the window function. Wavelet ridge is defined as:

$$P = \{(a_r, b) \in \mathbb{R}^2; M_s(a_r, b)\} = \max(|W_s(a_i, b)|) \tag{14.8}$$

where (a_r, b) and $|W_s(a_i, b)|$ are the ridge points at b and the wavelet coefficient modulus, respectively. Since in real applications the analytic form of the signal is rarely available, the extracted ridge is used to calculate instantaneous frequency of the signal:

$$f_{inst}(t) = \frac{\omega_0}{2\pi a_r(t)} \tag{14.9}$$

The instantaneous amplitude is calculated in the similar manner as:

$$A_{inst}(t) \approx \frac{2|W_s(a_r(t), t|}{|\hat{g}(0)|(a_r(t))^{\frac{1}{2}}} \tag{14.10}$$

where $\hat{g}(0)$ stands for the Fourier transform of $g(t)$ at $\omega = 0$.
WSST is aimed to address the issue of blurring in time-frequency maps. Denoting $f_{inst}(t)$ by f and $A_{inst}(t)$ by A:

$$W_s(a, b) = \frac{1}{a^{\frac{1}{2}}} \int s(\xi) \hat{\psi}(a\xi) e^{ib\xi} d\xi = \frac{A}{2\sqrt{a}} \hat{\psi}(af) e^{ibf} \tag{14.11}$$

$\hat{\psi}(\xi)$ is concentrated around $\xi = f_0$. Consequently, $W_s(a, b)$ should be concentrated around $a = \omega_0/\omega$, whereas $W_s(a, b)$ usually spreads out over a region around $a = f_0/f$. At b, regardless of values, $W_s(a, b)$ represents an oscillatory behavior with original frequency, f.

2. An initial estimation of the phase transform corresponding to each (a,b) is made as:

$$f_{inst}(a, b) = \frac{i}{W_s(a, b)} \partial W_s(a, b)/\partial b \qquad (14.12)$$

where $W_s(a, b) \neq 0$. Such a formulation will cancel out the impact of wavelet on W_s.

3. Reassignment of $W_s(a,b)$ results in the WSST which is calculated as:

$$S_{s,\bar{\varepsilon}}^{\alpha}(b, \omega) = \int_{A_{\bar{\varepsilon}, s}(b)} \alpha^{-1} W_s(a, b) h\left(\frac{\omega - \omega_s(a, b)}{\alpha}\right) a^{\frac{3}{2}} da \qquad (14.13)$$

where α is the accuracy value and $\bar{\varepsilon}$ represents the threshold, h is the smoothing function. and $A_{\bar{\varepsilon}, s}(b) = \{a; |W_s(a, b)| > \bar{\varepsilon}\}$

Scaling variables, a, b, and frequency, f, are discrete values. Therefore, $W_s(a, b)$ is just calculated in discrete values. $(b, a) \rightarrow (b, f_{inst}(a, b))$ is a mapping from time domain to the time-frequency domain. According to this mapping the synchro-squeezing transform, $S(f, b)$, is just computed at the center of the successive bins:

$$[f_l - 0.5(f_l - f_{l-1}), f_l + 0.5(f_l - f_{l-1})] \qquad (14.14)$$

Therefore, synchro-squeezing transform is defined as [26]:

$$S(f_l, b) = \frac{1}{\Delta f} \sum_{a_k: |f_s(a_k, b) - f_l| \leq \frac{\Delta f}{2}} W_s(a_k, b) a_k^{-\frac{3}{2}} (\Delta a)_k \qquad (14.15)$$

It is proven that WSST possesses the perfect concentration property via:

$$\int_0^\infty W_s(a, b) a^{-\frac{3}{2}} da = \frac{1}{2\pi} \int_{-\infty}^\infty \int_0^\infty \hat{s}(\xi) \overline{\hat{\phi}(a\xi)} e^{ib\xi}/a \, da d\xi$$

$$= \frac{1}{2\pi} \int_0^\infty \int_0^\infty \hat{s}(\xi) \overline{\hat{\phi}(a\xi)} e^{ib\xi}/a \, da d\xi \qquad (14.16)$$

14.3   SECOND-ORDER WAVELET-BASED SST

Wavelet-based SST (WSST) is proven as an effective approach to improve time-frequency representation. However, it is only applicable to a class of multi-component signals composed of slightly perturbed purely harmonic modes. An extension of WSST is proposed to address this issue. It is denoted as second order wavelet-based synchro-squeezing transform (WSST2). The WSST2 works based on a more accurate IF estimation [32]. First of all, we need to define a second order local modulation operator. Second, it will be used to calculate IF estimate. The mentioned modulation operator is corresponding to the first order derivatives (with respect to t) of the reassignment operators.

Assuming a signal $s \in L^\infty(\mathbb{R})$, the complex reassignment operators for any (t, a) are defined as:

$$\tilde{\omega}_f(t, a) = \frac{1}{2\pi i} \frac{\partial_t W_s^\psi(t, a)}{W_s^\psi(t, a)} \tag{14.17}$$

$$\tilde{\tau}_s(t, a) = \frac{\int_{\mathbb{R}} \tau s(\tau) a^{-1} \overline{\psi\left(\frac{\tau - t}{a}\right)} d\tau}{W_s^\psi(t, a)} = t + a \frac{W_s^{t\psi}(t, a)}{W_s^\psi(t, a)} \tag{14.18}$$

where $W_s^\psi(t, a) \neq 0$. The above operators are defined so that $t\psi \in L^1(\mathbb{R})$, and $\psi' \in L^1(\mathbb{R})$. Therefore, the second-order local complex modulation operator is defined as:

$$\tilde{q}_{t,s}(t, a) = \frac{\partial_t \tilde{\omega}_s(t, a)}{\partial_t \tilde{\tau}_s(t, a)} \tag{14.19}$$

where $\partial_t \tilde{\tau}_s(t, a) \neq 0$.

Another second order local modulation operator can be calculated based on partial derivatives with respect to a rather than t:

$$\tilde{q}_{a,s}(t, a) = \frac{\partial_a \tilde{\omega}_s(t, a)}{\partial_a \tilde{\tau}_s(t, a)} \tag{14.20}$$

$\tilde{q}_{a,s}(t, a)$ shares the same properties with $\tilde{q}_{t,s}(t, a)$. As a result, the improved IF estimate corresponding to the time-frequency representation of $s \in L^\infty(\mathbb{R})$ is

$$Re\{\tilde{\omega}_s^{[2]}(t, a)\} \tag{14.21}$$

which is the real part of $\tilde{\omega}_s^{[2]}(t, a)$, where:

$$\tilde{\omega}_s^{[2]}(t, a) = \begin{cases} \tilde{\omega}_s(t, a) + \tilde{q}_{t,s}(t, a)(t - \tilde{\tau}_s(t, a)) & \text{if } \partial_t \tilde{\tau}_s(t, a) \neq 0 \\ \tilde{\omega}_s(t, a) & \text{otherwise} \end{cases} \tag{14.22}$$

In [32] it is shown that in s being a Gaussian modulated linear chirp as $s(t) = A(t)e^{i2\pi\varphi(t)}$, where $\log A(t)$ and $\varphi(t)$ are both quadratic, $Re\{\tilde{\omega}_s^{[2]}(t, a)\}$ is an exact estimate of $\frac{d\varphi(t)}{dt}$. One can estimate instantaneous frequency corresponding to a more general mode with Gaussian amplitude using $Re\{\tilde{\omega}_s^{[2]}(t, a)\}$. In this case the estimation error just involves the phase derivatives of orders more than 3.

For a given $s \in L^\infty(\mathbb{R})$, can be calculated using just five CWTs as:

$$\tilde{\omega}_s(t, a) = -\frac{1}{i2\pi a} \frac{W_s^{\psi'}(t, a)}{W_s^{\psi}(t, a)} \tag{14.23}$$

Similarly, for $\tilde{q}_{t,f}(t, a)$ we have:

$$\tilde{q}_{t,f}(t, a) = \frac{1}{i2\pi a^2} \frac{W_s^{\psi''}(t, a)W_s^{\psi}(t, a) - W_s^{\psi'}(t, a)^2}{W_s^{t\psi}(t, a)W_s^{\psi''}(t, a) - W_s^{t\psi'}(t, a)W_s^{\psi'}(t, a)} \tag{14.24}$$

where $t \to W^{\psi'}$, $W^{t\psi}$, $W^{\psi''}$, $W^{t\psi'}$ are CWTs corresponding to s obtained in $L^1(\mathbb{R})$, using wavelets ψ', $t\psi$, ψ', $t\psi'$, respectively. The above formulation can be easily derived from:

$$\partial_t^p W_s^{\psi}(t, a) = (-a)^{-p} W_s^{\psi^p}(t, a) \tag{14.25}$$

WSST2, as the second-order WSST is obtained via replacing $\tilde{\omega}_s(t, a)$ with $\hat{\omega}_s^{[2]}(t, a)$ in [33]:

$$S_{2, W_s^{\psi}}^{\gamma}(t, \omega): = \int_{\left|W_s^{\psi}(t,a)\right|>\gamma} W_s^{\psi}(t, a)\delta(\omega - \hat{\omega}_s^{[2]}(t, a))da/a \tag{14.26}$$

Finally, s_k is retrieved via replacing $S_{W_s^{\psi}}^{\gamma}(t, \omega)$ by $S_{2, W_s^{\psi}}^{\gamma}(t, \omega)$ in [34].

14.3.1 NUMERICAL IMPLEMENTATION OF WSST2

Numerical implementation of WSST2 will be discussed in this section. Signal s is uniformly discretized in [0,1], at values $t_m = m/n$ with $m = 0, ..., n-1$, and $n = 2^L$, $L \in \mathbb{N}$. First of all, W_s^{ψ} is discretized at points $\left(\frac{m}{n}, a_j\right)$, where $a_j = \frac{1}{n}2^{\frac{j}{n_v}}, j = 0, ...,Ln_v$. n_v is the so-called voice number. It is a user-defined controlling parameter which manages the number of scales. In [30], 32 and 64 are proposed values for n_v. Corresponding to s, the discrete wavelet transform (DWT) in the Fourier domain is defined as:

$$W_s^{\psi}(t_m, a_j) \approx W_{d,s}^{\hat{\psi}}(m, j): =\left(\mathcal{F}_d^{-1}((\mathcal{F}_d(s) \odot \overline{\hat{\psi}_{j,.}}))\right)_m$$

where $\mathcal{F}_d(s)$ is the standard discrete Fourier transform (DFT), and $\mathcal{F}_d^{-1}(s)$ denotes the inverse of $\mathcal{F}_d(s)$, i.e., iDFT. $\hat{\psi}_{j,q} = \hat{\psi}(a_j q)$, $q = 0, 1, ..., n-1$. stands for the element-wise multiplication. The complex estimate of the second order modulation operator, $\tilde{q}_{t,s}$, is calculated as [35]:

$$\tilde{q}_{d,t,s}(m, j) = \frac{i2\pi \left(W_{d,s}^{\hat{\psi}}(m, j)W_{d,s}^{\xi^2\hat{\psi}}(m, j) - (W_{d,s}^{\xi\hat{\psi}}(m, j))^2\right)}{a_j^2 \left[(W_{d,s}^{\hat{\psi}}(m, j))^2 + W_{d,s}^{\hat{\psi}}(m, j)W_{d,s}^{\xi\hat{\psi}'}(m, j) - W_{d,s}^{\hat{\psi}'}(m, j)W_{d,s}^{\xi\hat{\psi}}(m, j)\right]}$$

(14.27)

where $W_{d,s}^{\xi^2\hat{\psi}}$, $W_{d,s}^{\xi\hat{\psi}}$, $W_{d,s}^{\xi\hat{\psi}'}$, $W_{d,s}^{\hat{\psi}'}$ stands for DWTs of s which are calculated based on wavelets $\xi \rightarrow \xi^2\hat{\psi}$, $\xi \rightarrow \xi\hat{\psi}$, $\xi \rightarrow \xi\hat{\psi}'$, and $\xi \rightarrow \hat{\psi}'$, respectively.

Considering the following definitions:

$$\tilde{\omega}_{d,s}(m, j) = \frac{W_{d,s}^{\xi\hat{\psi}}(m, j)}{a_j W_{d,s}^{\hat{\psi}}(m, j)}$$

(14.28)

$$\tilde{\tau}_{d,s}(m, j) = t + \frac{a_j}{i2\pi} \frac{W_{d,s}^{\hat{\psi}'}(m, j)}{W_{d,s}^{\hat{\psi}}(m, j)}$$

(14.29)

a discrete form of a second order complex instantaneous frequency estimate associated with s is computed as follows:

$$\tilde{\omega}_{d,s}^{[2]}(m, j) = \begin{cases} \tilde{\omega}_{d,s}(m, j) + \tilde{q}_{d,t,s}(m, j)(t - \tilde{\tau}_{d,s}(m, j)) & \text{if } \partial_t \tilde{\tau}_{d,s}(m, j) \neq 0 \\ \tilde{\omega}_{d,s}(m, j) & \text{otherwise} \end{cases}$$

(14.30)

where $\partial_t \tilde{\tau}_{d,s}(m, j) = \frac{W_{d,s}^{\hat{\psi}}(m,j)W_{d,s}^{\xi\hat{\psi}'}(m,j) - W_{d,s}^{\hat{\psi}'}(m,j)W_{d,s}^{\xi\hat{\psi}}(m,j) + (W_{d,s}^{\hat{\psi}}(m,j))^2}{W_{d,s}^{\hat{\psi}}(m,j)^2}$. The discrete IF estimate is the real part of $\tilde{\omega}_{d,s}^{[2]}(m, j)$ denoted as:

$$\hat{\omega}_{d,s}^{[2]}(m, j) = Re\{\tilde{\omega}_{d,s}^{[2]}(m, j)\}$$

(14.31)

14.3.2 Computing WSST2

Computing WSST2 is brought up in this section. The first topic which will be discussed is splitting the frequency domain. It should be mentioned that, each scale a_j is equal to the inverse of frequency; $f_j = (a_j)^{-1} = 2^{-\frac{j}{n_v}}n$. Frequency bins associated with the wavelet representation are defined as:

$$W_j = \left[\frac{1}{2}(f_{j+1} + f_j), \frac{1}{2}(f_j, +f_{j-1})\right]$$

(14.32)

where f_{Ln_v} and f_{-1} are considered 0 and ∞, respectively, and $0 \leq j \leq L_{n_v} - 1$. According to this, the second order synchro-squeezing operator is computed as:

$$S^{\gamma}_{d,\,2,\,s}\left(\frac{m}{n}\cdot f_j\right) = \sum_{\mathbb{G}_d(j)} W^{\hat{\psi}}_{d,s}(m,\,l)\frac{log2}{n_v} \tag{14.33}$$

where $\mathbb{G}_d(j) = \{0 \leq l \leq L_{n_v} \ s.\ t.\ \hat{\omega}^{[2]}_{d,s}(m,\,l) \in W_j \ and \ |W^{\hat{\psi}}_{d,s}(m,\,l)| > \gamma\}$
Corresponding to each t_m we have:

$$f_k\left(\frac{m}{n}\right) \approx \frac{1}{C'_{d,\,\psi,k}} \sum_{l\,\in\,\Upsilon_k(m)} S^{\gamma}_{d,\,2,\,s}(m,\,\omega_l) \tag{14.34}$$

where f_k denotes each mode, $C'_{d,\psi,k}$ stands for a discrete approximation of $C'_{\psi,k}$, $\Upsilon_k(m)$ represents a set of measures associated with a narrow frequency band around the ridge curve of the kth mode. For extracting this ridge an approach proposed in [35,36] is used.

It should be emphasized that the accuracy of the set $\Upsilon_k(m)$ is dependent to the frequency of the kth mode.

14.4 DETECTION OF SLEEP SPINDLES AND K-COMPLEXES (DETOKS)

Parekh et al. introduced a nonlinear approach for detecting sleep spindles and K-complexes (DETOKS) in 2015 [25]. In their proposed method, the EEG is modeled as a summation of three components including transient, low frequency, and oscillatory parts that are explained in the following:

1. The transient part is a sparse signal which has a sparse first-order derivative. Therefore, this component should essentially be composed of spikes on a zero base-line.
2. The low frequency part is the low frequency component of EEG.
3. The oscillatory part illustrates the oscillations of EEG which possess a sparse representation in time-frequency plane.

For the purpose of estimating the above components, an optimization problem is proposed. In [25], a convex objective function in addition to a fast algorithm as its solution is proposed. First of all, the above components are estimated. Then, low frequency components are used to detect K-complex patterns. Sleep spindles are detected using oscillatory components. The DETOKS separates the transient part from the two other parts. Therefore, the band-pass filtering with respect to the base-line can reveal the sleep spindle much more prominently. Consequently, DETOKS can provide robust sleep spindle detection using non-linear transient removal.

14.4.1 Sparse Optimization

Consider a noisy mixture of x as follows:

$$y = x + w \tag{14.35}$$

To estimate x which has a sparse or approximately sparse derivative, one minimizes the ℓ_1 norm of Dx subject to a data fidelity constraint [37]. Consequently, x is estimated using an optimization problem:

$$\hat{x} = \underset{x}{argmin}\left\{\frac{1}{2}y - x_2^2 + \lambda D x_1\right\} \tag{14.36}$$

where Dx is the first order difference of x. $\lambda > 0$ is used to control the sparsity of Dx. In addition, the ℓ_1 norm is employed as a convex proxy for sparsity. The solution for equation 14.36 in linear time is given in [38]. For a sparse x an approximate optimization problem is as follows:

$$\hat{x} = \underset{x}{argmin}\left\{\frac{1}{2}\|y - x\|_2^2 + \lambda_1 \|x\|_1 + \lambda_2 \|Dx\|_1\right\} \tag{14.37}$$

The solution for this problem is given by [39] as:

$$x = soft\,(tvd\,(y,\;\lambda 2),\,\lambda_1) \tag{14.38}$$

where tvd indicates the solution to the (14.36) problem. $soft$ represents the soft thresholding function for $\lambda > 0$, $\lambda \in \mathbb{R}$, which is defined as [40]:

$$soft\,(x,\;\lambda) := \begin{cases} x - \lambda\left(\frac{x}{|x|}\right) & |x| > \lambda \\ 0 & |x| \leq \lambda \end{cases},\; x \in \mathbb{c} \tag{14.39}$$

The above definition for soft thresholding function is valid for a complex valued x. $soft\,(x,\;\lambda)$ indicates that the soft thresholding function is element-wisely applied to x with a threshold λ.

14.5 WSST2-DETOKS FOR K-COMPLEX DETECTION

Using an appropriate transform enables us to describe signals which have sparse representation in terms of a small number of coefficients. If such a representation exists, it may account for the majority of the energy content of the signal [41]. A signal consisting of oscillatory components can be sparsely denoted by applying some approaches. Short time Fourier transform (STFT) has been applied in standard DETOKS, which is replaced with WSST and WSST2 in our proposed approach.

The nonlinear Teager-Kaiser energy operator (TKEO) was proposed by Kaiser in 1990. It quantifies instantaneous energy changes in signals consisting of a unique time-varying frequency. Its output is a combination of energy obtained from instantaneous amplitude and frequency [42,43]. The TKEO was proposed to improve signal to noise ratio, in addition to minimizing the error associated with the EMG onset detection [44]. The TEKO was used in abrupt changes detected in broadband biological signals [45]. The TKEO is similarly useful for finding the sharp rising and falling edges which are seen in the K-complex pattern. It should be mentioned that the TKEO is used to design a hardware for detecting sleep spindle and K-complex patterns [46]. Given a discrete time signal s, TKEO is defined as:

$$[T(s)]_n = s^2(n) - s(n+1)s(n-1) \qquad (14.40)$$

14.5.1 Problem Formulation

First of all, the EEG signal, y, is modeled as:

$$y = f + x + s + w$$
$$f, x, s, w \in \mathbb{R}^N \qquad (14.41)$$

where f is a low frequency signal, x represents a signal which is sparse and also has a sparse first order derivative, and w is the residual. Such a modeling is similar to the model used for removing and suppressing transient in [47], and s stands for an oscillatory signal that is sparse with respect to Φ. For a given signal y with the length of N, $\Phi : \mathfrak{c}^{M \times K} \to \mathfrak{c}^N$ is defined as:

$$\Phi c = WSST^{-1}(c) \qquad (14.42)$$

$\Phi^H : \mathfrak{c}^N \to \mathfrak{c}^{M \times K}$ is defined as:

$$\Phi^H y = WSST(y) \qquad (14.43)$$

where Φ^H is the Hermitian transpose of Φ and satisfies

$$\Phi \Phi^H = I \qquad (14.44)$$

where I is the identity matrix.

Corresponding to signal y, signals f, x, s, and w should be estimated. Signal s is formulated as:

$$s = \Phi c \qquad (14.45)$$

where $c \in \mathbb{c}^{M \times K}$ represents the WSST coefficient matrix. The high-pass filter H is defined based on a low-pass filter L:

$$H = I - L \qquad (14.46)$$

With the assumption of being zero-phase or approximately zero-phase for the low-pass filter frequency response [47], the matrix H corresponds to a high-pass filter with a $2d$-order zero at $z = 1$, is of size $(N - 2d) \times N$. N represents the signal length to which H is applied. Applying the high-pass filter to the above signal model results in:

$$H(y - x - \Phi c) \approx w \qquad (14.47)$$

The following unconstrained optimization problem is proposed to estimate x and c corresponding to a given y, and also minimizing the energy of residual, w:

$$\underset{x,c}{\mathrm{argmin}} \left\{ \frac{1}{2} \|H(y - x - \Phi c)\|_2^2 + \lambda_0 \|x\|_1 + \lambda_1 \|Dx\|_1 + \lambda_2 \|c\|_1 \right\} \qquad (14.48)$$

The objective function of this optimization problem improves the sparsity of $x = Dx$, and the WSST coefficient, making benefits from the ℓ_1 norm. λ_0, λ_1 and λ_2 are regularization scalar parameters. H is set to be a zero-phase recursive discrete-time filter:

$$H = A^{-1}B \qquad (14.49)$$

where $A_{(N-2d) \times (N-2d)}$ and $B_{(N-2d) \times N}$ are banded Toeplitz matrices [47]. The sizes of A and B are obtained from applying the $2d$-order high-pass filter to a signal of length N.

14.5.2 ALGORITHM

The objective function in 48 is a convex problem and the Douglas-Rachford splitting method [48] is used. By applying variable splitting to the objective function, it can be rewritten equivalently as:

$$\underset{u_1, u_2, x, c}{\mathrm{argmin}} \left\{ \frac{1}{2} \|H(y - u_1 - \Phi u_2)\|_2^2 + \lambda_0 \|x\|_1 + \lambda_1 \|Dx\|_1 + \lambda_2 \|c\|_1 \right\} \; s.\,t. \; \begin{cases} u_1 = x \\ u_2 = c \end{cases}$$

$$(14.50)$$

This equation can be minimized using the scaled augmented Lagrangian mechanics. It is minimized using the following iterative algorithm:

Repeat:

$$u_1, u_2 \leftarrow \underset{u_1, u_2}{argmin} \left\{ \frac{1}{2} \|H\,(y - u_1 - \Phi u_2)\|_2^2 + \frac{\mu}{2} \|u_1 - x - d_1\|_2 + \frac{\mu}{2} \|u_2 - c - d_2\|_2^2 \right\}$$

$$x, c \leftarrow \underset{x, c}{argmin} \left\{ \lambda_0 \|x\|_1 + \lambda_1 \|Dx\|_1 + \lambda_2 \|c\|_1 + \frac{\mu}{2} \|u_1 - x - d_1\|_2 \right.$$

$$\left. + \frac{\mu}{2} \|u_2 - c - d_2\|_2 \right\}$$

$$d_1 \leftarrow d_1 - u_1 + x$$

$$d_2 \leftarrow d_2 - u_2 + c$$

$$\tag{14.51}$$

where $\mu > 0$.

For the first optimization problem, the following substitutions is made:

$$u = [u_1, u_2]^T, \, d = [d_1, d_2]^T$$
$$\bar{x} = [x, c]^T, \, M = [I, \Phi] \tag{14.52}$$

where $d, \, u, \, \bar{x} \in \mathbb{R}^{2N}$. According to the this substitution, the problem can be rewritten as:

$$u \leftarrow \underset{u}{argmin} \left\{ \frac{1}{2} \|Hy - HMu\|_2^2 + \frac{\mu}{2} \|u - \bar{x} - d\|_2^2 \right\} \tag{14.53}$$

The solution to this problem is:

$$u \leftarrow [M^T H^T HM + \mu I_{2N}]^{-1} [M^T H^T HM + \mu (\bar{x} + d)] \tag{14.54}$$

Since the second optimization problem is separable, we can minimize x and c independently. Therefore, the problem can be rewritten as:

$$x \leftarrow \underset{x}{argmin} \left\{ \lambda_0 \|x\|_1 + \lambda_1 \|Dx\|_1 + \frac{\mu}{2} \|u_1 - x - d_1\|_2 \right\} \tag{14.55}$$

$$c \leftarrow \underset{c}{argmin} \left\{ \lambda_2 \|c\|_1 + \frac{\mu}{2} \|u_2 - c - d_2\|_2^2 \right\} \tag{14.56}$$

The solution to these problems are:

$$x \leftarrow soft\left(tvd\left(u_1 - d_1, \frac{\lambda_1}{\mu}\right), \lambda_0/\mu\right) \tag{14.57}$$

$$c \leftarrow soft\left(u_2 - d_2, \frac{\lambda_2}{\mu}\right) \qquad (14.58)$$

According to the definition of the high-pass filter, H, and the perfect reconstruction property of Φ, it can be concluded:

$$H^T H = B^T (AA^T)^{-1} B \qquad (14.59)$$

$$MM^T = 2I \qquad (14.60)$$

These equations can be converted to the following ones based on the matrix inverse lemma [49]:

$$
\begin{aligned}
(M^T H^T H M + \mu I_{2N})^{-1} &= (M^T B^T (AA^T)^{-1} BM + \mu I_{2N})^{-1} \\
&= \frac{I_{2N} - M^T B^T (\mu AA^T + 2BB^T)^{-1} BM}{\mu} \qquad (14.61)
\end{aligned}
$$

As A and B are banded matrices, $\mu AA^T + 2BB^T$ is a banded matrix, too. Consequently, the problem is solving a banded system of equations. Therefore, the solution would be:

$$G \leftarrow \mu AA^T + 2BB^T \qquad (14.62)$$

$$g_1 \leftarrow \frac{B^T (AA^T)^{-1} By}{\mu} + (x + d_1) \qquad (14.63)$$

$$g_2 \leftarrow \frac{\Phi B^T (AA^T)^{-1} By}{\mu} + (c + d_2) \qquad (14.64)$$

$$u_1 \leftarrow g_1 - B^T G^{-1} B (g_1 - \Phi g_2) \qquad (14.65)$$

$$u_2 \leftarrow g_2 - \Phi^H B^T G^{-1} B (g_1 + \Phi g_2) \qquad (14.66)$$

Components s and f are obtained according to the x and c estimations as follows:

$$f \leftarrow (y - x - s) - A^{-1} By (y - x - s) \qquad (14.67)$$

$$s \leftarrow \Phi c \qquad (14.68)$$

Summarizing this formulation, WSST-DETOKS algorithm is given next.

Algorithm 14.1: WSST algorithm [30]

Inputs

$y \in \mathbb{R}^N, \mu > 0, \lambda_i > 0, i = 0, 1, 2$

$h \leftarrow \dfrac{B^T (AA^T)^{-1} By}{\mu}$

Repeat

$G \leftarrow \mu AA^T + 2BB^T$

$g_1 \leftarrow h + x + d_1$

$g_2 \leftarrow \Phi h + c + d_2$

$u_1 \leftarrow g_1 - B^T G^{-1} B (g_1 + \Phi g_2)$

$u_2 \leftarrow g_2 - \Phi^H B^T G^{-1} B (g_1 + \Phi g_2)$

$x \leftarrow soft \left(tvd \left(u_1 - d_1, \dfrac{\lambda_1}{\mu} \right), \lambda_0 / \mu \right)$

$c \leftarrow soft(u_2 - d_2, \dfrac{\lambda_2}{mu})$

$d_1 \leftarrow d_1 - (u_1 - x)$

$d_2 \leftarrow d_2 - (u_2 - c)$

Till convergence

$s \leftarrow \Phi c$

$f \leftarrow (y - x - s) - A^{-1} B (y - x - s)$

Return x, s, f

K-complex is embedded in the low frequency part extracted from the EEG, f. Therefore, TKEO is used for K-complex detection. For a discrete time signal x we have:

$$[T(x)]_n = x^2(n) - x(n+1)x(n-1) \qquad (14.69)$$

where $T(.)$ denotes TEKO. A binary signal, b_{KC}, is obtained using a constant threshold as follows:

$$b_{KC}(t) = \begin{cases} 1 \ T(f) > c \\ 0 \ T(f) \le c \end{cases} \qquad (14.70)$$

Duration of the detected K-complexes are checked with its definition. Durations less than 500 ms are rejected.

It should be mentioned that the above algorithm is the same for CWT-DETOKS, WSST-DETOKS, and WSST2-DETOKS. The only difference is in 42 and 43. In other words, to obtain each of the CWT-DETOKS, WSST-DETOKS, and WSST2-DETOKS, the proper transform and its reverse would be substituted in 43 and 42, respectively.

14.6 DATA DESCRIPTION

The database used in this chapter is prepared and available online, via the so-called DREAMS project run by Université de Mons – TCTS Laboratory (Stéphanie Devuyst, Thierry Dutoit), Belgium, and Université Libre de Bruxelles – CHU de Charleroi Sleep Laboratory (Myriam Kerkhofs), Belgium [50]. A digital polygraph is used for data acquisition. Data was recorded in 32 channels in a Belgium hospital laboratory with the sampling rate of 200Hz. This database is composed of ten 30-minute EEG signals of ten healthy subjects. Signals are recorded from three EEG channels; moreover, in two EOG channels and a sub-mental EMG channel. These channels include O_1-A_1, FP_1-A_1, C_3-A_1, or C_z-A_1 for EEG and P_8-A_1 and P_{18}-A_1 for EOG. Signals are extracted from the whole night's polysomnography recordings. Signals recorded from each subject are accompanied by two experts' annotations. Annotations consist of sleep stages, unknown stages, movements, and also K-complex patterns. Two experts independently labeled the data. The following features have been considered in labeling: K-complex pattern should have a duration not less than 500 ms and not exceeding 1500 ms; it should be a bi-phasic wave in which a first negative sharp part is immediately followed by a slower positive part. The negative component should have an amplitude which is at least 50% of the height of the positive one. The K-complex amplitude should be at least twice in height compared to the background EEG. There should be a minimum 2000 ms interval between consecutive K-complexes. Moreover, K-complexes may occur in an isolated manner or by the pair. They might be accompanied with sleep spindles before, after, or even on them [50]. The number of K-complexes scored by experts are summarized in Table 14.1. The last column will be explained later. As can be seen, scoring made by the second expert is just available for the first five excerpts. Accordingly, some research used just the first five excerpts [17,25]. We use the same excerpts as well.

14.6.1 PROPOSED SCORING METHOD

As Table 14.1 indicates, scoring made by the two experts are different. As we cannot decide between them, we propose to consider the automatic results reported in [17] as another (third) expert's annotation. These results are displayed in the last column of Table 14.1.

We propose to use a voting decision-making procedure. Actually, in this work data is re-scored according to the majority. Table 14.2 illustrates the number of detected K-complex patterns in the first five excerpts of the DREAMS database, according to the annotations made by the two experts, in addition to the automatic detection results reported in [17] what is considered as the third expert's annotation.

As Figure 14.1 illustrates, there are 70 K-complexes which are just scored by the first expert. Similarly, 41 and 15 K-complexes are just scored by the second and third experts, respectively. At least two votes are available corresponding to other K-complexes. Our proposed approach for accepting a pattern as a K-complex is the existence of at least two votes for it. Therefore, we can say the total number of K-complexes are 145.

14.7 RESULTS

This section is dedicated to results. First of all, to have a visual sense, an EEG signal containing a K-complex is shown in Figure 14.2. Its WSST and WSST2 transforms are also provided. Figures are enlarged to show more detail from the region of interest. As can be inferred, WSST2 provided more details in comparison with

TABLE 14.1

Data description and annotations based on Cz-A1 channel [28]

Sub. No.	Sex	Age	No. of scored K-complexes according to Ex. 1	No. of scored K-complexes according to Ex. 2	No. of scored K-complexes according to Ex. 3
1	male	20	34	19	22
2	female	23	45	8	37
3	female	47	12	3	14
4	female	24	78	14	63
5	female	23	39	20	40
6	male	23	28	–	–
7	male	27	11	–	–
8	female	46	4	–	–
9	male	27	5	–	–
10	female	21	16	–	–

WSST. The superior performance of WSST compared to CWT is discussed in our previous work [29].

DETOKS, CWT-DETOKS, WSST-DETOKS and WSST2-DETOKS are applied to the data. The confusion matrix is summarized in Table 14.3. It contains the number of true positives, true negatives, false positives, and false negatives which are represented by TrP, TrN, FaP, and FaN, respectively. The confusion matrix is reported corresponding to the original DETOKS as well as its modified versions including CWT, WSST, and WSST2-DETOKS. The following formulation is used to compute T-N [17]:

$$TrN = 5 * 1800 - (TrP + FaP + FaN) \tag{14.71}$$

This expression is written according to the signals and their length in time. We have five signals with a length of 1,800 s. Now, considering a duration of 1,000 ms (1 s) for each K-complex, equation (14.71) is obtained [17].

14.7.1 STATISTICAL ANALYSIS

The following indices are used to evaluate the results:

$$sensitivity\,(recall) = \frac{TrP}{TrP + FaN} \tag{14.72}$$

$$specificity = \frac{TrN}{FaP + TrN} \tag{14.73}$$

TABLE 14.2

K-complex detection in the first five excerpts based on the experts' annotations [28]

Experts	Expert1	Expert2	Expert3	Only Expert1	Only Expert2	Only Expert3	Only Expert1 & Expert2	Only Expert1 & Expert3	Only Expert2 & Expert3	All Experts
No. of cored K-complexes	209	64	176	70	15	41	10	96	6	33

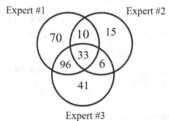

Expert #1   Expert #2

Expert #3

FIGURE 14.1 Scoring using a voting procedure among experts' annotations.

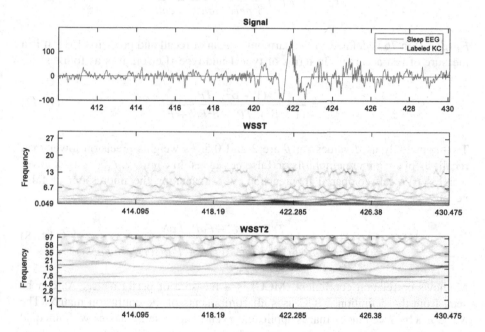

FIGURE 14.2 Signal containing K-complex and its WSST and WSST2 transforms.

TABLE 14.3

Confusion matrices associated with standard DETOKS and its modified versions CWT, WSST and WSST2-DETOKS

	DETOKS	CWT-DETOKS	WSST-DETOKS	WSST2-DETOKS
TrP	118	127	135	142
TrN	8729	8764	8772	8809
FaP	126	91	83	46
FaN	27	18	10	3

$$precision = \frac{TrP}{TrP + FaP} \qquad (14.74)$$

$$accuracy = \frac{TrP + TrN}{TrP + TrN + FaP + FaN} \qquad (14.75)$$

More than the above indices, results are evaluated using other measures:

$$F_\beta = (1 + \beta^2)\frac{percision.\ recall}{\beta^2 percision + recall} \qquad (14.76)$$

F_1 ($\beta = 1$) in 76 is defined as the harmonic mean of recall and precision [51]. It is a measure of test accuracy. In terms of type I and type II errors it is as follows:

$$F_\beta = \frac{(1 + \beta^2).\ TP}{(1 + \beta^2).\ TP + \beta^2 FN + FP} \qquad (14.77)$$

Two commonly used values for β are 2 and 0.5. F_2 weights precision lower than recall, by placing more emphasis on false negatives. In contrary, $F_{0.5}$ assigns lower weights to recall compared to precision, via attenuating the impression of false negatives.

$$MCC = \frac{TrP.\ TrN - FaP.\ FaN}{((TrP + FaP)(TrP + FaN)(TrN + FaP)(TrN + FaN))^{\frac{1}{2}}} \qquad (14.78)$$

Mathews correlation coefficient (MCC) is a measure of performance. As can be seen from the definition, MCC uses all components of the confusion matrix. The MCC is a balanced index that is applicable even in the case of classes with unequal sizes. Despite the other measures which have positive values, we have $-1 \leq MCC \leq 1$. -1 interpreted as the worst performance and 1 indicates the best one. Moreover, 0 represents that the obtained result is not better than random.

Table 14.4 illustrates recall, precision, specificity, and accuracy values based on DETOKS and its proposed modified versions, CWT-DETOKS, WSST-DETOKS, and WSST2-DETOKS. Moreover, Figure 14.3 displays the MCC and F1, F2, and F0.5 measures corresponding to these methods. MCC values are 61.98%, 70.89%, 75.48%, 85.76%, respectively. F1 score values are 60.67%, 69.97%, 74.38%, 85.28%, respectively. Moreover, F2 score values are 71.60%, 79.57%, 84.59%, and 92.45%, respectively. F0.5 score values are 52.63%, 62.44%, 66.37%, and 79.15%, respectively. As can be seen, using CWT-DETOKS results in a higher performance compared to DETOKS. Additionally, using WSST-DETOKS leads to higher performance. The WSST2-DETOKS outperforms all approaches. It should be emphasized that the big number of true negatives results in the high values foe specificity and accuracy which could not be discriminative. Therefore, MCC and F1, F2, and F0.5 measures are used to achieve better insights to the performance of studied methods.

TABLE 14.4

Recall, precision, specificity, and accuracy values corresponding to DETOKS and its modified versions

	DETOKS %	CWT-DETOKS %	WSST-DETOKS %	WSST2-DETOKS %
Recall	81.38	87.59	93.10	97.93
Precision	48.36	58.26	61.93	75.53
Specificity	98.58	98.97	99.06	99.48
Accuracy	98.30	98.79	98.97	99.46

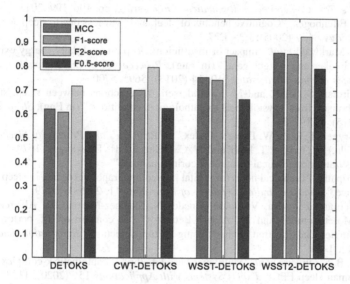

FIGURE 14.3   MCC and F1, F2, and F0.5 measures associated with DETOKS, CWT-DETOKS, WSST-DETOKS, and WSST2-DETOKS.

14.8   CONCLUSION

In this chapter a novel approach, called WSST2-DETOKS, for K-complex detection is proposed. Our proposed approach creates benefits from DETOKS as a recent powerful tool and second order synchro-squeezing transform. The WSST2 is a second order extension of WSST which is an EMD-like tool that benefits from continuous wavelet transform and reallocation methods. The WSST and WSST2 are described in Sections 14.2 and 14.3. DETOKS and WSST and WSST2-DETOKS are explained as well. Our proposed method is applied to an open source dataset called DREAMS. Data provides annotations were made by two experts. Due to the different scorings made by them, we proposed a voting approach by using an automatic scoring result as the third expert. Recall, precision, specificity, and accuracy results are reported as well as MCC measure and F1, F2, and F0.5 scores. Results demonstrated that WSST2-DETOKS had the highest performance compared to the standard DETOKS and CWT, and WSST-DETOKS.

ACKNOWLEDGMENT

The authors wish to express their appreciation to Professor Ankit Parekh (New York University) for his worthy advice.

REFERENCES

1. Z. Ghanbari, M. Najafi, and M. B. Shamsollahi. "Sleep spindles analysis using sparse bump modeling," in *2011 1st Middle East Conference on Biomedical Engineering*, pp. 37–40, 2011.
2. M. Najafi, Z. Ghanbari, B. Molaee-Ardekani, M. Shamsollahi, and T. Penzel. "Sleep spindle detection in sleep EEG signal using sparse bump modeling," in *2011 1st Middle East Conference on Biomedical Engineering*, pp. 196–199, 2011.
3. J. M. Ellenbogen. "Cognitive benefits of sleep and their loss due to sleep deprivation," *Neurology* 64, 7 (2005): E25–E27.
4. R. R. Markwald *et al.* "Impact of insufficient sleep on total daily energy expenditure, food intake, and weight gain," (in Eng), *Proceedings of the National Academy of Sciences of the United States* 110, 14 (2013): 5695–5700.
5. C. Hirotsu, S. Tufik, and M. L. Andersen. "Interactions between sleep, stress, and metabolism: from physiological to pathological conditions," (in Eng), *Sleep Science* 8, 3 (2015): 143–152.
6. M. Kryger, T. Roth, W. Dement."Index," in *Principles and Practice of Sleep Medicine* (6th edn.), M. Kryger, T. Roth, and W. C. Dement, Eds., Elsevier, pp. 1679–1730, 2017.
7. "https://aasm.org/clinical-resources/scoring-manual/."
8. M. Tripathi. "Technical notes for digital polysomnography recording in sleep medicine practice," *Annals of Indian Academy of Neurology* 11, 2 (2008): 129.
9. E. Hernández-Pereira, V. Bolón-Canedo, N. Sánchez-Maroño, D. Álvarez-Estévez, V. Moret-Bonillo, and A. Alonso-Betanzos. "A comparison of performance of K-complex classification methods using feature selection," *Information Sciences* 328 (2016): 1–14.
10. G. H. B. S. Oliveira *et al.* "Multitaper-based method for automatic k-complex detection in human sleep EEG," *Expert Systems with Applications* 151 (2020): 113331.
11. A. L. Pinto *et al.* "Localization of sleep spindles, k-complexes, and vertex waves with subdural electrodes in children," (in Eng), *Journal of Clinical Neurophysiology* 31, 4 (2014): 367–374.
12. T. Lajnef *et al.* "Sleep spindle and K-complex detection using tunable Q-factor wavelet transform and morphological component analysis," (in English), *Frontiers in Human Neuroscience, Original Research* 9, 414 (2015).
13. C. D. Nguyen, A. Wellman, A. S. Jordan, and D. J. Eckert. "Mild airflow limitation during N2 sleep increases K-complex frequency and slows electroencephalographic activity," (in Eng), *Sleep* 39, 3 (2016): 541–550.
14. A. Weigenand, M. Schellenberger Costa, H.-V. V. Ngo, J. C. Claussen, and T. Martinetz. "Characterization of K-complexes and slow wave activity in a neural mass model," (in Eng), *PLoS Computational Biology* 10, 11 (2014): e1003923–e1003923.
15. P. Halász. "The K-complex as a special reactive sleep slow wave - A theoretical update," (in Eng), *Sleep Medicine Reviews* 29 (2016): 34–40.
16. D. Moloney *et al.* "Detecting k-complexes for sleep stage identification using non-smooth optimization," *The ANZIAM Journal* 52, 4 (2011): 319–332.
17. S. Devuyst, T. Dutoit, P. Stenuit, and M. Kerkhofs. "Automatic K-complexes detection in sleep EEG recordings using likelihood thresholds," (in Eng), *Conference proceedings - IEEE Engineering in Medicine and Biology Society* 2010 (2010): 4658–4661.

18. L. K. Krohne, R. B. Hansen, J. A. E. Christensen, H. B. D. Sorensen, and P. Jennum. "Detection of K-complexes based on the wavelet transform," in *2014 36th Annual International Conference of the IEEE Engineering in Medicine and Biology Society*, pp. 5450–5453, 2014.

19. C. R. Patti *et al.* "K-complex detection based on pattern matched wavelets," in *2016 IEEE EMBS Conference on Biomedical Engineering and Sciences (IECBES)*, pp. 470–474, 2016.

20. A. Erdamar, F. Duman, and S. Yetkin. "A wavelet and Teager energy operator based method for automatic detection of K-complex in sleep EEG," *Expert Systems with Applications* 39, 1 (01/01/2012): 1284–1290.

21. S. Yazdani, S. Fallet, and J. Vesin. "A novel short-term event extraction algorithm for biomedical signals," *IEEE Transactions on Biomedical Engineering* 65, 4 (2018): 754–762.

22. T. A. Camilleri, K. P. Camilleri, and S. G. Fabri. "Automatic detection of spindles and K-complexes in sleep EEG using switching multiple models," *Biomedical Signal Processing and Control* 10 (2014): 117–127.

23. C. Yücelbaş, Ş. Yücelbaş, S. Özşen, G. Tezel, S. Küççüktürk, and Ş. Yosunkaya. "A novel system for automatic detection of K-complexes in sleep EEG," *Neural Computing and Applications* 29, 8 (2018): 137–157.

24. R. Ranjan, R. Arya, S. L. Fernandes, E. Sravya, and V. Jain. "A fuzzy neural network approach for automatic K-complex detection in sleep EEG signal," *Pattern Recognition Letters* 115 (2018): 74–83.

25. A. Parekh, I. W. Selesnick, D. M. Rapoport, and I. Ayappa. "Detection of K-complexes and sleep spindles (DETOKS) using sparse optimization," (in Eng), *Journal of Neuroscience Methods* 251 (2015): 37–46.

26. I. Daubechies, J. Lu, and H.-T. Wu. "Synchrosqueezed wavelet transforms: an empirical mode decomposition-like tool," *Applied and Computational Harmonic Analysis* 30, 2 (2011): 243–261.

27. H. T. Wu, S. S. Hseu, M. Y. Bien, Y. R. Kou, and I. Daubechies. "Evaluating physiological dynamics via synchrosqueezing: prediction of ventilator weaning," (in Eng), *IEEE Transactions on Biomedical Engineering* 61, 3 (2014): 736–744.

28. Z. Ghanbari and M. H. Moradi. "K-complex detection based on synchrosqueezing transform," *AUT Journal of Electrical Engineering* 49, 2 (2017): 214–222.

29. Z. Ghanbari and M. H. Moradi. "Synchrosqueezing transform: application in the analysis of the K-complex pattern," in *2016 23rd Iranian Conference on Biomedical Engineering and 2016 1st International Iranian Conference on Biomedical Engineering (ICBME)*, pp. 221–225, 2016.

30. D.-H. Pham and S. Meignen. "Second-order synchrosqueezing transform: the wavelet case, comparisons and applications," 2017.

31. I. Daubechies and S. H. Maes. "A nonlinear squeezing of the continuous wavelet transform based on auditory nerve models," 2017.

32. T. Oberlin and S. Meignen. "The second-order wavelet synchrosqueezing transform," *2017 IEEE International Conference on Acoustics, Speech and Signal Processing (ICASSP)*, pp. 3994–3998, 2017.

33. S. Meignen, T. Oberlin, and S. McLaughlin. "A new algorithm for multicomponent signals analysis based on synchrosqueezing: with an application to signal sampling and denoising," *IEEE Transactions on Signal Processing* 60, 11 (2012): 5787–5798.

34. P. Flandrin. *Time-Frequency/Time-Scale Analysis*. Academic Press, London, 10, 1998.

35. R. A. Carmona, W. L. Hwang, and B. Torresani. "Characterization of signals by the ridges of their wavelet transforms," *IEEE Transactions on Signal Processing* 45, 10 (1997): 2586–2590.

36. D. Pham and S. Meignen. "High-order synchrosqueezing transform for multi-component signals analysis—with an application to gravitational-wave signal," *IEEE Transactions on Signal Processing* 65, 12 (2017): 3168–3178.
37. L. I. Rudin, S. Osher, and E. Fatemi. "Nonlinear total variation based noise removal algorithms," *Physica D: Nonlinear Phenomena* 60, 1 (1992): 259–268.
38. L. Condat. "A direct algorithm for 1-D total variation denoising," *IEEE Signal Processing Letters* 20, 11 (2013): 1054–1057.
39. A. Rinaldo. "Properties and refinements of the fused lasso," *The Annals of Statistics* 37, 2008.
40. D. L. Donoho. "De-noising by soft-thresholding," *IEEE Transactions on Information Theory* 41, 3 (1995): 613–627.
41. M. Stéphane. "Chapter 1 — sparse representations," in *A Wavelet Tour of Signal Processing* (3rd edn.), M. Stéphane, Ed. Academic Press: Boston, pp. 1–31, 2009.
42. J. F. Kaiser. "On a simple algorithm to calculate the 'energy' of a signal," in *International Conference on Acoustics, Speech, and Signal Processing*, 1, pp. 381–384, 1990.
43. J. F. Kaiser. "Some useful properties of Teager's energy operators," in *1993 IEEE International Conference on Acoustics, Speech, and Signal Processing*, 3, pp. 149–152, 1993.
44. X. Li, P. Zhou, and A. S. Aruin. "Teager-Kaiser energy operation of surface EMG improves muscle activity onset detection," (in Eng), *Annals of Biomedical Engineering* 35, 9 (2007): 1532–1538.
45. S. Mukhopadhyay and G. C. Ray. "A new interpretation of nonlinear energy operator and its efficacy in spike detection," (in Eng), *IEEE Transactions on Biomedical Engineering* 45, 2 (Feb 1998): 180–187.
46. S. I. Khan, M. S. Diab, and S. A. Mahmoud. "Design of low power Teager energy operator circuit for sleep spindle and K-complex extraction," *Microelectronics Journal* 100, (2020): 104785.
47. I. W. Selesnick. "Resonance-based signal decomposition: a new sparsity-enabled signal analysis method," *Signal Processing* 91, 12 (2011): 2793–2809.
48. P. L. Combettes and J.-C. Pesquet. "Proximal splitting methods in signal processing," in *Fixed-Point Algorithms for Inverse Problems in Science and Engineering*, H. H. Bauschke, R. S. Burachik, P. L. Combettes, V. Elser, D. R. Luke, and H. Wolkowicz, Eds., Springer: New York, NY, pp. 185–212, 2011.
49. D. J. Tylavsky and G. R. L. Sohie. "Generalization of the matrix inversion lemma," *Proceedings of the IEEE* 74, 7 (1986): 1050–1052.
50. "http://www.tcts.fpms.ac.be/~devuyst/Databases/DatabaseKcomplexes/."
51. D. C. Blair. "Information Retrieval, 2nd ed. C.J. Van Rijsbergen. London: Butterworths; 1979: 208 pp. Price: $32.50," *Journal of the American Society for Information Science* 30, 6 (1979): 374–375.

15 Directed Functional Brain Networks

Characterization of Information Flow Direction during Cognitive Function Using Non-Linear Granger Causality

Md. Hedayetul Islam Shovon,
D. (Nanda) Nandagopal, Jia Tina Du, and
Vijayalakshmi Ramasamy

15.1 INTRODUCTION

The computational complexity of human brain surpasses any known system. It consists of densely populated neuronal cluster across all brain regions. The functioning of these networked neural clusters, also known as functional brain networks, underpin human cognition. The working principle of a single isolated neuron has been well investigated. However, our understanding in an integrated system, where billions of neuronal cells interact forming dynamic network of neuronal connections, is limited. The brain functioning at a systems level is completely different from the functioning of its fundamental unit (neuron) and thus exhibiting important properties such as cognition, emotion, and intelligence. Sum-of-parts analysis is not enough to explain these properties. Powerful computational techniques are needed to model and investigate the brain function during a particular brain function such as cognition. The brain hemispheres are further divided into lobes called frontal, occipital, temporal, and parietal, and each lobe performs different actions. For instance, the occipital lobe processes the visual action and the left hemisphere is related with language processing [1,2]. The human brain has approximately 86 billion neurons interacting, communicating, and processing information across brain regions [3], thus forming a complex communication network. The complex brain network is comprised of over one trillion of neuronal connections [4], with changing network topology exhibiting distinct functional activities at the neuronal level [5]. Many of these connections between neurons can be constant along the time [6], on the other side, many network patterns can establish and disappear in a few milliseconds time [7]. Therefore, in order to understand human cognition, the measurement and examination of neuronal connection with suitable temporal scale are essential.

The magnetoencephalography (MEG) and electroencephalography (EEG) appear to provide good temporal sensitivity [8]. In this study, EEG has been used to explore human cognition, as EEG is an economic noninvasive tool. Cognition is the coordination of mental processes in which the human brain converts the perceived information into respective action. During the cognitive activity, multiple brain regions are involved in processing the information that is being passed around. These mental processes include reasoning, problem-solving, language, memory, attention, decision making, learning, etc. Among the many paradigms under study, the visual search paradigm is a very useful tool for examining the attention of the participants. Prior studies have demonstrated that the visual search involves the brain region of occipital parietal, the frontal areas [9–13].

Web search is another example of a process involving searchers' cognition and cognitive load at both neuronal (brain) level and the behavioral level [14,15]. Interactive information retrieval is a cognitive neural information processing function. The EEG-based neuroimaging technique can be a useful tool to measure the human cognitive activity [15]. Recent papers have demonstrated that neuroscience can be helpful in interactive information retrieval research [16]. However, most existing studies in cognitive information retrieval have relied on searchers' behavioral performance, self-report, and reaction time. Such inferential methods as a dual-task approach [17], cognitive shifts in the Likert scale [14], and eye tracking [18] have been used to assess dynamic changes in the mental effort during the web searching while leaving the direct measure on brain activity under-studied. As pointed out by Shovon et al. (2015), how brain regions connect during web searching remains unknown [15].

Although the biological networks or World Wide Web are considered as directed network, most of the previous studies have not considered the direction of the edge in their algorithm. Recent researches have focused on the directional brain network analysis and proved that direction is very essential to identify important information from a complex network [19,20]. As a result, information flow analysis is gaining popularity in many different domains, including functional brain network studies. Recently, Dentico et al. (2014) explored the information flow in an occipital-parietal-frontal network during visual imagery and visual perception, and found a reversal of the information flow direction in the parieto-occipital regions in mental pictures when compared to perception [21].

The objective of this chapter is, therefore, to examine the neuronal information flow direction during the cognitive function in the human brain when people perform visual and web search tasks. The effects of visual and web-based searches on cognitive function are studied. Nonlinear Granger causality (GC) has been used to compute causality between pairs of EEG electrode data to create functional brain networks (FBNs) where the connections are directed. The GC is a largely accepted technique for deriving the effective connectivity in EEG and MEG signals. Most previous studies have considered a linear version of GC [22]. However, to capture the nonlinear interaction of the human brain, nonlinear GC analysis is essential. As such, in this study, we used nonlinear GC to compute the causality between EEG signals and, hence, derived the functional brain networks. The constructed FBNs were then analyzed using our proposed weighted Information Flow Direction Pattern (IFDP) algorithm along with the existing complex network measurement techniques such as clustering coefficient, connectivity density, and local information flow measures.

The remainder of this chapter has been structured as follows. Directed FBN construction techniques are discussed in the next section, then the research literature on GC and directed FBNs analysis techniques are discussed. Then the design of experimental, data collection techniques, preprocessing of data and the information flow direction pattern (IFDP) analysis framework is discussed, followed by a detailed explanation of the experimental results. The last section provides a short summary with recommendations for future direction and application of this research.

15.2 DIRECTED FUNCTIONAL BRAIN NETWORK CONSTRUCTION

A network or graph consists of two elements called nodes and edges. In EEG, FBN nodes represent the electrode regions on the head scalp, while the edges and weights on the edges reflect the functional connectivity and its strength among those regions [23], and the strengths between the connected nodes allow the creation of FBNs, respectively. In the past, statistical metrics including linear and nonlinear metrics were used to create FBNs. Simple metrics such as cross correlation, wavelet coherence, Pearson's product moment correlation, and magnitude squared coherence were also explored [24–27]. All the linear methods measure correlation between signals obtained from pairs of electrodes. These measures can provide linear connection among the brain regions whose strength is indicated by the degree of correlation between the signals. However, the linear measures are restricted to the linear function of the brain.

The nonlinear statistical metrics represent a measurement of brain function as brain is inherently nonlinear. Previous studies have used nonlinear GC [28,29], transfer entropy (TE) and mutual information (MI) [30,31] to construct FBNs. The MI technique produced only undirected networks. In contrast, GC and TE are helpful to generate directed brain networks. A general approach of constructing FBNs from EEG signals is illustrated in Figure 15.1. As GC-based effective connectivity from EEG and MEG signals is very popular, GC has been used in the present study to construct directed FBNs. Appropriate complex network analysis techniques can be applied once FBNs are constructed. The next section will describe GC and its usefulness for directed FBNs construction.

15.3 GRANGER CAUSALITY

Given two-time sequences, X and Y, if the previous information of X can be used to predict the future of Y, in addition to the information which is already in the past of Y then there exists a causal link between X and Y. The influence of X on Y is defined by Granger causality (GC). The GC analysis provides a very powerful

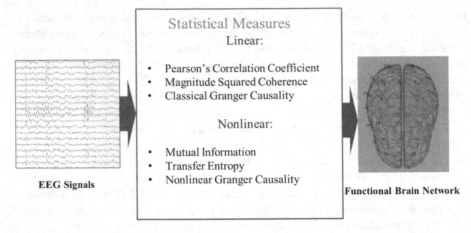

FIGURE 15.1   General approach to construct functional brain networks from EEG signals.

technique for identifying functional (causal) dependencies between time series data. The fundamental measurement of information is appropriated by Shannon entropy [32]. Like entropy, GC has a profound similarity to the directed information theory, as illustrated by Amblard and Michel (2012) [33]. They have presented conceptual and theoretical links between directed information theory and GC based on the causal influence between processes. However, an information-theoretic measure named transfer entropy, which measures the information transfer between jointly dependent systems, was studied extensively [31,34]. Barnett, Barrett, and Seth (2009) have shown that transfer entropy and Granger causality are similar for Gaussian variables, and they established that GC is an information-theoretic approach [35]. In this chapter, we have used Granger causality to measure the directed information flow across brain regions using EEG data.

Given two different signals $x(t)$ and $y(t)$ which are measured simultaneously, if one can predict the future of $y(t)$ better by including the previous information of $x(t)$ instead of using only information from $y(t)$, then $x(t)$ can be referred to as causal to the signal $y(t)$ [36]. Clive Granger, the Nobel Prize winner, gave a mathematical framework to describe his theory of causality. He proposed initially that if x regulates y then merging the previous information of $x(t)$ to the regression analysis yields an enhanced prediction of y [37].

The GC from y to x is given by:

$$GC_{y \to x} = ln\left(\frac{V_{x|\bar{x}}}{V_{x|\bar{x},\bar{y}}}\right) \tag{15.1}$$

where $var(.)$ is the variance $0 \leq GC_{Y \to X} < \infty$. If $GC_{y \to x}$ is zero then the previous state of $y(t)$ does not increase the prediction of $x(t)$. If the past of $y(t)$ increases the prediction of $x(t)$ then $GC_{y \to x}$ becomes greater than zero.

We have evaluated the directed functional connectivity from EEG signals using nonlinear GC. In the context of EEG signals, GC measures causal relationships between nodes. In this study, the kernel Granger causality (KGC) method has been used for the calculation of nonlinear GC, as described in Marinazzo et al. [38,39]. The KGC method is based on the theory of regenerating Kernel Hilbert spaces, which helps to measure neuronal information transfer between brain areas.

15.4 DIRECTED FBNs ANALYSIS

Although the behavior of the human brain as a networked system has been observed for awhile [40], the measurement and analysis of such networked neural activity gained serious research attention only recently. A comprehensive review of applying the complex network theory to study cognitive function was published in 2009 [23]. In this chapter, we have adopted the graph-theoretic approach to building functional brain networks.

A directed graph G normally has two sets V and E where the members of V and E are the nodes and edges respectively of the graph G. The nodes in a directed graph might have both outgoing and incoming edges [41]. For EEG-based directed FBNs, the electrodes sites are represented by node that identify the electrical activity of the respective neuronal cluster. Directed FBNs are created by quantifying the GC between EEG channels. Complex network parameters such as clustering coefficient, connectivity density, and local information flow measures, have been used to investigate the behavior of patterns of connection in brain networks during various cognitive conditions. Based on the existing complex network metrics, we propose a weighted Information Flow Direction Pattern (IFDP) algorithm for analyzing the directed FBNs, which is reported in the methods section.

15.4.1 CONNECTIVITY DENSITY

Connectivity density (CD), or physical cost of a network, is defined as a ratio of the real number of links and the total number of possible links in a graph [23]. Connectivity density is normally used to identify the global connectivity pattern of the graph [42]. Given a directed graph with N nodes with no loop, each node can link with at most $(N - 1)$ other nodes, and such a graph has total possible connections $N * (N - 1)$. The CD of the network is given in equation (15.2),

$$CD_d = \frac{e}{N(N - 1)} \tag{15.2}$$

where e is the real number of links in the network. CD has range 0 to 1. A complete directed graph has a connectivity density of 1.

15.4.2 CLUSTERING COEFFICIENT

The clustering coefficient (C) of a directed graph's node can be used to measure the ratio between total number of directed triangles actually formed and the number of all possible triangles that can form at that specific node. The ratio indicates how cohesively the neighbor of that node is connected within the network. The C is used for computing functional segregation in the network [23]. This concept of C in a directed graph was proposed by Fagiolo (2007) [19]. For a directed graph the clustering coefficient, C_d is averaged clustering coefficients across all the vertices in that graph:

$$C_d = \frac{1}{N} \sum_{i=1}^{N} C_i = \frac{1}{N} \sum_{i=1}^{N} \frac{\frac{1}{2} \sum_{j=1}^{N} \sum_{h=1}^{N} (a_{ij} + a_{ji})(a_{ih} + a_{hi})(a_{jh} + a_{hj})}{(k_i^{out} + k_i^{in})(k_i^{out} + k_i^{in} - 1) - 2 \sum_{j=1}^{N} a_{ij} a_{ji}} \quad (15.3)$$

where N: number of vertices, C_i represents clustering coefficient of vertex i, a_{ij} is the links (directed) from vertex i to vertex j. Out-degrees and in-degrees of the vertex i represented by k_i^{out} and k_i^{in}, respectively.

15.4.3 LOCAL INFORMATION MEASURE

The local information (LI) measure of a directed network (weighted) quantify the amount of information flows through each vertex locally. It represents the value of outgoing information minus incoming information of a particular node [43]. Outgoing information of node i, k_i^{out} can be represented as

$$k_i^{out} = \sum_{j \in V} a_{ij} \quad (15.4)$$

Accordingly, incoming information of node i, k_i^{in} can be represented as

$$k_i^{in} = \sum_{j \in V} a_{ji} \quad (15.5)$$

where a_{ij} is an element of the weighted connection matrix. a_{ij} will be greater than zero if edge found from i to j otherwise it is zero. The LI of node i is the difference between k_i^{out} and k_i^{in}, as shown in equation (15.6):

$$LI[i] = k_i^{out} - k_i^{in} = \sum_{j \in V} a_{ij} - \sum_{j \in V} a_{ji} \quad (15.6)$$

The range of LI: $[-\infty, +\infty]$. The LI is useful to identify the source and sink nodes from directed networks. A positive LI value of a vertex means that the information emitted by a vertex is more than what it receives. This phenomenon called "emittance contribution" reflects the strength of a source vertex. On the other hand, if the vertex receives more information than it normally emits (the LI value is negative) it shows the strength of a sink node. In this study, the LI measure helps to find the net information flow in the FBNs. It also helps to find the top-down or bottom-up information flow direction in the FBNs.

15.5 METHODS

15.5.1 PARTICIPANTS IN THE COGNITIVE EXPERIMENTS

Eight healthy (6 males, 2 females) and right-handed adults (age: 22–59) were selected for the cognitive experiments. EEG data was collected from these subjects by the cognitive neuro-engineering team at the University of South Australia. The student and staff community of the university are voluntarily engaged in the data collection. As a standard practice, all subjects were screened for normal or corrected-to-normal vision and normal hearing with no neurological abnormalities. We have mostly used about eight participants in our cognitive research studies. The published results using this sample size demonstrated statistical significance [44–48].

15.5.2 EEG DATA COLLECTION

A 40 channel Neuroscan Nuamps amplifier was used to collect EEG data from participants. Curry 7 software was used for signal preprocessing. The sampling rate for the data collection was 1,000 Hz. In this study, 30 electrode systems were chosen using the international 10–20 convention of electrode location. The EEG data acquisition and the experimental setup is illustrated in Figure 15.2.

The electrode layout is shown in Figure 15.3. The impedance values for all the used electrodes were checked and kept below 40 kΩ. A stimulus design software called STIM2 has been used to provide designed stimulus to the participants and track their response to the EEG recoding system. EEG data were collected during the baseline state (eyes open – looking at blank screen), visual search, and web search interaction cognitive tasks.

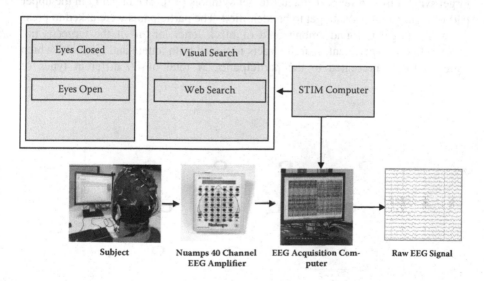

FIGURE 15.2 EEG data acquisition paradigm.

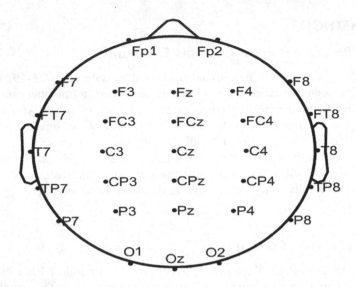

FIGURE 15.3   Electrode placement according to international 10–20 system.

15.5.2.1   Baseline – Eyes Open (EOP)

For baseline state or EOP, participants need to stare to the computer screen with a neutral symbol such as a blue colored star. This time, they do not need to do any cognitive tasks. Even though the participants do not perform any tasks, we still collected EEG data to get baseline EEG data for two minutes.

15.5.2.2   Cognitive Task Relating to Visual Search (VS)

In this cognitive experiment (visual search), participants were instructed to detect a target symbol from a set of distractor target symbols [49]. The target Q in the upper part of Figure 15.4 is the target to be identified. The participants were asked to press "y" if the target is found among field of black letter, or "n" if the target is not present. In our experiment, search targets included both letters and symbols, which were randomly presented to the participants. A total of 80 different types of

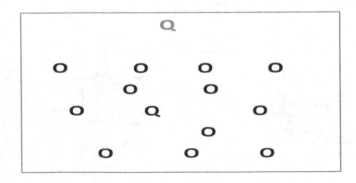

FIGURE 15.4   Visual search experiment.

distractor arrays were used where the targets randomly presented on the screen. All these visual stimuli were presented using a well-known stimulus presentation software, STIM2.

15.5.2.3 Web Search Cognitive Task (Around 5–10 Minutes)

In this web search cognitive task, the participants were asked to find online information on three given scenarios. The reason for choosing three search scenarios was to engage the participants in information searching for 5–10 minutes, and that would produce enough information search-related EEG data for further analysis. The participants were allowed to use any web-based browser of their choice (e.g., Mozilla, Firefox, Google, Chrome, or any web browser) and any search engine (e.g., Bing or Google). Participants have the liberty to decide which database they want to use for their search. The search scenarios are given below:

Scenario 1: *Finding a red-colored fuel-efficient car that will be sponsored you by your company.*
Scenario 2: *In travelling in Adelaide Hills, you get bitten. What you will do?*
Scenario 3: *Finding a movie to watch in the cinema. Which movie and which show and which cinema?*

In the web search session, three subtasks/cognitive states were individually examined: Formulation of query (Q), viewing the result of search list (L), and reading each content page (C'). These cognitive states were reported as important constructs of the cognitive aspects of human information interaction, including information relevance, browsing, and search in previous cognitive information retrieval studies [14,17,31]. The experimental descriptions about how the participants conducted the web search in the three scenarios (S1, S2, and S3) are presented in Table 15.1. This table represents searching activity such as the number of query issues (Q), the number of search result pages examined (L), and the number of content pages (C') accessed by each participant to obtain their expected information. In the table, search activity (Q, L, or C') is represented with a sequential number if it needs to be repeated.

15.5.3 EEG SIGNAL PRE-PROCESSING

The EEG primarily represents the nonstationary, nonlinear, and time-varying nature of the ongoing neuro-electric activity of underlying neuronal populations. The changes in EEG signals reflect the dynamic nature of communication and information exchange between the underlying neural structures. The EEG signals are a time series data that carry information about the ongoing interactions between underlying neuronal populations. Based on Shannon's information theory for communication signals, EEG signals from an electrode can be considered as a set of time-varying transactions taking place as a result of interactions between both underlying neuronal populations and distant neuronal populations. If an EEG electrode site can be represented by variable x taking

TABLE 15.1
Web search activity

Participant	Search Sequence
P1	S1-Q1 → S1-L1 → S1-C'1 → S1-C'2 → S2-Q1 → S2-L1 → S2-C'1 → S2-L2→ S3-Q1 → S3-L1 → S3-C'1
P2	S1-Q1 → S1-L1 → S1-C'1 → S1-C'2 → S1-C'3 → S1-C'4 → S2-Q1 → S2-L1 → S2-C'1 → S3-Q1 → S3-L1 → S3-C'1→ S3-C'2
P3	S1-Q1 → S1-L1 → S1-Q2 → S1-L2 → S1-C'1 → S2-Q1 → S2-L1 → S2-Q2 → S2-L2 → S2-C'1 → S2-L3→ S2-C'2 → S2-L4→ S3-Q1 → S3-L1 → S3-C'1
P4	S1-Q1 → S1-L1 → S1-C'1 → S1-L2 → S1-C'2 → S1-L3 → S1-C'3 → S2-Q1 → S2-L1 → S2-C'1 → S3-Q1 → S3-L1 → S3-C'1→ S3-Q2 → S3-L2
P5	S1-Q1 → S1-Q2 → S1-L1 → S1-C'1 → S2-Q1 → S2-L1 → S2-C'1 → S3-Q1 → S3-C'1 → S1-Q3 → S1-L2 → S1-C'2 → S3-C'2 → S2-C'2
P6	S1-Q1 → S1-L1 → S1-C'1 → S1-Q2 → S1-L2 → S1-Q3 → S1-L3→ S1-Q4 → S1-L4 → S1-C'2 → S1-Q5 → S2-Q1 → S2-L1 → S2-C'1 → S3-Q1 → S3-L1 → S3-Q2 → S3-L2 → S3-Q3 → S3-L3 → S3-C'1 → S3-L4 → S3-C'2
P7	S1-Q1 → S1-L1 → S1-C'1 → S1-L2 → S1-L3 → S1-C'2 → S2-Q1 → S2-L1→ S2-C'1 → S3-Q1 →S3-C'1→ S3-Q2 →S3-C'2
P8	S1-Q1 → S1-L1 → S1-C'1→ S2-Q1 → S2-L1 → S2-C'1 → S2-Q2 → S2-L2 → S2-C'2 → S3-Q1 → S3-L1 → S3-C'1

varying values {x1, x2, …, xn}, then Shannon's measure of information in x can be computed as:

$$H(x) = - \sum_{i=1}^{n} p(x_i)\log(x_i) \qquad (15.7)$$

where $H(x)$ is the average information produced in x, $p(x)$ are probability values of x. Therefore, any changes in the EEG signal could be related to changes of the information contained in them. As discussed earlier, GC is equivalent to transfer entropy for Gaussian variable; hence, we used GC to compute the directed information flow in this book chapter.

A band pass filter of 1–70 Hz was applied initially, then a notch filter centered at 50 Hz to separate main line noise. Principal component analysis was carried out to separate eye blink artifacts. Any residual bad blocks of EEG data was removed manually using visual inspection. During the visual search task, only those trial epochs with reaction time between 1.5 and 3.5 seconds were used in this analysis. The EEG data from selected epochs were taken from the stimulus onset points for two seconds length, and averaged. For every participant, 50 epochs of two seconds' length during the VS has been used. During the web search, each subtask was identified with a time marked on the EEG data using interaction session logs (mouse strokes and key presses on keyboard) of Camtasia Studio software. For each subtask, two-second epochs of EEG data were selected and averaged to make one averaged epoch data for

TABLE 15.2

Number of epochs in each cognitive state

Cognitive states	Epoch
EOP	50
VS	50
Q	50
L	50
C'	50

further analysis. To compare each cognitive load states with the baseline (EOP) state, 50 good epochs of two seconds' length during EOP were selected. The selected 50 epochs of EEG data were then averaged to produce a single two-second epoch. The averaged EEG data epochs during EOP, VS, Q, L, and C' were then utilized to compute the GC matrices. The number of epochs that were taken after cleaning the EEG data during each cognitive state for each participant is illustrated in Table 15.2.

15.5.4 A FRAMEWORK FOR THE COMPUTATION AND ANALYSIS OF INFORMATION FLOW DIRECTION PATTERNS

The preprocessed and averaged EEG data segments were extracted as described in the previous section for each of the cognitive states (EOP, VS, Q, L, and C'). These data segments were then utilized for further analysis and to create GC matrices. Each individual element of the GC matrix indicates the GC value from one node to another. From the computed GC matrix, both weighted and binary FBNs were constructed and subsequently utilized for analysis. Binary-directed FBNs have been analyzed using CD and C; whereas, weighted FBNs have been analyzed using our proposed IFDP algorithm and LI measures. An overall framework outlining the computational steps and analysis process of the IFDP algorithm is illustrated in Figure 15.5. The proposed IFDP algorithm is discussed in the next section.

15.5.5 INFORMATION FLOW DIRECTION PATTERNS (IFDP) FOR WEIGHTED DIRECTED NETWORK

A new algorithmic approach to detect information flow direction patterns in EEG based FBNs is proposed in this section. This approach, involving an integration of statistical and graph theoretical analysis, tracks the information transfer direction in FBNs in each of the cognitive tasks (visual search or web search) in comparison with the baseline (EOP) state. The primary motivation for the development of this algorithm is to construct an information flow network among lobes from the whole functional brain network, which also reflects the overall contribution of all the participants. Firstly, we constructed a subnetwork consisting of 12 electrodes from four different lobes from the whole FBNs. Then the subnetwork was averaged across the eight participants to construct a group subnetwork. We divided the 12

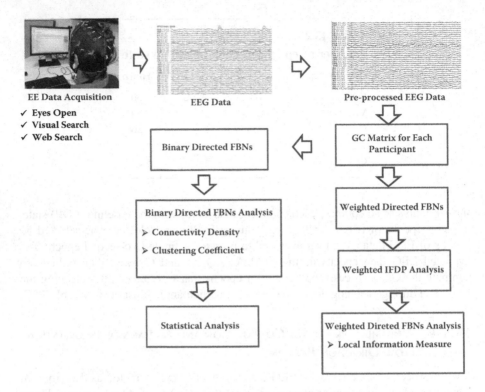

FIGURE 15.5 Information flow direction patterns (IFDP) analysis framework.

electrodes into four lobes based on their position on the head scalp. Thus, each lobe represents the aggregated/merged electrode's contribution, i.e., F (frontal lobe) represents all the frontal lobe electrodes (F3, Fz, and F4). The outline of the algorithm for investigating the information transfer direction is given next.

Algorithm: Information Flow Direction Patterns (IFDP). This algorithm takes EEG data (preprocessed) as input and produces a lobe-wise information flow network.

Input: EEG data (preprocessed) during any cognitive state (CS), e.g., EOP, VS, Q, L, C'.
Output: Information flow network among lobes

  i. For each participant:
    a. Compute GC:

For any CS, compute GC (CS) for all pairs of electrode sites.

    b. Extract subnetwork:

Extract subnetworks Sub_GC (CS) formed by electrodes: F3, Fz, F4, FT7, FT8, T7, C3, Cz, C4, T8, TP7, TP8, P3, Pz, P4, O1, Oz, and O2 from GC (CS).

  ii. Construct group GC:

Construct graphs Group_Sub_GC (CS) from Sub_GC (CS) by averaging the corresponding GC value of all participants.

iii. Calculate information transfer network for each lobe:

Merge the corresponding electrodes in each lobe into a vertex: F(F3, Fz, F4), C(C3, Cz, C4), P(P3, Pz, P4) and O(O1, Oz, O2). By merging each lobe, the aggregated/merged electrode's contribution, such as F (frontal lobe), represents all the frontal lobe electrodes (F3, Fz, and F4).

The total information flow from one lobe's nodes/electrodes to another lobe represents the respective link weights (See Figure 15.6). For instance, the link from F to C represents the summation of all the links from F3, Fz, F4 to C3, Cz, C4.

iv. Display the information transfer network of each lobe during each CS.

It should be noted that a limitation of the IFDP approach is the averaging of the GC values across the participants to construct a single information flow network for each cognitive state. The motivation for this is to reflect the contribution of each participant in the information flow network. There may have been some other alternative, which has not been addressed in this book chapter.

15.6   RESULTS AND DISCUSSION

15.6.1   BINARY DIRECTED FUNCTIONAL BRAIN NETWORK

In this study, a threshold of 0.04 was used to construct binary-directed FBNs from GC matrices. This threshold is an arbitrary value, which has been chosen to remove

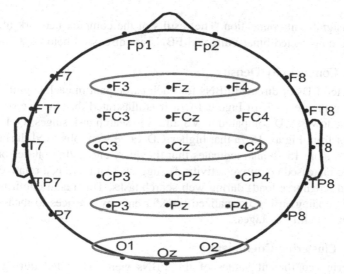

FIGURE 15.6   Electrodes of occipital, parietal, central and frontal lobes representing four nodes on the head scalp. The electrodes which have been chosen for analysis are highlighted in oval.

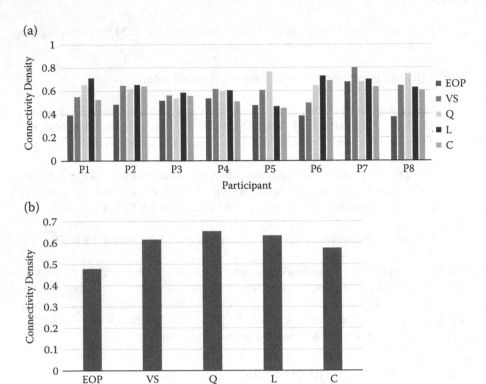

FIGURE 15.7 Connectivity density during EOP, VS, Q, L, and C': (a) across all the participants and (b) average across all the participants.

the very insignificant connection. The results of the complex network metrics applied to the constructed binary-directed FBNs are discussed below.

15.6.1.1 Connectivity Density

The computed CDs of directed FBNs for each participant in each cognitive state is illustrated in Figure 15.7. In Figure 15.7a it is illustrated that the eye open (EOP) state had the lowest CD compared to VS and web search task stages (Q, L, and C'). It is evident from Figure 15.7a that higher CD value were observed during VS, Q, L, and, C'. Figure 15.7b also indicates that the query and listing phases of the web search have increased cognitive activity. It suggests that there is a relatively higher mental load (cognitive load) during web search tasks. This result confirms Shovon et al.'s [15] findings using normalized transfer entropy matrices to measure FBNs during web search task stages.

15.6.1.2 Clustering Coefficient

The clustering coefficient values of the FBNs were calculated during different cognitive states for all participants. The clustering coefficient values of FBNs, illustrated in Figure 15.8, clearly demonstrates a consistent increase with induced

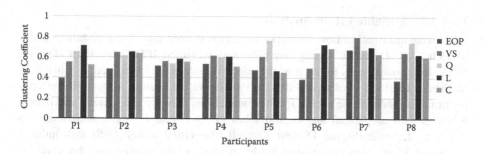

FIGURE 15.8 Clustering coefficient during EOP, VS, Q, L and C' across all the participants.

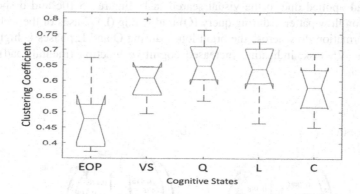

FIGURE 15.9 Box plot showing the median value of clustering coefficient during EOP, VS, Q, L and C'.

cognitive load states such as L, Q, and VS. This indicates the sensitivity of the clustering coefficient to the cognitive load.

A one-way variance (ANOVA) analysis was carried out using the clustering coefficient values computed for different cognitive states across all participants. As shown in Figure 15.9, the box plot result provides the visual comparison of the group clustering coefficient values during different cognitive states. For each box, the central mark represents the median clustering coefficient value. Figures 15.8 and 15.9 illustrate that the clustering coefficient, like the connectivity density, is also sensitive to cognitive activity. The results demonstrate increased cognitive function during the web search. On average, both the clustering coefficient and connectivity density show approximately 27% increase during cognitive activity.

15.6.2 WEIGHTED DIRECTED FUNCTIONAL BRAIN NETWORK

Weighted directed FBNs were also constructed from GC matrices computed using nonlinear GC with no threshold applied. The weighted IFDP algorithm discussed earlier was applied to the constructed weighted FBNs to identify and visualize changes in neuro-information patterns among the brain lobes/regions during EOP, VS, Q, L, and C'.

15.6.2.1 Weighted IFDP Analysis

Lobe-wise information flow networks were constructed during the cognitive states of EOP, VS, Q, and C' using our proposed weighted IFDP algorithm. The information flow patterns for each of the cognitive states are visualized, as illustrated in Figure 15.10. It is observed that during the visual search, almost all the connection weights increase except for the connections between the parietal and frontal lobes as well as parietal and central lobes ($P \to F$ and $P \to C$), which show a marginal decrease (Figure 15.10b). Overall, the visual search (VS) task induces increased information flow across the brain lobes while maintaining the same information flow directions as that of the EOP. This observation is consistent with increases in connectivity density and clustering coefficient during increased cognitive load applied due to the visual search task. Figure 15.10c and d shows the information flow patterns during query (Q) and listing (L) phases of the web search task. Information flow across the brain lobes during Q and L phases is higher than during the VS task, indicating increased cognitive function (mental load) during web search.

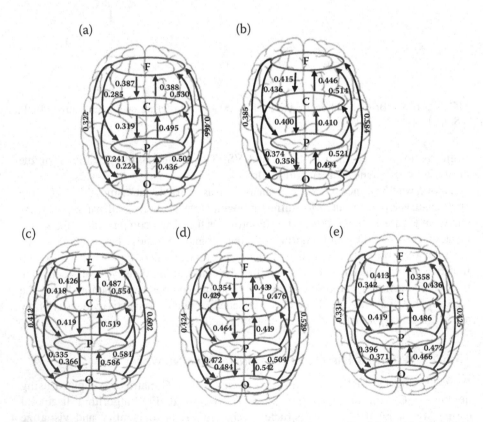

FIGURE 15.10 Information flow among occipital, parietal, central and frontal lobes during (a) EOP, (b) VS, (c) Q, (d) L, and (e) C'.

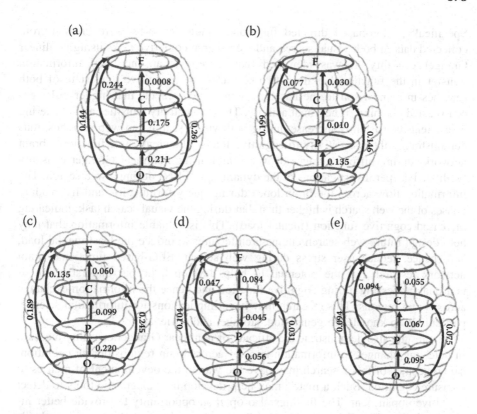

FIGURE 15.11 Net information flow direction among occipital, parietal, central and frontal lobes during (a) EOP, (b) VS, (c) Q, (d) L and (e) C'.

15.6.2.2 Local Information Measure

Net information flow has been calculated from the lobe-wise information flow network, as shown in Figure 15.11. In all the cognitive states, it appears that the occipital lobe (O) behaves as a source node where the information is flowing out, and the frontal lobe (F) acts as a sink node where the information is flowing in. On the other hand, the parietal lobe (P) serves both as a source and a sink node except during the listing phase of the web search, where it acts like a sink node only. The net information is observed to be flowing mostly from O to F via P and C' during all the cognitive states. Hence, the net information is flowing from bottom to top during all the cognitive activities, including the EOP state. The cognitive tasks are given to the brain visually. The occipital lobe processes the visually received information and shares the processed outcomes to other lobes, and this may be a reason for this bottom-up information flow phenomenon.

15.7 CONCLUSION

In the current study, direction of information transfer/flow among various brain regions (EEG electrode sites) during search-related cognitive activities was detected.

Specifically, EEG-based directed functional brain networks were created from collected data in both visual search and web search cognitive tasks using nonlinear Granger causality. It was identified that there was an increased information transfer in the functional brain networks during the cognitive load state of both searches in comparison to the baseline state, which reflects that higher order executive and planning of neuronal activity. The connectivity densities and clustering coefficients consistently increase during both visual search and web searches, thus demonstrating their sensitivity to cognitive loads. The creation of functional brain networks during different stages of web search using nonlinear Granger causality facilitated deeper investigations of the dynamics of FBNs during a web search. The information flow across the brain lobes during query formulation and list reading phases of the web search is higher than that during the visual search task, indicating increased cognitive function (mental load). This is valuable information that may help design future web search engine architectures to induce the least mental load, and, hence, reduce user stress during web search. EEG-based functional brain network research has the potential to help develop a deeper understanding of neuronal processing during cognitive function and hence the information exchange across brain regions. This research may have implications for information science, particularly to knowledge generation, storage, and retrieval.

The results also demonstrate the efficacy of nonlinear Granger causality measure in detecting changes in information transfer across brain regions during cognition. The outcomes of this research may pave the way to the development of metrics to measure cognition. Such a metric may help develop new diagnostic tools to detect cognitive impairment. The findings also open an opportunity to provide better insight on how to better design user-friendly search systems to reduce cognitive loads during web searches. Understanding the concepts of brain function during a web search is crucial to understanding the cognitive load imposed by the search tasks and search system. This chapter makes a valuable contribution to brain and behavior science in that, for the first time the nonlinear GC was applied in computational neuroscience to measure brain activities that are unobservable in traditional information retrieval as users perform information search. The unobservable cognitive loads were linked to web search constructs such as formulating search queries, relevance judgement of search results list, and relevance judgement of search content. In future research, it is worthwhile to explore the cognitive demands imposed by search systems as well as how brain activation can be used to measure the complexity of search tasks.

How the brain behaves or how the brain neural information flows during web searching (cognitive load) is very important in the neuro-information retrieval field. If we understand this or get some reliable results, then this may help to minimize the search effort of a person or cognitive load during web searches, and, hence, it may lead to a searcher's improved performance level. We call for further study with larger data samples to examine cognitive load levels in web search and how to improve searcher performance levels. It would also be interesting to explore whether a searcher's performance level could be enhanced by providing audio and visual dialogues with future search engines.

REFERENCES

1. Sperry, R.W., M.S. Gazzaniga, and J.E. Bogen. Interhemispheric relationships: the neocortical commissures; syndromes of hemisphere disconnection. In: *Disorders of Speech, Perception and Symbolic Behavior. Handbook of Clinical Neurology.* No. 4. North-Holland Publishing Co., Amsterdam, pp. 273–290, 1969.
2. Chilosi, A.M., P. Brovedani, and M. Moscatelli, et al. Neuropsychological findings in idiopathic occipital lobe epilepsies. *Epilepsia* 47 (2006): 76–78.
3. Azevedo, F.A., L.R. Carvalho, and L.T. Grinberg, et al. Equal numbers of neuronal and nonneuronal cells make the human brain an isometrically scaled-up primate brain. *Journal of Comparative Neurology* 513 (2009): 532–541.
4. Marois, R., and J. Ivanoff. Capacity limits of information processing in the brain. *Trends in Cognitive Sciences* 9 (2005): 296–305.
5. Bassett, D.S., A. Meyer-Lindenberg, and S. Achard, et al. Adaptive reconfiguration of fractal small-world human brain functional networks. *Proceedings of the National Academy of Sciences* 103 (2006): 19518–19523.
6. Batty, M., and M.J. Taylor. Early processing of the six basic facial emotional expressions. *Cognitive Brain Research* 17 (2003): 613–620.
7. Sergent, C., S. Baillet, and S. Dehaene. Timing of the brain events underlying access to consciousness during the attentional blink. *Nature Neuroscience* 8 (2005): 1391–1400.
8. Nunez, P.L. Electroencephalography (EEG). In V.S. Ramachandran (Ed.), *Encyclopaedia of the Human Brain* (pp. 169–179). Cambridge: Academic Press, 2002.
9. Ellison, A., K.L. Ball, and P. Moseley. Functional interaction between right parietal and bilateral frontal cortices during visual search tasks revealed using functional magnetic imaging and transcranial direct current stimulation. *PloS ONE* 9, 4 (2014): e93767.
10. Fairhall, S., I. Indovina, and J. Driver. The brain network underlying serial visual search: comparing overt and covert spatial orienting, for activations and for effective connectivity. *Cerebral Cortex* 19, 12 (2009): 2946–2958.
11. Leonards, U., S. Sunaert, and P. Van Hecke et al. Attention mechanisms in visual search—an fMRI study. *Journal of Cognitive Science* 12 (2000): 61–75.
12. Mechelli, A., C.J. Price, and K.J. Friston et al. Where bottom-up meets top-down: Neuronal interactions during perception and imagery. *Cerebral Cortex* 14 (2004): 1256–1265.
13. Nobre, A., J. Coull, and V. Walsh et al. Brain activations during visual search: Contributions of search efficiency versus feature binding. *Neuroimage* 18 (2003): 91–103.
14. Du, J.T., and A. Spink. Toward a web search model: Integrating multitasking, cognitive coordination, and cognitive shifts. *Journal of the American Society for Information Science and Technology* 62, 8 (2011): 1446–1472.
15. Shovon, M.H.I., D.N. Nandagopal, and J.T. Du et al. Cognitive activity during Web search. In *Proceedings of the 38th ACM International Conference on Research and Development in Information Retrieval* (pp. 967–970). New York: ACM, 2015.
16. Gwizdka, J., J. Mostafa, and Y. Moshfeghi et al. Applications of neuroimaging in information science: Challenges and opportunities. *Proceedings of the American Society for Information Science and Technology* 50 (2013): 1–4.
17. Gwizdka, J. Distribution of cognitive load in web search. *Journal of the American Society for Information Science and Technology* 61, 11 (2010): 2167–2187.
18. Cole, M.J., J. Gwizdka, and C. Lui et al. Dynamic assessment of information acquisition effort during interactive search. *Proceedings of the American Society for Information Science and Technology* 48 (2011): 1–10.

19. Fagiolo, G. Clustering in complex directed networks. *Physical Review E* 76 (2007): 026107.
20. Leicht, E.A., and M.E. Newman. Community structure in directed networks. *Physical Review Letters* 100, no. 11 (2008): 118703.
21. Dentico, D., B.L. Cheung, and J.-Y. Chang et al. Reversal of cortical information flow during visual imagery as compared to visual perception. *NeuroImage* 100 (2014): 237–243.
22. Marinazzo, D., W. Liao, and H. Chen et al. Nonlinear connectivity by granger causality. *Neuroimage* 58 (2011): 330–338.
23. Bullmore, E., and O. Sporns. Complex brain networks: Graph theoretical analysis of structural and functional systems. *Nature Reviews Neuroscience* 10 (2009): 186–198.
24. Ts'o, D.Y., C.D. Gilbert, and T.N. Wiesel. Relationships between horizontal interactions and functional architecture in cat striate cortex as revealed by cross-correlation analysis. *The Journal of Neuroscience* 6 (1986): 1160–1170.
25. Dobie, R.A., and M.J. Wilson. Objective detection of 40 Hz auditory evoked potentials: Phase coherence vs. magnitude-squared coherence. *Electroencephalography and Clinical Neurophysiology/Evoked Potentials Section* 92 (1994): 405–413.
26. Kowalski, C.J. On the effects of non-normality on the distribution of the sample product-moment correlation coefficient. *Applied Statistics* (1972): 1–12.
27. Sankari, Z., H. Adeli, and A. Adeli. Wavelet coherence model for diagnosis of Alzheimer disease. *Clinical EEG and neuroscience* 43 (2012): 268–278.
28. Friston, K., R. Moran, and A.K. Seth. Analysing connectivity with granger causality and dynamic causal modelling. *Current Opinion in Neurobiology* 23 (2013): 172–178.
29. Liao, W., J. Ding, and D. Marinazzo et al. Small-world directed networks in the human brain: multivariate Granger causality analysis of resting-state fMRI. *Neuroimage* 54 (2011): 2683–2694.
30. Jeong, J., J.C. Gore, and B.S. Peterson. Mutual information analysis of the EEG in patients with Alzheimer's disease. *Clinical Neurophysiology* 112 (2001): 827–835.
31. Shovon, M.H.I., D.N. Nandagopal, and R. Vijayalakshmi et al. Transfer entropy and information flow patterns in functional brain networks during cognitive activity. *Neural Information Processing, Lecture Notes in Computer Science (LNCS 8834).* Part I (2014): 1–10.
32. Shannon, C.E. A mathematical theory of communication. *The Bell System Technical Journal* 27, no. 3 (1948): 379–423.
33. Amblard, P.O., and O.J.J. Michel. On directed information theory and Granger Causality graphs. *Journal of Computational Neuroscience* 30, no. 1 (2011): 7–16.
34. Schreiber, T. Measuring information transfer. *Physical Review Letters* 85, no. 2 (2000): 461–464.
35. Barnett, L., A.B. Barrett, and A.K. Seth. Granger causality and transfer entropy are equivalent for Gaussian variables. *Physical Review Letters* 103, no. 23 (2009): 238701(4).
36. Wiener, N. The theory of prediction. In E. F. Beckenbach (Ed.), *Modern Mathematics for the Engineers* (pp. 165–190). New York: McGraw-Hill, 1956.
37. Granger, C.W. Investigating causal relations by econometric models and cross-spectral methods. *Econometrica: Journal of the Econometric Society* 37, no. 3 (1969): 424–438.
38. Marinazzo, D., M. Pellicoro, and S. Stramaglia. Kernel-Granger causality and the analysis of dynamical networks. *Physical review E* 77 (2008a): 056215.
39. Marinazzo, D., M. Pellicoro, and S. Stramaglia. Kernel method for nonlinear granger causality. *Physical Review Letters* 100, no. 14 (2008b): 144103.

40. McIntosh, A., and F. Gonzalez-Lima. Structural equation modeling and its application to network analysis in functional brain imaging. *Human Brain Mapping* 2, no. 1–2 (1994): 2–22.

41. Newman, M.E. The structure and function of complex networks. *SIAM Review* 45 (2003): 167–256.

42. Rubinov, M. and O. Sporns. Complex network measures of brain connectivity: Uses and Interpretations. *Neuroimage* 52, no. 3 (2010): 1059–1069.

43. Amini, L., C. Jutten, and S. Achard et al. Comparison of five directed graph measures for identification of leading interictal epileptic regions. *Physiological Measurement* 31, no. 11 (2010): 1529–1546.

44. Nandagopal, D., R. Vijayalakshmi, and B. Cocks et al. Computational neuroengineering approaches to characterising cognitive activity in EEG. *Knowledge, Systems and Technologies*. Springer International Publishing Switzerland, 2015. DOI: 10.1007/978-3-319-13545-8_8.

45. Shovon, M.H.I., D.N. Nandagopal, and R. Vijayalakshmi et al. Towards a cognitive metric using normalized transfer entropy. *ASE BigData/SocialInformatics/PASSAT/BioMedCom 2014 Conference*, Harvard University, December 14–16, 2014.

46. Shovon, M.H.I., D.N. Nandagopal, and R. Vijayalakshmi et al. Directed connectivity analysis of functional brain networks during cognitive activity using transfer entropy. *Neural Processing Letters* 45, no. 3 (2017): 807–824.

47. Thilaga, M., R. Vijayalakshmi, and R. Nadarajan et al. Shortest path based network analysis to characterize cognitive load states of human brain using EEG based functional brain networks. *Journal of Integrative Neuroscience* 17 (2018): 253–275.

48. Vijayalakshmi, R., D.N. Nandagopal, and B. Cocks et al. Minimum Connected Component - A Novel Approach to Detection of Cognitive Load Induced Changes in Functional Brain Networks. *Journal of Neuro Computing* 170 (2015): 15–31.

49. Luck, S.J., and S.A. Hillyard. Spatial filtering during visual search: Evidence from human electrophysiology. *Journal of Experimental Psychology: Human Perception and Performance* 20, no. 5 (1994): 1000–1014.

16 Student Behavior Modeling and Context Acquisition
A Ubiquitous Learning Framework

Anandi Giridharan and K.A. Venkatesh

16.1 INTRODUCTION

We have proposed a research study on the growth of mobile technologies, smart sensing devices, and ubiquitous learning environments that have led to the development of context-aware adaptive learning education. Our proposed context-aware system uses sensors that gathers student's useful context information that is exploited to retrieve the most suitable learning contents, benefiting student learning behavior. Various query keywords like who, what, where, when, why, and how are used for reframing and extracting students' semantic context information based on their knowledge level.

The proposed system consists of the students' behavior model, subject domain model [1,2] and context acquisition model in a ubiquitous learning environment organized to provide adaptive service to the students. This chapter consists of four sections: the first section, 16.2, discusses literature surveys on various context-modeling frameworks in an adaptive learning environment.

16.2 A SURVEY ON CONTEXT MODELING FRAMEWORKS

Ubiquitous systems gather student context, analyze this information, and determine a method to construct appropriate services dynamically [3]. A literature survey on some of the context modeling frameworks is discussed next.

16.2.1 CONTEXT MODELING APPROACHES

Some of the requirements of context modeling approaches:

- *Distributed composition*: In a distributed environment, the central instance is lacking which is essential for important core functionalities. Central instance is responsible for generation, placement, and up-keeping related data and services [4].

- *Partial validation*: Partial validation is essential for contextual knowledge to improve contextual interrelationships to rule out possible errors.
- *Quality of information*: Information acquired by sensors that define a student in a ubiquitous learning environment varies over time.
- *Incompleteness and ambiguity*: The information of a student should be complete without ambiguity.
- *Specification of information*: Specification of the contextual information is essential to describe the ability of a context model for cross-system knowledge sharing and reuse [5].
- *Reliability and realizable*: The context modeling approach should be reliable and realizable.

16.2.1.1 Various Context Modeling Approaches in Ubiquitous Learning Environments

A. *Ontology-based models:* This model represents a concept group and the relationship among them in a given ubiquitous learning domain. It is a domain with a graph of concepts; contextual relationships may be hierarchical or semantic.

Classification of ontologies depends on the level of generality [6]:

- *Domain ontologies*: It represents concepts for a specific subject domain.
- *Generic ontologies*: General concepts are described in generic ontologies, free of any task or learning domain (e.g., time, space, etc.).
- *Application ontologies*: This describes concepts related to a learning application that relies on both domain and generic ontologies.

There are many ubiquitous and pervasive computing systems that use ontology models including COBRA and SOCAM [7].

- *COBRA*: Common object request broker architecture (COBRA) computing is a broker-centric, agent-based architecture. Acquiring and keeping track and proper reasoning of context information is done by this architecture.
- *SOCAM*: The service-oriented context-aware middleware (SOCAM) is an architecture that constructs context-aware services in ubiquitous and pervasive computing environments. It uses CONON (CONtext ONtology) for modeling context hierarchical approaches for designing context ontologies. Two reasoning approaches are used, one is reasoning with description logic and others is user-defined reasoning.

B. *Spatial context models* [8,9]: Space is an important context in many ubiquitous context-aware learning applications. Context is defined as – where you are, who you are with, and what resources are nearby (e.g., location of student, in campus, library, etc., students with other classmates doing collaborative learning; resources like subject content with multimedia streams, etc.). There are two different spatial representations based on symbolic and geometric coordinates.

- *Symbolic coordinates* are identified by classroom number or access point in LAN. Specification of relationships among pairs of symbolic coordinates is a must, since there is an absence of spatial relation between spatial coordinates.
- *Geometric coordinates* represent areas or points in metric space like GPS. Mostly this type of spatial information is used in areas of location-based ubiquitous applications.

C. *Logic-based models:* The definition of context is done based on a certain set of observations and inferring beliefs; predictions with facts. The conditions are derived logically and context is represented as abstract mathematical entities.

D. *Graphical models*: Unified modeling language (UML) is a well-known technique that has developed based on graphical components (UML diagrams). Being a generic model, context modeling using UML structuring was well known. Another approach called object-role modeling (ORM) is another graphics oriented approach for the construction of context Modeling.

16.2.2 Context Acquisition, Reasoning, and Dissemination in Ubiquitous Learning Environments

Context modeling is the process of gathering student information related to a student's current situation. Context acquisition is done by proper analysis and classification to logically interpret the student's goals, skills, challenges, knowledge, etc.; and, finally, context dissemination delivers appropriate learning content as shown in Figure 16.1.

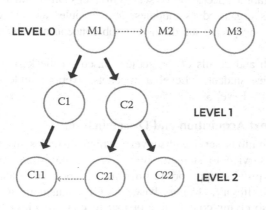

FIGURE 16.1 Subject domain modeling based on a student's knowledge level.

16.2.2.1 Student Learning Behavioral Model

In a context-aware ubiquitous learning system, student context is utilized and exploited to characterize the real-time situation based on student learning behavior. The system retrieves adaptive subject content to make it more suitable based on student learning behavior elements. In the student learning context, both static and dynamic elements related to physical, system, social, and application in the ubiquitous learning environments are exploited to retrieve suitable adaptive subject content matching the student's learning goal elements.

The student model keeps track of the student's contextual data and represents the student's current state of knowledge and psychological state. The student model (SM) consists of a set of prepositions P believed by the adaptive system (AS) [10].

Set of beliefs B_{As} of the adaptive system:

$$B_{As} = \{p|B_{As}P\} \tag{16.1}$$

then B_{As} p holds if adaptive system believes p.

$$sM = B_{As}p(S)\} \tag{16.2}$$

$$\text{Student Model}(SM) = KAS(S)UGAS(S)UCAS(S)U\ SkAS(S)LsAS(S) \tag{16.3}$$

where K is the knowledge of the student, G is the Goal, C is the challenge, Sk is the skill, and Ls is learning style of the student.

16.2.2.2 Subject Domain

Course domain should be designed by organizing relevant course modules along with associated concepts based on guidelines provided by standards and specifications for computer-mediated learning. The specification should follow the details on the construction of subject content; proper student data, like personal competencies; goal; skill; challenge; knowledge; etc. Specifications and standards are very essential to maintain interoperability, accessibility, scalability, reusability and also durability [11]. Subject content is organized as modules, and modules are classified as a set of concepts. Again, concepts are sub-divided as sub-concepts and again sub-sub-concept to
increase the depth and details of the subject based on the knowledge level of the student, i.e., novice student – Level 0 concepts, average student – Level 1, and advanced students – Level 3.

16.2.2.3 Context Acquisition and Dissemination

Systems use ubiquitous service discovery which provides the technique of detecting suitable service to students in a learning environment. Context-aware applications that provide appropriate information about the location of a student (e.g., campus, lab, library, etc.) are based on GPS sensor information in the student's device; also giving content in a proper format especially when a student is on the move (e.g., the context multimedia stream with audio, video, and text based

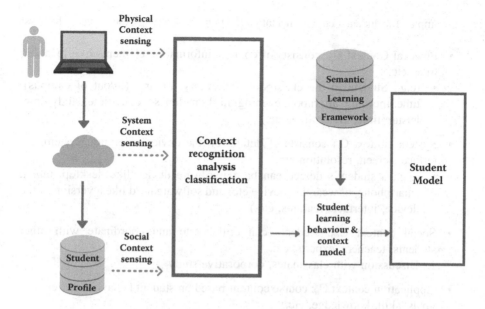

FIGURE 16.2 Context acquisition, modeling and dissemination.

on a suitable device). Figure 16.2 shows the context acquisition system that gathers student learning contexts from physical, system, application, and social context from a ubiquitous learning environment. Context recognition analysis and classification is done – based on a student's learning behavior like preference, knowledge level, time, location – the adaptive subject content is retrieved and presented to the student.

16.3 PROPOSED MODELING OF STUDENT LEARNING BEHAVIOR, SUBJECT DOMAIN, AND CONTEXT ACQUISITION IN UBIQUITOUS LEARNING ENVIRONMENTS

A ubiquitous system provides a method that identifies the automatic discovery of suitable subject content based on his/her preference. Context information representation, student modeling, subject domain modeling, and context modeling are discussed in the following section.

16.3.1 STUDENT CONTEXT INFORMATION REPRESENTATION

A student's context information is sensed from physical, system, application, and social environment based on a student's learning behavior elements like goal, knowledge, skill, psychological state, etc.

Context information is a tuple of physical context C_p, system context C_s, application context C_a, and social context C_{so}.

$CI(x) = \{C_p, C_s, C_a, C_{so}\}$ where x is categories of context.

Example of a student's environmental contexts in the learning system are as follows:

- Physical Context C_p: consists of context information elements like location, time, etc.
  - (e.g., Student in the classroom, laboratory, library, (in/out of campus); time: morning, afternoon, evening, night includes lecture time, study time, leisure time, break time, etc.)

- System context C_s: consists of details on the device, operation system, interface, screen, resolution etc.
  - (e.g., a student's device can be a hardware device like desktop, tablet, smartphone, or wearable device etc. and software used like a version of the device, interface, features, etc.)

- Social context C_{so}: students can collaborate and coordinate with other students, teachers, experts, etc.
  - Discussion with classmates, corporative study

- Application context C_a: course content based on student behavior, preference, goals, skill, knowledge, etc.
  - (e.g., student knowledge level like a novice, professional; skill to improve in oral/written communication; goal to complete relevant courses; preference is a multimedia stream with video recording, etc.).

Context modeling is done by describing each environment context of the student and relating it to the student's learning behavior goal elements to derive the appropriate learning application. Subject content retrieval may be static depending on the subjective property of the student like preference, profile etc., and dynamic depending on the objective property of the student like time, place, device, etc. Thus, it is motivating students to achieve their goals by giving attention to their psychological conditions as well.

16.3.2 SUPPORTING STRUCTURE OF CONTEXT ACQUISITION

The proposed model uses various queries like who, what, where, when, why, and how for reframing and extracting semantic context of a student without ambiguity. The query expansion method is an efficient technique to discover advanced content search in context-aware ubiquitous learning environments. The same query for different students' context will generate distinct results. While designing subject content, a student's learning behavior elements like goals, knowledge level, preference, etc. should be taken into consideration.

16.3.3 STUDENT MODELING

Student modeling updates a student's information to impart adaptivity and personalization [12]. The student model includes all context information of the student's learning behavioral elements like goal, skill, challenge, knowledge, preference, etc.,

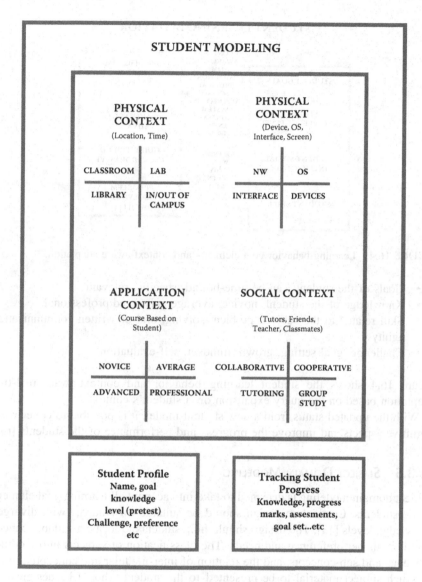

FIGURE 16.3 Student modeling.

which is essential for the course learning. When a student accesses the course, student modeling builds up slowly at run-time, since it is mainly through the validity provided by the student's input to the system that the student model is created.

Figure 16.3 shows the student's modeling relating to context reasoning for building an individualized student model.

16.3.4 LEARNING BEHAVIOR GOAL ELEMENTS OF A STUDENT

The learning behavior goal for a student is as follows:

STUDENT LEARNING BEHAVIOR

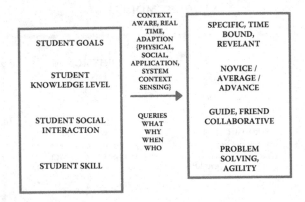

FIGURE 16.4   Learning behavior goal elements and context-aware adaptation.

- Goals of the student: can be time-bound, specific, relevant
- Knowledge of the student: novice, average, advanced/professional
- Skill related to the subject: problem-solving, oral or written communication, agility
- Challenge: goal setting, growth mindset, self-evaluation

Figure 16.4 shows the student learning behavior and context-aware real-time adaptation based on the query expansion on a student's context.

With the updated status from a new student model, it is possible to cover wider cognitive aspects and improve the progress and performance of the students [6].

16.3.5 SUBJECT DOMAIN MODELING

Subject domain modeling is designed to take into account all learning goal elements of the students. Curriculum design should be suitable for students with divergent knowledge levels [13]. The design should help students to locate a suitable concept based on his/her preference and needs. The classification of subjects into modules, concepts, and sub-concepts, and the relation of inter-modular and conceptual links, in which subject material to be presented to the students should be designed sequentially, as shown in Figures 16.5 and 16.6.

The arrangement of modules and concepts should be based on the perception of subject difficulty. Novice students can access links having less weightage and less difficulty; whereas, the average and expert students are provided access to links having more and complex modules, and concepts based on their knowledge levels.

After completion of each chapter, students are self-evaluated with automatic feedback. The test consists of multiple-choice questions with predefined answers. Students will be able to understand his/her status in that accessed chapter. Student's anxiety on a subject learning material was found to be reduced to increase their motivation. Self-evaluation encourages students to improve their psychological emotional dimension to motivate their skill ability.

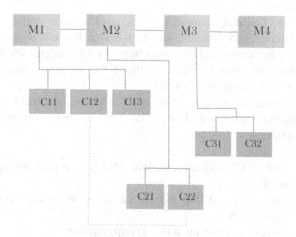

FIGURE 16.5 Inter-modular-inter-conceptual relationship.

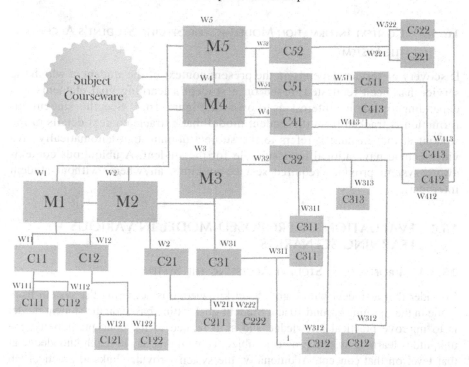

FIGURE 16.6 Course contents with weightage.

16.3.6 Context Information Modeling in Ubiquitous Learning Systems

Registration of the students to the course is done by service providers, who provide the required service based on a student's learning goal elements. Various details of these elements (goal, knowledge, challenge, skill, preference) required for the course are noted. The student model keeps track of the student's updates and progress, and motivates the student with self-evaluation and assessments. Service providers will be available anytime, anywhere, to the students requiring services, providing appropriate subject content without the student's intervention in the ubiquitous learning environment [14,15].

We have designed context acquisition in a ubiquitous learning environment using various queries (what, who, how, what, why, and when) based on a student's learning goal elements as follows:

- Physical context C_p = classroom, lab, library, campus; morning, afternoon, evening, night
- System context C_s = PDA, laptop, desktop, interface, screen resolution, network, application
- Social context C_{so} = friends, tutor, group, teacher
- Application context C_a = goal, knowledge, skill, challenge, applications

16.3.7 CONTEXT INFORMATION MODELING FOR SPECIFIC STUDENT'S ACCESSING THE SYSTEM

Discovery of service depends on the present context of the student at which the service has been requested, based on a student's learning goal elements and depending on choice/interest as shown in Figure 16.7. Specific student information is tracked from the student model that extracts context details of the student at that instant; it refers to the subject domain that automatically provides course navigational links suitable for the student. A ubiquitous context-aware system provides required service anytime, anywhere, without student intervention.

16.4 EVALUATION OF PROPOSED MODEL IN VARIOUS LEARNING SCENARIOS

16.4.1 PROFESSIONAL STUDENT ACCESSING THE SYSTEM

Consider that a student with higher-level knowledge is accessing the system from home in the morning around 10 am. Student goal setting based on the student model is to improve practical knowledge and skill related to the concept. Initially, the ubiquitous learning system provides subject content that has in-depth knowledge at that level on that concept. Additionally, the system provides links to practical lab experiments and provides lab timings to the student for his lab sessions. The system sends reminders to the student regarding lab sessions.

16.4.2 NOVICE STUDENT TO CHECK ON NEGATIVE EMOTIONS

When a novice student has negative emotions while accessing the course, a ubiquitous learning system should create a positive learning environment. The system

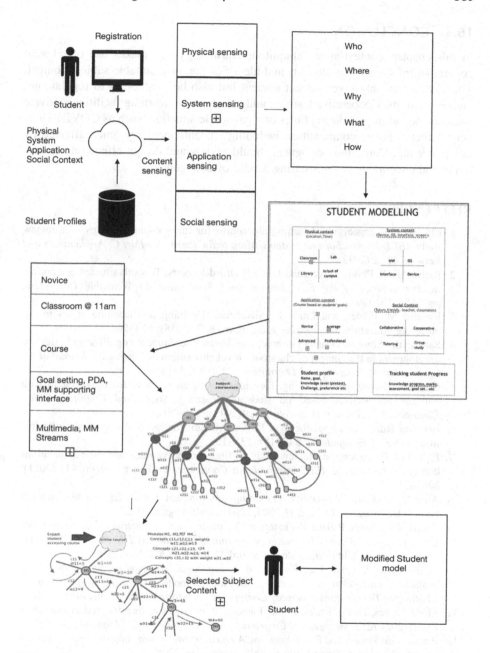

FIGURE 16.7 Context modeling in a ubiquitous learning environment.

could even motivate other students to encourage the student to continue with his course. The system recommends co-operative learning and provides links for tutors who provide counseling in collaborative learning. Evaluation is provided frequently to keep track of the student's emotional dimension.

16.5   CONCLUSION

In this chapter, context-aware ubiquitous learning system makes use of relevant contextual information of students and identifies the most suitable subject content. The system not only gives subject content but also helps students to regulate negative emotions. Cooperative learning and collaborative learning facilities motivate students. Social impact during times of a pandemic situation, such as COVID-19, is very pathetic. Entire communities, including students, are very much affected by this pandemic. Curriculum designers should review and design effectively to motivate and encourage students during a state of emergency.

REFERENCES

1. Elpiniki I. Papageorgiou. Learning algorithms for fuzzy cognitive maps — a review study. *IEEE Transactions on Systems, Man, and Cybernetics-Part C: Applications and Reviews* 42, 2 (2012).
2. Richard Hull, Philip Neaves, and James Bedford-Roberts. Towards situated computing. In: *Proceedings of the First International Symposium on Wearable Computers.* pp. 146–153. 1997.
3. Richard M. Felder, and Linda K. Silverman. Learning and teaching styles in engineering education. *Engineering Education* 78, 7 (1988): 674–668.
4. Saad Fathy Shawer, Deanna Gilmore, and Susan Rae. Student cognitive and affective development in the context of classroom-level curriculum development. *Journal of the Scholarship of Teaching and Learning* 8, 1 (2008): 1–28.
5. Gwo-Jen Hwang, and W. Hong. Development of an adaptive learning system with multiple perspectives based on students' learning. *Styles and Cognitive Styles, Educational Technology & Society* 16, 4(2013): 185–200.
6. Boryana Ruzhekova-Rogozherova. ESP curriculum design and cognitive skills formation, *BETA E-Newsletter* 8 (2015): 135–158.
7. Elpiniki I. Papageorgiou. Review study on fuzzy cognitive maps and their applications during the last decade. *IEEE International Conference on Fuzzy Systems* 444 (2011): 828–835.
8. Anandi Giridharan, "Adaptive eLearning environment for students with divergent knowledge levels", *ELELTECH* 2005, Hyderabad, August 2005.
9. Anandi Giridharan, Pallapa Venkataram. Organizing subject material in accordance with Ubiquitous student status. *International Journal of Education (EDU-15)* 3, 3 (2015). 10. 5121/ije.2015.330. https://zenodo.org/record/1220585#.YA28WugzZPY.
10. Zixing Shen, Songxin Tan, Keng Siau. Using cognitive maps of mental models to evaluate learning challenges: a case study, mental models. *Cognitive Maps, Learning Challenges Twenty-third Americas Conference on Information Systems, Boston,* 2017.
11. Márta Takács, Imre J. Rudas, Zoltán Lantos. Fuzzy cognitive map for student evaluation model. *2014 IEEE International Conference on System Science and Engineering (ICSSE).*
12. Anandi Giridharan, and P. Venkataram. *A causal model based subject domain creation for a web-based education. NSEE 2005,* Bangalore, 2005.
13. Anandi Giridharan, K.A. Venkatesh. *Machine consciousness: mind, machine, and society contributors,* Elsevier, 2020. Weiser.
14. Pallapa Venkataram, and M. Bharath. "A method of context-based services discovery in ubiquitous environment", *Lecture Notes of the Institute for Computer Sciences Social Informatics and Telecommunications Engineering,* 2014.
15. Luiz A. Amaral, Detmar Meurers. "On using intelligent computer-assisted language learning in real-life foreign language teaching and learning", *ReCALL,* 2011.

Index

Note: *Italicized* page numbers refer to figures, **bold** page numbers refer to tables

Printed in the United States
by Baker & Taylor Publisher Services

Printed in the United States
by Baker & Taylor Publisher Services